**RICHARD BELLAMY**
**ANGUS ROSS** *editors*

# A textual introduction
# to social and political theory

**Manchester University Press**

Manchester and New York

*distributed exclusively in the USA and Canada by St. Martin's Press*

*Published by* Manchester University Press
Oxford Road, Manchester M13 9NR, UK
*and* Room 400, 175 Fifth Avenue,
New York, NY 10010, USA

*Distributed exclusively in the USA and Canada*
*by* St. Martin's Press, Inc.,
175 Fifth Avenue, New York, NY 10010, USA

*British Library Cataloguing-in-Publication Data*
A catalogue record is available from the British Library

*Library of Congress Cataloging-in-Publication Data*
A textual introduction to social and political theory/edited by
   Richard Bellamy and Angus Ross.
       p.   cm.
    ISBN 0-7190-4916-4   ISBN 0-7190-4639-4 (pbk.)
    1. Political science--History.   2. Political sociology.
   I. Bellamy, Richard (Richard Paul)   II. Ross, Angus (Angus C.)
   JA81.T48   1996
   320'.01'1--dc20                                                            95-36976

ISBN 0 7190 4916 4 *hardback*
ISBN 0 7190 4639 4 *paperback*

First published in 1996

00  99  98  97  96                              10  9  8  7  6  5  4  3  2  1

Typeset in Palatino with Mixage
by Action Typesetting Limited, Gloucester

Printed in Great Britain
by Bell & Bain Limited, Glasgow

# Contents

# Notes on contributors

**Richard Bellamy** is Professor of Politics at the University of Reading. Recent publications include: *Liberalism and Modern Society: An Historical Argument* (Polity Press, 1992) and (with Darrow Schecter) *Gramsci and the Italian State* (Manchester University Press, 1993). He is currently editing (with Terence Ball) *The Cambridge History of Twentieth Century Political Thought*.

**Howard Caygill** is Professor of Cultural History at Goldsmiths College, University of London. Recent publications include: *Art of Judgement* (Blackwell, 1989) and *The Kant Dictionary* (Blackwell, 1995).

**John Greenaway** is a Lecturer in Politics in the School of Economic and Social Studies at the University of East Anglia (UEA). Recent publications include: (with Steve Smith and John Street) *Deciding Factors in British Politics: A Case-Studies Approach* (Routledge, 1992) and 'British Conservatism and Bureaucracy', *History of Political Thought*, 13, 1, 1992.

**Martin Hollis** is Professor of Philosophy in the School of Economic and Social Studies at the University of East Anglia (UEA). Recent publications include: (with Steve Smith) *Explaining and Understanding International Relations* (Oxford University Press, 1990) and *The Philosophy of Social Science* (Cambridge University Press, 1995). He is currently writing a book on the analysis of trust in social life.

**David Houghton** is a Lecturer in Philosophy in the School of Economic and Social Studies at the University of East Anglia (UEA). Recent publications include journal articles in the philosophy of language and the theory of rational choice.

**Tony Kemp-Welch** is a Senior Lecturer in International Relations in the School of Economic and Social Studies at the University of East Anglia (UEA). Recent publications include: *The Ideas of Nikolai Bukharin* (Oxford University Press, 1992), *Stalin and the Literary Intelligentsia* (Macmillan, 1991) and *The Birth of Solidarity* (Macmillan, 2nd edn, 1991).

**Timothy O'Hagan** is a Senior Lecturer in Philosophy in the School of Economic and Social Studies at the University of East Anglia (UEA). Recent publications include: *Enlightenment and Revolution in Europe* (editor) (Aberdeen University Press, 1991) and 'La morale sensitive de Jean-Jacques Rousseau' (*Revue de théologie et de philosophie*, 1993). He is currently completing a book on the philosophy of Jean-Jacques Rousseau.

**Angus Ross** is a Lecturer in Philosophy in the School of Economic and Social Studies at the University of East Anglia (UEA). Recent publications include: (edited with Shaun Hargreaves-Heap) *Understanding the Enterprise Culture: Themes in the Work of Mary Douglas* (Edinburgh University Press, 1992). He is currently writing a book on language and consciousness.

**Alan Scott** is a Lecturer in Sociology in the School of Economic and Social Studies at the University of East Anglia (UEA). Recent publications include: *Ideology and the New Social Movements* (Routledge, 1990) and (with Ahmed Gurnah) *The Uncertain Science* (Routledge, 1992). He is currently editing *The Limits of Globalization* for Routledge.

**John Street** is a Senior Lecturer in Politics in the School of Economic and Social Studies at the University of East Anglia (UEA). Recent publications include: *Politics and Technology* (Macmillan, 1992) and (with John Greenaway and Steve Smith) *Deciding Factors in British Politics* (Routledge, 1992). He is currently writing *Passionate Interests: The Politics of Popular Culture* for Polity Press.

**John Zvesper** is a Lecturer in Politics in the School of Economic and Social Studies at the University of East Anglia (UEA). He has published journal articles on Locke and on Aristotle. Recent publications include: *Nature and Liberty* (Routledge, 1993).

# Editors' introduction

Why should we accept the authority of the state? Is democracy possible? Do we live in a free society? Is communism dead? Have modern conservatives abandoned their ideological roots? Whenever we discuss contemporary political issues we employ ideas and concepts, and ways of thinking about the nature of society, which we have inherited from the past. These ideas and the languages in which they are expressed are deeply embedded in the institutions of Western liberal democracies. They inform our understanding of citizenship and shape our social and political ideals. There is no better way of making ourselves aware of the precise meanings and resonances of the terms involved than by becoming acquainted with the key thinkers who helped to shape the way we understand them now.

Thus the first aim of this book is to introduce the reader to some of the main thinkers of the Western political tradition from Plato onwards. A few classic works supply social and political theorists with a shared set of reference points. They provide a common currency in which to debate the problems facing modern societies. An acquaintance with these classic works puts one in a position to join in the dialogue. By combining expert commentary with carefully chosen extracts from the original texts, this collection allows the reader get to know these writings at first hand.

Second, the book offers an introduction to the key concepts of political debate and the ways in which they interconnect. Since different thinkers have interpreted these concepts in crucially different ways, each chapter focuses on a debate between two (or in one case three) thinkers, illustrating these differences of approach and assessing their significance.

Underlying most serious political disagreements, for example the difference between a liberal and a conservative outlook, lie different understandings of the nature of society, which in turn reflect the historical and intellectual context of the thinkers. Thus a third aim of this book is to alert the reader to these contextual differences, revealing our present way of understanding ideas like liberty and democracy as in part a response to dramatic changes in the nature of society itself. The Greek *polis* is not the modern state, whose main lineaments began to emerge only in the sixteenth and seventeenth centuries, and from Marx onwards our thinkers are conscious that they are focusing on problems peculiar to modern industrial society. Those who look to the ancient world for inspiration must allow for huge differences between ancient and modern society, though, as we shall see, the desire to recreate certain features of pre-modern society repeats itself throughout the history of social and political thought and inspires some of the most potent criticisms of contemporary politics.

This collection represents a collaboration between an interdisciplinary team of political scientists, philosophers and sociologists with a keen interest in the history of social and political thought. The boundaries between these intellectual disciplines are of relatively recent origin. Most of the thinkers represented in this volume made no such disciplinary distinctions, and only later commentators have sought to hive off bits of their work as contributions to particualr fields of study. An interdisciplinary approach not only provides a better understanding of the great thinkers of the past, but also, we believe, offers a model to adopt in our own thinking about politics and society.

# Acknowledgements

This volume grew out of a first year course on Social and Political Theory taught jointly by Philosophy, Politics and Sociology faculty at the University of East Anglia. Our students acted as guinea pigs for much of the material. We have certainly benefited from their comments, and trust that the book will prove more serviceable to other students as a result. The editors would like to thank all the contributors for their collaboration on this project, and are especially indebted to Tim O'Hagan and Martin Hollis for their support throughout. Anne Martin, Mary Robinson and Hazel Taylor provided wonderful secretarial back-up, as always. Richard Purslow made extremely helpful comments at the planning stage, and we are very grateful for the commitment which he and the staff at Manchester University Press have shown for this volume.

Permission has been granted to quote from translations as follows:
Plato, *Crito*, from *The Last Days of Socrates*, trans. Hugh Tredennick (Penguin 1954); Aquinas, *Summa Theologiae*, ed. Thomas Gilby (Blackfriars/Eyre & Spottiswoode 1966, 1975), Vols 28, 38; Machiavelli, *The Discourses* (Bk II, Ch. 2), ed. Bernard Crick, trans. L. J. Walker (Penguin Classics 1983); Rousseau, *Second Discourse* and *The Social Contract* (Bk I, Chs 6–8), from *The Collected Writings of Rousseau*, ed. R. D. Masters and C. Kelly, trans. J. R. Bush, R. D. Masters and C. Kelly (University Press of New England 1992, 1994), Vols 3, 4; Rousseau, *Emile*, trans. Allan Bloom (Basic Books 1979); Kant, 'On the Relationship of Theory to Practice in Political Right', from *Kant: Political Writings*, ed. Reiss (Cambridge University Press 1970); Hegel, *Lectures on the Philosophy of History*, trans. J. Sibree (Dover 1956); Marx, *On the Jewish Question*, from *Marx: Early Political Writings*, ed./trans. Joseph O'Malley (Cambridge University Press 1994); Lenin, *The State and Revolution*, trans. Robert Service (Penguin 1992); from *Bakunin: Selected Writings*, ed. Arthur Lehning (Jonathan Cape 1973); Kropotkin, 'The State: Its Historic Role' and a letter to Lenin, from *Kropotkin: Selected Writings on Anarchism and Revolution*, ed. Martin and Miller (MIT Press 1970); Durkheim, 'Individualism and the Intellectuals', from *Political Studies* 17 (1979), trans. S. and J. Lukes; Weber: 'Parlament und Regierung im neugeordneten Deutschland' in *Max Weber: Gesammelte politische Schriften*, ed. J. Winckelmann (J.C.B. Mohr, 1988), trans. Alan Scott (1994); Weber 'Socialism' from *Weber: Selections in Translation*, ed. W. Runciman, trans. E. Matthews (Cambridge University Press, 1978); Michels: 'Der konservative Grundzug der Partei-Organization' in *Monatsschrift für Sociologie*, 1, ed. A. Eleutheropulos and Baron von Engelhardt (1909), trans. Alan Scott (1994).

**RICHARD BELLAMY**

# Socrates and Locke
# on political obligation

Why should we obey the law? This is one of the oldest and most basic
questions of political theory. It forces us to confront not only the links
and tensions between morality and politics but also the very purpose
of belonging to a political society. It arises in an extreme form whenever the state requires us to do something we believe to be morally
wrong, such as serving in a war we think unjustified. Less urgently, but
perhaps more importantly, we also face this question whenever we pay
taxes or accept the state's authority to order our everyday lives in
numerous ways.

Theories of political obligation imply that a special moral relationship exists between a polity and its members. They focus on explaining
and justifying our membership of a political community, and specify-
ing the rights, duties and obligations that follow from it. Two features
of such theories need emphasising. First, they claim that a specifically
political commitment to a particular state creates a moral bond that
differs in important respects from the general moral rights and duties
that we possess or owe to others as human beings. For example, British
citizens are said to stand in a different and more special moral relationship both to each other and to their state than they do to either
non-nationals or to the states of foreign countries. As we shall see, this
contention is neither as straightforward nor as indisputable as many
thinkers, including Socrates and Locke, have assumed. Indeed, many
contemporary political philosophers claim that political obligation is
either an incoherent idea or practically unrealisable and in any case
unnecessary. We shall return to the arguments of these philosophical
anarchists in the conclusion.

Second, in most accounts political obligation is not just a matter of
prudence, it involves a moral or ethical relationship between individuals and their polity. The cynical view of why we obey the law suggests
that we do so either out of fear of being punished, or because we think
that anarchy would be worse than even the most tyrannical regime.
Hobbes, who is discussed in chapter 3, offers a sophisticated version of
this prudential view of political obligation. A common argument, it
suffers from serious weaknesses most of which were noted by Plato in
Book 1 of his masterpiece, *The Republic*. Of course, many people do

support certain odious regimes, such as Hitler's Germany, for merely prudential reasons. Extreme cases aside, though, states do not and could not rely on coercion alone to obtain the allegiance of their citizens – the costs of policing everyone, including the police, are simply too great. Nor is it enough to appeal to a generalised recognition that it is in our interest to live in a law-abiding society. Individuals have an unfortunate tendency either to free ride on, or defect from, collectively beneficial arrangements whenever it would be to their own advantage to do so, regardless of the consequences for everyone else. Even if Hobbes was correct to assert that no state would survive without a monopoly of force to compel obedience, political obligation requires a stronger bond to exist between citizens and the state than either force or self-interest alone.

This chapter examines two classic accounts of political obligation: that of Socrates as recounted in Plato's dialogue the *Crito*, and John Locke's in his *Second Treatise of Government*. The *Crito* offers a perfect starting-point for considering the issues raised by this concept. Socrates has been condemned to death and awaits his execution. Although he believes the decision to be unjust, he rejects the offer of his friend, Crito, to help him escape as equally unjustified, and so opts to meet his fate. Their discussion presents in dramatic form the ways general moral and more specifically political obligations intersect and potentially conflict. Socrates resolves the difficulties in part through linking our moral identity with membership of a political community – a position developed even more forcefully by Aristotle, as we shall see in chapter 2, but which also finds an echo in the theories of Machiavelli, Rousseau, Hegel and Durkheim, examined in later chapters.

By contrast Locke, in the extract from the *Second Treatise*, offers a more individualistic theory in which our obligations rest on various kinds of consent. In some respects, his thesis reflects a more modern sensibility. It suits an age that insists on the moral equality of human beings, endows their capacity for free choice with considerable moral significance, and so tends to play down the importance of our unchosen attachments, such as nationality. However, it would be quite false to suppose that such allegiances have lost all relevance today. Quite the contrary: it is their very strength that threatens to undermine the legitimacy not only of established nation states, as in the dissatisfaction of the Scots with the United Kingdom or the far more dramatic events in the former Yugoslavia, but also of attempts to build effective international political groupings, such as the European Union. Consequently, I shall conclude that a complete theory may require some integration of both the Platonic and the Lockean ways of understanding political obligation.

### Plato (c. 427–347 BC) and Socrates (c. 469–399 BC)

Socrates was the son of an Athenian sculptor and a midwife. Although he avoided participation in politics, he fulfilled his citizenly duties when required. He served on the executive council when chosen by lot to do so, though he never spoke in the Assembly. He also performed military service in the wars against Sparta. He owned sufficient property to serve as a hoplite. These heavy-armed infantrymen had to purchase their own arms, putting him in the class of farmers and craftsmen. Highly critical of democracy, he kept his distance from those who conspired against it - many of whom were among his admirers. When Athens fell to Sparta in 404 BC, he withheld support from the Spartan regime of the Thirty Tyrants. As he noted at his trial under a restored democracy, he even risked his life by disobeying the Tyrants' order to arrest Leon of Salamis on the grounds of its illegality. The oracle at Delphi is reputed to have said that no one in Greece was wiser than Socrates because, while other people thought they possessed wisdom, he was wise enough to know he knew nothing. Socrates's mission became that of showing people that they did not know what they presumed to have knowledge of – least of all themselves. His skill at debunking the pretensions of others brought him not only influential followers but also powerful enemies, who ultimately secured his downfall on the grounds of impiety towards the official gods of the *polis* and the corruption of young men.

Socrates wrote no works himself, so we know of his thought principally through the writings of his followers – especially Plato. Child of an upper-class family, Plato was embarking on a career in tragic drama when he met Socrates, who turned him to philosophy. Apart from a brief and ill-fated attempt to influence Dionysius II of Syracuse in 367 BC, he kept out of politics. The excesses of the Thirty Tyrants, with whom he initially sympathised, and the execution of Socrates by the democrats, led him to steer clear of such involvements. His philosophical achievement consists of a series of dialogues in which Socrates appears as the main protagonist. How much of the thought of this fictional Socrates belongs to the man himself and how much to Plato is hard to tell, although it is generally supposed that Plato's own views predominated as he got older. In 380 BC he founded the Academy, and from 367 until his death his most prominent student was Aristotle.

Fifth-century BC Athens comprised approximately 30–45,000 citizens, consisting of all Athenian-born males aged over 20, and around 80–100,000 slaves, as well as numerous immigrants. Its form of government was highly democratic, at least so far as the citizen body were concerned. Candidates for the legislative Assembly, which had a quorum of 6,000 citizens for plenary sessions, were elected by lot, from which members of the executive Council of 500, magistrates and juries were chosen – also by lot. The aim was to equalise everybody's chance of holding office and to achieve the principal aim of democracy – that of 'ruling and being ruled in turn' (Aristotle, 1981, p. 195). The jury that condemned Socrates would have been a relatively numerous body, probably with several hundred jurors. Socrates' fate has been held up by some commentators as highlighting the dangers of popular rule, a view almost certainly shared by Plato. Others have regarded Socrates' intellectual arrogance and elitism as having provoked his condemnation. Although democracy is conspicuous by its absence from Socrates' argument, it is important to remember that law in Athens essentially meant the sovereign will of the people – a notion later developed by Rousseau and discussed in chapter 5. To the extent that Socrates advocates obedience to the Laws, therefore, he is endorsing the legitimacy of democratic government.

The *Crito* reports a conversation between Socrates and Crito, a close friend, on the eve of his execution. The sentence has been delayed until the return from the island of Delos of the sacred ship dispatched each year to commemorate Theseus' victory over the Minotaur: during the time of its voyage all executions in Athens were suspended. Crito urges Socrates to seize the opportunity to escape. Not to do so would be to betray his duties towards his family and the love of his friends, whom common opinion would assume had failed to help him and damn accordingly. Socrates retorts that it would look ill for a seventy year old to seem so greedy for life as to appear ready to do anything to preserve himself. More important than mere living was to live well or justly. Justice could never entail committing an unjust act – even when that action was provoked by an injustice, as in the case of his own condemnation on trumped up charges. Two wrongs do not make a right. Nor was justice a matter of what ordinary people did or did not think. Rather, it involved acting according to what was right, regardless of the consequences.

It is worth remarking that these opening passages of the dialogue offer a brief sketch of some of the central themes of Socrates' and the early Plato's political philosophy. First, note the analogy Socrates draws between the physical health of an athlete's body and the moral health and efficient functioning of the body politic. Much as an athlete has to follow an approved diet and programme of training to keep fit and stave off illness or injury, so a polity supposedly needs an appropriate regimen to avoid corruption or political disasters – namely justice. Second and relatedly, just as the athlete will take the advice of a qualified trainer rather than consult any Tom, Dick or Harriet who cares to voice their ill-informed opinion, so a polity should take its orders from an expert on justice, in other words from a philosopher rather than the ignorant mass. To cite another favourite Platonic metaphor, the ship of state ought to be sailed under the direction of the captain rather than the passengers, otherwise it will founder on the rocks. Both these images, with their implicitly anti-democratic message, have had a powerful influence on how people conceive of politics. Plato developed these ideas in much greater detail in *The Republic*, once again using Socrates as his mouthpiece. For the present, however, it suffices to record that nothing Socrates says about political obligation directly turns on whether a state is democratic or not, only on what is just. As we noted above, Socrates's silence concerning democracy is odd given that Athens was ruled in a highly democratic manner for most of this period. I shall consider the issue of whether democracy makes a difference when discussing Locke's arguments in the next section.

Socrates pursues his analysis of our obedience to the law through an imaginary discussion with the Laws of Athens, in which they reply to his proposal to violate them by escaping. Their first response is to ask what would happen if everyone broke the law whenever they felt aggrieved. This argument appeals to a domino theory, whereby to break one law is tantamount to inviting revolution against the entire legal system. Taken literally, this thesis is demonstrably false. Almost everyone has broken the law in some way or other, say by speeding, without the state collapsing. Nor do ordinary criminals have any interest in inviting others to follow their example. Their success depends on others being law abiding, and on their not being detected. Once discovered, the only example they set is the salutary and law-reinforcing one of demonstrating that crime does not pay. An exception might be a criminal who gets found out and yet escapes the clutches of the law, such as the Great Train Robber Ronald Biggs. Socrates' depiction of Thessaly as a latter day Costa del Crime suggests that he may have wished to portray the course of action proposed by Crito as analogous to that of Biggs.

Socrates' apparent subservience to whatever the Laws require sits oddly with his reputation for bolshiness and a strict adherence to his principles. It hardly seems the appropriate attitude for the self-styled 'gadfly' of Athens to adopt. Indeed, at his trial, reported by Plato in the *Apology*, Socrates seemed to question the court's fitness to decide matters of justice. He even stated that if the court were to discharge him on condition that he gave up philosophical enquiry and debate, he would disobey the order: 'I owe a greater obedience to God than to you', he remarked, 'and so long as I draw breath and have my faculties, I shall never stop practising philosophy and exhorting you and elucidating the truth for everyone I meet' (Plato, 1954, p. 61). Some commentators have taken Socrates to mean that law is only valid to the extent that it accords with the higher law of God or morality, a position that apparently gains additional support from his earlier refusal to comply with the order of the Thirty Tyrants to arrest Leon of Salamis. However, it was clearly not Socrates's intention in either case to escape the legal consequences of his actions. Socrates merely declared that, if banned from philosophising, he would try to persuade Athens of the error of its decision by 'exhorting' and 'elucidating the truth', but if he failed then he was prepared to pay the penalty.

This stance has led many commentators to characterise Socrates as a civil disobedient. In some respects, the Laws' domino argument appears to have more force as an objection to civil disobedience than it has against revolutionaries or criminals. Unlike revolutionaries, who do wish to overturn the prevailing legal system, civil disobedients desire only to protest against a particular law. Moreover, they do so openly and so could be accused of inviting others to follow suit, thereby possibly encouraging the general collapse of legal authority feared by the Laws. However, the Laws themselves propose an answer to this dilemma. They tell Socrates that 'if you cannot persuade your country you must do whatever it orders, and patiently submit to any punishment'. This remark suggests that dissent is permissable so long as it remains persuasive in character and dissenters accept the normal penalty for their wrongdoing. In so acting, protesters can acknowledge the law's legitimacy and right to be obeyed, even if they challenge a particular law. As we saw, Socrates adopts this line. As always, he insisted two wrongs did not make a right. He refused to do an act he thought wrong, even when commanded by the law to do so. Yet he also refrained from committing what he regarded as a wrong against the Laws by challenging their authority to punish him for his disobedience.

Although a number of legal theorists, and most governments, continue to espouse such views, these criteria of permissible law-breaking are highly contentious. Some civil disobedience campaigns arise out of the fact that certain interests have not been taken into account by the usual political process, often because it is dominated by a powerful elite. In such cases, more might be required than mere persuasive strategies, such as demonstrations and public meetings. Working-class movements, for example, have typically had recourse to more costly tactics, such as strikes, to get their voice heard. Similarly, some forms of dissent depend on those who engage in it not getting caught. The classic case is the campaign against the Fugitive Slave Act in the United States in the nineteenth century. This law forbade northerners from helping southern slaves to escape. Only a secret network of helpers enabled it to be successfully evaded and eventually undermined.

Many civil disobedients go further and confront the Laws' arguments head on. They contend that the failure to remove an injustice is likely to delegitimise and so destabilise the rule of law far more than acting against it (see, for example, the argument employed by Durkheim in chapter 11). Indeed, civil disobedients often appeal to the underlying principles of the political regime to justify their actions. American civil rights campaigners during the 1960s, for example, argued that segregation infringed both the letter and the spirit of the Constitution of the United States. From this perspective, their actions serve to uphold and restore, rather than to undermine the laws. This strategy is not available in unjust regimes, of course. Yet even here a campaigner might believe that civil disobedience would be preferable to risking a descent into anarchy – many took this approach when seeking to overturn apartheid in South Africa.

Without qualification, then, the Laws' argument goes too far. It implies that we should never challenge even very tyrannical regimes, such as Saddam Hussein's Iraq. Yet a general collapse of law and order might be preferable to the continuance of such a highly unjust regime. The assumption that the Laws are basically just and beneficial plays a key role in their second response to Socrates, which stresses the gratitude he should show to them.

The Laws argue that we owe them an analogous duty to that which we owe to a parent who brings us into existence, nurtures and educates us. This analogy between the family and a *polis* highlights a major difficulty with the Lockean account, examined in the next section, with its stress on consent. Namely, that by and large we no more choose our nationality than we do our parents. Moreover, most people feel a lasting bond both to their parents and to their country of birth that can legitimately override various voluntarily incurred duties. If I renege on a dinner engagement to tend a sick relative, no one will think it odd – quite the reverse. Similarly, individuals who have found fame and fortune abroad often feel obliged to return to far less prestigious positions in their home country when called upon during a national crisis.

However, there are limits to how much work this analogy can do. We no longer regard children as the slaves or chattels of their parents, as the Laws appear to do. Although the strength of either our affection for, or sense of obligation towards, our parents does not simply depend on how caring or good they were to us, some relation exists between the two. A child may legitimately feel less obliged towards a cruel parent than a kind or solicitous one. Returning to Socrates's earlier argument that it is wrong to repay one injustice with another, the Laws maintain that to break the law of even a badly ordered state would be akin to retaliating against a parent who has beaten you by striking them in return. This complaint assumes that disobedience constitutes such an injury against the state, something we disputed above. And whilst it would be wrong perhaps to return harm for harm (although sometimes punishment might be appropriate), we would none the less wish to protect children against abuse by their parents and would quite understand if they wanted nothing further to do with them.

Perhaps for these reasons, the Laws subtly shift their ground and concentrate simply on the benefits they bestow on the people, such as law and order. Even so, the beneficial nature of the goods provided need not in themselves create an obligation to obey. An old lady who is officiously escorted across the road by a do-gooding boy scout may well object that she would rather have crossed at her own pace and at a place of her choosing. Similarly, citizens can reasonably ask for some control over what the Laws provide, and ought not to be expected to feel grateful for whatever service the Laws happen to offer them, regardless of whether they want it or not. Even when we acknowledge that someone has placed us in his or her debt by doing us a good turn, few feel bound to reciprocate in the manner of Friday to Robinson Crusoe with life-long obedience and devotion. Likewise, it remains obscure why gratitude to the Laws should mean total obedience rather than some more qualified recognition of their worth to us. The Laws might claim that they have a better idea of what we need than we do ourselves, rather as parents frequently have to direct young children in their own best interests. However, citizens do not remain eternal infants; the Laws cannot portray themselves as being *in loco parentis* throughout the whole course of one's life.

At some stage, the benefit will need to be accepted by choice, therefore, and the conditions of acceptance arrived at. The Laws imply such a negotiation has occurred when they argue that whoever willingly remains in a country 'when he can see how we administer justice and the rest of our public organisation ... has in fact undertaken to do anything we tell him.' Socrates's exceptional reluctance to leave Athens meant that few people had entered into this agreement as explicitly as he had. To run away would be in breach 'of the contracts and undertakings by which you agreed to live as a member of our State'. These arguments invoke the doctrine of consent, which Locke was to make the lynch-pin of his theory of political obligation.

### John Locke (1632–1704)

Details of Locke's life and political philosophy can be found in chapter 4. We shall restrict ourselves here to an examination of his theory of consent and a comparison with the views expressed in the *Crito*.

Consent theory holds that we are under an obligation to obey the law only if we have first agreed to do so. A number of important assumptions lie behind this idea. Namely, that individuals are naturally free and equal and so entitled to, as well as capable of, governing themselves. The Greeks believed that some people were born to be citizens and others to be slaves, and that human beings were by nature political animals (*zoa politika*), or members of a *polis*. Locke argued that no one is by nature the subordinate of anybody else, so that political society and the setting up of a system of government is an artificial arrangement created by individuals. Locke's argument was aimed against contemporary monarchical theories that contended that societies were naturally hierarchical and akin to families, with the King as a father figure. Indeed, much of the *Two Treatises* takes the form of an explicit critique of Sir Robert Filmer's defence of this thesis in his *Patriarcha*. This and other of Filmer's writings had been posthumously published in 1680 as part of a campaign to justify obedience to the Stuart monarchy against those seeking to exclude the future James II from the throne on the grounds of his being a Catholic. Locke was a member of the opposition camp, and his theory has decidedly revolutionary implications.

Locke portrays political society as the product of a social contract between free and equal individuals living in a state of nature – a device that has been employed by many theorists before and since. This account of the origin of political society raises the related questions of who consents, when, how, why and to what? We shall examine each in turn.

Who consents? Although controversy rages about whether Locke included the propertyless or women amongst the consenters, the main thrust of his argument suggests that he ought to have held (and in my view did hold) that all adults of sound mind signed up to the social contract. However, our second question – when are we to suppose they consented – presents greater problems. Filmer had raised two important objections to social contract theories in this regard. He pointed out that there is no historical record of any society ever coming into being in this fashion, and that everyone is now born into an already existing polity. Locke counters the first objection by remarking that although no written records of original charters exist, there is plenty of anthropological evidence – especially from the native American peoples – to show that independent, equal and free men commonly set rulers over themselves. Against the second objection, Locke denies that birth makes any difference: in his view there can be no natural subjection to any society. He claims that history offers plenty of examples of 'Men withdrawing themselves, and their Obedience, from the Jurisdiction they were born under and *setting up new Governments* in other places' (*Second Treatise*, para. 115). He insists that past generations cannot bind their successors or fathers their children. Once an individual reaches the 'Age of Discretion ... he is a Free-man, at liberty what Government he will put himself under; what Body Politick he will unite himself to' (para. 118).

Readers may find this contention surprising, for it implies that at some stage they must either have offered their consent or be stateless persons. Given that most people do regard themselves as citizens, how did they consent? Locke argues that we consent in two different ways: tacitly and expressly. Tacit consent bears a close resemblance to the last argument of the Laws examined above. It derives from simple enjoyment of the benefits provided by the laws of any state, such as the secure possession of property or even 'travelling freely on the Highway' (para. 116). However, Locke contends that tacit consent does not entail membership of the society in question. Rather, it places us under the sorts of obligations tourists have in visiting another country to obey its laws for the duration of their stay. Such consent neither entitles them to the full rights of citizenship, such as participation in elections, nor imposes such duties as military service. Only express consent can result in a person being 'perpetually and indispensably obliged to be and remain unalterably a Subject to' a given Commonwealth (para. 121). Such consent involves a 'positive Engagement, and express Promise and Compact', such as naturalised citizens are usually called upon to give today (para. 122).

Both tacit and express consent prove problematic. The first risks being impossible to avoid, whilst the second seems hard to give. With regard to the latter, historians have pointed out that explicit oaths of allegiance formed a common part of the covenanting tradition of contemporary Calvinist sects, and were widely practised in early modern Europe. Locke may have had in mind the fact that in 1650 Parliament had legitimised its victory in the recent Civil War by requiring all males aged over eighteen to signal their allegiance to the Cromwellian regime by subscribing to the following Engagement: 'I do declare and promise, That I will be true and faithful to the Commonwealth of England, as it is now established, without a king or House of Lords'. However, such oaths are unsatisfactory as examples of express consent. They were usually obligatory rather than voluntary and were taken with regard to certain religious or political doctrines.

They were not forms of consent to membership. On the contrary, refusal led not to expulsion or withdrawal of citizenship but to punishment as a citizen.

On closer inspection, Locke's distinction between tacit and express consent turns out to be less clear-cut than the passages cited above make it appear. He suggests that the inheritance of property can serve as both tacit (para. 120) and express (para. 117) consent, for example. This ambiguity reflects, on the one hand, Locke's concern to avoid any appeal to Filmer's argument that we incur political obligations by birth alone and, on the other, his desire to preserve the territorial integrity of the state, which requires binding landowners to it. Macpherson (1962, p. 250) famously argued that inheritance constitutes the only form of express consent, a thesis that fits his general interpretation of Locke as a defender of bourgeois possessive individualism. However, this view is contradicted by Locke's explicit declaration (at paras 120 and 122) that mere possession is insufficient. A confusion none the less remains. Locke wants to emphasise that a difference exists between mere travellers and those with some sort of ongoing stake in a country. He also wants to stress a distinction between general moral obligations and those we incur by joining a given political society. Both elements are important, but he does not offer satisfactory ways of establishing them.

Express consent is not necessary for every change of regime. It is only required to join or establish a given, territorially defined, political society. Thereafter, consenters are bound to abide by the determination of the majority as to the form of government and the composition of the executive, until such time as either their citizenship is revoked or the society dissolves. The personnel, policy and even the character of the regime may alter without requiring the express consent of each and every citizen, so long as it remains true to the purpose for which political societies come into being in the first place.

Here we come to the hardest questions posed by consent theory: why do we consent and to what? Locke believes that all rational individuals are capable of discovering the Law of Nature, by which he means the general rules of morality laying down our rights and obligations towards other human beings. As chapter 4 shows, Locke takes these rules to relate to the preservation of our 'property', by which Locke generally means our lives, liberties and estates. However, the application of these rules to particular cases is often difficult and contentious. As population grows and the pressure on resources increases, this fact becomes ever more troublesome. In addition to the inherent difficulty of agreeing on what the Law of Nature requires in particular cases, individuals have a tendency to be partial towards their own cause. Nor do they always have the power to enforce the Law against those that transgress it. The purpose of political society is to avoid all three of these sources of uncertainty by first, establishing settled and known laws embodying a set standard of right and wrong; second, appointing a 'known and indifferent judge' to resolve disputes; and third and last, to create a body with a monopoly of violence that has the power to enforce sentences once they are made (paras 124–6).

Locke insists that we only entrust governments with our right to adjudicate on and enforce the Law of Nature. We do not, as Hobbes had maintained, alienate that right completely to the sovereign power. Such alienation would leave the sovereign body outside political society, with the people unable to judge or punish it or him for violations of the natural law. This would be an extremely unwise decision, and he chides Hobbes for thinking men 'so foolish that they take care to avoid what Mischiefs may be done them by *Pole-Cats* or *Foxes* [in the state of nature], but are content, nay think it safety, to be devoured by *Lions* [absolute monarchs]' (para. 93). As a result, Locke allows not just for civil disobedience but even, in extreme cases, for revolution against an unjust government. Indeed, the *Two Treatises* were originally written with just such revolutionary intentions.

How satisfactory is Locke's argument? It remains unclear whether actual consent is either possible or necessary. The possibility of consenting turns on our ability to withhold it. As we noted above, whilst the tacit transfer of our consent may be reasonably easy, our opportunities for exercising express consent are decidedly limited. In Locke's day, white Europeans still had the chance to set up colonies whereas, on his somewhat idealised and convenient account, the indigenous peoples of colonised lands remained largely in the state of nature, submitting to government only in the case of war, when they elected a general. Today, immigration controls make it extremely hard even to change one's allegiance from one state to another. Although limited possibilities exist for political refugees, the case of the Vietnamese boat people reveals how restricted these are. Even so, many people would claim that, whilst the political systems of some countries are undoubtedly better than others, the available options merely allow us to choose the lesser of various evils rather than to give a positive expression of approval.

Some theorists assume that democracy allows the expression of consent. However, as Locke correctly observes, the acceptance of majority rule and democratic decision-making *assumes* that we have already expressly consented to being a member of political society governed by those rules. Only a very radical kind of direct democracy could embody a form of rolling express consent, one that allowed the electorate to vote on all the possible options surrounding every policy and required unanimity on all issues. As R. P. Wolff has pointed out (1970, p. 33), such a unanimous direct democracy is impractical and so this position is tantamount to anarchism (see chapter 10).

The only way nowadays to give express consent is by revolution and the explicit setting up of a new political society. However, the option of revolution when governments abuse their trust may be sufficient for Locke's purposes, provided we interpret his theory as involving hypothetical rather than actual consent. In other words, we ask whether a political regime is one to which a rational person *would* consent if they were given the option. A theory of hypothetical consent aims to provide criteria for assessing a polity's legitimacy. According to Locke, what rational consenters would agree to is a political society that upholds the Law of Nature and preserves our natural rights. Unlike Hobbes, Locke did not believe that genuine consent could be coerced (paras 175–6) or could be given to an unjust regime. Similarly, he thought that consent to slavery (para. 23); absolute or arbitrary government (paras 93, 131, 137–8) and the like was not binding. To this extent, he did not consider actual consent a sufficient condition for political obligation. However, he clearly held it to be a necessary condition. The doctrine of hypothetical consent can only stipulate general minimum moral standards. If the all important special tie between citizens and polity is to be created, then individuals must actually consent. Unfortunately, we have seen that Locke fails to offer a plausible account of how actual consent might be given. Whether political obligation is really necessary is a question to which we now turn.

## Conclusion

Many contemporary philosophers see no need for political obligation. Our general moral duty to do what is right provides all that is necessary to secure our obedience to most laws. Morality teaches us not to murder or steal, for example, and to obey those laws that prevent such acts. Similarly, we all have good reason to abide by traffic laws and other regulations designed to solve collective action problems for the common benefit. Once again, the risk of harming others by not obeying such rules, as when we drive through a red light, suffices to bind us to the legal order. Additional legal or political obligations are neither needed nor warranted. We are citizens of the world, and are under an obligation to pay taxes to, and obey the laws of, whatever country we happen to reside in, so long as the regime is morally legitimate. There are no peculiar moral requirements of a political nature which give rise to a special obligation to any one state in particular.

This argument seems too weak, however, to sustain the complex network of special ties and obligations which seem required for any political system to operate, and that bind each of us to one particular state. This view makes it appear morally arbitrary, for example, whether we send money to Oxfam or support the National Health Service, or whether we join the UN peace keeping force or do national service. Nor can it explain the clash which many people feel at times, between their general moral obligations as human beings and the more particular moral duties they have as citizens. War offers a good example of this sort of conflict. Most people, including many pacifists, regard themselves as having a stronger moral, and not merely a sentimental, obligation to defend their own country rather than another.

Our analysis of Locke's argument suggests that consent offers a poor explanation of how we incur such duties. In this respect, the communitarian thesis implicit in Socrates' analogy between the *polis* and our parents proves superior. Not only does it possess greater psychological and sociological plausibility than the consent theory, the notion that

certain duties arise less out of choice than from the human condition of
dependence on an existing social framework also captures the moral
significance of such obligations with greater clarity. Human beings are
not born autonomous and self-supporting; they achieve this status
through society. Our social duties are best seen as an acknowledgement
of this fact. However, not all societies are equally nurturing and benign.
This is where consent theories have a role to play. Elaborating the
theory of hypothetical consent is a way of setting limits to what a state
can oblige us to do and suggesting minimum moral standards of what
we can expect it to provide.

Whilst neither the communitarian theory nor consent theory makes
democracy a condition of political obligation, democratic practices can
reinforce both sorts of obligation. Political participation, as Aristotle
and Rousseau noted, builds identification with the community and
with the policies it enacts. However, as James Mill argued, democratic
political participation also helps place a check on government and
ensures that rulers exercise their power in the interests of the governed
rather than themselves (see chapter 5). Thus Socrates' and Locke's
accounts complement each other. If a communitarian theory of our
basic social duties provides the basis for our political obligations, hypothetical consent marks its legitimate limits and minimal content.

## References

Aristotle, *The Politics*, Harmondsworth: Penguin, 1981.
Locke, J., *Two Treatises of Government*, ed. P. Laslett, Cambridge: Cambridge
    University Press, 1960.
Macpherson, C. B., *The Political Theory of Possessive Individualism*, Oxford:
    Clarendon Press, 1962.
Plato, *The Apology* in *The Last days of Socrates*, Harmondsworth: Penguin, 1954.
Wolff, R. P., *In Defense of Anarchism*, New York: Harper & Row, 1970.

## Further reading

The *Crito*, together with the *Apology*, Plato's recreation of Socrates' trial, and the
*Phaedo*, an account of his final day in prison, can be found in Plato, *The Last Days
of Socrates* (trans. H. Tredennick, Harmondsworth: Penguin, 1954) and also in
John Ferguson (ed.), *Socrates: A Source Book* (Basingstoke: Macmillan, 1970).
Good discussions of the *Crito* are A. D. Woozley, *Law and Obedience: The
Arguments of Plato's 'Crito'* (London: Duckworth, 1979); R. Kraut, *Socrates and the
State* (Princeton, NJ: Princeton University Press, 1984), and I. F. Stone, *The Trial
of Socrates* (London: Picador, 1988). The first two largely defend Socrates' view,
the last attacks it. A full reading list for Locke can be found in chapter 4, to which
should be added J. Dunn, 'Consent in the Political Theory of John Locke', in the
same author's *Political Obligation in its Historical Context: Essays in Political Theory*
(Cambridge: Cambridge University Press, 1980), a collection of essays replete
with Lockean variations on this theme; H. Pitkin, 'Obligation and Consent'
(*American Political Science Review*, 59 & 60, 1965–66) and J. Zvesper, 'The Utility
of Consent in John Locke's Political Philosophy' (*Political Studies*, 32, 1984), who
put forward a hypothetical consent reading of Locke; and A. J. Simmonds, *On
the Edge of Anarchy: Locke, Consent and the Limits of Society* (Princeton, NJ:
Princeton University Press, 1993), who provides an exhaustive survey of the

literature and critical defence of Locke. Three useful discussions of political obligation are A. J. Simmonds, *Moral Principles and Political Obligations* (Princeton, NJ: Princeton University Press, 1979), who advocates a neo-Lockean viewpoint he describes as philosophical anarchism; J. Horton, *Political Obligation* (Basingstoke: Macmillan, 1992), who subscribes to a more communitarian position; and J. Charvet, 'Political Obligation: Individualism and Communitarianism', in P. Harris (ed.), *On Political Obligation* (London: Routledge, 1990), who offers an elegant synthesis of the two positions.

### Seminar questions

Do you think Socrates should have escaped, despite the fact that this would have meant breaking the law?

Is Socrates' argument for obedience to the law a gift to despots?

Is Socrates' thesis more appropriate to the Greek *polis* than a modern democratic state?

'Tacit consent is impossible to avoid, express consent impossible to give'. Is Locke's account of political obligation implausible?

Does Locke's theory drift into anarchism?

'The only obligation I have a right to assume, is to do at any time what I think right.' (Thoreau) Do you agree?

# PLATO
## The *Crito*

SOCRATES: Ought we to be guided and intimidated by the opinion of the many or by that of the one – assuming that there is someone with expert knowledge? Is it true that we ought to respect and fear this person more than all the rest put together; and that if we do not follow his guidance we shall spoil and mutilate that part of us which, as we used to say, is improved by right conduct and destroyed by wrong? Or is this all nonsense?

CRITO: No, I think it is true, Socrates.

SOCRATES: Then consider the next step. There is a part of us which is improved by healthy actions and ruined by unhealthy ones. If we spoil it by taking the advice of non-experts, will life be worth living when this part is once ruined? The part I mean is the body; do you accept this?

CRITO: Yes.

SOCRATES: Well, is life worth living with a body which is worn out and ruined in health?

CRITO: Certainly not.

SOCRATES: What about the part of us which is mutilated by wrong actions and benefited by right ones? Is life worth living with this part ruined? Or do we believe that this part of us, whatever it may be, in

14

which right and wrong operate, is of less importance than the body?

CRITO: Certainly not.

SOCRATES: It is really more precious?

CRITO: Much more.

SOCRATES: In that case, my dear fellow, what we ought to consider is not so much what people in general will say about us but how we stand with the expert in right and wrong, the one authority, who represents the actual truth. So in the first place your proposition is not correct when you say that we should consider popular opinion in questions of what is right and honourable and good, or the opposite. Of course one might object 'All the same, the people have the power to put us to death.'

CRITO: No doubt about that! Quite true, Socrates; it is a possible objection.

SOCRATES: But so far as I can see, my dear fellow, the argument which we have just been through is quite unaffected by it. At the same time I should like you to consider whether we are still satisfied on this point: that the realy important thing is not to live, but to live well.

CRITO: Why, yes.

SOCRATES: And that to live well means the same thing as to live honourably or rightly?

CRITO: Yes.

SOCRATES: Then in the light of this agreement we must consider whether or not it is right for me to try to get away without an official discharge. If it turns out to be right, we must make the attempt; if not, we must let it drop. As for the considerations you raise about expense and reputation and bringing up children, I am afraid, Crito, that they represent the relections of the ordinary public, who put people to death, and would bring them back to life if they could, with equal indifference to reason. Our real duty, I fancy, since the argument leads that way, is to consider one question only, the one which we raised just now: Shall we be acting rightly in paying money and showing gratitude to these people who are going to rescue me, and in escaping or arranging the escape ourselves, or shall we really be acting wrongly in doing all this? If it becomes clear that such conduct is wrong, I cannot help thinking that the question whether we are sure to die, or to suffer any other ill effect for that matter, if we stand our ground and take no action, ought not to weigh with us at all in comparison with the risk of doing what is wrong.

CRITO: I agree with what you say, Socrates; but I wish you would consider what we ought to *do*.

SOCRATES: Let us look at it together, my dear fellow; and if you can challenge any of my arguments, do so and I will listen to you; but if you can't, be a good fellow and stop telling me over and over again that I ought to leave this place without official permission. I am very anxious to obtain your approval before I adopt the course which I have in mind; I don't want to act against your convictions. Now give your attention to the starting point of this inquiry – I hope that you will be satisfied with my way of stating it – and try to answer my questions to the best of your judgement.

CRITO: Well, I will try.

SOCRATES: Do we say that one must never willingly do wrong, or does it depend upon circumstances? Is it true, as we have often agreed before, that there is no sense in which wrongdoing is good or honourable? Or have we jettisoned all our former convictions in these last few days? Can you and I at our age, Crito, have spent all these years in serious discussions without realizing that we were not better than a pair of children? Surely the truth is just what we have always said. Whatever the popular view is, and whether the alternative is pleasanter than the present one or even harder to bear, the fact remains that to do wrong is in every sense bad and dishonourable for the person who does it. Is that our view, or not?

CRITO: Yes, it is.

SOCRATES: Then in no circumstances must one do wrong.

CRITO: No.

SOCRATES: In that case one must not even do wrong when one is wronged, which most people regard as the natural course.

CRITO: Apparently not.

SOCRATES: Tell me another thing, Crito: ought one to do injuries or not?

CRITO: Surely not, Socrates.

SOCRATES: And tell me: is it right to do an injury in retaliation, as most people believe, or not?

CRITO: No, never.

SOCRATES: Because, I suppose, there is no difference between injuring people and wronging them.

CRITO: Exactly.

SOCRATES: So one ought not to return a wrong or an injury to any person, whatever the provocation is. Now be careful, Crito, that in making these single admissions you do not end by admitting something contrary to your real beliefs. I know that there are and always will be few people who think like this; and consequently between those who do think so and those who do not there can be no agreement on prin-ciple; they must always feel contempt when they observe one another's decisions. I want even you to consider very carefully whether you share my views and agree with me, and whether we can proceed with our discussion from the established hypothesis that it is never right to do a wrong or return a wrong or defend one's self against injury by retaliation; or whether you dissociate yourself from any share in this view as a basis for discussion. I have held it for a long time, and still hold it; but if you have formed any other opinion, say so and tell me what it is. If, on the other hand, you stand by what we have said, listen to my next point.

CRITO: Yes, I stand by it and agree with you. Go on.

SOCRATES: Well, here is my next point, or rather question. Ought one to fulfil all one's agreements, provided that they are right, or break them?

CRITO: One ought to fulfil them.

SOCRATES: Then consider the logical consequence. If we leave this place without first persuading the State to let us go, are we or are we not doing an injury, and doing it in a quarter where it is least justifiable? Are we or are we not abiding by our just agreements?

CRITO: I can't answer your question, Socrates; I am not clear in my mind.

SOCRATES: Look at it in this way. Suppose that while we were preparing to run away from here (or however one should describe it) The Laws and Constitution of Athens were to come and confront us and ask this question: 'Now, Socrates, what are you proposing to do? Can you deny that by this act which you are contemplating you intend, so far as you have the power, to destroy us, the Laws, and the whole State as well? Do you imagine that a city can continue to exist and not be turned upside down, if the legal judgements which are pronounced in it have no force but are nullified and destroyed by private persons?' – how shall we answer this question, Crito, and others of the same kind? There is much that could be said, especially by a professional advocate, to protest against the invalidation of this law which enacts that judgements once pronounced shall be binding. Shall we say 'Yes, I do intend to destroy the laws, because the State wronged me by passing a faulty judgement at my trial'? Is this to be our answer, or what?

CRITO: What you have just said, by all means, Socrates.

SOCRATES: Then what supposing the Laws say 'Was there provision for this in the agreement between you and us, Socrates? Or did you undertake to abide by whatever judgements the State pronounced?' If we expressed surprise at such language, they would probably say: 'Never mind our language, Socrates, but answer our questions; after all, you are accustomed to the method of question and answer. Come now, what charge do you bring against us and the State, that you are trying to destroy us? Did we not give you life in the first place? was it not through us that your father married your mother and begot you? Tell us, have you any complaint against those of us Laws that deal with marriage?' 'No, none', I should say, 'Well, have you any against the laws which deal with children's upbringing and education, such as you had yourself? Are you not grateful to those of us Laws which were instituted for this end, for requiring your father to give you a cultural and physical education?' 'Yes', I should say. 'Very good. Then since you have been born and brought up and educated, can you deny, in the first place, that you were our child and servant, both you and your ancestors? And if this is so, do you imagine that what is right for us is equally right for you, and that whatever we try to do to you, you are justified in retaliating? You did not have equality of rights with your father, or your employer (supposing that you had had one), to enable you to retaliate; you were not allowed to answer back when you were scolded or to hit back when you were beaten, or to do a great many other things of the same kind. Do you expect to have such licence against your country and its laws that if

17

we try to put you to death in the belief that it is right to do so, you on your part will try your hardest to destroy your country and us its Laws in return? and will you, the true devotee of goodness, claim that you are justified in doing so? Are you so wise as to have forgotten that compared with your mother and father and all the rest of your ancestors your country is something far more precious, more venerable, more sacred, and held in greater honour both among gods and among all reasonable men? Do you not realize that you are even more bound to respect and placate the anger of your country than your father's anger? that if you cannot persuade your country you must do whatever it orders, and patiently submit to any punishment that it imposes, whether it be flogging or imprisonment? And if it leads you out to war, to be wounded or killed, you must comply, and it is right that you should do so; you must not give way or retreat or abandon your position. Both in war and in the law courts and everywhere else you must do whatever your city and your country commands, or else persuade it in accordance with universal justice; but violence is a sin even against your parents, and it is a far greater sin against your country.' – What shall we say to this, Crito? – that what the Laws say is true, or not?

CRITO: Yes, I think so.

SOCRATES: 'Consider, then, Socrates,' the Laws would probably continue, 'whether it is also true for us to say that what you are now trying to do to us is not right. Although we have brought you into the world and reared you and educated you, and given you and all your fellow-citizens a share in all the good things at our disposal, nevertheless by the very fact of granting our permission we openly proclaim this principle: that any Athenian, on attaining to manhood and seeing for himself the political organization of the State and us its Laws, is permitted, if he is not satisfied with us, to take his property and go away wherever he likes. If any of you chooses to go to one of our colonies, supposing that he should not be satisfied with us and the State, or to emigrate to any other country, not one of us Laws hinders or prevents him from going away wherever he likes, without any loss of property. On the other hand, if any one of you stands his ground when he can see how we administer justice and the rest of our public organization, we hold that by so doing he has in fact undertaken to do anything that we tell him; and we maintain that anyone who disobeys is guilty of doing wrong on three separate counts: first because we are his parents, and secondly because we are his guardians; and thirdly because, after promising obedience, he is neither obeying us nor persuading us to change our decision if we are at fault in any way; and although all our orders are in the form of proposals, not of savage commands, and we give him the choice of either persuading us or doing what we say, he is actually doing neither. These are the charges, Socrates, to which we say that you will be liable if you do what you are contemplating; and you will not be the least culpable of your fellow-countrymen, but one of the most guilty.' If I said 'Why do you say that?' they would no doubt pounce upon me with perfect justice and point out that there are very few people in Athens who have entered into this agreement with them as explicitly as I have. They would say 'Socrates, we have substantial evidence that you are satisfied with us and with the State. You would not have been so exceptionally reluctant to cross the borders of your country if you had not been exceptionally attached to it. You have never left the city to attend a festival or for any other purpose, except on some military expedition; you have never travelled abroad as other people do, and you have never felt the impulse to acquaint yourself with another country or constitution; you have been content with us and with our city. You have definitely chosen us, and under-taken to observe us in all your activities as a citizen; and as the crowning proof that you are satisfied with our city, you have begot-ten children in it. Furthermore, even at the time of your trial you could have proposed the penalty of banishment, if you had chosen to do so; that is, you could have done then with the sanction of the State what you are now trying to do without it. But whereas at that time you made a noble show of indifference if you had to die, and in fact preferred death, as you said, to banishment, now you show no respect for your earlier professions, and no regard for us, the Laws, whom you are trying to destroy; you are behaving like the lowest type of menial, trying to run away in spite of the contracts and under-takings by which you agreed to live as a member of our State. Now first answer this question: Are we or are we not speaking the truth when we say that you have undertaken, in deed if not in word, to live your life as a citizen in obedience to us?' What are we to say to that, Crito? Are we not bound to admit it?

CRITO: We cannot help it, Socrates.

SOCRATES: 'It is a fact, then,' they would say, 'that you are breaking covenants and undertakings made with us, although you made them under no compulsion or misunderstanding, and were not compelled to decide in a limited time; you had seventy years in which you could have left the country, if you were not satisfied with us or felt that the agreements were unfair. You did not choose Sparta or Crete – your favourite models of good government – or any other Greek or foreign state; you could not have absented yourself from the city less if you had been lame or blind or decrepit in some other way. It is quite obvious that you stand by yourself above all other Athenians in your affection for this city and for us its Laws; – who would care for a city without laws? And now, after all this, are you not going to stand by your agreement? Yes, you are, Socrates, if you will take our advice; and then you will at least escape being laughed at for leaving the city.

'We invite you to consider what good you will do to yourself or your friends if you commit this break of faith and stain your conscience. It is fairly obvious that the risk of being banished and either losing their citizenship or having their property confiscated will extend to your friends as well. As for yourself, if you go to one of the neighbouring states, such as Thebes or Megara, which are both well governed, you will enter them as an enemy to their constitution, and all good patriots will eye you with suspicion as a destroyer of law and order. Incidentally you will confirm the opinion of the jurors who tried you that they gave a correct verdict; a destroyer of laws might very well be supposed to have a destructive influence upon young and foolish human beings. Do you intend, then, to avoid well governed states and the higher forms of human society? and if you do, will life be worth living? Or will you approach these people and have the impudence to converse with them? What arguments will you use, Socrates? The same which you used here, that goodness and integrity, institutions and laws, are the most precious possessions of mankind? Do you not think that Socrates and everything about him will appear in a disreputable light? You certainly ought to think so. But perhaps you will retire from this part of the world and go to Crito's friends in Thessaly? That is the home of indiscipline and laxity, and no doubt they would enjoy hearing the amusing story of how you managed to run away from prison by arraying yourself in some costume or putting on a shepherd's smock or some other conventional runaway's disguise, and altering your personal appearance. And will no one comment on the fact that an old man of your age, probably with only a short time left to live, should dare to cling so greedily to life, at the price of violating the most stringent laws? Perhaps not, if you avoid irritating anyone. Otherwise, Socrates, you will hear a good many humiliating comments. So you will live as the toady and slave of all the populace, literally 'roistering in Thessaly', as though you had left this country for Thessaly to attend a banquet there; and where will your discussions about goodness and uprightness be then, we should like to know? But of course you want to live for your children's sake, so that you may be able to bring them up and educate them. Indeed! by first taking them off to Thessaly and making foreigners of them, so that they may have that additional enjoyment? Or if that is not your intention, supposing that they are brought up here with you still alive, will they be better cared for and educated without you, because of course your friends will look after them? Will they look after your children if you go away to Thessaly, and not if you go away to the next world? Surely if those who profess to be your friends are worth anything, you must believe that they would care for them.

'No, Socrates; be advised by us your guardians, and do not think more of your children or of your life or of anything else than you think of what is right; so that when you enter the next world you may have all this to plead in your defence before the authorities there. It seems clear that if you do this thing, neither you nor any of your friends will be the better for it or be more upright or have a cleaner conscience here in this world, nor will it be better for you when you reach the next. As it is, you will leave this place, when you do, as the victim of a wrong done not by us, the Laws, but by your fellow-men.

But if you leave in that dishonourable way, returning wrong for
wrong and evil for evil, breaking your agreements and covenants
with us, and injuring those whom you least ought to injure – yourself, your friends, your country, and us – then you will have to face
our anger in your lifetime, and in that place beyond when the laws
of the other world know that you have tried, so far as you could, to
destroy even us their brothers, they will not receive you with a kindly
welcome. Do not take Crito's advice, but follow ours.'

That, my dear friend Crito, I do assure you, is what I seem to hear
them saying, just as a mystic seems to hear the strains of music; and
the sound of their arguments rings so loudly in my head that I cannot
hear the other side. I warn you that, as my opinion stands at present,
it will be useless to urge a different view. However, if you think that
you will do any good by it, say what you like.

CRITO: No, Socrates, I have nothing to say.

SOCRATES: Then give it up, Crito, and let us follow this course, since God
points out the way.

# JOHN LOCKE
## From *The Second Treatise of Government*

### CHAP. VIII   Of the Beginning of Political Societies

95. Men being, as has been said, by Nature, all free, equal and independent, no one can be put out of this Estate, and subjected to the
Political Power of another, without his own *Consent*. The only way
whereby any one devests himself of his Natural Liberty, and *puts on
the bonds of Civil Society* is by agreeing with other Men to joyn and
unite into a Community, for their comfortable, safe, and peaceable
living one amongst another, in a secure Enjoyment of their Properties,
and a greater Security against any that are not of it. This any number
of Men may do, because it injures not the Freedom of the rest; they
are left as they were in the Liberty of the State of Nature. When any
number of Men have so *consented to make one Community* or
Government, they are thereby presently incorporated, and make *one
Body Politick*, wherein the *Majority* have a Right to act and conclude
the rest.

96. For when any number of Men have, by the consent of every individual, made a *Community*, they have thereby made that *Community*
one Body, with a Power to Act as one Body, which is only by the will
and determination of the *majority*. For that which acts any
Community, being only the consent of the individuals of it, and it
being necessary to that which is one body to move one way; it is
necessary the Body should move that way whither the greater force
carries it, which is the *consent of the majority*: or else it is impossible
it should act or continue one Body, *one Community*, which the consent

of every individual that united into it, agreed that it should; and so every one is bound by that consent to be concluded by the *majority*. And therefore we see that in Assemblies impowered to act by positive Laws where no number is set by that positive Law which impowers them, the *act of the Majority* passes for the act of the whole, and of course determines, as having by the Law of Nature and Reason, the power of the whole.

97. And thus every Man, by consenting with others to make one Body Politick under one Government, puts himself under an Obligation to every one of that Society, to submit to the determination of the *majority*, and to be concluded by it; or else this *original Compact*, whereby he with others incorporates into *one Society*, would signifie nothing, and be no Compact, if he be left free, and under no other ties, than he was in before in the State of Nature. For what appearance would there by of any Compact? What new Engagement if he were no farther tied by any Decrees of the Society, than he himself thought fit, and did actually consent to? This would be still as great a liberty, as he himself had before his Compact, or any one else in the State of Nature hath, who may submit himself and consent to any acts of it if he thinks fit.

98. For if *the consent of the majority* shall not in reason, be received, as *the act of the whole*, and conclude every individual; nothing but the consent of every individual can make any thing to be the act of the whole: But such a consent is next impossible ever to be had, if we consider the Infirmities of Health, and Avocations of Business, which in a number, though much less than that of a Common-wealth, will necessarily keep many away from the publick Assembly. To which if we add the variety of Opinions, and contrariety of Interests, which unavoidably happen in all Collections of Men, the coming into Society upon such terms, would be only like *Cato*'s coming into the Theatre, only to go out again. Such a Constitution as this would make the mighty *Leviathan* of a shorter duration, than the feeblest Creatures; and not let it outlast the day it was born in: which cannot be suppos'd, till we can think, that Rational Creatures should desire and constitute Societies only to be dissolved. For where the *majority* cannot conclude the rest, there they cannot act as one Body, and consequently will be immediately dissolved again.

99. Whosoever therefore out of a state of Nature unite into a *Community*, must be understood to give up all the power, necessary to the ends for which they unite into Society, to the *majority* of the Community, unless they expressly agreed in any number greater than the majority. And this is done by barely agreeing to *unite into one Political Society*, which is *all the Compact* that is, or needs be, between the Individuals, that enter into, or make up a *Common-wealth*. And thus that, which begins and actually *constitutes any Political Society*, is nothing but the consent of any number of Freemen capable of a majority to unite and incorporate into such a Society. And this is that, and that only, which did, or could give *beginning* to any *lawful Government* in the World.

100. To this I find two Objections made.

First, *That there are no Instances to be found in Story of a Company of Men independent and equal one amongst another, that met together, and in this way began and set up a Government.*

Secondly, *'Tis impossible of right that Men should do so, because all men being born under Government, they are to submit to that, and are not at liberty to begin a new one.*

101. To the first there is this to Answer. That it is not at all to be wonder'd, that *History* gives us but a very little account of Men, *that lived together in the State of Nature.* The inconveniencies of that condition, and the love, and want of Society no sooner brought any number of them together, but they presently united and incorporated, if they designed to continue together. And if we may not suppose *Men* ever to have been *in the State of Nature*, because we hear not much of them in such a State, we may as well suppose the Armies of *Salmanasser*, or *Xerxes* were never Children, because we hear little of them, till they were Men, and imbodied in Armies. Government is every where antecedent to Records, and Letters seldome come in amongst a People, till a long continuation of Civil Society has, by other more necessary Arts provided for their Safety, Ease, and Plenty. And then they begin to look after the History of their *Founders*, and search into their *original*, when they have out-lived the memory of it. For 'tis with *Common-wealths* as with particular Persons, they are commonly *ignorant of their own Births* and *Infancies*: And if they know any thing of their *Original*, they are beholding, for it, to the accidental Records, that others have kept of it. And those that we have, of the beginning of any Polities in the World, excepting that of the *Jews*, where God himself immediately interpos'd, and which favours not at all Paternal Dominion, are all either plain instances of such a beginning, as I have mentioned, or at least have manifest footsteps of it.

102. He must shew a strange inclination to deny evident matter of fact, when it agrees not with his Hypothesis, who will not allow that the *beginning* of *Rome* and *Venice* were by the uniting together of several Men free and independent one of another, amongst whom there was no natural Superiority or Subjection. And if *Josephus Acosta's* word may be taken, he tells us, that in many parts of *America* there was no Government at all. *There are great and apparent Conjectures*, says he, *that these Men*, speaking of those of *Peru, for a long time had neither Kings nor Common-wealths, but lived in Troops, as they do this day in* Florida, *the* Cheriquanas, *those of* Bresil, *and many other Nations, which have no certain Kings, but as occasion is offered in Peace or War, they choose their Captains as they please*, I. t. c. 25. If it be said, that every Man there was born subject to his Father, or the head of his Family. That the subjection due from a Child to a Father, took not away his freedom of uniting into what Political Society he thought fit, has been already proved. But be that as it will, these Men, 'tis evident, were actually *free*; and whatever superiority some Politicians now would place in any of them, they themselves claimed it not; but by consent were all

23

*equal*, till by the same consent they set Rulers over themselves. So that their *Politick Societies* all *began* from a voluntary Union, and the mutual agreement of Men freely acting in the choice of their Governours, and forms of Government.

103. And I hope those who went away from *Sparta* with *Palantus*,. mentioned by *Justin l. 3. c. 4* will be allowed to have been *Freemen independent* one of another, and to have set up a Government over themselves, by their own consent. Thus I have given several Examples out of History, of *People free and in the State of Nature*, that being met together incorporated and *began a Common-wealth*. And if the want of such instances be an argument to prove that *Government* were not, nor could not be so *begun*, I suppose the Contenders for Paternal Empire were better let it alone, than urge it against natural Liberty. For if they can give so many instances out of History, of *Governments begun* upon Paternal Right, I think (though at best an Argument from what has been, to what should of right be, has no great force) one might, without any great danger, yield them the cause. but if I might advise them in the Case, they would do well not to search too much into the *Original of Governments*, as they have begun *de facto*, lest they should find at the foundation of most of them, something very little favourable to the design they promote, and such a power as they contend for.

104. But to conclude, Reason being plain on our side, that Men are naturally free, and the Examples of History shewing, that the *Governments* of the World, that were begun in Peace, had their beginning laid on that foundation, and were *made by the Consent of the People*; There can be little room for doubt, either where the Right is, or what has been the Opinion, or Practice of Mankind, about the *first erecting of Governments*.

105. I will not deny, that if we look back as far as History will direct us, towards the *Original of Common-wealths*, we shall generally find them under the Government and Administration of one Man. And I am also apt to believe, that where a Family was numerous enough to subsist by it self, and continued entire together, without mixing with others as it often happens, where there is much Land and few people, the Government commonly began in the Father. For the Father having, by the Law of Nature, the same Power with every Man else to punish, as he thought fit, any Offences against that Law, might thereby punish his transgressing Children even when they were Men, and out of their Pupilage; and they were very likely to submit to his punishment, and all joyn with him against the Offender, in their turns, giving him thereby power to Execute his Sentence against any transgression, and so in effect make him the Law-maker, and Governour over all, that remained in Conjunction with his Family. He was fittest to be trusted; Paternal affection secured their Property, and Interest under his Care, and the Custom of obeying him, in their Childhood, made it easier to submit to him, rather than to any other. If therefore they must have one to rule them, as Government is hardly

to be avoided amongst Men that live together; who so likely to be the
Man, as he that was their common Father; unless Negligence,
Cruelty, or any other defect of Mind, or Body made him unfit for it?
But when either the Father died, and left his next Heir for want of
Age, Wisdom, Courage, or any other Qualities, less fit for Rule: or
where several Families met, and consented to continue together:
There, 'tis not to be doubted, but they used their natural freedom, to
set up him, whom they judged the ablest, and most likely, to Rule
well over them. Conformable hereunto we find the People of *America*,
who (living out of the reach of the Conquering Swords, and spreading domination of the two great Empires of *Peru* and *Mexico*) enjoy'd
their own natural freedom, though, *ceteris paribus*, they commonly
prefer the Heir of their deceased King; yet if they find him any way
weak, or uncapable, they pass him by and set up the stoutest and
bravest Man for their Ruler.

106. Thus, though looking back as far as Records give us any account
of Peopling the World, and this History of Nations, we commonly
find the *Government* to be in one hand, yet it destroys not that, which
I affirm, (*viz.*) That the *beginning of Politick Society* depends upon the
consent of the Individuals, to joyn into and make one Society; who,
when they are thus incorporated, might set up what form of
Government they thought fit. But this having given occasion to Men
to mistake, and think, that by Nature Government was Monarchical,
and belong'd to the Father, it may not be amiss here to consider, why
people in the beginning generally pitch'd upon this form, which
though perhaps the Father's Preheminency might in the first institution of some Common-wealths, give a rise to, and place, in the
beginning, the Power in one hand; Yet it is plain, that the reason, that
continued the Form of *Government in a single Person*, was not any
Regard, or Respect to Paternal Authority; since all petty Monarchies,
that is, almost all *Monarchies*, near their Original, have been
commonly, at least upon occasion, *Elective*.

107. First then, in the beginning of things, the Father's Government of
the Childhood of those sprung from him, having accustomed them
to the *Rule of one Man*, and taught them that where it was exercised
with Care and Skill, with Affection and Love to those under it, it was
sufficient to procure and preserve to Men all the Political Happiness
they sought for, in Society. It was no wonder, that they should pitch
upon, and naturally run into that Form of Government, which from
their Infancy they had been all accustomed to; and which, by experience they had found both easie and safe. To which, if we add, that
*Monarchy* being simple, and most obvious to Men, whom neither
experience had instructed in Forms of Government, nor the Ambition
or Insolence of Empire had taught to beware of the Encroachments
of Prerogative, or the Inconveniences of Absolute Power, which
Monarchy, in Succession, was apt to lay claim to, and bring upon
them, it was not at all strange, that they should not much trouble
themselves to think of Methods of restraining any Exorbitances of

those, to whom they had given the Authority over them, and of ballancing the Power of Government, by placing several parts of it in different hands. They had neither felt the Oppression of Tyrannical Dominion, nor did the Fashion of the Age, nor their Possessions, or way of living (which afforded little matter for Covetousness or Ambition) give them any reason to apprehend or provide against it: and therefore 'tis no wonder they put themselves into such a *Frame of Government*, as was not only as I said, most obvious and simple, but also best suited to their present State and Condition; which stood more in need of defence against foreign Invasions and Injuries, than of multiplicity of Laws. The equality of a simple poor way of liveing confineing their desires within the narrow bounds of each mans smal propertie made few controversies and so no need of many laws to decide them: And there wanted not of Justice where there were but few Trespasses, and few Offenders. Since then those, who liked one another so well as to joyn into Society, cannot but be supposed to have some Acquaintance and Friendship together, and some Trust one in another; they could not but have greater Apprehensions of others, than of one another: And therefore their first care and thought cannot but be supposed to be, how to secure themselves against foreign Force. 'Twas natural for them to put themselves under a *Frame of Government*, which might best serve to that end; and chuse the wisest and bravest Man to conduct them in their Wars, and lead them out against their Enemies, and in this chiefly be their *Ruler*.

108. Thus we see, that the *Kings* of the *Indians* in *America*, which is still a Pattern of the first Ages in *Asia* and *Europe*, whilst the Inhabitants were too few for the Country, and want of People and Money gave Men no Temptation to enlarge their Possessions of Land, or contest for wider extent of Ground, are little more than *Generals of their Armies*; and though they command absolutely in War, yet at home and in time of Peace they exercise very little Dominion, and have but a very moderate Sovereignty, the Resolutions of Peace and War, being ordinarily either in the People, or in a Council. Though the War itself, which admits not of Plurality of Governours, naturally devolves the Command into the *King's sole Authority*.

109. And thus in *Israel* it self, the *chief Business of their Judges, and first Kings* seems to have been *to be Captains in War*, and Leaders of their Armies; which, (besides what is signified by *going out and in before the People*, which was, to march forth to War, and home again in the Heads of their Forces) appears plainly in the Story of *Jephtha*. The *Ammonites* making War upon *Israel*, the *Gileadites*, in fear send to *Jephtha*, a Bastard of their Family, whom they had cast off, and article with him, if he will assist them against the *Ammonites*, to make him their Ruler; which they do in these words, *And the People made him head and captain over them*, Judg. 11. 11. which was, as it seems, all one as to be *Judge. And he judged Israel*, Judge. 12. 7. that is, was their *Captain-General, six Years*. So when *Jotham* upbraids the *Schechemites* with the Obligation they had to *Gideon*, who had been their *Judge* and

Ruler, he tells them, *He fought for you, and adventured his life far, and delivered you out of the hands of Midian,* Judg. 9. 17. Nothing mentioned of him, but what he did as a *General,* and indeed that is all is found in his History, or in any of the rest of the Judges. And *Abimelech* particularly is called *King,* though at most he was but their *General.* And when, being weary of the ill Conduct of *Samuel's* Sons, the Children of *Israel* desired a King, *like all the nations to judge them, and to go out before them, and to fight their battels,* I Sam. 8. 20. God granting their Desire, says to *Samuel, I will send thee a Man, and thou shalt anoint him to be Captain over my People Israel, that he may save my People out of the hands of the Philistines,* c. 9. v. 16. As if the only *business of a King* had been to lead out their Armies, and fight in their Defence; and accordingly at his Inauguration, pouring a Vial of Oyl upon him, declares to *Saul,* that *the Lord had anointed him to be Captain over his inheritance,* c. 10. v. I. And therefore those, who after *Saul's* being solemnly chosen and saluted *King* by the *Tribes at Mispah,* were unwilling to have him their King, make no other Objection but this, *How shall this Man save us?* v. 27. as if they should have said, This Man is unfit to be our *King,* not having Skill and Conduct enough in War, to be able to defend us. And when God resolved to transfer the Government to *David,* it is in these Words, *But now thy Kingdom shall not continue: The Lord hath sought him a Man after his own heart, and the Lord hath commanded him to be Captain over his People,* c. 13. v. 14. As if the whole *Kingly Authority* were nothing else but to be their *General*: And therefore the *Tribes* who had stuck to *Saul's* Family, and opposed *David's* Reign, when they came to *Hebron* with terms of Submission to him, they tell him, amongst other Arguments they had to submit to him as to their King. That he was in effect their *King* in *Saul's* time, and therefore they had no reason but to receive him as their *King* now. *Also* (say they) *in time past, when Saul was King over us, thou wast he that leddest out and broughtest in Israel, and the Lord said unto thee, thou shalt feed my People Israel, and thou shalt be a Captain over Israel.*

110. Thus, whether *a Family* by degrees *grew up into a Commonwealth,* and the Fatherly Authority being continued on to the elder Son, every one in his turn growing up under it, tacitly submitted to it, and the easiness and equality of it not offending any one, every one acquiesced, till time seemed to have confirmed it, and settled a right of Succession by Prescription: or whether several Families, or the Descendants of several Families, whom Chance, Neighbourhood, or Business brought together, uniting into Society, the need of a General, whose Conduct might defend them against their Enemies in War, and the great confidence the Innocence and Sincerity of that poor but vertuous Age (such as are almost all those which begin Governments, that ever come to last in the World) gave Men one of another, made the first Beginners of Common-wealths generally put the Rule into one Man's hand, without any other express Limitation or Restraint, but what the Nature of the thing, and the End of Government required: which ever of these it was, that at first put the rule into the

hands of a single person, certain it is that no body was ever intrusted with it but for the publick Good and Safety, and to those Ends in the Infancies of Commonwealths those who had it, commonly used it: And unless they had done so, young Societies could not have subsisted: without such nursing Fathers tender and carefull of the publick weale, all Governments would have sunk under the Weakness and Infirmities of their Infancy; and the Prince and the People had soon perished together.

111. But though the *Golden Age* (before vain Ambition, and *amor sceleratus habendi*, evil Concupiscence, had corrupted Mens minds into a Mistake of true Power and Honour) had more Virtue, and consequently better Governours, as well as less vicious Subjects; and there was then *no stretching Prerogative* on the one side to oppress the People; *nor* consequently on the other any *Dispute about Priviledge*, to lessen or restrain the Power of the Magistrate; and so no contest betwixt Rulers and People about Governours or Government: Yet, when Ambition and Luxury, in future Ages would retain and increase the Power, without doing the business, for which it was given, and aided by Flattery, taught Princes to have distinct and separate Interests from their People, Men found it necessary to examine more carefully *the Original* and Rights of *Government*; and to find out ways to *restrain the Exorbitances*, and *prevent the Abuses* of that Power which they having intrusted in another's hands only for their own good, they found was made use of to hurt them.

112. Thus we may see how probable it is, that People that were naturally free, and by their own consent either submitted to the Government of their Father, or united together, out of different Families to make a Government, should generally put the *Rule into one Man's hands*, and chuse to be under the Conduct of a *single Person*, without so much as by express Conditions limiting or regulating his Power, which they thought safe enough in his Honesty and Prudence. Though they never dream'd of Monarchy being *Jure Divino*, which we never heard of among Mankind, till it was revealed to us by the Divinity of this last Age; nor ever allowed Paternal Power to have a right to Dominion, or to be the Foundation of all Government. And thus much may suffice to shew, that as far as we have any light from History, we have reason to conclude, that all peaceful beginnings of *Government* have been *laid in the Consent of the People*. I say *peaceful*, because I shall have occasion in another place to speak of Conquest, which some esteem a way of beginning of Governments.

*The other Objection I find urged against the beginning of Polities, in the way I have mentioned, is this, viz.*

113. *That all Men being born under Government, some or other, it is impossible any of them should ever be free, and at liberty to unite together, and begin a new one, or ever be able to erect a lawful Government.*

If this Argument be good; I ask, how came so many lawful Monarchies into the World? For if any body, upon this supposition,

can shew me any one Man in any Age of the World *free* to begin a
lawful Monarchy; I will be bound to shew him Ten other *free men* at
Liberty, at the same time to unite and begin a new Government under
a Regal, or any other Form. It being demonstration, that if any one,
*born under the Dominion* of another, may be so *free* as to have a right
to command others in a new and distinct Empire; every one that is
*born under the Dominion* of another may be so *free* too, and may
become a Ruler, or Subject, of a distinct separate Government. And
so by this their own Principle, either all Men, however *born*, are *free*,
or else there is but one lawful Prince, one lawful Government in the
World. And then they have nothing to do but barely to shew us,
which that is. Which when they have done, I doubt not but all
Mankind will easily agree to pay Obedience to him.

114. Though it be a sufficient Answer to their Objection to shew, that it
involves them in the same difficulties that it doth those they use it
against; yet I shall endeavour to discover the weakness of this
Argument a little farther.

*All Men*, say they, *are born under Government, and therefore they
cannot be at liberty to begin a new one. Every one is born a Subject to his
Father, or his Prince, and is therefore under the perpetual tye of Subjection
and Allegiance.* 'Tis plain Mankind never owned nor considered any
such natural *subjection, that they were born in*, to one or to the other,
that tied them, without their own Consents, to a Subjection to them
and their Heirs.

115. For there are no Examples so frequent in History, both Sacred and
Prophane, as those of Men withdrawing themselves, and their
Obedience, from the Jurisdiction they were born under, and the
Family or Community they were bred up in, and *setting up new
Governments* in other places; from whence sprang all that number of
petty Common-wealths in the beginning of Ages, and which always
multiplyed, as long as there was room enough, till the stronger, or
more fortunate swallowed the weaker; and those great ones again
breaking to pieces, dissolved into lesser Dominions. All which are so
many Testimonies against Paternal Sovereignty, and plainly prove,
That it was not the natural right of the Father descending to his Heirs,
that made Governments in the beginning, since it was impossible,
upon that ground, there should have been so many little Kingdoms;
all must have been but only one Universal Monarchy, if Men had not
been *at liberty to separate* themselves from their Families, and the
Government, be it what it will, that was set up in it, and go and make
distinct Common-wealths and other Governments, as they thought
fit.

116. This has been the practice of the World from its first beginning to
this day: Nor is it now any more hindrance to the freedom of
Mankind, that they are *born under constituted and ancient Polities*, that
have established Laws and set Forms of Government, than if they
were born in the Woods, amongst the unconfined Inhabitants that ran
loose in them. For those who would perswade us, that *by being born*

*under any Government, we are naturally Subjects to it*, and have no more any title or pretence to the freedom of the State of Nature, have no other reason (bating that of Paternal Power, which we have already answer'd) to produce for it, but only because our Fathers or Progenitors passed away their natural Liberty, and thereby bound up themselves and their Posterity to a perpetual subjection to the Government, which they themselves submitted to. 'Tis true, that whatever Engagements or Promises any one has made for himself, he is under the Obligation of them, but *cannot* by any *Compact* whatsoever, bind *his Children* or Posterity. For this Son, when a Man, being altogether as free as the Father, any *act of the Father can no more give away the liberty of the Son*, than it can of any body else: He may indeed annex such Conditions to the Land, he enjoyed as a Subject of any Common-wealth, as may oblige his Son to be of that Community, if he will enjoy those Possessions which were his Fathers; because that Estate being his Fathers Property, he may dispose or settle it as he pleases.

117. And this has generally given the occasion to mistake in this matter; because Commonwealths not permitting any part of their Dominions to be dismembred, not to be enjoyed by any but those of their Community, the Son cannot ordinarily enjoy the Possessions of his Father, but under the same terms his Father did; by becoming a Member of the Society: whereby he puts himself presently under the Government, he finds there established, as much as any other Subject of that Commonwealth. And thus *the Consent of Free-men, born under Government*, which only *makes them Members of it*, being given separately in their turns, as each comes to be of Age, and not in a multitude together; People take no notice of it, and thinking it not done at all, or not necessary, conclude they are naturally Subjects as they are Men.

118. But, 'tis plain, *Governments* themselves understand it otherwise; they *claim no Power over the Son, because of that they had over the Father*; nor look on Children as being their Subjects, by their Fathers being so. If a Subject of *England* have a Child by an *English* Woman in *France*, whose Subject is he? Not the King of *England*'s; for he must have leave to be admitted to the Priviledges of it. Nor the King of *France*'s; For how then has his Father a liberty to bring him away, and breed him as he pleases? And who ever was judged as a *Traytor* or *Deserter*, if he left, or warr'd against a Country, for being barely born in it of Parents that were Aliens there? 'Tis plain then, by the Practice of Governments themselves, as well as by the Law of right Reason, that *a Child is born a Subject of no Country or Government*. He is under his Fathers Tuition and Authority, till he come to Age of Discretion; and then he is a Free-man, at liberty what Government he will put himself under; what body Politick he will unite himself to. For if an *English-man*'s Son, born in *France*, be at liberty, and may do so, 'tis evident there is no Tye upon him by his Father being a Subject of this Kingdom; nor is he bound up, by any Compact of his Ancestors. And

why then hath not his Son, by the same reason, the same liberty, though he be born any where else? Since the Power that a Father hath naturally over his Children, is the same, where-ever they be born; and the Tyes of Natural Obligations, are not bounded by the positive Limits of Kingdoms and Common-wealths.

119. *Every Man* being, as has been shewed, *naturally free*, and nothing being able to put him into subjection to any Earthly Power, but only his own Consent; it is to be considered, what shall be understood to be *a sufficient Declaration of* a Mans *Consent, to make him subject* to the Laws of any Government. There is a common distinction of an express and a tacit consent, which will concern our present Case. No body doubts but an *express Consent*, of any Man, entring into any Society, makes him a perfect Member of that Society, a Subject of that Government. The difficulty is, what ought to be look'd upon as a *tacit Consent*, and how far it binds, *i.e.* how far any one shall be looked on to have consented, and thereby submitted to any Government, where he has made no Expressions of it at all. And to this I say, that every Man, that hath any Possession, or Enjoyment, of any part of the Dominions of any Government, doth thereby give his *tacit Consent*, and is as far forth obliged to Obedience to the Laws of that Government, during such Enjoyment, as any one under it; whether this his Possession be of Land, to him and his Heirs for ever, or a Lodging only for a Week; or whether it be barely travelling freely on the Highway; and in Effect, it reaches as far as the very being of any one within the Territories of that Government.

120. To understand this the better, it is fit to consider, that every Man, when he, at first, incorporates himself into any Commonwealth, he, by his uniting himself thereunto, annexed also, and submits to the Community those Possessions, which he has, or shall acquire, that do not already belong to any other Government. For it would be a direct Contradiction, for any one, to enter into Society with others for the securing and regulating of Property: And yet to suppose his Land, whose Property is to be regulated by the Laws of the Society, should be exempt from the Jurisdiction of that Government, to which he himself the Proprietor of the Land, is a Subject. By the same Act therefore, whereby any one unites his Person, which was before free, to any Commonwealth; by the same he unites his Possessions, which were before free, to it also; and they become, both of them, Person and Possession, subject to the Government and Dominion of that Commonwealth, as long as it hath a being. *Whoever* therefore, from thenceforth, by Inheritance, Purchase, Permission, or otherways *enjoys any part of the Land*, so annext to, and under the Government *of that Commonwealth, must take it with the Condition* it is under; that is, *of submitting to the Government of the Commonwealth*, under whose Jurisdiction it is, as far forth, as any Subject of it.

121. But since the Government has a direct Jurisdiction only over the Land, and reaches the Possessor of it, (before he has actually incorporated himself in the Society) only as he dwells upon, and enjoys

that: *The Obligation* any one is under, by Virtue of such Enjoyment, *to submit to the Government, begins and ends with the Enjoyment*; so that whenever the Owner, who has given nothing but such a *tacit Consent* to the Government, will, by Donation, Sale, or otherwise, quit the said Possession, he is at liberty to go and incorporate himself into any other Commonwealth, or to agree with others to begin a new one, *in vacuis locis*, in any part of the World, they can find free and unpossessed: Whereas he, that has once, by actual Agreement, and any *express* Declaration, given his *Consent* to be of any Commonweal, is perpetually and indispensably obliged to be and remain unalterably a Subject to it, and can never be again in the liberty of the state of Nature; unless by any Calamity, the Government, he was under, comes to be dissolved; or else by some publick Act cuts him off from being any longer a Member of it.

122. But submitting to the Laws of any Country, living quietly, and enjoying Priviledges and Protection under them, *makes not a Man a Member of that Society*: This is only a local Protection and Homage due to, and from all those, who, not being in a state of War, come within the Territories belonging to any Government, to all parts whereof the force of its Law extends. But this no more *makes a Man a Member of that Society*, a perpetual Subject of that Commonwealth, than it would make a Man a Subject to another in whose Family he found it convenient to abide for some time; though, whilst he continued in it, he were obliged to comply with the Laws, and submit to the Government he found there. And thus we see, that *Foreigners*, by living all their Lives under another Government, and enjoying the Priviledges and Protection of it, though they are bound, even in Conscience, to submit to its Administration, as far forth as any Denison; yet do not thereby come to be *Subjects or Members of that Commonwealth*. Nothing can make any Man so, but his actually entering into it by positive Engagement, and express Promise and Compact. This is that, which I think, concerning the beginning of Political Societies, and that *Consent which makes any one a Member* of any Commonwealth.

### CHAP. IX   Of the Ends of Political Society and Government

123. If Man in the State of Nature be so free, as has been said; If he be absolute Lord of his own Person and Possessions, equal to the greatest, and subject to no Body, why will he part with his Freedom? Why will he give up this Empire, and subject himself to the Dominion and Controul of any other Power? To which 'tis obvious to Answer, that though in the state of Nature he hath such a right, yet the Enjoyment of it is very uncertain, and constantly exposed to the Invasion of others. For all being Kings as much as he, every Man his Equal, and the greater part no strict Observers of Equity and Justice, the enjoyment of the property he has in this state is very unsafe, very unsecure. This makes him willing to quit this Condition, which however free, is full of fears and continual dangers: And 'tis not without reason,

that he seeks out, and is willing to joyn in Society with others who are already united, or have a mind to unite for the mutual *Preservation* of their Lives, Liberties and Estates, which I call by the general name, *Property*.

124. The great and *chief end* therefore, of Mens uniting into Commonwealths, and putting themselves under Government, *is the Preservation of their Property*. To which in the state of Nature there are many things wanting.

*First*, There wants an *establish'd*, settled, known *Law*, received and allowed by common consent to be the Standard of Right and Wrong, and the common measure to decide all Controversies between them. For though the Law of Nature be plain and intelligible to all rational Creatures; yet Men being biassed by their Interest, as well as ignorant for want of study of it, are not apt to allow of it as a Law binding to them in the application of it to their particular Cases.

125. *Secondly*, In the State of Nature there wants *a known and indifferent Judge*, with Authority to determine all differences according to the established Law. For every one in that state being both Judge and Executioner of the Law of Nature, Men being partial to themselves, Passion and Revenge is very apt to carry them too far, and with too much heat, in their own Cases; as well as negligence, and unconcernedness, to make them too remiss, in other Mens.

126. *Thirdly*, In the state of Nature there often wants *Power* to back and support the Sentence when right, and to *give* it due *Execution*. They who by any Injustice offended, will seldom fail, where they are able, by force to make good their Injustice: such resistance many times makes the punishment dangerous, and frequently destructive, to those who attempt it.

# TIMOTHY O'HAGAN

## Aristotle and Aquinas on community and natural law  2

In the aftermath of the French Revolution, Benjamin Constant argued that the evils of totalitarianism stem from a misconceived attempt to impose on the modern, pluralist world the 'liberty of the ancients' (see also chapter 3). According to Constant, the ancients valued the liberty to participate in the affairs of state but despised the liberty to engage in a private life. But it would be a mistake to attribute any simple-minded totalitarian view to either Aristotle or Aquinas, two of the greatest philosophers of the pre-modern world. As we shall see, the tension between these two poles of liberty was already a central problem for Aristotle, and in the *Politics* he provided the outlines of a realistic solution to it. It was equally important to Aquinas, who attempted to mediate between the demand to participate and the demand to be 'left alone' with his idea of a pluralist *communitas* and of a natural law that transcends human law. Though both thinkers are distant from us in time and in cultural context, they made an enduring contribution to our present-day debates about the relationship of the individual to society.

### Aristotle (384–322 BC)

Aristotle was born in Stagira, Thrace, a doctor's son. He lived most of his adult life in Athens, first as member of Plato's Academy (367–348 BC), then as a founder and director of his own school, the Lyceum (335–323), which was the first organised research institute in the Western world, whose members were trained and worked on a range of specified projects. Aristotle's own work was both encyclopaedic and original. He addressed every branch of knowledge: psychology, logic, language, literary theory, metaphysics, ethics, politics and all the natural sciences from astronomy to zoology. He applied the most rigorous rational and scientific methods to all domains, seeking always to 'preserve the phenomena' of the discipline in question. He strove to be systematic, but not reductionist and, above all, to integrate human behaviour into a naturalistic explanatory framework.

He spent his middle years travelling and teaching in different city states before accepting the post of tutor to the young Alexander (later

Emperor Alexander the Great) at the Macedonian Court. Alexander's death in 323 BC released a wave of anti-Macedonian feeling in Athens. Because of his association with the Macedonian royal house, Aristotle was suspected of disloyalty to Athens and to its democracy and, like Socrates before him, he was charged with impiety. So that the Athenians should not 'sin twice against philosophy', Aristotle left Athens and died a year later in Chalcis in Euboea.

In sharp contrast to Plato's *Republic*, the *Politics* is a realistic, anti-utopian treatise, applying Aristotle's naturalistic method to men and women within society, where they are seen as creatures endowed with an inbuilt tendency towards social life. Aristotle shows how the social drive is fostered or frustrated in well or badly ordered political systems.

Against the sophists, Aristotle maintained that the irreducible starting-point of our investigations is the phenomenon of *koinonia* or community. *Koinonia* is what is shared, held in common, as opposed to the private, the particular. Families and households are forms of *koinonia*, which together make up the highest form of community, the *polis*, or city state. Aristotle defined the human being as a political animal (*politikon zoon*). Since men and women are by nature gregarious rather than solitary creatures, fitted to live together in social groups, and since the *polis* is the most developed, comprehensive and rational form of social organisation, they are fitted by nature for life in a *polis*. Aristotle did not hold that all human beings do in fact live in city states. He was well aware that there existed many other forms of political and social order. The Persian Empire was close to hand, as was the emerging imperial power of Macedonia. When he argued that the *polis* is the natural form of human community, he was making a claim about how human beings can best fulfil their potential. His view was that we are so made that we will flourish best within a city state, since it alone provides the environment within which we can realise our natural potential for practical reason, by actively engaging in public affairs.

In Aristotle's schematic typology there are three possible forms of government (*politeia*) of a *polis*: monarchy, oligarchy and democracy. Within the *polis*, only full members are citzens (*politai*). Depending on the form of government, citizenship is distributed and exercised differently, most narrowly in a monarchy, most broadly in a democracy. But even in Athens, the most radical democracy of the ancient Greek world, only a small number of adult males, about one sixth of the total population, were citizens. Excluded were women, resident aliens and slaves. Even within these limits, Aristotle was suspicious of the unstable nature of a democratic regime, and favoured a mixed form of government, mid-way between oligarchy and democracy. We shall return to Aristotle's inegalitarianism later. For the moment let us concentrate on his idea that citizenship demands participation in running the affairs of the city state. To be a free citizen is to be active, not dependent. In particular, it is to share in deliberation, to debate and vote on political proposals in the assembly. It also involves participation in 'the administration of justice'. In the case of Athens, where an extreme version of direct democracy was practised, this meant that all citizens were available to serve on the vast juries, whose members were picked by lot and paid an attendance fee, and which passed down verdicts in both civil and criminal cases, including those against both Socrates and Aristotle.

Aristotle defines 'political justice' as 'justice between free and equal ... persons, living a common life for the purpose of satisfying their needs'. He continues:

Political justice is of two kinds, one natural, the other conventional. A rule of justice is natural that has the same validity everywhere, and does not depend on our accepting it or not. (*Nicomachean Ethics*, Book V)

The idea that there are rules of 'natural justice', universally valid, transcending local laws and conventions, gives a critical edge to Aristotle's political thought. Ultimately every law and every constitution must be judged against the standard of nature, to see how far it contributes to the flourishing of the well-ordered community. Flourishing takes different forms in different demographic, geographical and cultural environments, but there are certain constants, namely the shared universal features of human nature.

How are different kinds of social group held together? At one end of the spectrum, nearest 'nature', the extended household (*oikos*) is bound by ties of kinship and servitude. At the other end, there is the association based on legal-commercial transactions between individuals, or on a treaty between *poleis*, which is a purely instrumental arrangement. The *polis* itself is partly natural, partly instrumental. It is natural in that it consists of a community of households, of people who 'live in the same place and intermarry'. But it is more than that. A *polis*, for Aristotle, is concerned with public standards of virtue and vice, and aims at the common advantage. It involves the natural ties of kinship, but also the rational ties of choice, the choice of a form of living together (*syzen*), infused by a shared conception of a flourishing, noble life (*eudaimonia*). So Aristotle's idea of the social cohesion specific to a *polis* is a complex one. In order to flourish, a *polis* must have the natural ties of kinship and the religious-ideological links arising from shared ceremonial rites, 'common sacrifices'. It must also have an element of choice, since the citizens of a true *polis* 'choose to live together' in friendship. A unity based only on instrumental choice is a mere alliance or association. The choice of the citizens of a *polis* is a choice of friendship.

Aristotle's model of the *polis* is more cohesive, more ideologically integrated than the standard model of the modern liberal state. But it would be wrong to think that Aristotle was unreflectively 'totalitarian'. In fact he counterposed his relatively pluralist ideas to those of Plato in the *Republic* (see chapter 1), arguing against Plato that 'it is evident that a city is not by nature a unity in the sense which some affirm'. For Aristotle, the *Republic* was too much of a unity, for 'a *polis* is by nature a plurality, consisting of individuals differing in kind'. For him, the *polis* defines the parameters of the common good, within which countless private transactions can be made and relationships established. Within the *polis* both the liberty of the ancients (to govern themselves) and the liberty of the moderns (to be 'left alone') have room to flourish. The former is expressed most forcefully in a direct democracy, and that form of government has its natural home in the narrow confines of the city state. But it is not incompatible with greater size, any more than the pluralism of the moderns is excluded by the relative intimacy of the *polis*.

As we have seen, part of what it is to be a citizen is to share in 'the administration of justice'. In democratic Athens 'the people' (the *demos*), or at least the free citizens, were, through jury service, in direct control of the legal system from day to day. More than anywhere else before or since, the law became the expression of the popular will. But the cost of this direct democratic involvement was that the law became infinitely flexible, infinitely responsive to the people's passing whims. Aristotle envisaged an ideal of impersonal justice, where 'God and reason alone rule' and contrasted the rule of law to the rule of men. The former is appropriate to ordering the affairs of free, equal citizens. The latter is characteristic of despotism. So how, in a democracy, can the people be prevented from taking the law into its own hands and using it despotically against its own virtuous citizens, as it had done against Socrates? If 'the law is reason unaffected by desire', how can the people free itself from passion and prejudice, and administer the law by reason alone? Aristotle gave no direct answer to that question. On the one hand, he aimed to restrict direct democracy by tempering it with oligarchy. On the other hand, he hinted that expert draftsmen might be entrusted to sharpen and amend particular laws. But he did not envisage a constitutional arrangement in which the power of an independent judiciary might be endorsed by a formalised division of powers. In a world of direct democracy, one could prevent the people from misusing its judicial powers only by educating individuals in the virtues of responsible citizenship. Otherwise democracy itself must be restricted.

Notoriously, Aristotle maintained that human beings are born both naturally sociable and naturally unequal, destined for dominance or subservience. His discussions of natural inequalities occur in various contexts. Here we find a mind/body analogy grounding the relations between masters and slaves and between men and women:

It is in a living creature ... that it is first possible to discern the rule both of master and of statesman: the soul rules the body with the sway of a master, the intelligence the appetites with constitutional or royal rule ... it is natural and expedient for the body to be governed by the soul and for the emotional part to be governed by the intellect, ... whereas for the two parties to be on an equal footing or in the contrary positions is harmful in all cases. Again the same holds good between man and the other animals: tame animals are superior in their nature to wild animals, yet for all the former it is advantageous to be ruled by man, since this gives them security. Also, as between the sexes, the male is by nature superior and the female inferior, the male ruler and the female subject ... All men that differ as widely as the soul does from the body and the human being from the lower animal ... these are by

nature slaves, for whom to be governed by this kind of authority is advantageous ... (Below, p. 53)

How can Aristotle's belief that all human beings are endowed with reason be squared with such social inegalitariansm? His elusive answer is that the 'natural slave' lacks autonomy since he merely 'apprehends' reason, but does not 'possess' it, but he never satisfactorily developed the distinction.

In another context, Aristotle set himself this problem: does the slave have excellences (intellectual and moral capacities) 'beside his merits as an instrument and a servant ... or has he no excellence beside his bodily service?' Whether the answer is yes or no, it is problematic for Aristotle. If the slave has the same excellences (temperance, courage, justice, etc.) as the master, how will he differ from the master? If he does not, then 'that is odd, since slaves are human beings and participate in reason' (albeit passively, as we have seen above). With characteristic caution, Aristotle reached the conclusion that both ruler and ruled 'must share in excellence, but there are differences in that excellence', differences in kind, not just in degree, so that in the last analysis the moral, as well as the intellectual, unity of humanity is fragmented:

there are by nature various classes of rulers and ruled. For the free rules the slave, the male the female, the man the child in a different way. And all possess the various parts of the soul, but possess them in different ways; for the slave has not got the deliberative part at all, and the female has it, but without full authority, while the child has it, but in an undeveloped form. (Below, p. 54)

Plato had already divided the soul into functional parts and made reason the ruling part. But it was Aristotle who used the idea of the divided soul to argue that human beings are unalterably unequal, and that women, for instance, are by nature incapable of deliberating with 'full authority'. His thought that human beings fall into identifiably different psychological types with respect to autonomy and dependency may seem less bizarre to readers raised on Freud than to those raised on J. S. Mill. But Aristotle displayed a marked and uncharacteristic lack of imagination about the effect of differing socialisation on the capacity of individuals to transform themselves. Plato in contrast (at least in the *Republic*) saw no grounds for identifying intellectual difference with gender difference. For Plato, as for later rationalist thinkers, 'the mind has no sex'. Though he was no feminist, he applied that thesis to politics, and made radical proposals to liberate women members of the ruling class from the family and to recruit them for political service. The children of those women, though not of any others, would be cared for in public nurseries, and, for this small section of the female population, traditional family roles would be radically transformed. Aristotle, by contrast, propounded the mistaken thesis that women are by nature incapable of attaining the intellectual autonomy of men, and that, because of that incapacity, men are entitled to exclude women from the public domain. In this respect at least, the master's work is today more resonant than that of his more conservative pupil.

Aristotle sought the best environment to cultivate the human soul. The well ordered *polis*, would, he argued, ensure the *eudaimonia* of its members. Traditionally translated 'happiness', *eudaimonia* is better rendered as 'human flourishing'. To flourish, a person needs certain things not entirely within social control: good health, prosperity and a degree of good luck, the divine contribution of one's *daimon*, the impersonal power which controls one's destiny. But other elements of our fortune are the products of the social order to which we belong: 'the best life, both for individuals and for *poleis*, is the life of excellence, when excellence has external goods enough for the performance of good actions'. The word *arete*, though standardly translated 'virtue', denotes a broader range of excellence or proper function in classical Greek. In the *Nicomachean Ethics* Aristotle distinguished intellectual *aretai*, like wisdom, understanding and practical reasonableness (prudence), from ethical *aretai*, like generosity and self-control. All denote psychological states or faculties which individuals should strive to acquire if they are to flourish. In ordering our lives in society it is, interestingly, the intellectual excellence of *phronesis*, skill in practical reasoning, that plays the key role. Aristotle defined *phronesis* like this: 'a truth-attaining rational quality, concerned with actions in relation to things that are good and bad for human beings' (*Nicomachean Ethics*, Book VI). This excellence was attained by great statesmen who 'like Pericles are deemed prudent (*phronimoi*) because they possess a faculty of discerning what things are good for themselves and for humanity'. This intellectual excellence of practical reasoning enables us to rank-order the things which are good both generally ('for humanity'), and for us in particular. External goods contribute to a person's flourishing, but the key to *eudaimonia* lies within, in the ability effectively to organise one's life. An intellectual may still have to be convinced that a life of demanding public activity is preferable to the contemplative pursuits of the philosopher. Remembering the philosopher-kings of Plato's *Republic*, who are dragged unwillingly back into the cave to do their public duty, Aristotle poses the question starkly:

Now it is clear that the best constitution is the system under which anybody whatsoever would be best off and would live happily; but the question is raised even by those who agree that the life accompanied by excellence is the most desirable, whether the life of citizenship is desirable or rather a life released from all external affairs, for example some form of contemplative life ... For it is evident that these are the two modes of life principally chosen by the men most ambitious of attaining excellence ... I mean the life of politics and the life of philosophy. (Below, p. 54-5)

His somewhat evasive answer is that, given a broad and generous understanding of the word 'practical', even those engaged in 'pure' research, whose 'speculations and thoughts ... have their end in themselves and are pursued for their own sake', may be seen as living 'practical' or public lives. If we can develop that idea, then Aristotle's model of the *polis*, once purged of its grotesque inegalitarianism, may be seen as a realisable model of a social order which guarantees both a multiplicity of private projects, commercial and personal, and a true arena of intellectual freedom.

### Thomas Aquinas (1225–74)

Aquinas was born into the impoverished feudal nobility of southern Italy in the castle of Roccasecca near Aquino. His family intended him for the well-established and respected Benedictine order, but Thomas opted instead for the Dominicans, a new order of friars with radical aspirations, and entered their order in the face of opposition, and even a spell of incarceration, by his family. In the cosmopolitan order he had chosen, he pursued his studies in Naples, Cologne and Paris, where he was professor of theology from 1256–59. He was posted to Italy again in 1259–68. He spent a second term as professor in Paris in 1268–72, when he was summoned to Naples to found a new Dominican house. There he underwent a mystical experience which caused him to abandon philosophy. His master work is the immense *Summa theologiae*, a demonstration that Christian doctrine is compatible with Aristotelianism, which embodied the most advanced science and philosophy of the time. Aquinas died in 1274 and was canonised in 1323.

Most of the extracts in this chapter are drawn from the *Summa theologiae* II, written in 1268–72, which is generally acknowledged to be the most original part of Aquinas' work, and which addresses human psychology, morality and society. It shows the influence of Aristotle on every page, but Aquinas was no passive mouthpiece of his mentor. He produced subtle criticisms of his positions, both when Christian theology demanded them, and also, more interestingly, when his own philosophical genius led him beyond his master. Two other extracts are drawn from an earlier work, the Commentary on the *Sentences* of Peter Lombard, written in 1252–56, and from the Commentary on Aristotle's *Nicomachean Ethics*, written during the second Paris term. For Aquinas, as for Aristotle,

the fact that man is by nature a social animal – being compelled to live in society because of the many needs he cannot satisfy out of his own resources – has as a consequence the fact that man is destined by nature to form part of a community which makes a full and complete life possible for him (below, p. 55).

Here, commenting on the *Nicomachean Ethics*, Aquinas reproduces the central Aristotelian thesis without alteration. But, in translating it into the framework of Christian theology, he at once establishes a certain distance from the original, emphasising that the political unity to which the individual belongs is only a 'limited unity', that is, it is an entity which is legitimate, and fully real, if and only if it corresponds to a set

41

of higher norms. In the new context, human beings, bearers of immortal souls, are directly related to God, their creator. So the social order to which one belongs is 'a unity of order and not an unconditional unity'. Individuals are still irreducibly social, but they now have a more dramatic destiny than they had in Aristotle's secular *polis*. In our modern Godless world, it is hard to appreciate the importance of this shift. Access to a divine order, over and above any particular man-made order, permits individuals to take their distance from any given government, and to judge it by reference to external critical standards.

Within his model, Aquinas sometimes stresses the organic, sometimes the pluralist, aspect of community. There is a tension between these emphases, if not an outright inconsistency. The organic language is found in both social-political and theological contexts. In society, in the case of distributive justice, 'the private person ... may be compared to the community as a part to a whole', and capital punishment is justified by the sinister analogy of amputating the gangrenous limb to save the body. But in both cases Aquinas nuances the organic language: 'a part and the whole are identical in a sense ... every individual person is as it were a part of the whole ...' Aquinas gives three grounds for prohibiting suicide: first, it is against natural law which enjoins self-preservation;

second, every part belongs to the whole in virtue of what it is. But every man belongs to the community in virtue of what he is. Suicide therefore involves the damaging of the community, as Aristotle makes clear. Third, life is a gift made to man by God, and it is subject to him who is master of *death and life*. (Below, p. 56)

Of these grounds, only the second is strictly organic, and it is that which Aquinas correctly attributes to Aristotle. In theology, Aquinas conducts his discussion of original sin in organic language, and there, interestingly, he uses the political community to illustrate his theological position: 'All who are born of Adam can be considered as one man by reason of sharing the one nature inherited from the first parent, even as in political matters all belonging to one community are reckoned to be like one body and the whole community like one person...'. But here too the organic language ('reckoned to be like') is only analogical. Even when Aquinas comes closest to attributing absolute reality to the community he holds back from treating it as a person. In other contexts he uses a less organic, more individualistic vocabulary. Here, for instance, he maintains that individual human beings always preserve a moral autonomy due to their place in God's creation, an autonomy which transcends any political obligations:

A human being is not subordinate to the political community entirely within his whole self and with all he possesses and therefore it is not required that each of his acts should be well or ill deserving within the political order. But all that a man is, all that he can do, and all that he has is within God's order; and therefore every good or bad act deserves well or otherwise from God according to its character. (*Summa Theologiae*, 1a2ae.21.4)

The idea of law (*lex*) plays a central role in Aquinas' thought. In

scholastic terminology, this word covers a broad spectrum of meanings.
In the most general formulation, Aquinas defines law as 'a rule and
measure', applied both to 'the thing which is the rule and measure' and
to 'the thing which is ruled and measured'. The four forms of law which
he analyses are eternal, natural, human and divine. Eternal law is God's
ordering of the universe as a whole, his 'ordination for the governance
of things He foreknows'. Given the absolute generality of that definition, the other three forms of law can be seen as specifications of eternal
law. The focus of Aquinas' social and political theory is the interaction
between natural law and human law.

The precepts of natural law are general principles governing practical
reasoning, in the same way that the laws of thought govern theoretical
reasoning. Just as in our theoretical reasoning we seek truth and avoid
contradiction, so in practical affairs 'good is to be done and pursued and
evil to be avoided'. At this level of generality, the precepts of natural law
may sound platitudinous, but they are not. Together, they prohibit
consequentialist trade-offs which would allow us to pursue evils for the
sake of 'greater goods'. In short, they found a moral absolutism, which
would be hard to stick to in the real world of practical politics and dirty
hands. Once the precepts of natural law are integrated into a specific
model of human nature, they begin to bite. Human beings, for Aquinas,
(1) share with other created things the drive to self-preservation; (2)
share with other animals the drive to reproduce their species; (3) are
endowed, unlike other animals, with reason, which allows them to 'shun
ignorance [and] not offend others with whom [they] ought to live in
civility'. For human beings, 'all things that can be regulated by reason
fall under the law of reason'. By the use of reason they can embody the
principles of natural law in positive (human) legal codes, expressed as
commands backed by coercive force.

We pause here to head off a misreading of natural law theory, according to which all the laws which happen to be enacted in any given
society would automatically embody the principles of natural law. Such
a misreading would render the theory critically vacuous, a blatant
endorsement of any *status quo*. But nothing could be further from the
truth. Because men and women are innately free, rational and, also,
sinful, they, unlike the rest of God's creatures, are capable of pervert-
ing and misusing the drives which God implanted in them for their
personal and social well-being. Thus only 'the most general precepts',
those enjoining self-preservation, 'are known to all' and 'cannot be
cancelled in the human heart'. But even they can be misapplied
'because of lust or some other passion'. Secondary precepts, unlike the
primary ones, presuppose social institutions. Once an institution like
property is in place, then theft is seen to be against natural law, since it
conflicts with the goal of community, of living together with others 'in
civility'. At this level of applied natural law, it is only too frequent that
'human legislators have sometimes passed wrongful enactments'.

From his earliest work, the Commentary on the *Sentences* of Peter
Lombard, to the mature conclusions of the *Summa Theologiae*, Aquinas

maintains that an unjust human law, one contrary to natural law, has no binding force. In the early text he argues that tyrannicide is justified, indeed 'the one who liberates his country by killing a tyrant is to be praised and rewarded'. In the *Summa* he does not abandon that revolutionary doctrine, but modifies it somewhat. Within the framework of developed natural law theory, Aquinas now ties justice to reason and identifies tyrannical law both by its source and by its content, such that any law that is unjust and unreasonable is tyrannical. Source and content tend to coincide since it is in the nature of tyranny that one who lacks constitutional and moral restraints is likely to legislate in the interest of himself, not of his subjects, and so is likely to depart systematically from the precepts of natural law. Unjust laws 'are outrages rather than laws ... such commands do not oblige in the court of conscience, except perhaps to avoid scandal or riot'. The morally committed citizen has a prima facie obligation to obey the laws of the community, even inequitable ones, where the alternatives ('scandal or riot') are even worse. In other cases Aquinas' verdict is unequivocal: 'a man is not obliged to obey, if without scandal or greater damage he can resist'.

Natural law then operates as a critical standard against which philosophers and citizens alike can measure the adequacy of the particular legal systems by which they are ruled. In Aquinas' system, that standard is firm, but not over-rigid. He explains how its secondary precepts can be changed by changing social conditions, notoriously 'by addition'. Thus he suggests, plausibly, that wearing clothes is not contrary to natural law, even though clothes are made 'by art', not by nature. In wearing them, at least in cold climates, we are improving on nature, not opposing it. But it is only by an analogy, delivered by rapid sleight of hand, that Aquinas concludes that slavery is equally acceptable, since it too 'exist[s] by human contrivance for the convenience of social life', and thus 'does not change the law of nature except by addition'. Natural law must be flexible and adaptable. On the other hand, if it is expanded by 'additions', natural law will, as in the case of slavery, become too porous, too tolerant of unjust human laws. When later writers came to mount more egalitarian political programmes within a natural law framework, they had to rethink their model of human nature and divorce it more clearly from Aristotle's. But the seed of the new egalitarianism is planted in the Christian doctrine of the equality of all human souls before God. From this perspective, skin-colour cannot be a relevant difference in ordering society: 'Soul is either rational or non-rational, and therefore you divide animals essentially and properly into rational and non-rational animals, not into blacks and whites, which is a division irrelevant to the subject' (*Summa Theologiae*, 1a2ae.95.4). Later writers argued that the contingent fact that societies are ordered into radically inegalitarian relations between master and slave was equally 'irrelevant to the subject'.

There is one final problem which besets any theological version of natural law theory. In a world governed by an omnipotent God, God's command has, in the last instance, overriding authority. That makes the

precepts of natural law even more porous, at least at the point of application. For example, it is objected that 'you find God changing [the]
rules, as when he commanded Abraham to put his son to death, the
people of Israel to spoil the Egyptians, and Hosea to take a wife of
harlotry'. To this Aquinas gives the cheerfully offhand reply that

without injustice God's command can inflict death on anybody whether he
be guilty or innocent. Adultery is intercourse with a woman to whom you
are not married in accordance with divinely given law; nevertheless to go
unto any woman by divine command is neither adultery nor fornication.
(Below, p. 59)

The problem of Abraham and Isaac would dog theologians up to
Kierkegaard. But long before him, William of Ockham in the fourteenth
century and Thomas Hobbes in the seventeenth would take up a similar
'voluntarist' line in both theology and political theory, arguing that
there is strictly nothing beyond the command of God which founds
natural law, and nothing beyond the command of temporal sovereigns
which founds the laws of nations.

## Conclusion

Natural law theory provides the critic of the established political order
with a powerful armoury, in which *jus* or 'right' is an important
weapon. In later legal and political discourse *jus* would come to be
identified with a claim right, asserted by a legal person as a claim to
property, and by a citizen as a claim to liberties and provisions on the
part of government. In this later vocabulary, *jus* and *lex*, right and law,
would be seen as at least potentially opposed to one another. Aquinas,
in contrast, understands *jus* as an objective property of 'the just thing
… the objective interest of justice'. The word *jus* would be applied in
the first instance to the just situation, to the relationship holding
between parties within a shared community, whether public or private.
That situation would be right, would embody *jus*, to the extent that,
substantively, it promoted the flourishing of the parties, and, formally,
observed the spirit and the letter of the law in their transactions. In the
natural law tradition, the norms of substantive and procedural justice
have never been rigidly separated. The idea of *jus* links the two dimen-
sions of justice, so that a just outcome must be procedurally just, but
must also presuppose a fair distribution of resources between the
parties, so that all parties have a real, and not merely formal, 'equality
before the law'. There is an egalitarian drive within the natural law
programme which is constantly at odds with the inegalitarian model of
human nature which it inherited from Aristotle.

## References

The Aristotle extracts are taken from the *Politics*, trans. H. Rackham, London:
Heinemann, 1932 (The Loeb Classical Library). Other citations in the text are
from Aristotle, *Nicomachean Ethics*, trans. H. Rackham, London: Heinemann,

Aristotle       1926 (The Loeb Classical Library).

Aquinas         Most of the Aquinas extracts are taken from the *Summa Theologiae*, Blackfriars,
                in conjunction with Eyre & Spottiswoode, London, 1964, vols 23, 37, 38, 41.
                The remainder are from the Commentary on Aristotle's *Nicomachean Ethics*
                and the Commentary on the *Sentences* of Peter Lombard, both in Aquinas,
                *Selected Political Writings*, ed. A. P. d'Entrèves, trans. J. G. Dawson, Oxford:
                Blackwell, 1959.

## Further reading

There are a number of good translations of Aristotle's *Politics*. For commentaries
on Aristotle's political and ethical theory, see J. M. Cooper, *Reason and Human
Good in Aristotle* (Cambridge, MA: Harvard University Press, 1975); W. F. R.
Hardie, *Aristotle's Ethical Theory* (2nd edn, Oxford: Clarendon Press, 1980); M. C.
Nussbaum, *The Fragility of Goodness: Luck and Ethics in Greek Tragedy and
Philosophy* (Cambridge: Cambridge University Press, 1986, part 3); and J. Lear,
*Aristotle: the Desire to Understand* (Cambridge: Cambridge University Press, 1988,
ch. 5).

On Aquinas, see his *Selected Political Writings* (ed. d'Entrèves, Oxford:
Blackwell, 1959). Commentaries on his political thought include T. Gilby,
*Between Community and Society: a Philosophy and Theology of the State* (London:
Longmans, 1953); F. C. Copleston, *Aquinas* (Harmondsworth: Penguin, 1955, ch.
5); M. Wilks, *The Problem of Sovereignty in the Later Middle Ages* (Cambridge:
Cambridge University Press, 1963, ch. 4); G. G. Grisez, 'The First Principle of
Practical Reason ...' (in A. Kenny (ed.), *Aquinas: a Collection of Critical Essays*,
London: Macmillan, 1969); W. Ullmann, *Medieval Political Thought*
(Harmondsworth: Penguin, 1975, ch. 7).

F. C. Copleston, *A History of Philosophy* (vols 1, 2, 3 (1946, 1950, 1953), reprinted
in one volume, New York: Doubleday, 1985) provides a useful discussion of both
Aristotle and Aquinas in the context of the history of philosophy. Discussions of
the natural law tradition can be found in J. Finnis, *Natural Law and Natural Rights*
(Oxford: Clarendon Press, 1980); A. P. d'Entrèves, *Natural Law* (London:
Hutchinson, 1970); and R. P. George (ed.), *Natural Law Theory: Contemporary
Essays* (Oxford: Clarendon Press, 1992).

## Seminar questions

Do you agree that 'the human being is a political animal'?

As advocate for the devil, can you devise a defence of Aristotle's
inegalitarianism?

Can an atheist learn anything from Aquinas' natural law theory?

# ARISTOTLE
## From the *Politics*

### [NATURAL SOCIABILITY, COMMUNITY, THE CITY STATE]

Every state is [...] a sort of community and every community is formed with a view to some good (since all the actions of all mankind are done with a view to what they think to be good). It is therefore evident that, while all partnerships aim at some good, the partnership that is the most supreme of all and includes all the others does so most of all, and aims at the most supreme of all goods; and this is the community entitled the state, the political association.

In this subject as in others the best method of investigation is to study things in the process of development from the beginning. The first coupling together of persons then to which necessity gives rise is that between those who are unable to exist without one another, namely the union of female and male for the continuance of the species (and this not of deliberate purpose, but with man as with the other animals and with plants there is a natural instinct to desire to leave behind one another being of the same sort as oneself), and the union of natural ruler and natural subject for the sake of security (for one that can foresee with his mind is naturally ruler and naturally master, and one that can do these things with his body is subject and naturally a slave; so that master and slave have the same interest). Thus the female and the slave are by nature distinct (for nature makes nothing as the cutlers make the Delphic knife, in a niggardly way, but one thing for one purpose; for so each tool will be turned out in the finest perfection, if it serves not many uses but one).

The community finally composed of several villages is the city-state; it has at last attained the limit of virtually complete self-sufficiency, and thus, while it comes into existence for the sake of life, it exists for the good life. Hence every city-state exists by nature, inasmuch as the first communities so exist; for the city-state is the end of the other communities, and nature is an end, since that which each thing is when its growth is completed we speak of as being the nature of each thing, for instance of a man, a horse, a household. Again, the object for which a thing exists, its end, is its chief good; and self-sufficiency is an end, and a chief good. From these things therefore it is clear that the city-state is a natural growth, and that man is by nature a political animal, and a man that is by nature and not merely by fortune citiless is either low in the scale of humanity or above it (like the 'clanless, lawless, hearthless' man reviled by Homer, for he is by nature citiless and also a lover of war) inasmuch as he resembles an isolated piece at draughts. And why man is a political animal in a greater measure than any bee or any gregarious animal is clear. For nature, as we declare, does nothing without purpose; and man alone of the animals possesses speech. The mere voice, it is true, can indicate pain and pleasure, and therefore is possessed by the other animals as well (for their nature has been developed so far as to have sensations of what is painful and pleasant and to signify those sensations to one another), but speech is designed to indicate the advantageous and the harmful, and therefore also the right and the wrong; for it is the special property of man in distinction from the other animals that he alone has perception of good and bad and right and wrong and the other moral qualities, and it is partnership in these things that makes a household and a city-state. [Book I, 1252–3]

Thus also the city-state is prior in nature to the household and to each of us individually. For the whole must necessarily be prior to the part; since when the whole body is destroyed, foot or hand will not exist except in an equivocal sense, like the sense in which one speaks of a hand sculptured in stone as a hand; because a hand in those circumstances will be a hand spoiled, and all things are defined by their function and capacity, so that when they are no longer such as to perform their function they must not be said to be the same things, but to bear their names in an equivocal sense. It is clear therefore that the state is also prior by nature to the individual; for if each individual when separate is not self-sufficient, he must be related to the whole state as other parts are to their whole, while a man who is incapable of entering into community, or who is so self-sufficing that he has no need to do so, is no part of a state, so that he must be either a lower animal or a god.

Therefore the impulse to form a community of this kind is present in all men by nature; but the man who first united people in such a community was the greatest of benefactors. For as man is the best of the animals when perfected, so he is the worst of all when sundered from law and justice. For unrighteousness is most pernicious when possessed of weapons, and man is born possessing weapons for the use of wisdom and virtue, which it is possible to employ entirely for the opposite ends. Hence when devoid of virtue man is the most unscrupulous and savage of animals, and the worst in regard to sexual indulgence and gluttony. Justice on the other hand is an element of the state; for judicial procedure, which means the decision of what is just, is the regulation of the political community. [Book I, 1253]

### [CITIZENSHIP]

We must first inquire into the nature of a citizen; for a state is a collection of citizens, so that we have to consider who is entitled to the name of citizen, and what the essential nature of a citizen is. For there is often a difference of opinion as to this: people do not all agree that the same person is a citizen; often somebody who would be a citizen in a democracy is not a citizen under an oligarchy.

[...]

A citizen pure and simple is defined by nothing else so much as by the right to participate in judicial functions and in office.

What constitutes a citizen is [...] clear from these considerations: we now declare that one who has the right to participate in deliberative or judicial office is a citizen of the state in which he has that right, and a state is a collection of such persons sufficiently numerous, speaking broadly, to secure independence of life. [Book III, 1275]

## [THE MORAL COMMUNITY]

The state was formed not for the sake of life only but rather for the good life (for otherwise a collection of slaves or of lower animals would be a state, but as it is, it is not a state, because slaves and animals have no share in well-being or in purposive life), and its object is not military alliance for defence against injury by anybody, and it does not exist for the sake of trade and of business relations – for if so, Etruscans and Carthaginians and all the people that have commercial relations with one another would be virtually citizens of a single state; at all events they have agreements about imports and covenants as to abstaining from dishonesty and treaties of alliance for mutual defence; but they do not have officials common to them all appointed to enforce these covenants, but different officials with either party, nor yet does either party take any concern as to the proper moral character of the other, nor attempt to secure that nobody in the states under the covenant shall be dishonest or in any way immoral, but only that they shall not commit any wrong against each other. All those on the other hand who are concerned about good government do take civic virtue and vice into their purview. Thus it is also clear that any state that is truly so called and is not a state merely in name must pay attention to virtue; for otherwise the community becomes merely an alliance, differing only in locality from the other alliances, those of allies that live apart. And the law is a covenant or, in the phrase of the sophist Lycophron, a guarantee of men's just claims on one another, but it is not designed to make the citizens virtuous and just. And that this is how the matter stands is manifest. For if one were actually to bring the sites of two cities together into one, so that the city-walls of Megara and those of Corinth were contiguous, even so they would not be one city; nor would they if they enacted rights of intermarriage with each other, although intermarriage between citizens is one of the elements of community which are characteristic of states. And similarly even if certain people lived in separate places yet not so far apart as not to have intercourse, but had laws to prevent their wronging one another in their interchange of products – for instance, if one man were a carpenter, another a farmer, another a shoemaker and another something else of the kind, – and the whole population numbered ten thousand, but nevertheless they had no mutual dealings in anything else except such things as exchange of commodities and military alliance, even then this would still not be a state. What then exactly is the reason for this? for clearly it is not because their intercourse is from a distance; since even if they came together for intercourse of this sort (each nevertheless using his individual house as a city) and for one another's military aid against wrongful aggressors only, as under a defensive alliance, not even then would they seem to those who consider the matter carefully to constitute a state, if they associated on the same footing when they came together as they did when they were apart. It is manifest therefore that a state is not merely the sharing of a common locality for the purpose of preventing mutual injury and exchanging goods. These are necessary pre-conditions of a state's existence, yet nevertheless, even if all these conditions are present, that does not therefore make a state, but a state is a partnership of families and of clans in living well, and its object is a full and independent life. At the same time this will not be realized unless the partners do inhabit one and the same locality and practise intermarriage; this indeed is the reason why family relationships have arisen throughout the states, and brotherhoods and clubs for sacrificial rites and social recreations. But such organization is produced by the feeling of friendship, for friendship is the motive of social life, these things are means to that end. And a state is the partnership of clans and villages in a full and independent life, which in our view constitutes a happy and noble life; the political community must therefore be deemed to exist for the sake of noble actions, not merely for living in common. [Book III, 1279–80]

## [PLURALISM]

There are three possible systems of property: either all the citizens must own everything in common, or they must own nothing in common, or some things must be common property and others not. To have nothing in common is clearly impossible; for the state is essentially a form of community, and it must at any rate have a common locality: a single city occupies a single site, and the single city belongs to its citizens in common. But is it better for a city that is to be well ordered to have community in everything which can possibly be made common property, or is it better to have some things in common and others not? For example, it is possible for the citizens to have children, wives and possessions in common with each other, as in Plato's *Republic*, in which Socrates says that there must be community of children, women and possessions. Well then, which is preferable, the system that now obtains, or one conforming with the regulation described in *The Republic*?

[...]

It is not an outcome of nature for the state to be a unity in the manner in which certain persons say that it is, and that what has been said to be the greatest good in states really destroys states; yet surely a thing's particular good acts as its preservative. – Another line of consideration also shows that to seek to unify the state excessively is not beneficial. In point of self-sufficiency the individual is surpassed by the family and the family by the state, and in principle a state is fully realized only when it comes to pass that the community of numbers is self-suffices; if therefore the more self-suffices a community is, the more desirable is its condition, then a less degree of unity is more desirable than a greater.

Again, even granting that it is best for the community to be as complete a unity as possible, complete unity does not seem to be proved by the formula 'if all the citizens say 'Mine' and 'Not mine' at the same time,' which Socrates thinks to be a sign of the city's being completely one. 'All' is an ambiguous term. If it means 'each severally,' very likely this would more fully realize the state of things which Socrates wishes to produce (for in that case every citizen will call the same boy his son and also the same woman his wife, and will speak in the same way of property and indeed of everything that falls to his lot); but *ex hypothesi* the citizens, having community of women and children, will not call them 'theirs' in this sense, but will mean theirs collectively and not severally, and similarly they will call property 'theirs' meaning the property of them all, not of each of them severally. We see then that the phrase 'all say' is equivocal (in fact the words 'all,' 'both,' 'odd,' 'even,' owing to their ambiguity, occasion argumentative quibbling even in philosophical discussions); hence really for 'all' to say the same thing is in one sense admirable, although impracticable but in another sense is not at all a sign of concord. And furthermore, the proposal has another disadvantage. Property that is common to the greatest number of owners receives the least attention; men care most for their private possessions, and for what they own in common less, or only so far as it falls to their own individual share; for in addition to the other reasons, they think less of it on the ground that someone else is thinking about it, just as in household service a large number of domestics sometimes give worse attendance than a smaller number. And it results in each citizen's having a thousand sons, and these do not belong to them as individuals but any child is equally the son of anyone, so that all alike will regard them with indifference. [Book II, 1260–1]

## [JUSTICE AND THE LAW]

It is wrong for those who are equal to have inequality, owing to which it is just for no one person to govern or be governed more than another, and therefore for everybody to govern and be governed alike in turn. And this constitutes law; for regulation is law. Therefore it is preferable for the law to rule rather than any one of the citizens, and according to this same principle, even if it be better for certain men to govern, they must be appointed as guardians of the laws and in subordination to them; for there must be some government, but it is clearly not just, men say, for one person to be governor when all the citizens are alike. It may be objected that any case which the law appears to be unable to define, a human being also would be unable to decide. But the law first specially educates the magistrates for the purpose and then commissions them to decide and administer the matters that it leaves over 'according to the best of their judgement,' and furthermore it allows them to introduce for themselves any amendment that experience leads them to think better than the established code. He therefore that recommends that the law shall govern seems to recommend that God and reason alone shall govern, but he that would have man govern adds a wild animal also; for appetite is like a wild animal, and also passion warps the rule even of the best men. Therefore the law is wisdom without desire. [Book III, 1287]

## [INEQUALITIES]

Let us begin by discussing the relation of master and slave, in order to observe the facts that have a bearing on practical utility, and also in the hope that we may be able to obtain something better than the notions at present entertained, with a view to a theoretic knowledge of the subject. For some thinkers hold the function of the master to be a definite science, and moreover think that household management, mastership, statesmanship and monarchy are the same thing, as we said at the beginning of the treatise; others however maintain that for one man to be another man's master is contrary to nature, because it is only convention that makes the one a slave and the other a freeman and there is no difference between them by nature, and that therefore it is unjust, for it is based on force.

Since therefore property is a part of a household and the art of acquiring property a part of household management (for without the necessaries even life, as well as the good life, is impossible), and since, just as for the definite arts it would be necessary for the proper tools to be forthcoming if their work is to be accomplished, so also the manager of a household must have his tools, and of tools some are lifeless and others living (for example, for a helmsman the rudder is a lifeless tool and the look-out man a live tool – for an assistant in the arts belongs to the class of tools), so also an article of property is a tool for the purpose of life, and property generally is a collection of tools, and a slave is a live article of property.

[…]

We must next consider whether or not anyone exists who is by nature of this character, and whether it is advantageous and just for anyone to be a slave, or whether on the contrary all slavery is against nature. And it is not difficult either to discern the answer by theory or to learn it empirically. Authority and subordination are conditions not only inevitable but also expedient; in some cases things are marked out from the moment of birth to rule or to be ruled. And there are many varieties both of rulers and of subjects (and the higher the type of the subjects, the loftier is the nature of the authority exercised over them, for example to control a human being is a higher thing than to tame a wild beast; for the higher the type of the parties to the performance of a function, the higher is the function, and when one party rules and another is ruled, there is a function performed between them) – because in every composite thing, where a plurality of parts, whether continuous or discrete, is combined to make a single common whole, there is always found a ruling and a subject factor

[…] [Book I, 1253–4]

The soul rules the body with the sway of a master, the intelligence the appetites with constitutional or royal rule; and in these examples it is manifest that it is natural and expedient for the body to be governed by the soul and for the emotional part to be governed by the intellect, the part possessing reason, whereas for the two parties to be on an equal footing or in the contrary positions is harmful in all cases. Again, the same holds good between man and the other animals: tame animals are superior in their nature to wild animals, yet for all the former it is advantageous to be ruled by man, since this gives them security. Also, as between the sexes, the male is by nature superior and the female inferior, the male ruler and the female subject. And the same must also necessarily apply in the case of mankind generally; therefore all men that differ as widely as the soul does from the body and the human being from the lower animal (and this is the condition of those whose function is the use of the body and from whom this is the best that is forthcoming) – these are by nature slaves, for whom to be governed by this kind of authority is advantageous, inasmuch as it is advantageous to the subject things already mentioned.

The intention of nature therefore is to make the bodies also of freemen and of slaves different – the latter strong for necessary service, the former erect and unserviceable for such occupations, but serviceable for a life of citizenship (and that again divides into the employments of war and those of peace); though as a matter of fact often the very opposite comes about – slaves have the bodies of freemen and freemen the souls only; since this is certainly clear, that if freemen were born as distinguished in body as are the statues of the gods, everyone would say that those who were inferior deserved to be these men's slaves; and if this is true in the case of the body, there is far juster reason for this rule being laid down in the case of the soul, but beauty of soul is not so easy to see as beauty of body. It is manifest therefore that there are cases of people of whom some are freemen and the others slaves by nature, and for these slavery is an institution both expedient and just.

But at the same time it is not difficult to see that those who assert the opposite are also right in a manner. The fact is that the terms 'slavery' and 'slave' are ambiguous; for there is also such a thing as a slave or a man that is in slavery by law, for the law is a sort of agreement under which the things conquered in war are said to belong to their conquerors.

It is clear […] that there is some reason for this dispute, and that in some instances it is not the case that one set are slaves and the other freemen by nature; and also that in some instances such a distinction does exist, when slavery for the one and mastership for the other are advantageous, and it is just and proper for the one party to be governed and for the other to govern by the form of government for which they are by nature fitted, and therefore by the exercise of mastership, while to govern badly is to govern disadvantageously for both parties (for the same thing is advantageous for a part and for the whole body or the whole soul, and the slave is a part of the master – he is, as it were, a part of the body, alive but yet separated from it; hence there is a certain community of interest and friendship between slave and master in cases when they have been qualified by nature for those positions, although when they do not hold them in that way but by law and by constraint of force the opposite is the case). [Book I, 1254–5]

As to slaves the difficulty might be raised, does a slave possess any other excellence, besides his merits as a tool and a servant, more valuable than these, for instance temperance, courage, justice and any of the other moral virtues, or has he no excellence beside his bodily service? For either way there is difficulty; if slaves do possess moral virtue, wherein will they differ from freemen? or if they do not, this is strange, as they are human beings and participate in reason. And nearly the same is the question also raised about the woman and the child: have they too virtues, and ought a woman to be temperate, brave and just, and can a child be intemperate or temperate, or not? [...]

There are by nature various classes of rulers and ruled. For the free rules the slave, the male the female, and the man the child in a different way. And all possess the various parts of the soul, but possess them in different ways; for the slave has not got the deliberative part at all, and the female has it, but without full authority, while the child has it, but in an undeveloped form. Hence the ruler must possess intellectual virtue in completeness (for any work, taken absolutely, belongs to the master-craftsman, and rational principle is a master-craftsman); while each of the other parties must have that share of this virtue which is appropriate to them. We must suppose therefore that the same necessarily holds good of the moral virtues: all must partake of them, but not in the same way, but in such measure as is proper to each in relation to his own function. Hence it is manifest that all the persons mentioned have a moral virtue of their own, and that the temperance of a woman and that of a man are not the same, nor their courage and justice, as Socrates throught, but the one is the courage of command, and the other that of subordination, and the case is similar with the other virtues. [Book I, 1259–60]

## [HUMAN FLOURISHING]

The best life, whether separately for an individual or collectively for states, is the life conjoined with virtue furnished with sufficient means for taking part in virtuous actions
[...]

The best constitution is the system under which anybody whatsoever would be best off and would live in felicity; but the question is raised even on the part of those who agree that the life accompanied by virtue is the most desirable, whether the life of citizenship and activity is desirable or rather a life released from all external affairs, for example some form of contemplative life, which is said by some to be the only life that is philosophic. For it is manifest that these are the two modes of life principally chosen by the men most ambitious of excelling in virtue, both in past times and at the present day – I mean the life of politics and the life of philosophy.

If happiness is to be defined as well-doing, the active life is the best life both for the whole state collectively and for each man individually. But the active life is not necessarily active in relation to other men, as some people think, nor are only those processes of thought active that are pursued for the sake of the objects that result from action, but far more those speculations and thoughts that have their end in themselves and are pursued for their own sake. [Book VII, 1323–5]

# AQUINAS
# From the *Political Writings* and from the *Summa Theologiae*

## [COMMUNITY]

### [The Aristotelian heritage]

The fact that man is by nature a social animal – being compelled to live in society because of the many needs he cannot satisfy out of his own resources – has as a consequence the fact that man is destined by nature to form part of a community which makes a full and complete life possible for him. The help of such a communal life is necessary to him for two reasons. In the first place it is necessary to provide him with those things without which life itself would be impossible. For this purpose there is the domestic community of which man forms a part. We all get life and food and education from our parents, and it is thus that the various individuals of a family assist one another with what is necessary to existence. But life in a community further enables man to achieve a plenitude of life; not merely to exist, but to live fully, with all that is necessary to well-being. In this sense the political community, of which man forms a part, assists him not merely to obtain material comforts, such as are produced by the many diverse industries of a state, but also spiritual well-being, as when youthful intemperance, which paternal admonishment is unable to control, is restrained by public authority.

But it must be noted that this unity which is the political community or the unity of the family, is only a unity of order and not an unconditional unity. Consequently the parts which form it can have a sphere of action which is distinct from that of the whole; just as in an army a soldier can perform actions which are not proper to the whole army. At the same time the whole has a sphere of action which is not proper to any of its parts; as for example the general action in battle of the

55

entire army: or again like the movement of a ship which results from the combined action of the rowers. There is on the other hand a whole which has not only a unity of order but also of composition, of aggregation, or of physical continuity; a unity which can be called absolute. In such a case there is no action of the parts which is not also action of the whole. In continuous things the movement of the whole is in fact identical with that of the part: and similarly in a composite or aggregate the action of any part is principally that of the whole; and in consequence the study of the part should be included in that of the whole. On the other hand it is not right that the study of what is only a unity of order, and of the parts which so compose it, should be undertaken under one head. For this reason moral philosophy should be divided into three parts. The first studies men as individuals and as ordered to a certain end: this is called monastic. The second is concerned with the domestic community and is called economic; and the third studies the action of the civil community and is called political. [Commentary on Aristotle's *Nicomachean Ethics*, in *Political Writings*, pp. 191, 193]

### [Distributive justice]

Particular justice is directed towards the private person, who may be compared to the community as a part to a whole. Now with a part we may note a twofold relationship. First, that of one part to another, and this corresponds to the ordering of private persons among themselves. This is governed by commutative justice, which is engaged with their mutual dealings one with another. Second, that of the whole to a part, which goes with the bearing of the community on individual persons. This is governed by distributive justice which apportions proportionately to each his share from the common stock. [...]

As a part and the whole are identical in a sense, so too in a sense that which is of the whole is also of a part. Accordingly when something is given to each from the goods of the community each in a way receives what is his own. [*Summa Theologiae*, 2a2ae.61.1, vol. 37, p. 89]

### [Suicide]

Suicide is completely wrong for three reasons. First, everything naturally loves itself, and it is for this reason that everything naturally seeks to keep itself in being and to resist hostile forces. So suicide runs counter to one's natural inclination, and also to that charity by which one ought to cherish oneself. Suicide is, therefore, always a mortal sin in so far as it stultifies the law of nature and charity. Second, every part belongs to the whole in virtue of what it is. But every man is part of the community, so that he belongs to the community in virtue of what he is. Suicide therefore involves damaging the community, as Aristotle makes clear. Third, life is a gift made to man by God, and it is subject to him who is *master of death and life*. Therefore a person who takes his own life sins against God, just as he who kills another's slave injures the slave's master, or just as he who usurps judgement in a matter outside his authority also commits a sin. And God alone has authority to decide about life and death, as he declares in *Deuteronomy*, *I kill and I make alive*. [*Summa Theologiae*, 2a2ae.64.5, vol. 38, p. 33]

### [Capital punishment]

Men may kill brute animals in so far as they are naturally ordained for man's own use, on the principle that the imperfect is for the sake of the perfect. But every part is related to the whole precisely as imperfect to perfect, which is the reason why every part is naturally for the sake of the whole. If, therefore, the well-being of the whole body demands the amputation of a limb, say in the case where one limb is gangrenous and threatens to infect the others, the treatment to be commended is amputation. Now every individual person is as it were a part of the whole. Therefore if any man is dangerous to the community and is subverting it by some sin, the treatment to be commended in his execution in order to preserve the common good. [*Summa Theologiae*, 2a2ae.64.2, vol. 38, p. 23]

### [LAW]

### [Law defined]

Law is a rule and measure ... and therefore can exist in two manners, first as in the thing which is the rule and measure, second as in the thing that is ruled and measured, and the closer the second to the first the more regular and measured it will be. Since all things are regulated and measured by Eternal Law, as we have seen, it is evident that all somehow share in it, in that their tendencies to their own proper acts and ends are from its impression.

Among them intelligent creatures are ranked under divine Providence the more nobly because they take part in Providence by their own providing for themselves and others. Thus they join in and make their own the Eternal Reason through which they have their natural aptitudes for their due activity and purpose. Now this sharing in the Eternal Law by intelligent creatures is what we call 'natural law'. [*Summa Theologiae*, 1a2ae.91.2, vol. 28, p. 23]

### [Natural law and practical reason]

Now we discover that the things which enter into our apprehension are ranged in a certain order. That which first appears is *the real*, and some insight into this is included in whatsoever is apprehended. This first indemonstrable principle, 'There is no affirming and denying the same simultaneously', is based on the very nature of the real and the non-real: on this principle, as Aristotle notes, all other propositions are based.

To apply the analogy: as to be *real* first enters into human apprehending as such, so to be *good* first enters the practical reason's apprehending when it is bent on doing something. For every agent acts on account of an end, and to be an end carries the meaning of to be good. Consequently the first principle for the practical reason is based on the meaning of good, namely that it is what all things seek after. And so this is the first command of law, 'that good is to be sought and done, evil to be avoided'; all other commands of natural law are based on this. Accordingly, then, natural-law commands extend to all doing or avoiding of things recognized by the practical reason of itself as being human goods.

Now since being good has the meaning of being an end, while being an evil has the contrary meaning, it follows that reason of its nature apprehends the things towards which man has a natural tendency as good objectives, and therefore to be actively pursued, whereas it apprehends their contraries as bad, and therefore to be shunned.

Let us continue. The order in which commands of the law of nature are ranged corresponds to that of our natural tendencies. Here there are three stages. There is in man, first, a tendency towards the good of the nature he has in common with all substances; each has an appetite to preserve its own natural being. Natural law here plays a corresponding part, and is engaged at this stage to maintain and defend the elementary requirements of human life.

Secondly, there is in man a bent towards things which accord with his nature considered more specifically, that is in terms of what he has in common with other animals; correspondingly those matters are said to be of natural law which nature teaches all animals, for instance the coupling of male and female, the bringing up of the young, and so forth.

Thirdly, there is in man an appetite for the good of his nature as rational, and this is proper to him, for instance, that he should know truths about God and about living in society. Correspondingly whatever this involves is a matter of natural law, for instance that a man should shun ignorance, not offend others with whom he ought to live in civility, and other such related requirements. [*Summa Theologiae*, 1a2ae.94.2, vol. 28, pp. 81, 83]

### [Can natural law be effaced?]

As we noticed when speaking of what belongs to natural law, to begin with there are certain most general precepts known to all; and next, certain secondary and more specific precepts which are like conclusions lying close to the premises. As for these first common principles in their universal meaning, natural law cannot be cancelled in the human heart, nevertheless it can be missing from a particular course of action when the reason is stopped from applying the general principle there, because of lust or some other passion, as we have pointed out.

As for its other and secondary precepts, natural law can be effaced, either by wrong persuasions – thus also errors occur in theoretical matters concerning demonstrable conclusions – or by perverse customs and corrupt habits; for instance robbery was not reputed to

be wrong among some people, nor even, as the Apostle mentions,
some unnatural sins. [*Summa Theologia*, 1a2ae.94.6, vol. 28, p. 97]

## [Theological voluntarism]

Objection: the killing of the innocent is against natural law, and so is adultery and theft. Yet you find God changing these rules, as when he commanded Abraham to put his son to death, the people of Israel to spoil the Egyptians, and Hosea to take a wife of harlotry. Natural law, then, can be altered.

Reply: A change can be understood to mean either addition or subtration. As for the first, there is nothing against natural law being changed, for many things over and above natural law have been added, by divine law as well as by human laws, which are beneficial to social life.

As for change by subtraction, meaning that something that once was of natural law later ceases to be so, here there is room for a distinction. The first principles of natural law are altogether unalterable. But its secondary precepts, which we have described as being like particular conclusions close to first principles, though not alterable in the majority of cases where they are right as they stand, can nevertheless be changed on some particular and rare occasions, as we have mentioned in the preceding article, because of some special cause preventing their unqualified observance.

Hence:

1. The written Law is said to have been for the correction of natural law because it supplied what was wanting there, or because parts of natural law were decayed in the hearts of those who reckoned that some things were good which by nature are evil. This called for correction.

2. All men without exception, guilty and innocent alike, have to suffer the sentence of natural death from divine power because of original sin, according to the words, *The Lord kills and brings to life.* Consequently without injustice God's command can inflict death on anybody whether he be guilty or innocent. Adultery is intercourse with a woman to whom you are not married in accordance with divinely given law; nevertheless to go unto any woman by divine command is neither adultery nor fornication. The same applies to theft, the taking of what belongs to another, for what is taken by God's command, who is the owner of the universe, is not against the owner's will, and this is of the essence of theft. ...

3. You speak of something being according to natural right in two ways. The first is because nature is set that way; thus the command that no harm should be done to another. The second is because nature does not bid the contrary; thus we might say that it is of natural law for man to be naked, for nature does not give him clothes; these he has to make by art. In this way common ownership and universal liberty are said to be of natural law, because private property and slavery exist by human contrivance for he convenience of social life, and not

by natural law. This does not change the law of nature except by addition. [*Summa Theologiae*, 1a2ae, 94.5, vol. 28, pp. 93, 95]

## [JUS]

Something is said to be just because it has the rightness of justice; it is this that engages the activity of justice, even abstracting from the temper in which it is done; by contrast, the rightness of the other moral virtues is not determined apart from the frame of mind of the person acting. This is why for justice expecially, in comparison with other virtues, an impersonal objective interest is fixed. We call it *the just thing*, and this indeed is a right: clearly, then, right is the objective interest of justice.

[...]

By customary usage words are twisted from their original application to signify other things; 'medicine', for instance, first applied to a healing remedy for the sick, was afterwards extended to the art which procures this. Likewise the word 'right' [jus] was first applied to the just thing itself, and then derivatively to the art which discerns what this is; then further to the courts where justice is administered, thus when somebody is said to appear juridically, *in jure*, and further when we speak of *jus* being delivered by one holding the office of administering justice, even when his decision is wicked. [*Summa Theologiae*, 2a2ae.57.1, vol. 37, pp. 5, 7]

## [TYRANNICAL AND UNJUST LAWS]

### [Tyrannicide justified]

We must observe that ... in the observance of a certain precept, obedience is connected with the obligation to such observance. But such obligation derives from the order of authority which carries with it the power to constrain, not only from the temporal, but also from the spiritual point of view, and in conscience; as the Apostle says (*Romans* XIII): and this because the order of authority derives from God, as the Apostle says in the same passage. For this reason the duty of obedience is, for the Christian, a consequence of this derivation of authority from God, and ceases when that ceases. But, as we have already said, authority may fail to derive from God for two reasons: either because of the way in which authority has been obtained, or in consequence of the use which is made of it. There are two ways in which the first case may occur. Either because of a defect in the person, if he is unworthy; or because of some defect in the way itself by which power was acquired, if, for example, through violence, or simony or some other illegal method. The first defect is not such as to impede the acquisition of legitimate authority; and since authority derives always, from a formal point of view, from God (and it is this which produces the duty of obedience), their subjects are always obliged to obey such superiors, however unworthy they may be. But the second defect prevents the establishment of any just authority:

for whoever possesses himself of power by violence does not truly become lord or master. Therefore it is permissible, when occasion offers, for a person to reject such authority; except in the case that it subsequently became legitimate, either through public consent or through the intervention of higher authority. With regard to abuse of authority, this also may come about in two ways. First, when what is ordered by an authority is opposed to the object for which that authority was constitued (if, for example, some sinful action is commanded or one which is contrary to virtue, when it is precisely for the protection and fostering of virtue that authority is instituted). In such a case, not only is there no obligation to obey the authority, but one is obliged to disobey it, as did the holy martyrs who suffered death rather than obey the impious commands of tyrants.
[...]
Those who attain power by violence are not truly rulers; therefore their subjects are not bound to obey them except in the cases already noted. ... [in] a case where a person had possessed himself of power through violence, either against the will of his subjects or by compelling their consent, and where there was no possibility of appeal to a higher authority who could pass judgement on such action. In such a case, one who liberates his country by killing a tyrant is to be praised and rewarded. [Commentary on the *Sentences* of Peter Lombard, *Political Writings*, pp. 183, 185]

### [A perversion of the law]
A tyrannical law is not according to reason, and therefore is not straightforwardly a law, but rather a sort of perversion of the law. It does however possess some quality of law in intending that the citizens should be good. This it does as being the decree of a presiding authority set on making its subjects obedient, i.e. making them good from the point of view of the government, not thoroughly good in themselves. [*Summa Theologiae*, 1a2ae.92.2 vol. 28, p. 45]

### [A corruption of the law]
Augustine observes that *there never seems to have been a law that was not just*: hence a command has the force of law to the extent that it is just. In human matters we call something 'just' from its being right according to the rule of reason. The first rule of reason is natural law, as appears from what has been stated. Hence in so far as it derives from this, every law laid down by men has the force of law in that it flows from natural law. If on any head it is at variance with natural law, it will not be law, but a corruption of the law. [*Summa Theologiae*, 1a2ae.95.2, vol. 28, p. 105]

### [Unjust laws]
Laws are unjust in two ways, as being against what is fair in human terms and against God's rights. They are contrary to human good on the three counts made above; from their end, when the ruler taxes his

subjects rather for his own greed or vanity than the common benefit; from their author, when he enacts a law beyond the power committed to him; and from their form, when, although meant for the common good, laws are inequitably dispensed. These are outrages rather than laws; Augustine remarks, *There never seems to have been a law where justice was not present.* Such commands do not oblige in the court of conscience, unless perhaps to avoid scandal or riot; on this account a man may be called to yield his rights, according to the text of *Matthew, If any one forces you to go one mile, go with him two miles, and if any one would sue you and take your coat, let him have your cloak as well.*

Laws can be unjust because they are contrary to God's rights; such are the laws of tyrants which promote idolatry or whatsoever is against divine law. To observe them is in no wise permissible, for as is said in the *Acts, We must obey God rather than men.*

Hence:

1. According to St Paul, *There is no authority*, that is, human authority, *except from God*, and *therefore he who resists the authorities*, that is in what lies within the order of their power, *resists what God has appointed*, and consequently is made guilty in conscience.

2. This argument is put forward about human laws which are directed against God's commandments. They then go beyond the order of power, and are not to be submitted to.

3. This argument is about a law which inflicts an unjust grievance on its subjects; here also it exceeds the power of command divinely granted, and in such cases a man is not obliged to obey, if without scandal or greater damage he can resist. [*Summa Theologiae*, 1a2ae. 96.4, vol. 28, pp. 131, 133]

**MARTIN HOLLIS**

# Machiavelli, Milton and Hobbes on liberty

3

The key to liberty in the republican tradition is self-government: free states are those 'which are far from all external servitude, and are able to govern themselves according to their own will', as Niccolò Machiavelli puts it in *The Discourses* (Book I, chapter 2). No republic can remain independent of its neighbours and free within its borders, unless citizens accept civic obligations as an integral part of their personal liberty. But Machiavelli does not hold that political liberty can flourish only in republics. For that strand in republicanism we shall look to John Milton's *The Readie and Easie Way to Establish a Free Commonwealth.* Having denounced monarchy in all its forms, Milton then argues, like Machiavelli, that the key to liberty lies in civic-mindedness within a constitutional framework. Both writers thus stand in contrast to Thomas Hobbes in *Leviathan*, who is sceptical of republican forms of government and measures liberty primarily by whether individuals can pursue their personal ends without interference. Yet Hobbes's more modern and apparently liberal view cannot merely supplant the older one. Benjamin Constant's distinction between 'the liberty of the ancients' and 'the liberty of the moderns' crystallises a debate which remains very much alive.

The theme of the chapter is thus a dispute about the nature of liberty and the form of government best able to ensure it. To trace its strands, we need to distinguish our three authors.

### Niccolò Machiavelli (1469–1527)

Machiavelli was a citizen of Florence in a period when Italy was a land of small states and political upheavals. He came to prominence in 1498, when Savonarola was replaced by a republican government in Florence, and he served the republic as second chancellor and secretary to the chief foreign relations committee until 1512. In that year the republic was overthrown and the Medici family returned to power. Machiavelli was dismissed and, in 1513, was accused of conspiring against the new regime, tortured and imprisoned. He was then released, however, and allowed to retire from public life. Despite several efforts, he never regained favour and lived as man of letters until his death in 1527.

Some five centuries later he remains so notorious for his reflections on the nature of politics that no political leader cares to be called machiavellian. There are, he held, only two viable kinds of state, principalities and republics, and he wrote a book about each. *The Prince*, composed in 1513, is a handbook of statecraft for rulers of principalities, full of cool advice on how to gain and hold power by whatever means is necessary. For example, a successful prince must be 'a great feigner and dissembler'. To keep the trust of his subjects, he must cultivate a high moral reputation; to keep the state great and prosperous, he must break faith and deceive its enemies without scruple. Such advice has earned Machiavelli a place in the demonology of political thought as a friend of wicked rulers and a tempter to corruption in politics.

This reputation is misleading. *The Prince* does indeed argue that a wise prince with the good of his people at heart cannot be bound by ordinary moral rules. But Machiavelli does not thereby absolve princes from all moral concern. They are to be judged by whether they practise a proper princely virtue (*virtú*), no less genuinely virtuous for differing from common morality. That may be a dangerous line of thought, but it is not one which simply gives rulers moral *carte blanche*.

The book about republics was also written around 1513. *The Discourses* is a commentary on the first ten books of Livy's history of Rome, which cover the ancient Roman republic. With accompanying reflections on other republics, Machiavelli firmly recommends republican forms of government, if and when they are viable, as in this passage:

It is easy to see how this affection of peoples for self-government (*del vivere libero*) comes about, for experience shows that cities have never increased either in dominion or wealth, unless they have been independent. It is truly remarkable to observe the greatness which Athens attained in the space of a hundred years after it has been liberated from the tyranny of Pisistratus. But most marvellous of all is to observe the greatness which Rome attained after freeing itself from its kings. The reason is easy to understand; for it is not the well-being of individuals that makes cities great, but the well-being of the community; and it is beyond question that it is only in republics that the common good is looked to properly in that all that promotes it is carried out ... (*The Discourses*, II, 2)

The connecting idea here is that liberty is a collective good. Hence the best way for a republic to remain independent of neighbouring states is to have a citizen militia, since that involves the citizens collectively in the defence of their freedom. (This is one reason why the citizen's right to bear arms is enshrined in the American constitution.) Internally, the best way to avoid domination by sectional interests is to achieve a self-governing balance between the interests of the people (*plebe*) and the rulers (*grandi*), secured by an impartial system of law. Only in a flourishing republic are there these direct connections between liberty and the common good.

But republics were fragile in the Italy of the early sixteenth century and Machiavelli holds that it is better to be governed by a suitable prince than to lose one's liberty altogether. A principality, wisely governed, can be free and independent. While it remains secure from enemies without and corruption within, it too can increase in dominion and wealth. Since this requires the prince visibly to embody its greatness, no self-denial on his part is involved. Sometimes, moreover, only a prince can act with the duplicity and ruthlessness which the flourishing of an independent state may demand. Principalities may be second best, but they are sometimes better than unsuccessful republics.

Although both books were written at the same time, it would be a mistake to read *The Prince* as a cynical attempt to curry favour with the new rulers by praising their vices, on the off-chance that they would not get to hear about *The Discourses*. The books have major themes in common, notably the connectedness of greatness, power, prosperity, virtue and liberty. The crucial element is *virtú*, which does not have the connotations of today's 'virtue'. *Virtú*, often best translated as 'public spiritedness', does indeed carry a moral charge, but one more ancient than modern. The core idea is that of proper function, of the qualities needed for realising one's proper ends. It originated in Aristotle's definition of a human being as a social animal (*politikon zoon*) whose flourishing depends on participation in the life of the *polis*. The idea was then refined by Latin writers, notably by Cicero in *De Officiis*, who specified virtue (*virtus*) in a man (*vir*) as possession of wisdom, justice, courage and temperance. Later authors added magnanimity and liberality. The list then became standard in Renaissance handbooks of advice for rulers.

*The Prince* belongs to this genre and invokes this list of virtues. But as we have noted, Machiavelli deems them virtues to be paraded rather than practised officiously. *Virtú* in those seeking to govern a great and free state, in a world where human nature is unreliable and fortune favours the bold, consists in doing whatever is needed to achieve the proper ends of government. Success depends partly on having a reputation for the classic virtues, and partly on knowing when to ignore them. That creates a tension and a constant temptation for the prince to pursue his personal interest in the name of the real public interest. But then republics, which are less prone to this conflict, are also less able to act ruthlessly in defending their freedom.

By thinking in terms of sovereign authority, as distinct from the rulers who embody it, Machiavelli can make these connections for republics and principalities alike. Citizens are subjects of the sovereign in both cases, although in republics they, or some of them, also wield its authority, whereas in principalities that authority is wielded by the prince. In both kinds of government public spirit is what prevents corruption, secures independence and keeps the people free: 'it is not the well-being of individuals that makes cities great, but the well-being of the community'.

The message is clear in *The Prince* and is presented more reflectively in *The Discourses*. In both books, however, it takes the form of scattered comments interspersed among historical observations on the fortunes of states past and present. The nearest Machiavelli comes to putting it shortly is in the second chapter of Book II of *The Discourses*, which is reproduced below. Even there, the message is not easy to discern. Yet republican ideas of liberty are too enduringly important to go by default, and no other thinker in the period is a match for Machiavelli. When other authors discuss liberty in a republican spirit, they are crude by comparison, although we shall find that John Milton's vision has a refreshing directness.

### John Milton (1608–74)

Those reared on *Paradise Lost* and Milton's other poetic works are often surprised by his prose. He was a copious author of tracts on political, religious and social matters, especially between 1640 and 1660, a period which included the English civil war, the execution of Charles I, the Protectorate and the restoration of the monarchy. Best known of these political writings is *Areopagitica* (1644), a passionate defence of a free press, written in prose which still reverberates. Other works are as passionate for a free commonwealth, whose religious and civil liberties are sustained by an elected elite. Milton wrote as a Protestant who held that the Bible speaks directly to individuals and does not require interpretation by the dogmatic authority of the church – especially not the Roman Catholic Church. He advocated the separation of church and state and a citizenry educated to practise a responsible individualism. Since these views were couched in language which excoriated kings and popes, the restoration of Charles II in 1660 put his life and property in danger. But thanks to his blindness (since 1652) and the influence of powerful friends, he was allowed to retire into private life and his greatest poetry was all published before his death.

The *Readie and Easie Way to Establish a Free Commonwealth* appeared in 1660, the very year of the Restoration. It denounces monarchy it all its forms and urges that the Rump Parliament become a perpetual Supreme Council consisting of freely (but not democratically) elected Knights and Burgesses. There would also be local government by committees of 'the nobilitie and chief gentry' with educational and judicial functions. Although no profound piece of political theory, it breathes republican fire.

Milton starts by appealing to 'the law of nature', which is 'the only law of laws truly and properly to all mankinde fundamental; the beginning and end of all Government'. Thus armed, he describes a free commonwealth as one

wherein they who are greatest are perpetual servants and drudges to the public at their own cost and charges, neglect their own affairs; yet are not elevated above their brethren; live soberly in their families, walk the streets as other men, may be spoken to freely, familiarly, friendly, without adoration. Whereas a king must be adored like a Demigod, with a dissolute and haughty court about him, of vast expense and luxury, masks and revels, to the debauching of our prime gentry both male and female; not in their pastimes only, but in earnest, by the loose employments of court service, which will then be thought honourable.

The two extracts reproduced on pp. 79 and 81 expand on the theme. The first proposes the institution of a perpetual Council as a 'readie and easie way' to extend the fruits of the civil war. The second discusses spiritual and civil liberty, the latter consisting in 'the civil rights and advancements of every person according to his merit'. The general line is that 'of all governments a Commonwealth aims most to make the people flourishing, vertuous, noble and high-spirited', whereas monarchs want sycophants about them and a people that is 'softest, basest, servilest, easiest to be kept under'.

## Thomas Hobbes (1588–1679)

Machiavelli and Milton held that a free state requires citizens who are 'vertuous' in contributing to the common good. Hobbes, writing like Milton in the aftermath of the civil war, had a strikingly different idea of liberty, more philosophical in origin and more modern in its implications. Setting out as a classical scholar, he presently became fascinated with geometry, which he came to see as a model for a general scientific method for deriving significant theorems from self-evidently true axioms. He also became convinced of the truth of materialism, the thesis that all mental operations can be explained by or as physical motions in the body. His first philosophical work, the *Little Treatise* (1637), tried to account for sense experience in purely bodily terms. This materialist theme recurs throughout his political writings.

The first of these, *Elements of Law*, not published until 1650, was completed in 1640 and then circulated in manuscript. It proved so contentious that, fearing the wrath of Parliament, Hobbes fled to France, before *De Cive* appeared in 1642. He was taken up by the royal court in exile and, in 1646, appointed tutor in mathematics to the future Charles II. There he stayed until the publication of *Leviathan* in 1651. This seminal text, notorious from the start, offended his hosts and Hobbes returned to England, where he continued to work on scientific questions. When the monarchy was restored in 1660, he feared for his safety, but Charles II welcomed him at court and awarded him a pension of £100. His writings, which included *Behemoth* (a history of the civil war period), an autobiography and translations of the *Iliad* and *Odyssey*, continued until his death at the age of ninety-two.

*Leviathan* opens by remarking that 'life is but motion of Limbs' (Introduction) and by deploying a materialist analysis of human action. Human beings are rational machines, driven by their passions, steered by reason and bent on 'felicity' or 'continuall successe in obtaining those things which a man from time to time desireth' (chapter VI). Having anatomised the passions, Hobbes moves on to analyse judgements, beliefs, virtues, *mores*, social aspirations and religion.

Not until chapter XIII does he set about expounding his crucial theory

67

of the social contract. The root problem of social order, as Hobbes sees it, is that men by nature seek their own preservation and felicity, and become enemies whenever any two of them 'desire the same thing, which neverthelesse they cannot both enjoy'. On becoming enemies, they 'endeavour to destroy, or subdue one another'. In a state of nature they quarrel so readily that no one is safe, and the felicity which all desire is unattainable. That requires domestic peace but 'during the time men live without a common Power to keep them all in awe, they are in that condition which is called warre; and such a warre, as is of every man, against every man'. Then follows an unforgettable paragraph:

Whatsoever therefore is consequent to a time of Warre, where every man is Enemy to every man; the same is consequent to the time, wherein men live without other security, than what their own strength, and their own invention shall furnish them withall. In such condition, there is no place for Industry; because the fruit thereof is uncertain: and consequently no Culture of the Earth; no Navigation, nor use of the commodities that may be imported by Sea; no commodious Building; no Instruments of moving, and removing, such things as require much force; no Knowledge of the face of the Earth; no account of Time; no Arts; no Letters; no Society; and which is worst of all, continuall feare, and danger of violent death; And the life of man, solitary, poore, nasty, brutish, and short.

The only way of escape for these quarrelsome individuals is to create a common power to keep them all in awe, which is

that great LEVIATHAN called a COMMONWEALTH, or STATE, (in latin CIVITAS) which is but an Artificiall Man. (Introduction)

The idea is nicely caught in the frontispiece to the original edition, which shows a crowned king, armed with all the weapons of church and state. The king seems to be wearing chain mail. Looking closer, however, we see that the sovereign's body is made up of tiny human individuals. Leviathan is an artifact created by the social contract and composed of all those party to it.

This sovereign, armed with a sword, wields absolute authority but only for the limited purpose of solving the original problem. The state provides protection against foreign enemies and safety at home. It arbitrates disputes and, crucially, sees to it that people keep whatever contracts they make with one another. But it does not otherwise interfere in their pursuit of their ends, by telling them how to live or by concerning itself with their misfortunes. Its rationale is summed up in a famous remark in chapter XVII: 'Covenants, without the Sword, are but Words, and of no strength to secure a man at all.'

Chapter XXI, which is reproduced below, is titled 'Of the LIBERTY of Subjects'. Liberty or freedom, it begins, 'signifieth (properly) the absence of Opposition', by which Hobbes means the absence of 'externall Impediments of motion'. Hence laws, while an impediment to law-breakers, do not restrict the freedom of those who obey them willingly, even if through fear. Rational individuals realise that they can attain their ends only if others can be relied on to keep their promises.

This will not happen unless there is a framework of laws and a sword to enforce them. Therefore each rational individual obeys willingly, since universal enforcement is a guarantee that others will obey. Thus a war of every man against every man is replaced by a condition of peace where rational individuals can trust one another and hope to benefit from the fruits of industry. Since a free man *'is he, that in those things, which by his strength and wit he is able to do, is not hindred to doe what he has a will to'*, the result is a commonwealth of free individuals.

Like Machiavelli, Hobbes thus makes liberty depend on law. He differs, however, in leaving individuals to their own ends and does not seek to tie their freedom to public participation. Republics can be as tyrannous as principalities, in Hobbes's view, the test being whether they impose duties on their citizens which go beyond the original purpose of the social contract. So the rest of the chapter concerns the liberty of subjects in their dealings with Leviathan itself. The basic theme is that, whatever the sovereign does, he can do no injury or injustice to a subject, 'because every Subject is Author of every act the Soveraign doth'. Any injury is therefore self-inflicted and not grounds for complaint. A king who abuses his authority has offended against God but has not wronged his victims. Since the sovereign has the power of life and death, this is an alarming principle for a free commonwealth, but Hobbes means what he says. The sovereign is not party to the social contract and is not bound by laws which stem from the sovereign body thus created. Since there is injustice only where there is a breach of a law by someone who is subject to it, the sovereign cannot act unjustly.

Nevertheless, subjects are sometimes entitled to disobey. Here the principle is that there is no obligation to do what one has not authorised the sovereign to command. In assenting to the social contract, I have not given up my natural right to defend my own body. I therefore have no obligation to kill, wound or maim myself or to go without food, air, medicine or anything without which I shall die. I am not obliged to confess my crimes or incriminate myself – a principle now enshrined in the American constitution as the Fifth Amendment. In general, I have an obligation to do what is dangerous or dishonourable only when refusal 'frustrates the End for which Soveraignty was ordained'.

These are limited exceptions. We may act in self-defence, but 'to resist the Sword of the Commonwealth, in defence of another man, guilty or innocent, no man hath Liberty'. Other liberties 'depend on the Silence of the Law' and thus vary from place to place depending on what is locally permitted or forbidden. Hobbes does not think the overall reckoning oppressive. Whatever is not forbidden I may do, and the whole is governed by whether the sovereign achieves its primary purpose:

The Obligation of Subjects to the Soveraign, is understood to last as long as, and no longer than, the power lasteth, by which he is able to protect them ... The end of Obedience is Protection.

In that case, however, it is hard to see how a society whose *raison d'être* is mutual self-interest can resist the attrition of its public realm by self-interested individuals, each seeking to contribute as little as possible. Hobbes squarely poses the question in *Leviathan*; whether he can answer it remains an urgent matter of debate.

## Conclusion

Machiavelli and Milton speak for the liberty of the ancients and Hobbes for the liberty of the moderns. The enduring issue is not one of constitutional forms. Although Milton denounces kings, Machiavelli, as we saw, holds that a free state can have a single ruler and, indeed, may need one when times are treacherous. Conversely, Hobbes grants that the sovereignty of Leviathan can be embodied in an oligarchy or parliament, although he commends monarchy as less prone to conflicts of authority which can destroy the unity of the state. All three writers are discussing sovereignty and, in principle, the sovereign body of a free commonwealth can take several forms.

The crucial disagreement turns on a contrast between the ancient liberty of citizens and the modern liberty of individuals. This contrast was famously defined by Benjamin Constant (1767–1830) in a speech on 'The Liberty of the Ancients Compared with that of the Moderns' made in 1819:

The aim of the ancients was the sharing of social power among the citizens of the same fatherland: this is what they called liberty. The aim of the moderns is the enjoyment of security in private pleasures; and they call liberty the guarantees accorded by institutions to these pleasures.

Having warned that the liberty of the ancients could deprive citizens of all private life (especially in the versions reinvented by the French Revolution), he noted that the liberty of the moderns threatens the public life of society. Hence we must 'learn to combine the two together'. We need institutions which respect the individual rights of citizens and yet secure their moral education.

The question remains whether and how this can be done. The republican tradition ties freedom to self-government and assigns citizens a primary duty to participate. They are citizens first and private persons second, when their public obligations have been performed. They have rights as well as duties, but these rights are akin to opportunities to lead a complete life, which includes their public contribution. 'Modern' thinkers, by contrast, regard citizens as private individuals who form political associations for mutual advantage. Although the benefits may depend on contributions in tax or service and perhaps on some measure of public-spiritedness, ends remain individual and personal. Associates retain rights against one another and – although not in Hobbes's version – against the state. Rights are prior to obligations, since it is not rational to be bound by a contract unless it works to one's overall advantage. Freedom is typically freedom from interference in one's private pursuits and enjoyments.

The difference between these concepts of liberty is often generalised as one between 'freedom from' and 'freedom to', with the moderns favouring 'negative' liberty – freedom from impediments – and the ancients 'positive' liberty – freedom to flourish in some prescribed manner. But that way of presenting the contrast is too neat. A minor snag is that it now seems a merely verbal distinction. Freedom *from* interference is freedom *to* do what one wants; freedom *to* flourish is freedom *from* impediments to one's flourishing. More seriously, this way of making the contrast between the liberty of the ancients and the liberty of the moderns runs together two very different debates.

One debate turns on whether the concept of freedom is neutral between competing ideas of the good life. Here the 'negative' view is that it is indeed neutral, since whether one is free has nothing to do with whether one is good or wicked. The rise of liberalism has tended to favour this line. In the Introduction to *On Liberty* (1859), John Stuart Mill remarks:

The only liberty which deserves the name, is that of pursuing our own good in our own way, so long as we do not attempt to deprive others of theirs, or impede their efforts to obtain it.

Liberals commonly hold that the choice of our own good is up to each of us and that, whatever good we choose, we are free in so far as we are unimpeded in pursuing it. Sinners can be as free as saints, short-order cooks as free as nomads. But this answer is not definitive. Even liberals can be tempted, like Mill himself, into connecting the extent or quality of one's freedom to one's degree of self-mastery or to the development of one's higher faculties or to one's possession of virtues of character, including concern for others. On the collective front, even liberals can wonder, like Mill himself, whether a free society can do without a moral cement of shared values, especially those implicit in liberalism itself. In other words, if liberty has anything to do with liberality, there may be a minimal set of virtues and values which are requisite for an autonomous life in a free society. In that case liberty is not merely the absence of external impediments to the will, even if caveats are kept to a minimum (see also the discussion of J. S. Mill in chapter 11). Meanwhile the 'ancient' view has never faded away. It remains ready to pounce on the use of concepts like 'autonomy' in the previous paragraph, with their suggestion that freedom is subject to a regulative ideal or to virtues of character which echo old Stoic virtues. It has always been espoused by religions claiming to offer true freedom, as in Thomas Cranmer's sixteenth-century prayer invoking 'God, whose service is perfect freedom'. Here freedom is a matter of willing obedience to the demands of a Christian life, but similar claims are made by other religions. Political versions tend towards communitarianism, or at least towards making collective liberty primary. For instance in Rousseau's *The Social Contract* (1762) 'freedom is obedience to a law which we prescribe to ourselves', with the stress on a collective 'we' who do the prescribing (below p. 218). In obeying the 'General Will' of a well-ordered society, I am doing what I *truly* want; if I dissent from the General Will, I have misread my own will, and, in being forced to conform, am being 'forced to be free' (below p. 217). Such theories are 'positive' either in defining true freedom with an eye to *inner* impediments to living a virtuous life, or in insisting that we are social beings whose collective freedom and self-realisation are true guides to our individual liberty.

The other debate is between what could be termed 'thin' and 'thick' concepts of liberty. It occurs within each camp. For negative theories, the question is whether freedom depends solely on the absence of formal, especially legal, impediments or whether resources are involved. Thus libertarians argue that, since there is nothing in the American constitution to forbid it, a pauper is free to buy a Cadillac or to become President of the United States: rights which guarantee liberty are formal rights and permissions. Others, including many liberals, retort that we cannot pursue our own good in our own way without resources: opportunities are for those with the education, money or whatever else is needed to grasp them. This dispute has fierce ramifications, for example over the role of a welfare state in a free society.

Within the 'positive liberty' camp, the crux is whether service to a General Will or common good is consistent with individuality. A 'thick' view holds that total subordination, willingly made, brings self-realisation. But this tends to be so alarmingly careless about the human ants who comprise the collective ant-hill that it is rare in its pure form. More commonly, debate turns on attempts to connect public and private commitments without letting either absorb the other. Individuality is to be protected by deeming us social but not fully social. Whether this delicate balance can be struck is a crux of current debate between liberal communitarians and communally minded liberals.

That sets a fine line between a 'thick negative' contention that a free society must distribute resources so as to make opportunities real and a 'thin positive' contention that freedom entails virtuous acceptance of limited obligations to the common good. Resources are always scarce and one use excludes another. If a just society implies a socially just pattern in their distribution (as libertarians deny but liberals usually assert), then claims to moral neutrality are precarious. For example, the pattern of resources devoted to education can hardly fail to entrench a specific conception of the skills, needs and values suited to a flourishing life in that particular society. Conversely, if civic obligations are not to undermine the basis of individuality, persons must be kept distinct from citizens and their autonomy respected, thus giving substance to Mill's fervent apothegm: 'Over himself, over his own body and mind, the individual is sovereign' (below p. 294).

There is thus a clear contrast between a 'thin negative' view that freedom is the absence of external, especially legal, impediments to pursuing one's private ends and a 'thick positive view' that it is obedience to the demands of the common good. But the relation of 'thick negative' to 'thin positive' is so problematic that one wonders whether a line between them can finally be drawn.

Berlin, I., 'Two Concepts of Liberty', in D. Miller, (ed.), *Liberty*, Oxford: Oxford University Press, 1981.

Constant, B. (1819),'The Liberty of the Ancients Compared with that of the Moderns', in *Political Writings*, trans. and ed. B. Fontana, Cambridge: Cambridge University Press, 1988, pp. 307–28.

Hobbes T. (1651), *Leviathan*, ed. J. Plamenatz, London: Fontana Books, 1962.

Hobbes T. (1651), *Leviathan*, ed. R. Tuck, Cambridge: Cambridge University Press, 1991.

Machiavelli, N., *The Discourses*, ed. B. Crick, London: Penguin Classics, 1983.

Machiavelli, N., *The Prince*, ed. Q. Skinner, Cambridge: Cambridge University Press, 1988.

Mill, J. S. (1859), *On Liberty*, in *Utilitarianism*, ed. M. Warnock, London: Fontana Books, 1962.

Miller, D. (ed.), *Liberty*, Oxford: Oxford University Press, 1991.

Milton, J. (1660), *The Readie and Easie Way to Establish a Free Commonwealth*, in volume VII of *The Complete Prose Works of John Milton*, New Haven and London: Yale University Press, 1980.

Skinner, Q. R. D., *Machiavelli*, Oxford: Oxford University Press, 1981.

Skinner, Q. R. D., 'The Paradoxes of Political Liberty', in Miller, *Liberty*.

Tuck, R., *Hobbes*, Oxford: Oxford University Press, 1989.

## Further reading

There are excellent introductions to Machiavelli's *The Discourses* by Bernard Crick (London, Penguin Classics, 1983) and *The Prince* by Quentin Skinner (Cambridge: Cambridge University Press, 1988). *Machiavelli* by Quentin Skinner in the *Past Masters* series (Oxford: Oxford University Press, 1981) is also excellent. *The Complete Prose Works of John Milton*, volume VII (New Haven and London: Yale York University Press, 1980) contains *The Readie and Easie Way* and useful editorial comments. *Hobbes* by Richard Tuck in the *Past Masters* series is a fine guide and John Plamenatz's introduction to the Fontana edition of *Leviathan* (London, 1962) is especially helpful. For the general topic of liberty, see *Liberty*, edited and well introduced by David Miller (Oxford: Oxford University Press, 1991), which includes especially Isaiah Berlin's 'Two Concepts of Liberty' and Quentin Skinner's 'The Paradoxes of Political Liberty'.

## Seminar questions

Why does Machiavelli hold that 'it is not the well-being of individuals that makes cities great, but the well-being of the community'? What follows for the idea of a free state?

Milton claims that 'of all governments a Commonwealth aims most to make the people flourishing, vertuous, noble and high spirited'. Comment on his choice of these qualities.

'The end of Obedience is protection.' In what ways is Hobbes a 'modern' theorist of liberty?

What connections are there between individual liberties and political obligations?

# NICCOLÒ MACHIAVELLI
## From *The Discourses*, Book II

**[CHAPTER 1, final paragraph]**

That everyone may the better know how much more virtue helped the Romans to acquire their empire than did fortune, we shall in the next chapter discuss the character of the peoples with whom they had to fight, and show how obstinate they were in defending their liberty.

**[CHAPTER 2]**

Nothing made it harder for the Romans to conquer the peoples of the central and outlying parts of Italy than the love which in those times many peoples had for liberty. So obstinately did they defend it that only by outstanding virtue could they ever have been subjugated. For numerous instances show to what dangers they exposed themselves in order to maintain or to recover it, and what vendettas they kept up against those who had taken it away. The study of history reveals, too, the harm that servitude has done to peoples and to cities. There is, indeed, in our own times only one country which can be said to have in it free cities, whereas in ancient times quite a number of genuinely free peoples were to be found in all countries. One sees how in the times of which we are speaking at present the peoples of Italy from the Apennines which now divide Tuscany from Lombardy, right down to its toe, were all of them free. The Tuscans, the Romans, the Samnites were, for instance, and so were many other peoples who dwelt in other parts of Italy. One never hears of there being any kings, apart from those who reigned in Rome, and Porsenna, the king of Tuscany, whose stock became extinct, though history does not tell us how. It is quite clear, however, that at the time when the Romans laid siege to Veii, Tuscany was free. Moreover, it enjoyed its freedom so much, and so hated the title of prince, that, when the people of Veii appointed a king in that city for the purpose of defence, and asked the Tuscans to help them against the Romans, the Tuscans after many consultations had been held, decided not to give help to the people of Veii so long as they lived under a king, since they held that they could not well defend a country whose people had already placed themselves in subjection to someone else.

It is easy to see how this affection of peoples for self-government[1] comes about, for experience shows that the cities have never increased either in dominion or wealth, unless they have been independent. It is truly remarkable to observe the greatness which Athens attained in the space of a hundred years after it had been liberated from the tyranny of Pisistratus. But most marvellous of all is it to observe the greatness which Rome attained after freeing itself from its kings. The reason is easy to understand; for it is not the well-being of individuals that makes cities great, but the well-being of the

[1]*del vivere libero*

community; and it is beyond question that it is only in republics that the common good is looked to properly in that all that promotes it is carried out; and, however much this or that private person may be the loser on this account, there are so many who benefit thereby that the common good can be realized in spite of those few who suffer in consequence.

The opposite happens where there is a prince; for what he does in his own interests usually harms the city, and what is done in the interests of the city harms him. Consequently, as soon as tyranny replaces self-government[2] the least of the evils which this tyranny brings about are that it ceases to make progress and to grow in power and wealth: more often than not, nay always, what happens is that it declines. And should fate decree the rise of an efficient[3] tyrant, so energetic and so proficient in warfare[4] that he enlarges his dominions, no advantage will accrue to the commonwealth, but only to himself, for he cannot bestow honours on the valiant and good citizens over whom he tyrannizes, since he does not want to have any cause to suspect them. Nor yet can he allow the cities he acquires to make their submission to, or to become the tributaries of, the city of which he is the tyrant, for to make it powerful is not to his interest. It is to his interest to keep the state divided so that each town and each district may recognize only him as its ruler. In this way he alone profits by his acquisitions, not his country. Should anyone desire to confirm this view by a host of further arguments, let him read Xenophon's treatise *On Tyrannicide*.

It is no wonder, then, that peoples of old detested tyrants and gave them no peace, or that they were so fond of liberty and held the word itself in such esteem, as happened when Hieronymus, the grandson of Hiero, the Syracusan, was killed in Syracuse, and the news of his death came to his army which was then not very far from Syracuse. At first there was a tumult, and men took up arms against those who had killed him, but when they perceived that in Syracuse the cry was for liberty, they were so delighted to hear the word, that all became quiet, and, setting aside their anger against the tyrannicides, they began to consider how self-government could be organized in that city.

Nor is it surprising that peoples are so extraordinarily revengeful towards those who have destroyed their liberty. Of this there are numerous examples, but I propose to give but one, which happened in Corcyra, a city of Greece, during the Peloponnesian war. Greece was then divided into two parties, of which one supported the Athenians, the other the Spartans. The result was that in many cities internal dissensions arose, some advocating an alliance with Sparta, others an alliance with Athens. This happened in Corcyra, where the nobles got the upper hand, and deprived the populace of its liberty.

[2]*uno vivere libero*
[3]*virtuoso*
[4]*per virtù d'arme*

But with the help of the Athenians the populace regained their strength, laid hands on all the nobles, and shut them up in one prison which held them all. Then they took them, eight or ten at a time, on the plea of banishing them to various parts, and then to set an example put them to death with much cruelty. When those who were left heard of this, they considered whether there was any possible way in which they could escape this ignominious death. So, having armed themselves with anything at hand, they defended the entrance to the prison, and fought with those who tried to get in. The result was that, when rumours of this reached the populace, they came in a crowd, removed the upper storey and roof from the building, and smothered the inmates beneath the ruins. Many well-known instances of a like horrible nature happened later in this country. We thus see how true it is that a liberty which you have actually had taken away is avenged with much greater ferocity than is a liberty which someone has only tried to take away.

If one asks oneself how it comes about that peoples of old were more fond of liberty than they are today, I think the answer is that it is due to the same cause that makes men today less bold than they used to be; and this is due, I think, to the difference between our education and that of bygone times, which is based on the difference between our religion and the religion of those days. For our religion, having taught us the truth and the true way of life, leads us to ascribe less esteem to worldly honour. Hence the gentiles, who held it in high esteem and looked upon it as their highest good, displayed in their actions more ferocity than we do. This is evidenced by many of their institutions. To begin with, compare the magnificence of their sacrifices with the humility that characterizes ours. The ceremonial in ours is delicate rather than imposing, and there is no display of ferocity or courage. Their ceremonies lacked neither pomp nor magnificence, but, conjoined with this, were sacrificial acts in which there was much shedding of blood and much ferocity; and in them great numbers of animals were killed. Such spectacles, because terrible, caused men to become like them. Besides, the old religion did not beatify men unless they were replete with worldly glory: army commanders, for instance, and rulers of republics. Our religion has glorified humble and contemplative men, rather than men of action. It has assigned as man's highest good humility, abnegation, and contempt for mundane things, whereas the other identified it with magnanimity, bodily strength, and everything else that conduces to make men very bold. And, if our religion demands that in you there be strength, what it asks for is strength to suffer rather than strength to do bold things.

This pattern of life, therefore, appears to have made the world weak, and to have handed it over as a prey to the wicked, who run it successfully and securely since they are well aware that the generality of men, with paradise for their goal, consider how best to bear, rather than how best to avenge, their injuries. But, though it looks as if the world were become effeminate and as if heaven were power-less, this undoubtedly is due rather to the pusillanimity of those who have interpreted our religion in terms of *laissez faire*, not in terms of *virtù*. For, had they borne in mind that religion permits us to exalt and defend the fatherland, they would have seen that it also wishes us to love and honour it, and to train ourselves to be such that we may defend it.

This kind of education, then, and these grave misinterpretations account for the fact that we see in the world fewer republics than there used to be of old, and that, consequently in peoples we do not find the same love of liberty as there then was. Yet I can well believe that it was rather the Roman empire, which, with its armed forces and its grandiose ideas, wiped out all republics and all their civic institutions, that was the cause of this. And though, later on, Rome's empire disintegrated, its cities have never been able to pull themselves together nor to set up again a constitutional regime, save in one or two parts of that empire.

Anyhow, however this may be, the Romans encountered in all parts of the world, however small, a combination of well-armed republics, extremely obstinate in the defence of their liberty; which shows that, if the virtue of the Roman people had not been of a rare and very high order, they would never have been able to overcome them. Of instances which bear this out, I shall cite but one case, that of the Samnites. It is a remarkable thing, as Livy admits, that they should have been so powerful and their arms so strong that they were able to withstand the Romans right up to the time of Papirius Cursor, the consul, son of the first Papirius; i.e. to withstand them for the space of forty-six years in spite of many disastrous defeats, the destruction of towns, and the slaughter of the inhabitants of their country, a slaughter so great that this country, in which there were formerly seen so many cities and so many inhabitants, was now almost deserted, whereas at one time, it was so well ordered and so strong that it would have been insuperable if it had not been confronted with a virtue such as Rome's.

It is easy, moreover, to see whence arose that order and how this disorder came about. For it is all due to the independence which then was and to the servitude which now is. Because, as has been said before, all towns and all countries that are in all respects free, profit by this enormously. For, wherever increasing populations are found, it is due to the freedom with which marriage is contracted and to its being more desired by men. And this comes about where every man is ready to have children, since he believes that he can rear them and feels sure that his patrimony will not be taken away, and since he knows that not only will they be born free, instead of into slavery, but that, if they have virtue, they will have a chance of becoming rulers. One observes, too, how riches multiply and abound there, alike those that come from agriculture and those that are produced by the trades. For everybody is eager to acquire such things and to obtain property, provided he be convinced that he will enjoy it when it has been acquired. It thus comes about that, in competition one with the other, men look both to their own advantage and to that of the public; so that in both respects wonderful progress is made. The contrary of this happens in countries which live in servitude; and the harder the servitude the more does the well-being to which they are accustomed dwindle.

Of all forms of servitude, too, that is the hardest which subjects you to a republic. First because it is more lasting, and there is no hope of escape; secondly because the aim of a republic is to deprive all other corporations of their vitality and to weaken them, to the end that its own body corporate may increase. A prince who makes you his subject, does not do this unless he be a barbarian who devastates the country and destroys all that man has done for civilization, as oriental princes do. On the contrary, if his institutions be humane and he behave constitutionally, he will more often than not be equally fond of all the cities that are subject to him, and will leave them in possession of all their trades and all their ancient institutions. So that, if they are unable to increase, as free cities do, they will not be ruined like those that are enslaved. I refer here to the servitude that befalls cities which are subject to a foreigner, for of those that are subject to one of their own citizens I have already spoken.

He who reflects, therefore, on all that has been said, will not wonder at the power the Samnites had when free, or at the weakness that befell them later, when they became a subject state. This Titus Livy attests in several places, particularly in his account of the war with Hannibal, where he shows how the Samnites, when they had been maltreated by a legion which lay at Nola, sent messengers to Hannibal to ask him to come to their aid. In their address they told him that for a hundred years they had been fighting the Romans with their own troops and their own officers, and that often they had held up two consular armies and two consuls, but that now they had come to such a pass that they could scarce hold their own against the small Roman legion that was at Nola.

# JOHN MILTON
## *The Readie and Easie Way to Establish a Free Commonwealth; and the Excellence Thereof Compared with the Inconveniences and Dangers of Readmitting Kingship in this Nation*

[...]

I doubt not but all ingenuous and knowing men will easily agree with me, that a free Commonwealth without single person or house of lords, is by far the best government, if it can be had; but we have all this while, say they, been expecting it, and cannot yet attain it.

'Tis true indeed that, when monarchy was dissolved, the form of a commonwealth should have forthwith been framed; and the practice thereof immediately begun; so that the people might have soon been satisfied and delighted with the decent order, ease and benefit thereof. We would have been then by this time firmly rooted past fear of commotions or mutations, and now flourishing. This care for timely settling a new government instead of the old, too much neglected, has been our mischief. Yet the cause thereof may be ascribed with most reason to the frequent disturbances, interruptions and dissolutions, which the Parliament has had, partly from the impatience of disaffected people, partly from some ambitious leaders in the army; much contrary, I believe, to the mind and approbation of the army itself and their other commanders, once undeceived or in their own power. Now is the opportunity, now the very season wherein we may obtain a free Commonwealth and establish it for ever in the land, without difficulty or much delay. Writs are sent out for elections, and, which is worth observing, in the name not of any king but of the keepers of our liberty, to summon a free Parliament: which then only will indeed be free, and deserve the true honour of that supreme title, if they preserve us a free people. Which never Parliament was more free to do; being now called not as heretofore by the summons of a king, but by the voice of liberty. And, if the people, laying aside prejudice and impatience, will seriously and calmly now consider their own good both religious and civil, their own liberty and the only means thereof, as shall be here laid before them, and will elect as their Knights and Burgesses able men, and according to the just and necessary qualifications (which, for aught I hear, remain yet in force unrepealed, as they were formerly decreed in Parliament), men not addicted to a single person or house of lords, the work is done; at least the foundation firmly laid of a free Commonwealth and good part also erected of the main structure. For the ground and basis of every just and free government (since men have smarted so often for committing all to one person) is a general council of the ablest men, chosen by the people to consult on public affairs from time to time for the common good. In this Grand Council must the sovereignty reside, not transferred but delegated only and, as it were, deposited: with this caution, that they must have the forces by sea and land committed to them for preservation of the common peace and liberty; must raise and manage the public revenue, at least with some inspectors deputed for satisfaction of the people in how it is employed; must make or propose, as more expressly shall be said anon, civil laws; treat of commerce, peace, or war with foreign nations; and, for the carrying on some particular affairs with more secrecy and expedition, must elect, as they have already out of their own number and others, a Council of State.

And, although it may seem strange at first hearing, by reason that men's minds are prepossessed with the notion of successive parliaments, I affirm that the Grand or General Council, being well chosen, should be perpetual: for so their business is or may be, and oft times urgent; the opportunity of affairs gained or lost in a moment. The day of council cannot be set as the day of a festival; but must be ready always to prevent or answer all occasions. By this continuance they will become every way skillfullest, best provided of intelligence from abroad, best acquainted with the people at home, and the people with them. The ship of the Commonwealth is always under sail. They sit at the stern and, if they steer well, what need is there to change them, it being rather dangerous? Add to this, that the Grand Council is both foundation and main pillar of the whole State; and to move pillars and foundations, not faulty, cannot be safe for the building. I see not, therefore, how we can be advantaged by successive and transitory Parliaments; which are much likelier continually to unsettle rather then to settle a free government; to breed commotions, changes, novelties and uncertainties; to bring neglect upon present affairs and opportunities, while all minds are in suspense with expectation of a new assembly, and the assembly for a good space taken up with the new settling of itself. After which, if they find no great work to do, they will make it, by altering or repealing former acts, or making and multiplying news; so that they may seem to see what their predecessors saw not, and not to have assembled for nothing: till all law be lost in the multitude of clashing statutes. [...]

Having thus far shown with what ease we may now obtain a free Commonwealth, and by it with as much ease all the freedom, peace, justice, plenty that we can desire, and, on the other side, the difficulties, troubles, uncertainties, nay rather impossibilities, to enjoy these things constantly under a monarch, I will now proceed to show more particularly wherein our freedom and flourishing condition will be more ample and secure to us under a free Commonwealth than under kingship.

The whole freedom of man consists either in spiritual or civil liberty. As for spiritual, who can be at rest, who can enjoy anything in this world with contentment, who has not liberty to serve God and to save his own soul, according to the best light which God has planted in him to that purpose, by the reading of His revealed will and the guidance of

His holy spirit? That this is best pleasing to God, and that the whole Protestant Church allows no supreme judge or rule in matters of religion but the scriptures, and these to be interpreted by the scriptures themselves, which necessarily infers liberty of conscience, I have heretofore proved at large in another treatise,[1] and might yet further by the public declarations, confessions and admonitions of whole churches and states, obvious in all history since the Reformation.

[…]

The other part of our freedom consists in the civil rights and advancements of every person according to his merit: the enjoyment of those never more certain, and the access to these never more open, than in a free Commonwealth. Both of which in my opinion may be best and soonest obtained, if every county in the land were made a kind of subordinate Commonalty or Commonwealth, and one chief town or more, according as the shire is in circuit, made cities, if they be not so called already; where the nobility and chief gentry from a proportionable compass of territory annexed to each city may build houses or palaces befitting their quality, may bear part in the government, make their own judicial laws, or use those existing, and execute them by their own elected judicatures and judges without appeal, in all things of civil government between man and man. So they shall have justice in their own hands, law executed fully and finally in their own counties and precincts, long wished and spoken of but never yet obtained. They shall have none then to blame but themselves, if it be not well administered; and fewer laws to expect or fear from the supreme authority. For those that shall be made, if of any great concernment to public liberty, they may without much trouble in these commonalties, or in more general assemblies called to their cities from the whole territory on such occasion, declare their assent or dissent by deputies sent, within a time limited, to the Grand Council. Yet their judgment so declared shall submit to the greater number of other counties or commonalties, and not avail them to any exemption of themselves or refusal of agreement with the rest, as it may in any of the United Provinces, where each is sovereign within itself often to the great disadvantage of that union. In these employments they may much better than they do not exercise and fit themselves, till their lot fall to be chosen into the Grand Council, according as their worth and merit shall be taken notice of by the people. As for controversies that shall happen between men of several counties, they may repair, as they do now, to the capital city or any other more commodious, neutral place and even-handed judges. And this I find to have been practised in the old Athenian Commonwealth, reputed the first and ancientest place of civility in all Greece: that they had in their several cities a peculiar, in Athens a common, government; and the right, as it befell them, to the administration of both.

[1] *Of Civil Power* (1659 edn)

They should have here also schools and academies at their own choice, wherein their children may be bred up in their own sight to all learning and noble education, not in grammar only but in all liberal arts and exercises. This would soon spread much more knowledge and civility, yea religion, through all parts of the land, by communicating the natural heat of government and culture more distributively to all extreme parts, which now lie numb and neglected; would soon make the whole nation more industrious, more ingenious at home, more potent, more honourable abroad. To this a free Commonwealth will easily assent (nay the Parliament has had already some such thing in design).

For, of all governments, a Commonwealth aims most to make the people flourishing, virtuous, noble and high spirited. Monarchs will never permit: whose aim is to make the people wealthy indeed perhaps and well fleeced, for their own shearing and the supply of regal prodigality; but otherwise softest, basest, vitiousest, servilest, easiest to be kept under; and not only in fleece, but in mind also sheepishest; and will have all the benches of judicature annexed to the throne, as a gift of royal grace that we have justice done us. Hence nothing can be more essential to the freedom of a people than to have the administration of justice and all public ornaments in their own election and within their own bounds, without long travelling or depending on remote places to obtain their right or any civil accomplishment; provided that it be not supreme, but subordinate to the general power and union of the whole Republic. In which happy firmness, as in the particular above mentioned, we shall also far exceed the United Provinces, by having, not as they (often to the retarding and distracting of their counsels on urgentest occasions) many Sovereignties united in one Commonwealth, but many Commonwealths under one united and entrusted Sovereignty. And, when we have our forces by sea and land, either of a faithful army or a settled militia, in our own hands to the firm establishing of a free Commonwealth, public accounts under our own inspection, general laws and taxes with their causes in our own domestic suffrages, judicial laws, offices and ornaments at home in our own ordering and administration, all distinction of lords and commoners, that may in any way divide or sever the public interest, removed, then what can a perpetual senate have wherein to grow corrupt, wherein to encroach upon us to usurp; or, if they do, wherein to be formidable? Yet, if all this avail not to remove the fear or envy of a perpetual sitting, it may be easily provided to change a third part of them yearly or every two or three years, as was above mentioned; or that it be at those times in the people's choice whether they will change them or renew their power, as they shall find cause.

I have no more to say at present: a few words will save us, well considered; a few and easy things, now seasonably done. But, if the people be so affected as to prostitute religion and liberty to the vain and groundless apprehension that nothing but kingship can restore trade, not remembering the frequent plagues and pestilences that then wasted this city, such as through God's mercy we never have felt since, and forgetting that trade flourishes nowhere more than in the free Commonwealths of Italy, Germany, and the Low-Countries before their eyes at this day; and if trade be grown so craving and importunate through the profuse living of tradesmen that nothing can support it but the luxurious expenses of a nation upon trifles or superfluities, so that, if the people generally should betake themselves to frugality, it might prove a dangerous matter, lest tradesmen should mutiny for want of trading, and so that we must therefore forgo and set to sale religion, liberty, honour, safety and all concernments Divine or human, to keep up trading; and if, lastly, after all this light among us, the same reason shall pass for current to put our necks again under kingship as was made use of by the Jews to return back to Egypt and to the worship of their idol queen, because they falsely imagined that they then lived in more plenty and prosperity; then our condition is not sound but rotten, both in religion and all civil prudence; and will bring us soon, the way we are marching, to those calamities which attend, always and unavoidably on luxury, all national judgments under foreign or domestic slavery: and we shall be so far from mending our condition by monarchizing our government, whatever new conceit now possesses us. However with all hazard I have ventured what I though my duty to speak in season, and to forewarn my country in time: wherein I doubt not but there be many wise men in all places and degrees, but am sorry the effects of wisdom are so little seen among us.

# THOMAS HOBBES
## From *Leviathan*

### CHAP. XXI   OF THE LIBERTY OF SUBJECTS

Liberty, or Freedome, signifieth (properly) the absence of Opposition; (by Opposition, I mean externall Impediments of motion;) and may be applyed no lesse to Irrationall, and Inanimate creatures, than to Rationall. For whatsoever is so tyed, so environed, as it cannot move, but within a certain space, which space is determined by the opposition of some externall body, we say it hath not Liberty to go further. And so of all living creatures, whilest they are imprisoned, or restrained, with walls, or chayns; and of the water whilest it is kept in by banks, or vessels, that otherwise would spread it selfe into a larger space, we use to say, they are not at Liberty, to move in such manner, as without those externall impediments they would. But when the impediment of motion, is the constitution of the thing it selfe, we use not to say, it wants the Liberty; but the Power to move; as when a stone lyeth still, or a man is fastned to his bed by sicknesse.

And according to this proper, and generally received meaning of the word, *A FREE-MAN, is he, that in those things, which by his strength and wit he is able to do, is not hindred to doe what he has a will to*. But when the words *Free*, and *Liberty*, are applyed to any thing but *Bodies*, they are abused; for that which is not subject to Motion, is not subject to Impediment: And therefore, when 'tis said (for example) The way is Free, no Liberty of the way is signified, but of those that walk in it without stop. And when we say a Guift is Free, there is not meant any Liberty of the Guift, but of the Giver, that was not bound by any law, or Covenant to give it. So when we *speak Freely*, it is not the Liberty of voice, or pronunciation, but of the man, whom no law hath obliged to speak otherwise than he did. Lastly, from the use of the word *Free-will*, no Liberty can be inferred of the will, desire, or inclination, but the Liberty of the man; which consisteth in this, that he finds no stop, in doing what he has the will, desire, or inclination to doe.

Feare, and Liberty are consistent; as when a man throweth his goods into the Sea for *feare* the ship should sink, he doth it neverthelesse very willingly, and may refuse to doe it if he will: It is therefore the action, of one that was *free*: so a man sometimes pays his debt, only for *feare* of Imprisonment, which because no body hindred him from detaining, was the action of a man at *liberty*. And generally all actions which men doe in Common-wealths, for *feare* of the law, are actions, which the doers had *liberty* to omit.

*Liberty*, and *Necessity* are consistent, as in the water, that hath not only *liberty*, but a *necessity* of descending by the Channel; so likewise in the Actions which men voluntarily doe: which, because they proceed from their will, proceed from *liberty*; and yet, because every act of mans will, and every desire, and inclination proceedeth from some cause, and that from another cause, in a continuall chaine, (whose first link is in the hand of God the first of all causes,) they proceed from *necessity*. So that to him that could see the connexion of those causes, the *necessity* of all mens voluntary actions, would appeare manifest. And therefore God, that seeth, and disposeth all things, seeth also that the *liberty* of man in doing what he will, is accompanied with the *necessity* of doing that which God will, & no more, nor lesse. For though men may do many things, which God does not command, nor is therefore Author of them; yet they can have no passion, nor appetite to any thing, of which appetite Gods will is not the cause. And did not his will assure the *necessity* of mans will, and consequently of all that on mans will dependeth, the *liberty* of men would be a contradiction, and an impediment to the omnipotence and *liberty* of God. And this shall suffice, (as to the matter in hand) of that naturall *liberty,* which only is properly called *liberty*.

But as men, for the atteyning of peace, and conservation of themselves thereby, have made an Artificiall Man, which we call a Common-wealth; so also have they made Artificiall Chains, called *Civill Lawes*, which they themselves, by mutuall covenants, have fastned at one end, to the lips of that Man, or Assembly, to whom they have given the Soveraigne Power; and at the other end to their own Ears. These Bonds in their own nature but weak, may neverthelesse be made to hold, by the danger, though not by the difficulty of breaking them.

In relation to these Bonds only it is, that I am to speak now, of the *Liberty of Subjects*. For seeing there is no Common-wealth in the world, wherein there be Rules enough set down, for the regulating of all the actions, and words of men, (as being a thing impossible:) it followeth necessarily, that in all kinds of actions, by the laws praetermitted, men have the Liberty, of doing what their own reasons shall suggest, for the most profitable to themselves. For if wee take Liberty in the proper sense, for corporall Liberty; that is to say, freedome from chains, and prison, it were very absurd for men to clamor as they doe, for the Liberty they so manifestly enjoy. Againe, if we take Liberty, for an exemption from Lawes, it is no lesse absurd, for men to demand as they doe, that Liberty, by which all other men may be masters of their lives. And yet as absurd as it is, this is it they demand; not knowing that the Lawes are of no power to protect them, without a Sword in the hands of a man, or men, to cause those laws to be put in execution. The Liberty of a Subject, lyeth therefore only in those things, which in regulating their actions, the Soveraign hath praetermitted: such as is the Liberty to buy, and sell, and other-wise contract with one another; to choose their own aboad, their own diet, their own trade of life, and institute their children as they them-selves think fit: & the like.

Neverthelesse we are not to understand, that by such Liberty, the Soveraign Power of life, and death, is either abolished, or limited. For it has been already shewn, that nothing the Soveraign Representative can doe to a Subject, on what pretence soever, can properly be called Injustice, or Injury; because every Subject is Author of every act the Soveraign doth; so that he never wanteth Right to any thing, other-wise, than as he himself is the Subject of God, and bound thereby to observe the laws of Nature. And therefore it may, and doth often happen in Common-wealths, that a Subject may be put to death, by the command of the Soveraign Power; and yet neither doe the other wrong: As when *Jeptha* caused his daughter to be sacrificed: In which, and the like cases, he that so dieth, had Liberty to doe the action, for which he is neverthelesse, without Injury put to death. And the same holdeth also in a Soveraign Prince, that putteth to death an Innocent Subject. For though the action be against the law of Nature, as being contrary to Equitie, (as was the killing of *Uriah*, by *David*;) yet it was not an Injurie to *Uriah*; but to *God*. Not to *Uriah*, because the right to doe what he pleased, was given him by *Uriah* himself: And yet to *God*, because *David* was Gods Subject; and prohibited all Iniquitie by the law of Nature. Which distinction, *David* himself, when he repented the fact, evidently confirmed, saying, *To thee only have I sinned*. In the same manner, the people of *Athens*, when they banished the most potent of their Common-wealth for ten years, thought they committed no Injustice; and yet they never questioned what crime he had done; but what hurt he would doe: Nay they commanded the banishment of they knew not whom; and every Citizen bringing his Oystershell into the market place, written with the name of him he desired should be banished, without actuall accusing him, sometimes banished an *Aristides*, for his reputation of Justice; And sometimes a scurrilous Jester, as *Hyperbolus*, to make a Jest of it. And yet a man cannot say, the Soveraign People of *Athens* wanted right to banish them; or an *Athenian* the Libertie to Jest, or to be Just.

The Libertie, whereof there is so frequent, and honourable mention, in the Histories, and Philosophy of the Antient Greeks, and Romans, and in the writings, and discourse of those that from them have received all their learning in the Politiques, is not the Libertie of Particular men; but the Libertie of the Common-wealth: which is the same with that, which every man then should have, if there were no Civil Laws, nor Common-wealth at all. And the effects of it also be the same. For as amongst masterlesse men, there is perpetuall war, of every man against his neighbour; no inheritance, to transmit to the Son, nor to expect from the Father; no propriety of Goods, or Lands; no security; but a full and absolute Libertie in every Particular man: So in States, and Common-wealths not dependent on one another, every Common-wealth, (not every man) has an absolute Libertie, to doe what it shall judge (that is to say, what that Man, or Assemblie that representeth it, shall judge) most conducing to their benefit. But withall, they live in the condition of a perpetuall war, and upon the confines of battel, with their frontiers armed, and canons planted against their neighbours round about. The *Athenians*, and *Romanes* were free; that is, free Common-wealths: not that any particular man had the Libertie to resist their own Representative; but that their Representative had the Libertie to resist, or invade other people. There is written on the Turrets of the city of *Luca* in great characters at this day, the word *LIBERTAS*; yet no man can thence inferre, that a particular man has more Libertie, or Immunitie from the service of the Commonwealth there, than in *Constantinople*. Whether a Common-wealth be Monarchicall, or Popular, the Freedome is still the same.

But it is an easy thing, for men to be deceived, by the specious name of Libertie; and for want of Judgement to distinguish, mistake that for their Private Inheritance, and Birth right, which is the right of the Publique only. And when the same errour is confirmed by the authority of men in reputation for their writings in this subject, it is no wonder if it produce sedition, and change of Government. In these westerne parts of the world, we are made to receive our opinions concerning the Institution, and Rights of Common-wealths, from *Aristotle*, *Cicero*, and other men, Greeks and Romanes, that living under Popular States, derived those Rights, not from the Principles of Nature, but transcribed them into their books, out of the Practise of their own Common-wealths, which were Popular; as the

Grammarians describe the Rules of Language, out of the Practise of the time; or the Rules of Poetry, out of the Poems of *Homer* and *Virgil*. And because the Athenians were taught, (to keep them from desire of changing their Government,) that they were Free-men, and all that lived under Monarchy were slaves; therefore *Aristotle* puts it down in his *Politiques*, (lib.6.cap.2.) *In democracy*, Liberty *is to be supposed: for 'tis commonly held, that no man is* Free *in any other Government.* And as *Aristotle*; so *Cicero*, and other Writers have grounded their Civill doctrine, on the opinions of the Romans, who were taught to hate Monarchy, at first, by them that having deposed their Soveraign, shared amongst them the Soveraignty of *Rome*; and afterwards by their Successors. And by reading of these Greek, and Latine Authors, men from their childhood have gotten a habit (under a falseshew of Liberty,) of favouring tumults, and of licentious controlling the actions of their Soveraigns; and again of controlling those controllers, with the effusion of so much blood; as I think I may truly say, there was never any thing so deerly bought, as these Western parts have bought the learning of the Greek and Latine tongues.

To come now to the particulars of the true Liberty of a Subject; that is to say, what are the things, which though commanded by the Soveraign, he may neverthelesse, without Injustice, refuse to do; we are to consider, what Rights we passe away, when we make a Common-wealth; or (which is all one,) what Liberty we deny our selves, by owning all the Actions (without exception) of the Man, or Assembly we make our Soveraign. For in the act of our *Submission*, consisteth both our *Obligation*, and our *Liberty*; which must therefore be inferred by arguments taken from thence; there being no Obligation on any man, which ariseh not from some Act of his own; for all men equally, are by Nature Free. And because such arguments, must either be drawn from the expresse words, *I Authorise all his Actions*, or from the Intention of him that submitteth himselfe to his Power, (which Intention is to be understood by the End for which he so submitteth;) The Obligation, and Liberty of the Subject, is to be derived, either from those Words, (or others equivalent;) or else from the End of the Institution of Soveraignty; namely, the Peace of the Subjects within themselves, and their Defence against a common Enemy.

First therefore, seeing Soveraignty by Institution, is by Covenant of every one to every one; and Soveraignty by Acquisition, by Covenants of the Vanquished to the Victor, or Child to the Parent; It is manifest, that every Subject has Liberty in all those things, the right whereof cannot by Covenant by transferred. I have shewn before in the 14. Chapter, that Covenants, not to defend a mans own body, are voyd. Therefore,

If the Soveraign command a man (though justly condemned,) to kill, wound, or mayme himselfe; or not to resist those that assault him; or to abstain from the use of food, ayre, medicine, or any other thing, without which he cannot live; yet hath that man the Liberty to disobey.

If a man be interrogated by the Soveraign, or his Authority, concerning a crime done by himselfe, he is not bound (without assurance of Pardon) to confesse it; because no man (as I have shewn in the same Chapter) can be obliged by Covenant to accuse himselfe.

Again, the Consent of a Subject to Soveraign Power, is contained in these words, *I Authorise, or take upon me, all his actions*; in which there is no restriction at all, of his own former naturall Liberty: For by allowing him to *kill me*, I am not bound to kill my selfe when he commands me. 'Tis one thing to say, *Kill me, or my fellow, if you please*; another thing to say, *I will kill my selfe, or my fellow*. It followeth therefore, that

No man is bound by the words themselves, either to kill himselfe, or any other man; And consequently, that the Obligation a man may sometimes have, upon the Command of the Soveraign to execute any dangerous, or dishonourable office, dependeth not on the Words of our Submission; but on the Intention; which is to be understood by the End thereof. When therefore our refusall to obey, frustrates the End for which the Soveraignty was ordained; then there is no Liberty to refuse: otherwise there is.

Upon this ground, a man that is commanded as a Souldier to fight against the enemy, though his Soveraign have Right enough to punish his refusall with death, may neverthelesse in many cases refuse, without Injustice; as when he substituteth a sufficient Souldier in his place: for in this case he deserteth not the service of the Commonwealth. And there is allowance to be made for naturall timorousnesse, not onely to women, (of whom no such dangerous duty is expected,) but also to men of feminine courage. When Armies fight, there is on one side, or both, a running away; yet when they do it not out of trechery, but fear, they are not esteemed to do it unjustly, but dishonourably. For the same reason, to avoyd battell, is not Injustice, but Cowardice. But he that inrowleth himselfe a Souldier, or taketh imprest mony, taketh away the excuse of a timorous nature; and is obliged, not onely to go to the battell, but also not to run from it, without his Captaines leave. And when the Defence of the Commonwealth, requireth at once the help of all that are able to bear Arms, every one is obliged; because otherwise the Institution of the Common-wealth, which they have not the purpose, or courage to preserve, was in vain.

To resist the Sword of the Common-wealth, in defence of another man, guilty, or innocent, no man hath Liberty; because such Liberty, takes away from the Soveraign, the means of Protecting us; and is therefore destructive of the very essence of Government. But in case a great many men together, have already resisted the Soveraign Power unjustly, or committed some Capitall crime, for which every one of them expecteth death, whether have they not the Liberty then to joyn together, and assist, and defend one another? Certainly they have: For they but defend their lives, which the Guilty man may as well do, as the Innocent. There was indeed injustice in the first breach of

their duty; Their bearing of Arms subsequent to it, though it be to
maintain what they have done, is no new unjust act. And if it be onely
to defend their persons, it is not unjust at all. But the offer of pardon
taketh from them, to whom it is offered, the plea of self-defence, and
maketh their perseverance in assisting, or defending the rest, unlaw-
full.

As for other Lyberties, they depend on the Silence of the Law. In cases
where the Soveraign has prescribed no rule, there the Subject hath
the Liberty to do, or forbeare, according to his own discretion. And
therefore such Liberty is in some places more, and in some lesse; and
in some times more, in other times lesse, according as they that have
the Soveraignty shall think most convenient. As for Example, there
was a time, when in *England* a man might enter in to his own Land,
(and dispossesse such as wrongfully possessed it,) by force. But in
after-times, that Liberty of Forcible Entry, was taken away by a
Statute made (by the King) in Parliament. And in some places of the
world, men have the Liberty of many wives: in other places, such
Liberty is not allowed.

If a Subject have a controversie with his Soveraigne, of debt, or of right
of possession of lands or goods, or concerning any service required
at his hands, or concerning any penalty, corporall, or pecuniary,
grounded on a precedent Law; he hath the same Liberty to sue for
his right, as if it were against a Subject; and before such Judges, as
are appointed by the Soveraign. For seeing the Soveraign demandeth
by force of a former Law, and not by vertue of his Power; he declar-
eth thereby, that he requireth no more, than shall appear to be due by
that Law. The sute therefore is not contrary to the will of the
Soveraign; and consequently the Subject hath the Liberty to demand
the hearing of his Cause; and sentence, according to that Law. But if
he demand, or take any thing by pretence of his Power; there lyeth,
in that case, no action of Law: for all that is done by him in Vertue of
his Power, is done by the Authority of every Subject, and consequently, he that brings an action against the Soveraign, brings it
against himselfe.

If a Monarch, or Soveraign Assembly, grant a Liberty to all, or any of
his Subjects, which Grant standing, he is disabled to provide for their
safety, the Grant is voyd; unlesse he directly renounce, or transferre
the Soveraignty to another. For in that he might openly, (if it had been
his will,) and in plain terms, have renounced, or transferred it, and
did not; it is to be understood it was not his will; but that the Grant
proceeded from ignorance of the repugnancy between such a Liberty
and the Soveraign Power: and therefore the Soveraignty is still
retayned; and consequently all those Powers, which are necessary to
the exercising thereof; such as are the Power of Warre, and Peace, of
Judicature, of appointing Officers, and Councellours, of levying
Mony, and the rest named in the 18th Chapter.

The Obligation of Subjects to the Soveraign, is understood to last as
long, and no longer, than the power lasteth, by which he is able to

protect them. For the right men have by Nature to protect themselves, when none else can protect them, can by no Covenant be relinquished. The Soveraignty is the Soule of the Common-wealth; which once departed from the Body, the members doe no more receive their motion from it. The end of Obedience is Protection; which, wheresoever a man seeth it, either in his own, or in anothers sword, Nature applyeth his obedience to it, and his endeavour to maintaine it. And though Soveraignty, in the intention of them that make it, be immortall; yet is it in its own nature, not only subject to violent death, by forreign war; but also through the ignorance, and passions of men, it hath in it, from the very institution, many seeds of a naturall mortality, by Intestine Discord.

If a Subject be taken prisoner in war; or his person, or his means of life be within the Guards of the enemy, and hath his life and corporall Libertie given him, on condition to be Subject of the Victor, he hath Libertie to accept the condition; and having accepted it, is the subject of him that took him; because he had no other way to preserve himself. The case is the same, if he be deteined on the same termes, in a forreign country. But if a man be held in prison, or bonds, or is not trusted with the libertie of his bodie; he cannot be understood to be bound by Covenant to subjection; and therefore may, if he can, make his escape by any means whatsoever.

If a Monarch shall relinquish the Soveraignty, both for himself, and his heires; His Subjects returne to the absolute Libertie of Nature; because, though Nature may declare who are his Sons, and who are the nerest of his Kin; yet it dependeth on his own will, (as hath been said in the precedent chapter,) who shall be his Heyr. If therefore he will have no Heyre, there is no Soveraignty, nor Subjection. The case is the same, if he dye without known Kindred, and without declaration of his Heyre. For then there can no Heire be known, and consequently no Subjection be due.

If the Soveraign Banish his Subject; during the Banishment, he is not Subject. But he that is sent on a message, or hath leave to travell, is still Subject; but it is, by Contract between Soveraigns, not by vertue of the covenant of Subjection. For whosoever entreth into anothers dominion, is Subject to all the Laws thereof; unlesse he have a privelege by the amity of the Soveraigns, or by speciall licence.

If a Monarch subdued by war, render himself Subject to the Victor; his Subjects are delivered from their former obligation, and become obliged to the Victor. But if he be held prisoner, or have not the liberty of his own Body; he is not understood to have given away the Right of Soveraigntie; and therefore his Subjects are obliged to yield obedience to the Magistrates formerly placed, governing not in their own name, but in his. For, his Right remaining, the question is only of the Administration; that is to say, of the Magistrates and Officers; which, if he have not means to name, he is supposed to approve those, which he himself had formerly appointed.

JOHN ZVESPER

# Locke and Aristotle
# on property

**4**

Property has always been a critical issue in political philosophy. Every political philosopher has something to say about it. However, the theme of property has become particularly central in modern political thought; at times the whole science of politics has seemed to be subordinate to, or even identical with, the science of economics. As Rousseau complained in his *First Discourse* (1750), while 'ancient politicians incessantly talked about morals and virtue, those of our time talk only of business and money'. Arguably, the most important step in this change from the ancient to the modern world was John Locke's novel account of the relationship between political life and property in his *Two Treatises of Government* (1689). In the importance that Locke attaches to property as the motive for establishing and maintaining political society, Locke 'departs from all his predecessors, classical and medieval' (Laslett, 1963, p. 114). With his focus on questions of property, his insistence that legitimate government must be based on consent, and his elaboration of clearly limited ends for government, Locke set modern liberalism in motion.

## John Locke (1632–1704)

Locke was the son of a country attorney. As a student in Oxford, he was attracted by the new natural science of his day, and (as he later recalled) repelled by scholastic disputes. He refused the opportunity to be ordained in the Church of England (a usual next step in the scholarly career that he was following), and became instead a medical academic, although one who also cautiously studied politics, in particular the relationship between church and state. (In Restoration England, writing about politics or religion could be a dangerous activity, leading to exile or even on occasion to capital punishment.) In 1666 he became a friend, and a medical and political consultant, of Anthony Ashley Cooper, later the first earl of Shaftesbury. Locke's close relationship with Shaftesbury, who was a leading Whig opponent of the restored Stuart monarchy, helped to end his academic career; he was watched closely by his fellow Oxford dons, and although their attempts to entrap him failed and they were unable to produce for the government any incriminating evidence against the taciturn Locke, he left Oxford, never to return, in 1683. A royal order to his college to dismiss him from his job soon followed. From 1683 until after the Revolution of 1688–89, Locke lived in Holland. The Revolution replaced the Stuart regime with a constitutionally more limited monarchy and a more tolerant policy. Upon his return to England in 1689, Locke was transformed from a political exile into a man with friends in high places. He gave advice on political and commercial matters, and much of his advice became government policy. His intellectual reputation was also established at this time with the publication of *An Essay Concerning Human Understanding* (1690).

His more political work, *Two Treatises of Government*, was published anonymously, for Locke was always cautious, only acknowledging authorship in a codicil appended to his will the same year that he died. The work was understood and welcomed as a philosophical justification for the Revolution of 1688, although in fact Locke must have written most of it during the years before 1688. It presents itself as a polemic against the work of Sir Robert Filmer. Filmer, basing his arguments on the assertion that political authority descended directly from Adam, was an apologist for the divine right of kings (and therefore a vigorous opponent of the more secular political thinking of Thomas Hobbes (see chapter 3). The *First Treatise* demolishes and ridicules Filmer's arguments, and the *Second* presents Locke's own principles: it is subtitled 'An Essay Concerning the True Original, Extent, and End of Civil Government' (and was probably largely completed before the *First*, and before Filmer's work attracted so much attention). Locke evidently felt it would be desirable for the principles of limited government based on consent to be more widely accepted as the right way of thinking about the Revolution; he was troubled by the tendency for the Revolution settlement to be accepted merely on pragmatic grounds (Ashcraft, 1986, pp. 590–601).

Against the defence of absolute monarchy mounted by Filmer (but also departing from Filmer's opponent, Hobbes), Locke set the framework for liberal political arguments ever since, maintaining that legitimate government has certain specified and limited purposes, and that constitutional limitations are needed in order to keep government limited to these proper ends. In particular, he defends a greater and more definite separation of public and private spheres, and a constitutional arrangement that will safeguard that more clearly defined separation. Most immediately, Locke is concerned to establish that government has secular rather than religious purposes. (His political principles were thus as opposed to the Whig partisans as to the Tory partisans of seventeenth-century Britain.) He urges that both religion and politics will be healthier if they are disentangled from each other. This is the theme of his first published work, *A Letter Concerning Toleration*. (This too was published anonymously in 1689, first in Holland, in Latin, then in translations – though not by Locke – into Dutch, French and English.) Here he insists that 'political society is entered upon only to preserve to each individual the possession of the things of this life, and for no other end. The care of his soul, and of the things of heaven, (which neither belongs to the state [*civitatem*] nor can be subjected to it) is kept back and retained by each individual.' This distinct separation of state and church is the primary meaning of 'liberty' in Locke's thinking. The purpose of political society is not the salvation of souls, but the 'comfortable preservation' of bodies (*First Treatise*, chapter 9). The first chapter of the *Second Treatise* thus offers a definition of political power as '*a Right* of making Laws … for the Regulating and Preserving of Property, and of employing the force of the Community, in the Execution of such Laws, and in the defence of the Common-wealth from Foreign Injury …' Especially in the last third of the *Second Treatise*, Locke makes it clear that by 'property' he means life and liberty as well as material possessions; however, he starts with the narrower definition of the word, and property understood as 'estate' remains central to his political thought.

One of the advantages of not acknowledging authorship of the *Two Treatises* was that Locke could enthusiastically recommend his book; in a letter to a relative in 1703, Locke declared, 'Property I have nowhere found more clearly explained, than in a book entitled, Two Treatises of Government' (quoted in Laslett, 1963, p. 15). It is not just hindsight, then, that makes us think of Locke's political writing as particularly concerned to establish an understanding of the politics of property, as well as to promote religious toleration. The two concerns naturally go together: if one wishes to take religion out of politics, then perhaps it will help if citizens can be encouraged to focus more energetically on more mundane affairs. The connection of the two themes is apparent in the *Letter Concerning Toleration*, which briefly summarises Locke's thinking about property and civil society, alongside his thoughts about religious toleration. 'The commonwealth [*res publica*],' he here declares, 'seems to me to be constituted only for preserving and advancing civil goods,' i.e. 'life, liberty, and bodily integrity and freedom from pain; and the possession of outward things, such as estate, money, furniture, etc.'

The view that religious toleration went hand in hand with commercial freedom and prosperity had found ample support in English and Dutch experience in the sixteenth and seventeenth centuries. However, Locke wished to establish the link between the two at the level of universal principle. As events in Locke's own lifetime showed, without a basis in universal principles, these policies are always subject to disruption by appeals to the universal principles of revealed religion. Locke's attempt was remarkably successful. The political principles of the *Second Treatise* became the elements of a liberal philosophical 'creed' (as David Hume caustically called it: Hume, 1969, p. 593) in the eighteenth century, and they had a great influence on liberal revolutionary acts in America as well as in Europe; for example, the American Declaration of Independence of 1776 repeats some of Locke's argument. Locke's reasoning continues to engage political thinkers in the twentieth century, even though the natural basis of his thought has been widely questioned in nineteenth- and twentieth-century philosophy (ironically, often on the grounds of the sceptical epistemology that Locke himself proposed in his *Essay Concerning Human Understanding*).

Locke's most elaborate statement on property is chapter 5 of the *Second Treatise* (this chapter is reprinted in full on pp. 104–14). Here Locke uses the word 'property' only in the narrower sense, meaning legitimate material possessions. Like Hobbes, Locke bases his reasoning about the purposes of political life on the undeniable and irreproachable fact that humans will seek to preserve themselves, 'God and Nature never allowing a Man so to abandon himself, as to neglect his own preservation' (chapter 14); individuals agree to become members of a political community 'for their comfortable, safe, and peaceable living one amongst another, in a secure Enjoyment of their Properties, and a greater Security against any that are not of it' (chapter 8). But in contrast to Hobbes, Locke emphasises that the defects of the state of nature have at least as much to do with the material poverty and insecurity found there, as with the threat of violent death that is emphasised by Hobbes. The two problems cannot be separated: the threat of violent death cannot be effectively overcome unless competition for scarce necessities can be overcome, for that competition will compel even the good Hobbesian subject to return to fighting other subjects, to avoid death by starvation. One of the major themes of the chapter is the extent to which human effort is needed to transform natural materials into useful products. In the end, we learn that the invention of money is essential to make this transformation work as well as it can: this piece of human ingenuity helps make human effort worthwhile, and thereby makes property more abundant, while making government even more necessary in order to protect it. Economic and financial development, fostered by enlightened government, is the thing most needed in order to avoid the evils of the state of nature.

Near the end of his chapter on property, Locke reminds us that in civil society positive laws 'regulate the right of property' (section 50; notice the preparation for this statement that Locke had made in sections 30, 38, and 45, and recall the definition of political power, quoted above, p. 93). This chapter discusses property in the state of nature rather than property regulated by positive laws in civil society. Nevertheless, the argument of this chapter is crucial for understanding the purposes of the political regulation of property. Locke here tells us a story about how individuals in a state of nature can come to have property in things, why and with what effects they consent to the use of money, and why finally they consent to civil society.

Property means entitlement to exclusive use. Locke starts with the idea that the earth belongs to 'mankind in common' (sections 25–6), but immediately notes that this gift of God or Nature cannot be made 'use of ... to the best advantage of Life, and convenience' unless *individual* 'men' (not 'mankind') can rightly 'appropriate' parts of it (section 26). Reason – the law of nature – makes it clear that the right to self-preservation implies the right to the means of subsistence. But how can one individual justly exclude others from using particular items? Locke's argument (rather contradicting the suggestion he had made in chapter 2 that God owns everyone) is that individuals, even in the primitive natural state in which no individual owns anything, naturally own their own persons or bodies. They therefore own their own labour, and by extension also own things that they take from the natural commons through their labour, as long as 'there is enough, and as good left in common for others' (section 27), and as long as they do not take more than they can use before it spoils (section 31). Locke applies this reasoning to the ownership of land as well: cultivating the land mixes labour with it, and therefore creates ownership of it in the cultivator, as long as there remains 'enough, and as good left' for others, and as long as the cultivator can use the product of the land (sections 32–8).

Why should labour be thought to be so central in the creation of property? Why should mixing something that one owns (one's labour) with something that one does not own make the mixture all one's own? Locke's argument is that it is human labour (rather than natural plenty) that creates most of what is useful and valuable to humans. Cultivation of otherwise waste land increases 'the stock of Corn' (section 36); improving land is equivalent to creating land, because it makes it far more productive (section 37); in short, ''tis *Labour* indeed that *puts the difference of value* on everything' (section 40). Locke is so enthusiastic about this proposition that he soon revises his original estimate of the proportion of the value added by labour to that given by '*Nature*' from 90 per cent up to 99 per cent, and eventually raises it to 99.9 per cent (sections 40 and 43). It is important that labour be valued, because it is necessary in order to relieve the 'penury' of the natural human condition, with its 'needy and wretched inhabitants' (sections 32, 35 and 37). Nature furnishes us not with plenty but only 'the materials of Plenty', useless without improvement 'by labour' (section 40). 'Nature and the Earth furnished only the almost worthless Materials, as in themselves' (section 43). That is why properly speaking, the earth belongs to mankind, but primarily 'to the use of the Industrious and Rational' (section 34).

How can the poverty of the state of nature be overcome? Why do people have any incentive to labour beyond their immediate needs? In the original condition, no one has any motive to take more than they can use; taking more would be 'foolish' and 'useless' (sections 46 and 51). While that level of economic activity may be as conducive to peaceful human relations as Locke here suggests, it is unlikely to lead to great improvements in the general level of wealth because it is unlikely to lead to great improvements in the level of wealth of any individual. Even agriculture will be very limited because of the perishable nature of agricultural products. No one has a rational incentive to be very industrious, unless for some reason they take a fancy to hoarding such durable things as 'a piece of Metal, pleased with its colour; ... Shells, or ... a sparkling Pebble or a Diamond' (section 46). But a solid reason for desiring such durable items appears only when, by tacit consent, they become *money*, exchangeable 'for the truly useful, but perishable Supports of Life' (section 47). The use of money soon eliminates the lying in waste of potentially useful land (section 45), for it gives people the incentive and 'the opportunity to continue to enlarge' their possessions (section 48).

The invention of money also increases the inequality of private possessions, already a fact of life before money came on to the scene, because of the 'different degrees of Industry' of different humans (section 48). Locke bluntly states that in this new situation, money 'may be hoarded up without injury to any one', since it does not spoil; and therefore individuals may now fairly possess more than they can use (section 50). The '*Invention of Money*, and the tacit Agreement of Men to put a value on it, introduced (by Consent) larger Possessions, and a Right to them' (section 36). The conditions and rules existing before the advent of money and government (rehearsed in section 51) no longer obtain: money does not spoil, and everyone can pursue it honestly and lawfully without injury to anyone else's ability and right to do so as well. Although labour remains the source of wealth, and therefore 'in great part, *the measure*' of the value of useful things, labour soon ceases to create property rights; with the advent of government, property rights come under the jurisdiction of positive laws (section 50) – laws which, however, as we can see from the rest of the *Second Treatise*, should be designed to preserve the conditions of this new situation.

Why does Locke think it is fair to sanction such inequalities of private possessions? Why does he imagine that anyone but the rich or the potentially rich would consent to such rules as he here describes? Does justice not demand that in the new situation, with common land disappearing and population increasing, the right of individuals to appropriate should be restricted rather than enlarged? These questions are related to others that are often raised about the political arrangements that Locke recommends in the subsequent chapters of the *Second Treatise*. For example, why does Locke suggest that wealth as well as numbers might fairly be counted in the electoral system (chapter 13)? And why does he place so much emphasis on the principle that active consent must always be given for taxation (chapter 11)?

The answer to such questions that is suggested by the chapter on property is simply that such rules and 'laws of liberty' are necessary in order 'to secure protection and incouragement to the honest industry of Mankind' (section 42). Lockean government is less *laissez-faire* than *encouragez-faire*. And the reason that this encouragement is necessary is that otherwise humans will remain in economically undeveloped societies (and in Locke's world, in societies ruined by religious conflicts). Encouraging and rewarding 'the Industrious and Rational' actually rewards everyone, even the poor: 'a King of a large fruitful Territory there [among 'several Nations of the *Americans*'] feeds, lodges, and is clad worse than a day Labourer in *England*' (section 40). Economic competition need not be a zero-sum activity. Even if a system of private property rights does not produce exact justice, it does make general prosperity possible. This is the basic argument of liberal political economics; it is repeated, for example, in the Introduction to the *Wealth of Nations* (Smith, 1910 edn, p. 2), where Adam Smith remarks, 'Among civilised and thriving nations ... a workman, even of the lowest and poorest order, if he is frugal and industrious, may enjoy a greater share of the necessaries and conveniences of life than it is possible for any savage to acquire.' (Consider also John Rawls's 'difference principle', which holds that social and economic inequalities must work 'to the greatest benefit of the least advantaged' (Rawls, 1971, p. 302); Rawls's theory, however, is more concerned with the distribution than with the production of wealth.) In contrast to many twentieth-century 'neo-Lockeans' (see e.g. Nozick, 1974, p. 177), this basic Lockean argument is that a system of private property – which is subject to prudent legislative regulation – serves the common good – the 'wealth of nations' – not just the private interests of individuals.

Even though natural property is replaced by civil property in civil society, the understanding of natural property that Locke has taken us through remains politically relevant, because the important fact about property remains true: that desirable objects – in particular, things that go beyond what is naturally and immediately useful – are created not by civil society but by individual industry, inspired by the individual acquisitiveness that the existence of money, and the acceptance of Locke's story about property, encourage. Prudent civil societies will defer to 'charity', and anticipate the just claims that could otherwise be made on anyone's property by anyone else who becomes so poor that they have 'no means to subsist' (*First Treatise*, section 42). But the most effective means of true charity is encouragement of economic entrepreneurs, industry and commerce.

Many later political thinkers condemn Locke's thoughts about the justice of protecting private property rights as a defence of bourgeois class interests. (A neo-Marxist interpretation of Locke was developed by Macpherson, 1962.) Locke's own discussion of property reminds us of the unpleasant fact that in developed societies labour can be alienated (note one of the examples he gives in section 28, where the labour of someone else – 'my servant' – becomes 'mine'). However, Locke promotes not 'possessive individualism' (Macpherson's phrase) so much as *acquisitive* individualism. Locke defends possessiveness in order to defend further acquisitiveness, and he defends acquisitiveness in order to promote economic growth that benefits everyone. He defends not the existing or emerging class structure, but the ethics of an acquisitive society, in which individuals in every class can participate.

Although Locke can be acquitted from the charge of defending the haves against the have-nots, it does seem to be Locke's intention to defend what can be called a bourgeois way of life, in which the virtues of 'the Industrious and Rational' are favoured, on the ground that they contribute most to the public good. Without these types of human character, Locke argues, the fact that 'God gave the World to Men in

Common' would be a far less useful fact, for natural abundance is only potential, and takes individual human effort to actualise. But the question arises, will humans actually be happier in an acquisitive society? Such a society may provide 'enough' for all, but will that 'enough' really be 'as good'? For example, will the position of a wage labourer, dependent on labour markets and employers, not be in some sense inferior to that of a less wealthy but more independent savage? And will the 'better off' truly be as good and as happy as it is humanly possible to be? Even if the science of economics succeeds in bringing forth wealth and is not economically 'dismal', is it not still morally dismal?

Locke writes as if the alternative facing humans is either the poverty of primitive underdevelopment or the prosperity of modern commercial society. But many pre-modern societies were somewhere in between. In assessing the strength of Locke's argument, and simply in appreciating the novelty of an argument that has become familiar if not always dominant in modern liberal regimes, it can be more helpful to look not at the later modern (Marxist and other) critics of Locke – who share many of his premises – but at pre-modern (and pre-Christian) thoughts about property. One of the best ways of understanding modernity is by contrasting it with antiquity, and the best representative of a tradition of thought that Locke and other early moderns implicitly or explicitly either rejected or revised is Aristotle.

## Aristotle (384–322 BC)

(For details of Aristotle's life, see chapter 2.) Two extracts from Aristotle's *Politics* appear below. The first, from his discussion of household management ('economics' in the original sense of the word) in Book I, reproduces some of his moral strictures against the unlimited pursuit of wealth by private households. The second extract, from Book II, criticises the communism advocated in Plato's *Republic*. While Aristotle agrees with Locke about the usefulness of private property, his assumptions and reasoning are very different, reflecting a very different conception of the nature and purpose of society.

In the *Republic*, Plato's Socrates (perhaps ironically, but Aristotle here takes him seriously) prescribed a comprehensive system of communism for the rulers – the 'guardians' – of the perfect political community. Not just possessions but family life and privacy itself are to be abolished in this perfect regime. These abolitions are proposed in the interest of the unity of the regime, and to promote the spiritedness and warrior virtues of the rulers. If the guardians were allowed to develop family life and private property, this would greatly reduce their loyalty to the community as a whole, and acquisitiveness would soften their martial education. Socrates' prescriptions, made in the middle of the dialogue, are developments of arguments introduced near its beginning, at the point where Socrates gently but firmly refutes the respectable old Cephalus. Cephalus had suggested that justice means returning property to its owner. Socrates asks Cephalus whether

it would be just to return a weapon to a friend who had become mad;
in other words, Socrates adds to Cephalus' idea of justice as respect for
legally-defined property the idea that justice should be good for people.
How can it be right for anyone to possess something that they cannot
use well, making themselves and others better or happier? Socrates'
enlargement of the idea of justice implies that legal property is very
limited as a fair way of determining possessions; perfect justice requires
rather that wise rulers – philosopher kings – should determine 'who
gets what and when', and that supposed 'rights' to private property
should not be allowed to interfere with this wise determination. From
this point of view, even Locke's seemingly uncontroversial assumption
that one has an undeniable right to one's own body (and the labour of
that body) becomes questionable; it all depends on how wisely one uses
it.

Aristotle spends a long time criticising Plato's political philosophy:
nearly half of Book II of the *Politics*. Much of this criticism is devoted
specifically to the question of whether material possessions should be
held in common or privately. This question is answered in the context
of a more general discussion of the nature of the political community.
What kind of unity is natural for politics? Is it better for a political
community to hold everything in common that can be so held, or is it
better for some of these things to be held in common and some
privately? Aristotle argues that Socrates' proposal for radical commu-
nisation is based on the erroneous assumption that the greater the
amount of unity, the more perfect will be political life. This assumption,
says Aristotle, by overemphasising the need for unity, treats political
life as if it were the life of a family or of a single individual. Even if this
degree and kind of unity were possible in politics, it would not improve
but would destroy political life, because political communities are
made up of different kinds of individuals. This diversity and the division of labour it implies help make political communities more
self-sufficient than the individuals and the families out of which these
communities grow. Moreover, by treating the political community as if
it were a family – by Socrates' proposal that everyone should say 'mine'
and 'not mine' of the same persons – husbands, wives and children –
the social bonds would be weakened rather than strengthened, just as
the material things held in common would be less well cared for. No
one would know who their real relations were, so in effect no one
would have any real relations. Diluting family affection by making
everyone a member of the same family would water it down so much
that it would effectively disappear. Abolishing the family would therefore abolish the space in which human beings develop the basics of
affection and morality. In Aristotle's way of thinking, human friendship
and virtues are first developed in family life, and can then be extended
and perfected in relationships with one's fellow citizens. Paradoxically,
but naturally and necessarily, the extreme communism proposed by
Socrates would produce more uncaring and individualistic beings, less
suited to political life.

Having established this crucial point about the nature of political life and the necessary and beneficial complexity of political unity, Aristotle then turns to the question of whether it is best to possess things – as distinguished from persons – in common. He points out that one difficulty found with various communal arrangements is that the effect of the different and unequal abilities of the individuals involved is bound to lead to quarrels. Even fellow travellers, who merely share a direction of travel and perhaps a means of conveyance, develop friction among themselves about the most trivial matters, so it is not surprising that individuals sharing their means of livelihood should develop rather serious disputes. He suggests that one could get the benefit of both private and common ownership by communising the *use* of certain property – as in Sparta, he points out, they use each other's slaves, horses and dogs, and freely take from the fields what they need to eat when they travel. Such laws, adorned by good character, would be possible and desirable improvements on the existing arrangement of private property – unlike Socrates' superficially attractive proposal for complete communism, which would be impossible and, to the extent that it could be implemented, counterproductive. After all, Aristotle contends, the ills sometimes charged to private ownership are actually caused by moral depravity; so what one needs to institute is not communism but good moral education. Education is the best method of bringing to political life the kind of unity that is appropriate to it. This education would condemn selfishness, but not the proper love of the good things of life. The pleasurable love of these things is natural and healthy, if not carried to excess. Moreover, there is an element of pleasure felt by individual bodies that cannot be truly shared, so perfect communism is impossible. Besides, the moral virtues of moderation and liberality, which are good for humans, would become impossible to develop if private property were abolished. The practice of morality requires a certain amount of material equipment. (That is why, in Aristotle's technologically undeveloped world, it seemed to require slavery; but Aristotle was not the crass apologist for slavery that he is often made out to be (on this troubling issue, see Jaffa, 1973, pp. 342–6).)

This fundamental concern with morality – visible throughout Aristotle's political philosophy – is clear in his discussion of money and family life in Book I of the *Politics* (the first *Politics* extract printed below). Aristotle would treat with some suspicion Locke's failure to introduce rules of moral restraint into his discussion of the acquisition of property by individuals and families. Aristotle recognises that money can all too easily become an end in itself, and that households do often engage, like merchants, in the limitless acquisition of money. But this, he claims, is an example of perhaps the most common basic error in political and moral practice, that of mistaking means for ends. The natural end of humanity – living well and happily – is (wrongly) subordinated to the means: mere life, 'comfortable preservation'. Good relations with other human beings depend on the practice of moral virtues, and these relations are more essential than wealth to an individual's happiness; therefore, an exaggerated concern with the acquisition of wealth must be avoided by individuals if they are to be happy. According to Aristotle, it is more suitable for the political community itself to engage in the art of unlimited acquisition than for private households to do so. The art of commerce, with its end as the unlimited acquisition of money, must be distinguished from the art of household management, which aims to satisfy limited needs. Otherwise, the morals learned in the family will be oligarchic and plutocratic. At best such morals will produce characters like Crito, so concerned with bodily preservation and money that they can be taught to appreciate at most only the rule of law, not the more complete morality that the law should help to create (Congleton, 1974, pp. 442–5). The commercial elements of the community – necessary though they are – must not be allowed to set its moral tone.

## Conclusion

In spite of his profound criticism of Plato's Socrates on the character of political unity, and on the possibility and desirability of communism, Aristotle shares Plato's pre-modern view of the relatively unlimited scope of politics (with no sharp distinction between state and society), and of the desirability of subordinating the economic acquisitiveness of individuals and families to moral considerations. In Aristotle's view, political communities grow not (as Locke has it) out of individual consent, but as a natural progression from family life. Therefore the strict limits of the purposes of government that Locke insists on would not seem right to Aristotle: political life exists not for the sake of mere life – not merely for 'comfortable preservation' – but for living well, for perfecting the human virtues that begin to develop in families and require political life for their completion. Politics is thus a part of ethics.

For Locke, the protection of natural property rights is one of the major purposes of government, and he gives the claims of the 'Industrious and Rational' great political weight. These claims are based on the view that the main purpose of political society is economic prosperity. Aristotle would see this primarily as an oligarchical view, grasping only part of the truth. Like the opposing democratic claim to political equality, based on the partial view that the purpose of politics is personal security, the oligarchical view mistakes some of the necessary means of political life (wealth) for the end of political life (living well).

By treating the origins of political life as its end, Locke makes economics the central theme of politics. In the twentieth century, conservative liberals and welfare state liberals have disagreed about the extent to which government should 'interfere' with private property and markets (a question that Locke himself left open), but they have accepted Locke's elevation of such economic policy questions to the top of the political agenda, and have agreed that economic welfare is the purpose of politics.

Critics of liberalism from left and right have pursued a rather aristocratic, Aristotelian way of thinking, by questioning the desirability as well as the feasibility of the Lockean liberal attempt to cut politics down to size, to narrow the scope of political life. Even if it were possible, does it not seem likely to lead to an inhumanly prosaic public and private life? This is what Rousseau was complaining about when he noticed the modern tendency to reduce politics to economics: taking the soulcraft out of politics may lead to a safer political life, but can politics be de-animated in this way without promoting societies of miserable *bourgeois* creatures, whose lives may be long, but still (recalling Hobbes's description of the state of nature, quoted in chapter 3) 'solitary, poor, nasty, [and] brutish'?

Locke might reply, first of all, by pointing out that if we recognise human equality, then we should be wary of any criticism of modern politics and ethics that builds on the ancient case for aristocracy. Socialist as well as conservative critics of liberalism often seem oddly keen to revive what are essentially aristocratic prejudices against commercial life and hard work. Intellectuals should remember that they, as well as business entrepreneurs, benefit from Lockean political liberty. Secondly, Locke would point out that he was not a libertarian or an advocate of 'negative liberty'. He did not call for the creation of an absolute 'wall of separation' between government and society. He did favour a greater separation between state and society – between political power and moral education – but this was not because of any indifference to morality, but because of his interest in advancing the morality of free and equal human beings. Similarly, his case for separating church and state was meant to promote the health of both. Finally, Locke might point to what he and Aristotle have in common, and contend that Aristotle – the great philosopher of prudence – would surely be the first to recognise that the modern world is different from the ancient, and that political philosophy therefore has to adapt itself accordingly. In particular, it had to respond to the challenge that universal revealed religion posed to the integrity of political life, by developing the universal secular political principles of the *Second Treatise*.

## References

Ashcraft, Richard, *Revolutionary Politics and Locke's Two Treatises of Government*, Princeton: Princeton University Press, 1986.

Congleton, Ann, 'Two Kinds of Lawlessness', *Political Theory*, 2, 4 (1974) pp. 432–46.

Hume, David, *A Treatise of Human Nature*, ed. Ernest C. Mossner, Harmondsworth: Penguin, 1969.

Jaffa, Harry V., *Crisis of the House Divided*, (2nd edn) Seattle and London: University of Washington Press, 1973.

Laslett, Peter, 'Introduction', in Peter Laslett (ed.), *John Locke's Two Treatises of Government*, Cambridge: Cambridge University Press, 1963, pp. 15–161.

Macpherson, C. B., *The Political Theory of Possessive Individualism: Hobbes to Locke*, Oxford: Oxford University Press, 1962.

Nozick, Robert, *Anarchy, State and Utopia*, Oxford: Basil Blackwell, 1974.
Rawls, John, *A Theory of Justice*, Cambridge, MA: Harvard University Press, 1971.
Smith, Adam, *An Inquiry Into the Nature and Causes of the Wealth of Nations* (1st pub. 1776), London and Toronto: J. M. Dent & Sons, 1910.

## Further reading

See Aristotle, *Politics*, especially Books I–IV, and *Nicomachean Ethics*, especially Books I and IV; and John Locke, *A Letter Concerning Toleration*, Two Treatises of Government, especially I, chapters 7–9, and II, chapters 1–4, 7–15, and 18–19, and *Questions concerning the Law of Nature* (trans. D. Clay, Ithaca and London: Cornell University Press, 1990). Interesting introductory commentaries on both Locke and Aristotle can be found in Larry Arnhart, *Political Questions: Political Philosophy from Plato to Rawls* (New York: Macmillan, 1987). For more detailed analyses, on Locke, see Richard Ashcraft, *Revolutionary Politics and Locke's Two Treatises of Government* (Princeton: Princeton University Press, 1986); Thomas L. Pangle, *The Spirit of Modern Republicanism* (Chicago and London: University of Chicago Press, 1988), part three: 'The Lockean Conception of Human Nature'; Geraint Parry, *John Locke* (London: Allen & Unwin, 1978); and Nathan Tarcov, *Locke's Education for Liberty* (Chicago: University of Chicago Press, 1984); and on Aristotle, see Harry V. Jaffa, 'What Is Politics? An Interpretation of Aristotle's *Politics*', in *The Conditions of Freedom: Essays in Political Philosophy* (Baltimore and London: Johns Hopkins University Press, 1975); and Mary P. Nichols, *Socrates and the Political Community: An Ancient Debate* (Albany: State University of New York Press, 1987), part III (on Aristotle's critique of Plato). Alan Ryan, *Property* (Milton Keynes: Open University Press, 1987) combines historical and philosophical analysis in a concise and very readable book that discusses Locke and Aristotle alongside several other writers.

## Seminar questions

Are the conclusions Locke draws from his reflections on the state of nature more defensible than those of Hobbes?

How successfully does Locke establish property rights on universal principles?

How reasonable is the liberal attempt to separate state and society?

What are the best arguments for and against communal ownership of property?

Who has the better view of the role of private property in political life: Locke or Aristotle?

# JOHN LOCKE
## From *Second Treatise of Government*

### CHAP. V  Of Property

25. Whether we consider natural *Reason*, which tells us, that Men, being once born, have a right to their Preservation, and consequently to Meat and Drink, and such other things, as Nature affords for their Subsistence: Or *Revelation*, which gives us an account of those Grants God made of the World to *Adam*, and to *Noah*, and his Sons, 'tis very clear, that God, as King *David* says, *Psal*. CXV. xvj. *has given the Earth to the Children of Men*, given it to Mankind in common. But this being supposed, it seems to some a very great difficulty, how any one should ever come to have a *Property* in any thing: I will not content my self to answer, That if it be difficult to make out *Property*, upon a supposition, that God gave the World to *Adam* and his Posterity in common; it is impossible that any Man, but one universal Monarch, should have any *Property*, upon a supposition, that God gave the World to *Adam*, and his Heirs in Succession, exclusive of all the rest of his Posterity. But I shall endeavour to shew, how Men might come to have a *property* in several parts of that which God gave to Mankind in common, and that without any express Compact of all the Commoners.

26. God, who hath given the World to Men in common, hath also given them reason to make use of it to the best advantage of Life, and convenience. The Earth, and all that is therein, is given to Men for the Support and Comfort of their being. And though all the Fruits it naturally produces, and Beasts it feeds, belong to Mankind in common, as they are produced by the spontaneous hand of Nature; and no body has originally a private Dominion, exclusive of the rest of Mankind, in any of them, as they are thus in their natural state: yet being given for the use of Men, there must of necessity be a means *to appropriate* them some way or other before they can be of any use, or at all beneficial to any particular Man. The Fruit, or Venison, which nourishes the wild *Indian*, who knows no Inclosure, and is still a Tenant in common, must be his, and so his, *i.e.* a part of him, that another can no longer have any right to it, before it can do him any good for the support of his Life.

27. Though the Earth, and all inferior Creatures be common to all Men, yet every Man has a *Property* in his own *Person*. This no Body has any Right to but himself. The *Labour* of his Body, and the *Work* of his Hands, we may say, are properly his. Whatsoever then he removes out of the State that Nature hath provided, and left it in, he hath mixed his *Labour* with, and joyned to it something that is his own, and thereby makes it his *Property*. It being by him removed from the common state Nature placed it in, it hath by this *labour* something annexed to it, that excludes the common right of other Men. For this *Labour* being the unquestionable Property of the Labourer, no Man

but he can have a right to what that is once joyned to, at least where there is enough, and as good left in common for others.

28. He that is nourished by the Acorns he pickt up under an Oak, or the Apples he gathered from the Trees in the Wood, has certainly appropriated them to himself. No Body can deny but the nourishment is his. I ask then, When did they begin to be his? When he digested? Or when he eat? Or when he boiled? Or when he brought them home? Or when he pickt them up? And 'tis plain, if the first gathering made them not his, nothing else could. That *labour* put a distinction between them and common. That added something to them more than Nature, the common Mother of all, had done; and so they became his private right. And will any one say he had no right to those Acorns or Apples he thus appropriated, because he had not the consent of all Mankind to make them his? Was it a Robbery thus to assume to himself what belonged to all in Common? If such a consent as that was necessary, Man had starved, notwithstanding the Plenty God had given him. We see in *Commons*, which remain so by Compact, that 'tis the taking any part of what is common, and removing it out of the state Nature leaves it in, which *begins the Property*; without which the Common is of no use. And the taking of this or that part, does not depend on the express consent of all the Commoners. Thus the Grass my Horse has bit; the Turfs my Servant has cut; and the Ore I have digg'd in any place where I have a right to them in common with others, become my *Property*, without the assignation or consent of any body. The *labour* that was mine, removing them out of that common state they were in, hath *fixed* my *Property* in them.

29. By making an explicit consent of every Commoner, necessary to any ones appropriating to himself any part of what is given in common, Children or Servants could not cut the Meat which their Father or Master had provided for them in common, without assigning to every one his peculiar part. Though the Water running in the Fountain be every ones, yet who can doubt, but that in the Pitcher is his only who drew it out?: His *labour* hath taken it out of the hands of Nature, where it was common, and belong'd equally to all her Children, and *hath* thereby *appropriated* it to himself.

30. Thus this Law of reason makes the Deer, that *Indian's* who hath killed it; 'tis allowed to be his goods who hath bestowed his labour upon it, though before, it was the common right of every one. And amongst those who are counted the Civiliz'd part of Mankind, who have made and multiplied positive Laws to determine Property, this original Law of Nature for the *beginning of Property*, in what was before common, still takes place; and by vertue thereof, what Fish any one catches in the Ocean, that great and still remaining Common of Mankind; or what Ambergriese any one takes up here, is *by* the *Labour* that removes it out of that common state nature left it in, *made* his *Property* who takes that pains about it. And even amongst us the Hare that any one is Hunting, is thought his who pursues her during

the Chase. For being a Beast that is still looked upon as common, and no Man's private Possession; whoever has imploy'd so much *labour* about any of that kind, as to find and pursue her, has thereby removed her from the state of Nature, wherein she was common, and hath *begun a Property.*

31. It will perhaps be objected to this, That if gathering the Acorns, or other Fruits of the Earth, etc. makes a right to them, then any one may *ingross* as much as he will. To which I Answer, Not so. The same Law of Nature, that does by this means give us property, does also *bound* that *Property* too. *God has given us all things richly,* I Tim. vi. 17. is the Voice of Reason confirmed by Inspiration. But how far has he given it us? *To enjoy.* As much as any one can make use of to any advantage of life before it spoils; so much he may by his labour fix a Property in. Whatever is beyond this, is more than his share, and belongs to others. Nothing was made by God for Man to spoil or destroy. And thus considering the plenty of natural Provisions there was a long time in the World, and the few spenders, and to how small a part of that provision the industry of one Man could extend it self, and ingross it to the prejudice of others; especially keeping within the *bounds*, set by reason of what might serve for his *use*; there could be then little room for Quarrels or Contentions about Property so establish'd.

32. But the *chief matter of Property* being now not the Fruits of the Earth, and the Beasts that subsist on it, but the *Earth it self*; as that which takes in and carries with it all the rest: I think it is plain, that *Property* in that too is acquired as the former. *As much Land as a Man Tills, Plants, Improves, Cultivates, and can use the Product of, so much is his Property.* He by his Labour does, as it were, inclose it from the Common. Nor will it invalidate his right to say, Every body else has an equal Title to it; and therefore he cannot appropriate, he cannot inclose, without the Consent of all his Fellow-Commoners, all Mankind. God, when he gave the World in common to all Mankind, commanded Man also to labour, and the penury of his Condition required it of him. God and his Reason commanded him to subdue the Earth, *i.e.* improve it for the benefit of Life, and therein lay out something upon it that was his own, his labour. He that in Obedience to this Command of God, subdued, tilled and sowed any part of it, thereby annexed to it something that was his *Property*, which another had no Title to, nor could without injury take from him.

33. Nor was this *appropriation* of any parcel of *Land*, by improving it, any prejudice to any other Man, since there was still enough, and as good left; and more than the yet unprovided could use. So that in effect, there was never the less left for others because of his inclosure for himself. For he that leaves as much as another can make use of, does as good as take nothing at all. No Body could think himself injur'd by the drinking of another Man, though he took a good Draught, who had a whole River of the same Water left him to quench his thirst. And the Case of Land and Water, where there is

enough of both, is perfectly the same.

34. God gave the World to Men in Common; but since he gave it them for their benefit, and the greatest Conveniencies of Life they were capable to draw from it, it cannot be supposed he meant it should always remain common and uncultivated. He gave it to the use of the Industrious and Rational, (and *Labour* was to be *his Title* to it;) not to the Fancy or Covetousness of the Quarrelsom and Contentious. He that had as good left for his Improvement, as was already taken up, needed not complain, ought not to meddle with what was already improved by another's Labour: If he did, 'tis plain he desired the benefit of another's Pains, which he had no right to, and not the Ground which God had given him in common with others to labour on, and whereof there was as good left, as that already possessed, and more than he knew what to do with, or his Industry could reach to.

35. 'Tis true, in *Land* that is *common* in *England*, or any other Country, where there is Plenty of People under Government, who have Money and Commerce, no one can inclose or appropriate any part, without the consent of all his Fellow-Commoners: Because this is left common by Compact, *i.e.* by the Law of the Land, which is not to be violated. And though it be Common, in respect of some Men, it is not so to all Mankind; but is the joint property of this Country, or this Parish. Besides, the remainder, after such inclosure, would not be as good to the rest of the Commoners as the whole was, when they could all make use of the whole: whereas in the beginning and first peopling of the great Common of the World, it was quite otherwise. The Law Man was under, was rather for *appropriating.* God Commanded, and his Wants forced him to *labour.* That was his *Property* which could not be taken from him where-ever he had fixed it. And hence subduing or cultivating the Earth, and having Dominion, we see are joyned together. The one gave Title to the other. So that God, by commanding to subdue, gave Authority so far to *appropriate.* And the Condition of Humane Life, which requires Labour and Materials to work on, necessarily introduces *private Possessions.*

36. The measure of Property, Nature has well set, by the Extent of Mens *Labour, and the Conveniency of Life*: No Mans Labour could subdue, or appropriate all: nor could his Enjoyment consume more than a small part; so that it was impossible for any Man, this way, to intrench upon the right of another, or acquire, to himself, a property, to the Prejudice of his Neighbour, who would still have room, for as good, and as large a Possession (after the other had taken out his) as before it was appropriated. This *measure* did confine every Man's *Possession*, to a very moderate Proportion, and such as he might appropriate to himself, without Injury to any body in the first Ages of the World, when Men were more in danger to be lost, by wandering from their Company, in the then vast Wilderness of the Earth, than to be straitned for want of room to plant in. And the same *measure* may be allowed still, without prejudice to any Body, as full as the World seems. For supposing a Man, or Family, in the state they were, at first

peopling of the World by the Children of *Adam*, or *Noah*; let him plant in some in-land, vacant places of *America*, we shall find that the *Possessions* he could make himself upon the *measures* we have given, would not be very large, nor, even to this day, prejudice the rest of Mankind, or give them reason to complain, or think themselves injured by this Man's Incroachment, though the Race of Men have now spread themselves to all the corners of the World, and do infinitely exceed the small number [which] was at the beginning. Nay, the extent of *Ground* is of so little value, *without labour*, that I have heard it affirmed, that in *Spain* it self, a Man may be permitted to plough, sow, and reap, without being disturbed, upon Land he has no other Title to, but only his making use of it. But, on the contrary, the Inhabitants think themselves beholden to him, who, by his Industry on neglected, and consequently waste land, has increased the stock of Corn, which they wanted. But be this as it will, which I lay no stress on; This I dare boldly affirm, That the same *Rule of Propriety*, (*viz.*) that every man should have as much as he could make use of, would hold still in the World, without straitning any body, since there is Land enough in the World to suffice double the Inhabitants had not the *Invention of Money*, and the tacit Agreement of Men to put a value on it, introduced (by Consent) larger Possessions, and a Right to them; which, how it has done, I shall, by and by, shew more at large.

37. This is certain, That in the beginning, before the desire of having more than Men needed, had altered the intrinsick value of things, which depends only on their usefulness to the Life of Man; or [Men] had *agreed, that a little piece of yellow Metal*, which would keep without wasting or decay, should be worth a great piece of Flesh, or a whole heap of Corn; though Men had a Right to appropriate, by their Labour, each one to himself, as much of the things of Nature, as he could use: Yet this could not be much, nor to the Prejudice of others, where the same plenty was still left, to those who would use the same Industry. To which let me add, that he who appropriates land to himself by his labour, does not lessen but increase the common stock of mankind. For the provisions serving to the support of humane life, produced by one acre of inclosed and cultivated land, are (to speak much within compass) ten times more, than those, which are yielded by an acre of Land, of an equal richnesse, lyeing wast in common. And therefor he, that incloses Land and has a greater plenty of the conveniencys of life from ten acres, than he could have from an hundred left to nature, may truly be said, to give ninety acres to Mankind. For his labour now supplys him with provisions out of ten acres, which were but the product of an hundred lying in common. I have here rated the improved land very low in making its product but as ten to one, when it is much nearer an hundred to one. For I ask whether in the wild woods and uncultivated wast of America left to nature, without any improvement, tillage or husbandry, a thousand acres will yield the needy and wretched inhabitants as

many conveniencies of life as ten acres of equally fertile land doe in Devonshire where they are well cultivated?

Before the Appropriation of Land, he who gathered as much of the wild Fruit, killed, caught, or tamed, as many of the Beasts as he could; he that so employed his pains about any of the spontaneous products of Nature, as any way to alter them, from the state which Nature put them in, *by* placing any of his *Labour* on them, did thereby *acquire a Propriety in them*: But if they perished, in his Possession, without their due use; if the Fruits rotted, or the Venison putrified, before he could spend it, he offended against the common Law of Nature, and was liable to be punished; he invaded his Neighbour's share, for he had *no Right, farther than his Use* called for any of them, and they might serve to afford him Conveniencies of Life.

38. The same *measures* governed the *Possession of Land* too: Whatsoever he tilled and reaped, laid up and made use of, before it spoiled, that was his peculiar Right; whatsoever he enclosed, and could feed, and make use of, the Cattle and Product was also his. But if either the Grass of his Inclosure rotted on the Ground, or the Fruit of his planting perished without gathering, and laying up, this part of the Earth, notwithstanding his Inclosure, was still to be looked on as Waste, and might be the Possession of any other. Thus, at the beginning, *Cain* might take as much Ground as he could till, and make it his own Land, and yet leave enough to *Abel*'s Sheep to feed on; a few Acres would serve for both their Possessions. But as Families increased, and Industry inlarged their Stocks, their *Possessions inlarged* with the need of them; but yet it was commonly *without any fixed property in the ground* they made use of, till they incorporated, settled themselves together, and built Cities, and then, by consent, they came in time, to set out the *bounds of their distinct Territories*, and agree on limits between them and their Neighbours, and by Laws within themselves, settled the *Properties* of those of the same Society. For we see, that in that part of the World which was first inhabited, and therefore like to be best peopled, even as low down as *Abraham*'s time, they wandred with their Flocks, and their Herds, which was their substance, freely up and down; and this *Abraham* did, in a Country where he was a Stranger. Whence it is plain, that at least, a great part of the *Land lay in common*; that the Inhabitants valued it not, nor claimed Property in any more than they made use of. But when there was not room enough in the same place, for their Herds to feed together, they, by consent, as *Abraham* and *Lot* did, *Gen.* xiii. 5. separated and inlarged their pasture, where it best liked them. And for the same Reason *Esau* went from his Father, and his Brother, and planted in *Mount Seir*, Gen. xxxvi. 6.

39. And thus, without supposing any private Dominion, and property in *Adam*, over all the World, exclusive of all other Men, which can no way be proved, nor any ones Property be made out from it; but supposing the *World* given as it was to the Children of Men *in common*, we see how *labour* could make Men distinct titles to several

parcels of it, for their private uses; wherein there could be no doubt of Right, no room for quarrel.

40. Nor is it so strange, as perhaps before consideration it may appear, that the *Property of labour* should be able to over-ballance the Community of Land. For 'tis *Labour* indeed that *puts the difference of value* on every thing; and let any one consider, what the difference is between an Acre of Land planted with Tobacco, or Sugar, sown with Wheat or Barley; and an Acre of the same Land lying in common, without any Husbandry upon it, and he will find, that the improvement of *labour makes* the far greater part of *the value*. I think it will be but a very modest Computation to say, that of the *Products* of the Earth useful to the Life of Man ⁹/₁₀ are the *effects of labour*: nay, if we will rightly estimate things as they come to our use, and cast up the several Expences about them, what in them is purely owing to *Nature*, and what to *labour*, we shall find, that in most of them ⁹⁹/₁₀₀ are wholly to be put on the account of *labour*.

41. There cannot be a clearer demonstration of any thing, than several Nations of the *Americans* are of this, who are rich in Land, and poor in all the Comforts of Life; whom Nature having furnished as liberally as any other people, with the materials of Plenty, *i.e.* a fruitful Soil, apt to product in abundance, what might serve for food, rayment, and delight; yet for want of improving it by labour, have not one hundreth part of the Conveniencies we enjoy: And a King of a large and fruitful Territory there feeds, lodges, and is clad worse than a day Labourer in *England*.

42. To make this a little clearer, let us but trace some of the ordinary provisions of Life, through their several progresses, before they come to our use, and see how much they receive of their *value from Humane Industry*. Bread, Wine and Cloth, are things of daily use, and great plenty, yet notwithstanding, Acorns, Water, and Leaves, or Skins, must be our Bread, Drink and Clothing, did not *labour* furnish us with these more useful Commodities. For whatever *Bread* is more worth than Acorns, *Wine* than Water, and *Cloth* or *Silk* than Leaves, Skins, or Moss, that is wholly *owing to labour* and industry. The one of these being the Food and Rayment which unassisted Nature furnishes us with; the other provisions which our industry and pains prepare for us, which how much they exceed the other in value, when any one hath computed, he will then see, how much *labour makes the far greatest part of the value* of things, we enjoy in this World: And the ground which produces the materials, is scarce to be reckon'd in, as any, or at most, but a very small, part of it; So little, that even amongst us, Land that is left wholly to Nature, that hath no improvement of Pasturage, Tillage, or Planting, is called, as indeed it is, *wast*; and we shall find the benefit of it amount to little more than nothing. This shews, how much numbers of men are to be preferd to largenesse of dominions, and that the increase of lands and the right imploying of them is the great art of government. And that Prince who shall be so wise and godlike as by established laws of liberty to secure

protection and incouragement to the honest industry of mankind against the oppression of power and narrownesse of Party will quickly be too hard for his neighbours. But this bye the bye. To return to the argument in hand.

43. An Acre of Land that bears here Twenty Bushels of Wheat, and another in *America*, which, with the same Husbandry, would do the like, are, without doubt, of the same natural, intrinsick Value. But yet the Benefit Mankind receives from the one, in a Year, is worth 5 *l.*, and from the other possibly not worth a Penny, if all the Profit an *Indian* received from it were to be valued, and sold here; at least, I may truly say, not $\frac{1}{1000}$. 'Tis *Labour* then which *puts the greatest part of Value upon Land*, without which it would scarcely be worth any thing: 'tis to that we owe the greatest part of all its useful Products: for all that the Straw, Bran, Bread, of that Acre of Wheat, is more worth than the Product of an Acre of as good Land, which lies wast, is all the Effect of Labour. For 'tis not barely the Plough-man's Pains, the Reaper's and Thresher's Toil, and the Bakers Sweat, is to be counted into the *Bread* we eat; the Labour of those who broke the Oxen, who digged and wrought the Iron and Stones, who felled and framed the Timber imployed about the Plough, Mill, Oven, or any other Utensils, which are a vast Number, requisite to this Corn, from its being seed to be sown to its being made Bread, must all be *charged on* the account of *Labour*, and received as an effect of that: Nature and the Earth furnished only the almost worthless Materials, as in themselves. 'Twould be a strange *Catalogue of things, that Industry provided and made use of, about every Loaf of Bread*, before it came to our use, if we could trace them; Iron, Wood, Leather, Bark, Timber, Stone, Bricks, Coals, Lime, Cloth, Dying-Drugs, Pitch, Tar, Masts, Ropes, and all the Materials made use of in the Ship, that brought any of the Commodities made use of by any of the Workmen, to any part of the Work, all which, 'twould be almost impossible, at least too long, to reckon up.

44. From all which it is evident, that though the things of Nature are given in common, yet Man (by being Master of himself, and *Proprietor of his own person*, and the Actions or *Labour* of it) had still in himself *the great Foundation of Property*; and that which made up the great part of what he applyed to the Support or Comfort of his being, when Invention and Arts had improved the conveniencies of Life, was perfectly his own, and did not belong in common to others.

45. Thus *Labour*, in the Beginning, *gave a Right of Property*, where-ever any one was pleased to imploy it, upon what was common, which remained, a long while, the far greater part, and is yet more than Mankind makes use of. Men, at first, for the most part, contented themselves with what un-assisted Nature offered to their Necessities: and though afterwards, in some parts of the World, (where the Increase of People and Stock, with the *Use of Money*) had made Land scarce, and so of some Value, the several *Communities* settled the Bounds of their distinct Territories, and by Laws within themselves,

regulated the Properties of the private men of their Society, and so, *by Compact* and Agreement, *settled the Property* which Labour and Industry began; and the Leagues that have been made between several States and Kingdoms, either expressly or tacitly disowning all Claim and Right to the Land in the others Possession, have, by common Consent, given up their Pretences to their natural common Right, which originally they had to those Countries, and so have, by *positive agreement, settled a Property* amongst themselves, in distinct Parts and parcels of the Earth: yet there are still *great Tracts of Ground* to be found, which (the Inhabitants thereof not having joyned with the rest of Mankind, in the consent of the Use of their common Money) *lie waste*, and are more than the People, who dwell on it, do, or can make use of, and so still lie in common. Tho' this can scarce happen amongst that part of Mankind, that have consented to the Use of Money.

46. The greatest part of *things really useful* to the Life of Man, and such as the necessity of subsisting made the first Commoners of the World look after, as it doth the *Americans* now, *are* generally things *of short duration*; such as, if they are not consumed by use, will decay and perish of themselves: Gold, Silver, and Diamonds, are things, that Fancy or Agreement hath put the Value on, more then real Use, and the necessary Support of Life. Now of those good things which Nature hath provided in common, every one had a Right (as hath been said) to as much as he could use, and had a Property in all that he could affect with his Labour: all that his Industy could extend to, to alter from the State Nature had put it in, was his. He that *gathered* a Hundred Bushels of Acorns or Apples, had thereby a *Property* in them; they were his Goods as soon as gathered. He was only to look that he used them before they spoiled; else he took more than his share, and robb'd others. And indeed it was a foolish thing, as well as dishonest, to hoard up more than he could make use of. If he gave away a part to any body else, so that it perished not uselesly in his Possession, these he also made use of. And if he also bartered away Plumbs that would have rotted in a Week, for Nuts that would last good for his eating a whole Year, he did no injury; he wasted not the common Stock; destroyed no part of the portion of Goods that belonged to others, so long as nothing perished uselesly in his hands. Again, if he would give his Nuts for a piece of Metal, pleased with its colour; or exchange his Sheep for Shells, or Wool for a sparkling Pebble or a Diamond, and keep those by him all his Life, he invaded not the Right of others, he might heap up as much of these durable things as he pleased; the *exceeding of the bounds of his* just *Property* not lying in the largeness of his Possession, but the perishing of any thing uselesly in it.

47. And thus *came in the use of Money*, some lasting thing that Men might keep without spoiling, and that by mutual consent Men would take in exchange for the truly useful, but perishable Supports of Life.

48. And as different degrees of Industry were apt to give Men

Possessions in different Proportions, so this *Invention of Money* gave them the opportunity to continue and enlarge them. For supposing an Island, separate from all possible Commerce with the rest of the World, wherein there were but a hundred Families, but there were Sheep, Horses and Cows, with other useful Animals, wholsome Fruits, and Land enough for Corn for a hundred thousand times as many, but nothing in the Island, either because of its Commonness, or Perishableness, fit to supply the place of *Money*: What reason could any one have there to enlarge his Possessions beyond the use of his Family, and a plentiful supply to its Consumption, either in what their own Industry produced, or they could barter for like perishable, useful Commodities, with others? Where there is not something both lasting and scarce, and so valuable to be hoarded up, there Men will not be apt to enlarge their *Possessions of Land*, were it never so rich, never so free for them to take. For I ask, What would a Man value Ten Thousand, or an Hundred Thousand Acres of excellent *Land*, ready cultivated, and well stocked too with Cattle, in the middle of the in-land Parts of *America*, where he had no hopes of Commerce with other Parts of the World, to draw *Money* to him by the Sale of the Product? It would not be worth the inclosing, and we should see him give up again to the wild Common of Nature, whatever was more than would supply the Conveniencies of Life to be had there for him and his Family.

49. Thus in the beginning all the World was *America*, and more so than that is now; for no such thing as *Money* was any where known. Find out something that hath the *Use and Value of Money* amongst his Neighbours, you shall see the same Man will begin presently to *enlarge* his *Possessions*.

50. But since Gold and Silver, being little useful to the Life of Man in proportion to Food, Rayment, and Carriage, has its *value* only from the consent of Men, whereof Labour yet makes, in great part, *the measure*, it is plain, that Men have agreed to disproportionate and unequal Possession of the Earth, they having by a tacit and voluntary consent found out a way, how a man may fairly possess more land than he himself can use the product of, by receiving in exchange for the overplus, Gold and Silver, which may be hoarded up without injury to any one, these metalls not spoileing or decaying in the hands of the possessor. This partage of things, in an inequality of private possessions, men have made practicable out of the bounds of Societie, and without compact, only by putting a value on gold and silver and tacitly agreeing in the use of Money. For in Governments the Laws regulate the right of property, and the possession of land is determined by positive constitutions.

51. And thus, I think, it is very easie to conceive without any difficulty, *how Labour could at first begin a title of Property* in the common things of Nature, and how the spending it upon our uses bounded it. So that there could then be no reason of quarrelling about Title, nor any doubt about the largeness of Possession it gave. Right and

conveniency went together; for as a Man had a Right to all he could imploy his Labour upon, so he had no temptation to labour for more than he could make use of. This left no room for Controversie about the Title, nor for Incroachment on the Right of others; what Portion a Man carved to himself, was easily seen; and it was useless as well as dishonest to carve himself too much, or take more than he needed.

# ARISTOTLE
## From the *Politics*

### BOOK I, III, 15–20

So when currency had been now invented as an outcome of the necessary interchange of goods, there came into existence the other form of wealth-getting, trade, which at first no doubt went on in a simple form, but later became more highly organized as experience discovered the sources and methods of exchange that would cause most profit. Hence arises the idea that the art of wealth-getting deals specially with money, and that its function is to be able to discern from what source a large supply can be procured, as this art is supposed to be creative of wealth and riches; indeed wealth is often assumed to consist of a quantity of money, because money is the thing with which business and trade are employed. But at other times, on the contrary, it is thought that money is nonsense, and entirely a convention but by nature nothing, because when those who use it have changed the currency it is worth nothing, and because it is of no use for any of the necessary needs of life and a man well supplied with money may often be destitute of the bare necessities of subsistence, yet it is absurd that wealth should be of such a kind that a man may be well supplied with it and yet die of hunger, like the famous Midas in the story, when owing to the insatiable covetousness of his prayer all the viands served up to him turned into gold. Hence people seek for a different definition of riches and the art of getting wealth, and rightly; for natural wealth-getting and natural riches are different; natural wealth-getting belongs to household management, whereas the other kind belongs to trade, producing wealth not indiscriminately but by the method of exchanging goods. It is this art of wealth-getting that is thought to be concerned with money, for money is the first element and limit of commerce. And these riches, that are derived from this art of wealth-getting, are truly unlimited; for just as the art of medicine is without limit in respect of health, and each of the arts is without limit in respect of its end (for they desire to produce that in the highest degree possible), whereas they are not without limit as regards the means to their end (for with all of them the end is a limit to the means), so also this wealth-getting has no limit in respect of its end, and its end is riches and the acquisition of goods in the commercial sense. But the household branch of wealth-getting has a limit, inasmuch as the acquisition of money is not the function of household management. Hence from this point of view it appears necessary that there should be a limit to all riches, yet in actual fact we observe that the opposite takes place; for all men engaged in wealth-getting try to increase their money to an unlimited amount. The reason of this is the close affinity of the two branches of the art of business. Their common ground is that the thing that each makes use of is the same; they use the same property, although not in the same way – the one has another end in view, the aim of the other is the increase of the property. Consequently some people suppose that it is the function of household management to increase property, and they are continually under the idea that it is their duty to be either safeguarding their substance in money or increasing it to an unlimited amount. The cause of this stage of mind is that their interests are set upon life but not upon the good life; as therefore the desire for life is unlimited, they also desire without limit the means productive of life. And even those who fix their aim on the good life seek the good life as measured by bodily enjoyments, so that inasmuch as this also seems to be found in the possession of property, all their energies are occupied in the business of getting wealth; and owing to this the second kind of the art of wealth-getting has arisen. For as their enjoyment is in excess, they try to discover the art that is productive of enjoyable excess; and if they cannot procure it by the art of wealth-getting, they try to do so by some other means, employing each of the faculties in an unnatural way. For it is not the function of courage to produce wealth, but to inspire daring; nor is it the function of the military art nor of the medical art, but it belongs to the former to bring victory and to the latter to cause health. Yet these people make all these faculties means for the business of providing wealth, in the belief that wealth is the end and that everything must conspire to the end.

## BOOK II, I, 1–18 and II, 1–10

I. And since we take for our special consideration the study of the form of political community that is the best of all the forms for a people able to pursue the most ideal mode of life, we must also examine the other constitutions actually employed by certain of the states said to be well governed, as well as any others propounded by certain thinkers and reputed to be of merit, in order that we may discern what there is in them that is right and expedient, and also in order that it may not be thought that to seek for something different from them springs entirely from a desire to display ingenuity, but that we may be thought to enter upon this inquiry because these forms of constitution that already exist are not satisfactory.

We must first adopt as a starting-point that which is the natural point of departure for this inquiry. There are three possible systems of property: either all the citizens must own everything in common, or they must own nothing in common, or some things must be common property and others not. To have nothing in common is clearly impossible; for the state is essentially a form of community, and it must at any rate have a common locality: a single city occupies a single site, and the single city belongs to its citizens in common. But is it better for a city that is to be well ordered to have community in everything which can possibly be made common property, or is it better to have some things in common and others not? For example, it is possible for the citizens to have children, wives and possessions in common with each other, as in Plato's *Republic*, in which Socrates says that there must be community of children, women and possessions. Well then, which is preferable, the system that now obtains, or one conforming with the regulation described in *The Republic*?

Now for all the citizens to have their wives in common involves a variety of difficulties; in particular, (1) the object which Socrates advances as the reason why this enactment should be made clearly does not follow from his arguments; also (2) as a means to the end which he asserts should be the fundamental object of the city, the scheme as actually set forth in the dialogue is not practicable; yet (3) how it is to be further worked out has been nowhere definitely stated. I refer to the ideal of the fullest possible unity of the entire state, which Socrates takes as his fundamental principle.

Yet it is clear that if the process of unification advances beyond a certain point, the city will not be a city at all; for a state essentially consists of a multitude of persons, and if its unification is carried beyond a certain point, city will be reduced to family and family to individual, for we should pronounce the family to be a more complete unity than the city, and the single person than the family; so that even if any lawgiver were able to unify the state, he must not do so, for he will destroy it in the process. And not only does a city consist of a multitude of human beings, it consists of human beings differing in kind. A collection of persons all alike does not constitute a state. For a city is not the same thing as a league; a league is of value by its quantity, even though it is all the same in kind (since the essential object of the league is military strength), just as a weight would be worth more if it weighed more, whereas components which are to make up a unity must differ in kind (and it is by this characteristic that a city will also surpass a tribe of which the population is not scattered among villages but organized like the Arcadians). Hence reciprocal equality is the preservative of states, as has been said before in *Ethics*. For even among the free and equal this principle must necessarily obtain, since all cannot govern at once: they must hold office for a year at a time or by some other arrangement or period; and in this manner it does actually come about that all govern, just as all shoemakers would be also carpenters if the shoemakers and the carpenters kept on changing trades instead of the same persons being shoemakers and carpenters always. But since such permanence of function is better for the political community also, it is clear that it is better for the same persons to govern always, if possible; and among peoples where it is impossible because all the citizens are equal in their nature, yet at the same time it is only just, whether governing is a good thing or a bad, that all should partake in it, then for equals thus to submit to authority in turn imitates their being originally dissimilar; for some govern and others are governed by turn, as though becoming other persons; and also when they hold office in the same way different persons hold different offices. It is clear then from these considerations that it is not an outcome of nature for the state to be a unity in the manner in which certain persons say that it is, and that what has been said to be the greatest good in states really destroys states; yet surely a thing's particular good acts as its preservative. – Another line of consideration also shows that to seek to unify the state excessively is not beneficial. In point of self-sufficiency the individual is surpassed by the family and the family by the state, and in principle a state is fully realized only when it comes to pass that the community of numbers is self-sufficing; if therefore the more self-sufficing a community is, the more desirable is its condition, then a less degree of unity is more desirable than a greater.

Again, even granting that it is best for the community to be as complete a unity as possible, complete unity does not seem to be proved by the formula 'if all the citizens say "Mine" and "Not mine" at the same time,' which Socrates thinks to be a sign of the city's being completely one. 'All' is an ambiguous term. If it means 'each severally,' very likely this would more fully realize the state of things which Socrates wishes to produce (for in that case every citizen will call the same boy his son and also the same woman his wife, and will speak in the same way of property and indeed of everything that falls to his lot); but *ex hypothesi* the citizens, having community of women and children, will not call them 'theirs' in this sense, but will mean theirs collectively and not severally, and similarly they will call property 'theirs' meaning the property of them all, not of each of them severally. We see then that the phrase 'all say' is equivocal (in fact the words 'all,' 'both,' 'odd,' 'even,' owing to their ambiguity, occasion argumentative quibbling even in philosophical discussions); hence really for 'all' to say the same thing is in one sense admirable, although impracticable, but in another sense is not at all a sign of concord. And furthermore, the proposal has another disadvantage. Property that is common to the greatest number of owners receives the least attention; men care most for their private possessions, and for what they own in common less, or only so far as it falls to their own individual share; for in addition to the other reasons, they think less of it on the ground that someone else is thinking about it, just as in household service a large number of domestics sometimes give worse attendance than a smaller number. And it results in each citizen's having a thousand sons, and these do not belong to them as individuals but any child is equally the son of anyone, so that all alike will regard them with indifference.

Again, each speaks of one of his fellow-citizens who is prospering or getting on badly as 'my son' only in the sense of the fractional part which he forms of the whole number, meaning 'mine or so-and-so's,' indicating by 'so-and-so' each of the thousand citizens or whatever the number be of which the state consists, and even this dubiously, for it is uncertain who has chanced to have had a son born to him and when born safely reared. Yet which is the better way to use the word 'mine' – this way, each of two thousand or ten thousand people applying it to the same thing, or rather the way in which they say 'mine' in the actual states now? for the same person is called 'my son' by one man and 'my brother' by another, and another calls him 'nephew,' or by some other relationship, whether of blood or by affinity and marriage, the speaker's own in the first place, or that of his relations; and in addition someone else calls him 'fellow-clansman' or 'fellow-tribesman.' For it is better for a boy to be one's own private nephew than one's son in the way described. Moreover it would also be impossible to avoid men's supposing certain persons to be their real brothers and sons and fathers and mothers; for they would be bound to form their belief about each other by the resemblances which occur between children and parents. This indeed is said by some of those who write of travels round the world actually to occur; they say that some of the people of Upper Libya have their wives in common, yet the children born are divided among them according to their personal resemblances. And there are some females both of the human race and of the other animals, for instance horses and cattle, who have a strong natural tendency to produce offspring resembling the male parents, as was the case with the mare at Pharsalus named Honest Lady.

Moreover it is not easy for those who institute this communism to guard against such objectionable occurrences as outrage, involuntary and in some cases voluntary homicide, fights, abusive language; all of which are violations of piety when committed against fathers, mothers and near relatives as if they were not relatives; but these are bound to occur more frequently when people do not know their relations than when they do, and also, when they do occur, if the offenders know their relationship it is possible for them to have the customary expiations performed, but for those who do not no expiation is possible. Also it is curious that a theorist who makes the sons common property only debars lovers from intercourse and does not prohibit love, nor the other familiarities, which between father and son or brother and brother are most unseemly, since even the fact of love between them is unseemly. And it is also strange that he deprives them of intercourse for no other reason except because the pleasure is too violent; and that he thinks it makes no difference that the parties are in the one case father or son and in the other case brothers of one another. And it seems more serviceable for the Farmers to have this community of wives and sons than the Guardians; for there will be less friendship among them if their children and women are in common, and unfriendliness in the subject classes is a good thing with a view to their being submissive to authority and not making revolution. But speaking generally such a law is bound to bring about the opposite state of things to that which rightly enacted laws ought properly to cause, and because of which Socrates thinks it necessary to make these regulations about the children and women. For we think that friendship is the greatest of blessings for the state, since it is the best safeguard against revolution, and the unity of the state, which Socrates praises most highly, both appears to be and is said by him to be the effect of friendship, just as we know that Aristophanes in the discourses on love describes how the lovers owing to their extreme affection desire to grow together and both become one instead of being two. In such a union both personalities, or at least one, would be bound to be obliterated; and in the state friendship would inevitably become diluted in consequence of such association, and the expressions 'my father' and 'my son' would quite go out. For just as putting a little sugar into a quantity of water makes the mixture imperceptible, so it also must come about that the mutual relationship based on these names must become imperceptible, since in the republic described by Plato there will be the least possible necessity for people to care for one another as father for sons or as son for father or as brother for brother. For there are two motives that most cause men to care for things and be fond of them, the sense of ownership and the sense of preciousness; and neither motive can be present with the citizens of a state so constituted. Again, as to the transference of some of the children at birth from the Farmers and Artisans to the Guardians and of others from the Guardians to the Farmers and Artisans, there is much confusion as to how it is to be done; and the parents who give the children and the officials who transfer them are bound to know which they give to whom. And again, the things spoken of above are bound to occur even more with these transferred children, such as outrage, love-making and murder; for the children of the Guardians transferred to the other citizens will no longer speak of the Guardians as brothers and children and fathers and mothers, nor yet will those living among the Guardians so speak of the other classes, so as to be careful not to commit any such offence because of their relationship.

Such therefore may be our decision as to community of children and women.

II. In connexion with this we have to consider the due regulation of property in a community that is to have the best political institutions: should property be owned in common or privately? This question might indeed be considered separately from the system laid down by law with regard to the children and the women: I mean, even if there be separate families as is now the case with all nations, is it better for both the ownership and the employment of property to be in common..., for example, should the farms be separate property but the farm-produce be brought into the common stock for consumption (as is the practice with some non-Greek races); or on the contrary should the land be common and farmed in common, but the produce be divided for private use (and this form of communism also is said to prevail among some of the barbarians); or should both farms and produce be common property? Now if the tillers of the soil be of a different class[1] it would work differently and be easier, but if the citizens do the work for themselves, the regulations for the common ownership of property would give more causes for discontent; for if both in the enjoyment of the produce and in the work of production they prove not equal but unequal, complaints are bound to arise between those who enjoy or take much but work little and those who take less but work more. And in general to live together and share all our human affairs is difficult, and especially to share such things as these. And this is shown in the partnerships of fellow-travellers, for it may be said that most of them quarrel because they come into collision with one another as a result of ordinary matters and trifles; and also we come into collision most with those of our servants whom we employ most often for ordinary attendance. Community of property therefore involves these and other similar difficulties; and the present system, if further improved by good morals and by the regulation of correct legislation, would be greatly superior. For it will possess the merit of both systems, by which I mean the advantage of property being common and the advantage of its being private. For property ought to be common in a sense but private speaking generally. For the superintendence of properties being divided among the owners will not cause these mutual complaints, and will improve the more because each will apply himself to it as to private business of his own; while on the other hand virtue will result in making 'friends' goods common goods,' as the proverb goes, for the purpose of use. Such a system exists even now in outline in some states, so it is not deemed impracticable, and especially in the ones that are well-administered parts of it are realized already and parts might be realized; for individuals while owning their property privately put their own possessions at the service of their friends and make use of their friends' possessions as common property; for instance in Sparta people use one another's slaves as virtually their own, as well as horses and hounds, and also use the produce in the fields throughout the country if they need provisions on a journey. It is clear therefore that it is better for possessions to be privately owned, but to make them common property in use; and to train the citizens to this is the special task of the legislator. And moreover to feel that a thing is one's private property makes an inexpressibly great difference in one's pleasure; for the universal feeling of love for oneself is surely not purposeless, but a natural instinct. Selfishness on the other hand is justly blamed; but this is not to love oneself but to love

120  [1] As in Plato's *Republic*, or like the Helots at Sparta.

oneself more than one ought, just as covetousness means loving money to excess – since some love of self, money and so on is practically universal. Moreover, to bestow favours and assistance on friends or visitors or comrades is a great pleasure, and a condition of this is the private ownership of property. These advantages therefore do not come to those who carry the unification of the state too far; and in addition to this they manifestly do away with the practice of two virtues, temperance in relation to women (for it is a noble deed to refrain from one through temperance when she belongs to another) and liberality in relation to possessions (for one will not be able to show one's liberality nor perform a single liberal action, since the active exercise of liberality takes place in the use of possessions).

Such legislation therefore has an attractive appearance, and might be thought to be humane; for he who is told about it welcomes it with gladness, thinking that it will result in a marvellous friendliness of everybody towards everybody, especially when somebody denounces the evils at present existing in states as due to the fact that wealth is not owned in common – I mean lawsuits between citizens about breach of contract, and trials for perjury, and the flattery of the rich. But the real cause of all these evils is not the absence of communism, but wickedness, since we see far more quarrels occurring among those who own or use property in common than among those who have their estates separate; but we notice that those who quarrel as a result of their partnerships are few when compared with the total number of private owners. And again it is just to state not only all the evils that men will lose by adopting communism, but also all the good things; and life in such circumstances is seen to be utterly impossible.

The cause of Socrates' error must be deemed to be that his fundamental assumption was incorrect. It is certain that in a way both the household and the state should be a unit, but they should not be so in every way. For in one way the state as its unification proceeds will cease to be a state, and in another way, though it continues a state, yet by coming near to ceasing to be one it will be a worse state, just as if one turned a harmony into unison or a rhythm into a single foot. The proper thing is for the state, while being a multitude, to be made a partnership and a unity by means of education, as has been said before; and it is strange that the very philosopher who intends to introduce a system of education and thinks that this will make the city morally good should fancy that he can regulate society by such measures as have been mentioned instead of by manners and culture and laws.

# TIMOTHY O'HAGAN

## Rousseau and Wollstonecraft on sexual equality

**5**

Rousseau's reputation as a man of paradoxes is not wholly undeserved, and in his dealings with women, both in his life and in his writings, he was at his most paradoxical. According to the *Discourse on Inequality* (1755), all significant differences, and in particular all significant inequalities, between human beings are the result of a historically specific process of socialisation, in which people adapt to a combination of fortuitous external circumstances. None are based on physiological differences between individuals or sets of individuals. Yet in *Emile*, Book V (1762), entitled 'Sophie, ou de la femme', Rousseau advocates radically different forms of education for Sophie and for Emile, on the traditional grounds that the two sexes essentially perform contrasting functions, and that the woman's function is 'entirely dependent on maternity', a physical dependence which would be transformed, in the ideal social order, into a moral duty.

In her *Vindication of the Rights of Woman* (1792), pioneering feminist Mary Wollstonecraft undertakes a detailed critique of *Emile*, Book V, analysing much of it page by page, often sentence by sentence. She strips away the surface rhetoric of complementary spheres for the two sexes and lays bare the inner core of Rousseau's anti-feminism, which excludes women from public life and subjects them to a wholly domestic role.

### Jean-Jacques Rousseau (1722–78)

Rousseau was born in Calvinist Geneva, his father a watchmaker, later a dancing-master, and his mother the daughter of a clergyman. She died days after his birth, and he was raised by an aunt and his cultivated, feckless father, who abandoned him when ten years old, entrusting him to a wealthy uncle, who had him tutored by a pastor and a delightful governess, whose spankings he shamefully enjoyed. After three miserable years of apprenticeship to an engraver, he found himself locked out of the city after curfew. He spent the rest of his life as an outsider, dependent on the fickle patronage of the mighty. He was inveigled, with little resistance, into the Catholic Church by the religious but erotic Mme de Warens, with whom he formed his first and

123

deepest romantic attachment. Thereafter he worked as tutor, research assistant, diplomatic attaché, composer, music copier, fellow traveller of the *Encyclopédistes*, with whom he later quarrelled bitterly. After his readmission into the Calvinist Church in 1754, religion became increasingly important in his work, but his was an anti-authoritarian creed, anathema to established believers and unbelievers alike.

With little formal schooling, Rousseau published some of the most influential books of the century, including the *Social Contract* (see chapter 8) and the educational treatise *Emile*, which, with its denial of original sin, incurred the wrath of the French hierarchy and a warrant for his arrest. Rousseau fled to Switzerland, thence to England. Returning from exile, he lived out his last eleven years in France, again as the protégé of noble patrons, his literary output undiminished. Throughout his life Rousseau was wracked by ill health, particularly by an agonising retention of the urine. His common-law wife, the illiterate Thérèse Levasseur, bore him five children, all of whom he consigned to the Foundlings Home.

The first group of extracts reproduced below is from the *Discourse on the Origin of Inequality among Men* (known as the *Second Discourse*) (1755) which Rousseau wrote in response to the prize essay question set by the Academy of Dijon: 'What is the source of inequality among men and is it authorised by natural law?'. The *Discourse* failed to win the prize, but in it Rousseau developed his fundamental ideas about society and the individual, progress and decadence, time and history. The second group is from the *Emile* (1762) which applies the idea of the corrupting effect of society to the individual. Rousseau outlines an elaborate educational programme, initially negative, to keep at bay the influences of a badly ordered society, and to permit an autonomous individual to flourish.

The central thesis of the *Second Discourse* is that social forms are not founded in nature. The family is the test case for this radical thesis. If Rousseau can 'denature' the family, the most 'natural' of all social forms, he should have little difficulty with other 'higher' forms. John Locke had argued that the institutions of marriage and the family are natural because they are rooted in needs, in that human children need long-term care from their parents, and their mother needs long-term protection by the father of her children. Rousseau responds with his own account of how things would have been in the state of nature. There would have been no family because (1) speedily repeated pregnancy is unlikely in the absence of institutionalized marriage, (2) before the 'abuse' of reproductive faculties in society, women could conceive and bear children later in life, (3) before children were 'softened' in society, they were able to 'shift for themselves' at a younger age. Rousseau concludes that in the state of nature a mother could look after a child adequately on her own, and would need to devote less time to that task. There would therefore be no *natural* function for the father to provide continuing support for mother or child. Before the biological sex drive has been socialised, while it has not yet become love, the man does not connect the sexual act with procreation.

Where memory is short and there is no social context within which one can form preferences, another partner will, for both sexes, be as good as the last for purely animal satisfaction. For women, Rousseau's conclusion is particularly liberating. Outside society both continuing passion and need are absent:

if, in the state of Nature, the woman no longer feels the passion of love after the conception of the child, then the obstacle to her Society with the man thereby becomes much greater still, since she then no longer needs either the man who impregnated her or any other. (Below, p. 137)

As he approaches the end of Part 1 of the *Second Discourse*, Rousseau momentarily abandons the chronological narrative to 'distinguish between the moral and the Physical in the feeling of love' (p. 38). As he draws up the balance sheet, the physical elements shrink almost to vanishing point. In the pure state of nature complete indifference reigns: 'The Physical is that general desire which inclines one sex to unite with the other. The moral is that which determines this desire and fixes it exclusively on a single object ...' (p. 38). The male lacks the resources of discrimination and memory with which to make enduring comparisons between women, so that any woman is equally good for him. Rousseau's picture of the pure state of nature indicates that exactly the same argument applies to the female. Nothing suggests any asymmetry between the sexes. The passage to civil society, from the physical to the moral, is the passage to comparisons and preferences, 'founded on certain notions of merit and beauty'. In this context, for the first time, Rousseau's sexism emerges. 'The moral element of love', he says, is an 'artificial feeling, born of the usage of society, and extolled with much skill and care by women in order to establish their empire and to make dominant the sex that ought to obey' (pp. 38–9). The passage to society is also marked by the development of imagination, which gives rise to jealousy, aggression and disputes between suitors. None of the latter are based in nature, since there is a rough balance of numbers between the sexes, and the human female, unlike other mammals, is permanently in season. The outcome of socialising love in a bad social order is catastrophic, equivalent on the personal plane to the Hobbesian state of war on the political. Only with society does sexual passion become 'an ardent impetuous one ... a terrible passion which braves all dangers, overcomes all obstacles, and which, in its fury, seems fitted to destroy the human Race it is destined to preserve' (p. 38).

Sexuality makes its next appearance in the *Second Discourse* at the stage of the Youth of the World, after men and women have moved into their first permanent homes, the *cabanes*. The negative and positive effects of the first step to society are evenly balanced. On the one side come 'quarrels and combats' between families seeking the best places of residence, on the other come 'the first developments of the heart ... the habit of living together gave rise to the sweetest sentiments known to men: conjugal love and paternal love' (p. 46). It is only now, for the first time, that *difference* between the sexes emerges. Its development is

125

slow, it is contingent on the circumstances of a changed lifestyle, and is not rooted in nature:

it was then that the first difference was *established* in the way of life of the two Sexes, which until this time had had but one. Women became more sedentary and *grew accustomed* to tend the Hut and the Children, while the man went off to seek their common subsistence. (p. 46, my italics)

The passage from the physical to the moral element of sexuality, anticipated at the end of Part I, is now set in its historical context. 'Everything begins to change its appearance' (p. 47). The transition from a nomadic to settled way of life produces 'some link (liaison) between families', and that 'link' finds sexual expression:

Young people of different sexes live in neighbouring Huts; the passing intercourse demanded by Nature soon leads to another kind no less sweet and through mutual frequentation (p. 47).

Rousseau proceeds to paint in the detail of the earlier sketch of the arrival of discrimination:

People grow accustomed to consider different objects and to make comparisons; imperceptibly they acquire ideas of merit and beauty which produce sentiments of preference.

The outcome is in the balance. *Amour propre* has arrived, and one now begins to find oneself in the eyes of others. But that transition to social interaction can take a healthy or an unhealthy turn. One becomes personally dependent on others in relationships which may become either one-way obsession or mutual love. The point at which *amour propre* develops is the point at which sexuality becomes socialised. It is the point where people come to fix, to institutionalise, by convention the place of singing and dancing, the place of sexual encounter. Only in that public, social forum could *amour propre* flower: 'Each one began to look at the others and to want to be looked at himself, and public esteem had a value' (below, p. 138). That is the story of the origin of sexuality in the *Second Discourse*. The normative implication of the story is that social inequality between the two sexes is not grounded in nature. The justification for it must be found in what Rousseau calls in the *Social Contract* (I.8) that 'remarkable change in man' (and presumably in woman) which is brought about by socialisation.

Rousseau returns to the theme of the socialisation of sexuality in *Emile*, Book IV. *Amour propre* develops in the individual at adolescence. However long postponed, adolescence leads to sexuality, and it is in encountering someone of the opposite sex that Emile makes the final step to the social world:

As soon as man has need of a companion, he is no longer an isolated being. His heart is no longer alone. All his relations with his species, all the affections of his soul are born with this one. (Below, p. 138)

Rousseau assigns a key role to love and sexuality in the socialisation of the individual, but he is profoundly ambivalent in his attitudes towards them. This mirrors his underlying ambivalence about the role of *amour propre* in all our interactions. But in treating sexuality, Rousseau swings with more than usual violence between optimism and pessimism. On balance his verdict is finally pessimistic about the possibility of an egalitarian, non-exploitative outcome of the battle of the sexes. He professes complete ignorance of the mechanism which connects the advent of sexuality to that of morality. Sexuality spans nature and culture, our physical being and our moral being. Sexual needs receive physical satisfaction, but differ from the physical needs of hunger and thirst. When the latter are not satisfied, we die, whereas celibates survive, often prosper. Thus the three sources of needs which Rousseau distinguishes are survival, sensuality and opinion ('Fragments politiques', pp. 53–4), and he assigns 'the union of the sexes' to the second. At the same time, our sexuality, as soon as it advances from the ideal-typical abstraction of chance encounter in 'the forest', engages us in the play of *amour propre*, in which we project and find our identities by interacting with others. In most of our dealings, this play involves domination and subordination. One of Rousseau's fundamental goals is to reconstruct the conditions of our lives so that, at least in our political and economic interactions, they might be transformed into a play of freedom, equality and reciprocity. Yet our sexual relations remain brutally resistant to that transformation.

Why is that? Rousseau does not tell us, for he never theorised an answer, but he leaves us clues. Intense sexual relations are so unstable just because they span the two worlds which cannot peacefully coexist, the natural and the social. That is why love is 'accompanied by a constant disquiet caused by jealousy or by privation'. According to Julie, the heroine of Rousseau's romantic novel, *Julie, ou la nouvelle Héloïse*, 'there is no passion which produces such strong illusions in us as love'. For Julie, sexual passion is the enemy of order and reason:

Disordered affections corrupt [our] judgment as well as [our] will ... Everything that depends on the senses and is not necessary to life alters its nature as soon as it becomes a habit, it ceases to be a pleasure as soon as it becomes a need (*Nouvelle Héloïse*, V, 2, p. 541).

In sexual passion, physical drives are mediated through the imagination. It is the imagination which transforms love into jealousy, and, in the feelings of her lover, sets up 'inexplicable contradictions', so that he becomes 'at once submissive and bold, impetuous and shy'.

Rousseau opens *Emile*, Book V on a note of high rhetoric, heralding the final passage from childhood to the adult world, from nature to society.

We have reached the last act of the play of youth, but we are not yet at its dénouement. It is not good that man should be alone. Emile is a man; we have promised him a companion, we must give her to him. (*Emile*, V, p. 357)

The conclusion of this sentence marks a clear departure from the egalitarianism of the *Second Discourse*. The first four books of the Emile have addressed the education of a boy, who has been guarded against premature contact with members of the opposite sex. Now that Sophie makes her belated appearance, it is not in her own right, but as 'a companion' to be 'given' to Emile, and she retains this subordinate role throughout the dialectic of Book V. But the sexual inegalitarianism is complex. The theme of the interplay of identity and difference is no less dominant here than it is in the *Second Discourse*, and here as before, it is identity that takes first place:

In everything not connected with sex, woman is man. She has the same organs, the same needs, the same faculties. The machine is constructed in the same way; its parts are the same; the one functions as does the other; the form is similar; and in whatever respect one considers them, the difference between them is only one of more or less. (*Emile*, V, p. 357)

But now comes the crucial change: 'In everything connected with sex, woman and man are in every respect related and in every respect different.' There had been no hint of this move in the *Second Discourse*. There, any differences that might be 'connected with sex' were minimal. In the *Emile*, in contrast, Rousseau locates three differences within and around the sex act.

At the purely physiological level, in order for the sex act to be consummated, Rousseau holds, the two parties must have different drives. The man must (a) be 'active and strong', and (b) both 'want and be able' to perform. The woman must (c) 'put up little resistance', and (d) be 'passive and weak'. But a moment's reflection shows that this distribution of drives is odd. While (a), (b) and (c) can be said to be naturally, biologically required for consummation, which in turn is required by the 'biological imperative' to reproduce the species, (d) is rather different. Rousseau might have said that the imperative would be satisfied even if the woman were 'passive and weak' in sexual intercourse, so long as the man were not. But he goes further. He suggests, without quite saying it, that women are required by the imperative to be 'passive and weak', and that suggestion is evidently false. In making that suggestion, in slipping from (c) 'put up little resistance' to (d) 'be passive and weak', Rousseau has deprived women of activity and power in the sex act, and thereby assigned to them a certain 'moral' duty which extends beyond it. He then proceeds:

Once this principle is established, it follows that the woman is created to please the man; if the man has to please her in his turn, it is by a less direct necessity, his merit lies in his power, and he pleases by the very fact that he is strong. This is not the law of love, I agree, but it is the law of nature, prior to love itself. (Below, p. 140)

There seems no reason to accept the speculative biology of this passage. It is certainly not true of other species, in which the males engage in elaborate courtship behaviour apparently to please the females. Even if Rousseau were right, it is still not clear how the natural differences are to 'influence' the moral ones. So his next step, which has a particularly sinister resonance, is hardly supported by the run of the argument: 'If the woman is created to please and to be subjugated, she must make herself agreeable to the man in stead of provoking him.' Yet this is not the final step in the dialectic of sexuality through nature to society.

Finally Rousseau turns the tables on the relation of strength and weakness, domination and subjugation. 'Here then is the third consequence of the constitution of the sexes', he says, it is

that the stronger is always master in appearance, but in fact is dependent on the weaker. This is due not to a frivolous practice of gallantry or to the proud generosity of a protector, but to an invariable law of nature which gives women more ability to excite desires than men to satisfy them. This causes the latter, whether he likes it or not, to depend on the former's wish and constrains him to seek to please her in turn, *so that she will consent to let him be the stronger.* (Below, p. 142, italics added)

Mary Wollstonecraft quotes this passage and adds a brief footnote of her own to the last (italicised) words: 'Perfect nonsense!' (p. 176). Every other point she makes against *Emile*, Book V is unanswerable. But this passage is defensible as an insight into the dynamics of our sexual dealings. At the heart of the play of love, the natural difference between men and women, their relative strength and weakness, itself becomes a token in the game. It gains value only if it is freely granted, otherwise it constitutes rape, which is 'not only the most brutal of all acts, but the one most contrary to its end …' (p. 359). How can this sophisticated understanding of sexual love, as a perilous play of physiological and socially negotiated tokens, coexist with the crudely inegalitarian picture of the social relations between men and women? I shall return to that question at the end. Even on this page of the *Emile* Rousseau proceeds in the remainder of the paragraph to ruin the point he has just made. Mary Wollstonecraft mercilessly quotes his next words:

Then what is sweetest for man in his victory is the doubt whether it is weakness which yields to strength or the will which surrenders. And the woman's usual ruse is always to leave this doubt between her and him. In this the spirit of women corresponds perfectly to their constitution. Far from blushing at their weakness, they make it their glory. Their tender muscles are without resistance. They pretend to be unable to lift the lightest burdens. They would be ashamed to be strong. Why is that? It is not only to appear delicate; it is due to a shrewder precaution. They prepare in advance excuses and the right to be weak in case of need. (Below, p. 142)

Rousseau claims that women's essential function is child-bearing, and he argues, not unreasonably, that, given a 50 per cent infant mortality rate, each woman will need to produce an average of four children in order to sustain the population. This in itself would not justify the unequal treatment of women in society. The passage to that inegalitarianism runs through the family:

Doubtless it is not permitted to anyone to violate his faith, and every unfaithful husband who deprives his wife of the only reward of the austere duties of her sex is an unjust and barbarous man. But the unfaithful woman does more; she dissolves the family and breaks all the bonds of nature. (Below, p. 143)

Given his own insights in the *Second Discourse*, Rousseau's arguments here are confused. In so far as the family is a creation of society, not of nature, then even if the woman, by committing adultery, 'dissolves the family', she does not thereby 'break all the bonds of nature', only the bonds of society, albeit the fundamental ones. Rousseau is right to hold that adultery introduces distrust and contempt, makes the family into 'a society of secret enemies', but he holds that the woman is guiltier than the man in this respect because of the possible effects of her betrayal:

If there is a frightful condition in the world it is that of an unhappy father who, lacking confidence in his wife, does not dare to yield to the sweetest sentiments of his heart, who wonders, when embracing his child, whether he is embracing another's, the token of his dishonour, the plunderer of his own children's property. (Below, p. 143)

All this rings true, but true of a highly developed society, governed by a legal code and a system of property mediated through the family.

In what follows Rousseau departs further from the model of the *Second Discourse* in distributing natural faculties between the sexes. The distribution is not equal, but 'taken together, they balance out' (p. 363). The distribution owes something to the tradition, and something to Rousseau's own idiosyncratic views about psychology: to men reason, to women shame; to men immoderate passions, to women infinite desires. In stark contrast to the *Second Discourse*, Rousseau derives women's alleged timidity from their need to be protected during pregnancy. Most importantly, Rousseau holds that women in society should be absolutely dependent on the opinion of others, whereas men should form that opinion. And that dependence is natural: 'By the very law of nature women are at the mercy of men's judgments' (below, p. 00). Why should that be? Rousseau links women's dependence to his view of adultery: 'It is important ... not only that a woman be faithful, but that she be judged to be faithful by her husband, by those near her, by everyone' (below, p. 00). Beyond that, no argument is given for women's incapacity to form autonomous moral codes.

Rousseau paints a grotesque picture of the passivity of women. One must educate girls into women by teaching them to subordinate themselves to men:

To please them, to be useful to them, to make themselves loved and honored by them, to raise them when young, to look after them when grown, to advise them, to console them, to make their lives agreeable and sweet: those are women's duties in every age, and they must be taught them from childhood on. (Below, p. 147)

From there Rousseau proceeds to advocate a return to the ways of ancient Sparta, in which women lived public lives before marriage, but thereafter were shut up in their houses, 'as value and reason prescribe' (p. 366).

How then are we to explain the transition from the *Second Discourse* to *Emile*, Book V? A general response would be that Rousseau is simply using the schema of transition from nature to society, and applying it to relations between the sexes. In every such transition there must be a radical change in which the individual becomes a fraction of the whole, a numerator of the social denominator. But in politics that transformation is seen as *restoring* a certain autonomy which had been lost in a despotic social order. It replaces personal dependence by dependence on the whole. That dependence in turn is legitimate only in a context of radical equality between citizens. But in relations between men and women no such *restoration* takes place. The reason is that in the personal relationship between a man and a woman the move from personal to universal dependence cannot be total. And in the resulting mix between personal and universal dependence, the allocation of dependence between the two partners is asymmetrical. Both are (personally) dependent on the love and esteem of the other partner. Each must please the other, but the woman must please and obey, whereas the man must please and command. Each is also (universally) dependent on public opinion, but each is differently related to that public opinion. Women earn public approval entirely for their private conduct, for their reputation for fidelity to their husbands, whereas men compete for civic glory. At the same time, women are the passive recipients of public opinion, whereas men help shape it. So men engage in the play of autonomous citizens, seeking and offering recognition in the public forum. In that forum women are only seekers. If equality is restored at the most intimate moment of their dealings, in the sexual play of strength and 'permitted strength', that equality is kept strictly confined, to the seraglio. One might doubt whether equality could continue to flourish there, within a public sexual order which is little short of despotism.

### Mary Wollstonecraft (1759–97)

Mary Wollstonecraft was born in Epping Forest near London, the eldest of six children. Her father was a small farmer, unsuccessful, impoverished, ill-tempered and tyrannical towards his wife and family, whose life was spent moving round England, from one farm to another. Like Rousseau, Wollstonecraft received virtually no formal education. Leaving home in 1778, she took different unsatisfactory jobs to support herself and her family. Moving in 1783 to the liberal, nonconformist community of Newington Green, she set up a school and teacher-training institute. It failed, but her literary career took off. After working as a governess in Dublin, Wollstonecraft returned to London, and had a novel published. She was soon established as an independent, self-supporting writer, contributing to the dissenting press and moving in the cosmopolitan, progressive political circles influenced by William Godwin.

True to the spirit of the Enlightenment, Wollstonecraft published both *A Vindication of the Rights of Men*, defending the French Revolution against Burke's attack, and *A Vindication of the Rights of Woman*. The establishment reacted hysterically to her combination of republicanism and feminism: a 'hyena in petticoats', in Hugh Walpole's words. Wollstonecraft spent 1792–95, at the height of the Revolution, in Paris, engaged publicly in republican politics, and personally with her worthless lover George Imlay. By him she bore a daughter, and travelled to Scandinavia as his business representative. She returned to London, where he finally abandoned her. After an unsuccessful suicide attempt, she spent her last years, happily, with William Godwin. She died of complications following the birth of their daughter Mary, who would later write *Frankenstein* and marry Shelley.

The extracts reproduced below are taken from *A Vindication of the Rights of Woman*, Mary Wollstonecraft's feminist manifesto, written at speed for a publisher's deadline in 1792. In it she elaborates three themes. First, she claims that women should have the same rights as men on the grounds that they are identical to men in all relevant respects, in particular their possession of reason. Second, she addresses the inadequacies of contemporary women's education which inculcates weakness, immorality, triviality and dependence, and advocates a radically different approach, designed to produce women who will be strong, autonomous, capable of dealing with men as equals, raising families and at the same time engaging in public life. Third, she subjects previous writers, particularly Rousseau, to sustained and detailed criticism, laying bare their fallacious and self-serving arguments and shows how readers, both men and women, have been lured into mistaking the effects of nurture for those of nature.

For Mary Wollstonecraft, this is Rousseau's cardinal error in *Emile*, Book V. Women's 'dependence' is called natural, though it is evidently the product of education. Rousseau of all people should have avoided that error, having devoted the whole of the *Second Discourse* to combating it.

The absurdity ... of supposing that a girl is naturally a coquette, and that a desire connected with the impulse of nature to propagate the species, should appear even before an improper education has, by heating the imagination, called it forth prematurely, is so unphilosophical, that such a sagacious observer as Rousseau would not have adopted it, if he had not been accustomed to make reason give way to his desire of singularity, and truth to a favourite paradox. (Wollstonecraft, 1992, p. 129)

She dissects Rousseau's views on the difference in physical strength between the sexes. As Rousseau himself observed in the *Second Discourse*, that difference is less great in the state of nature than it is in society, since it is fostered in society by different educational systems for boys and girls and different expectations of behaviour for men and women. Wollstonecraft continues:

should it be proved that woman is naturally weaker than man, whence does it follow that it is natural for her to labour to become still weaker than nature intended her to be? Arguments of this cast are an insult to common sense, and savour of passion. (Wollstonecraft, 1992, p. 128)

It is still less natural that women should exploit their relative weakness, using it as a ploy to gain dominance over their physically stronger male partners. That dominance, as Wollstonecraft rightly points out, is itself a kind of despotism. It is power wielded through the degraded passion of licentiousness, not through reason.

Mary Wollstonecraft attributes Rousseau's error in part to his literary and philosophical pretentions, in his capricious 'desire of singularity' and his eagerness to 'sacrifice truth to a favourite paradox'. But beneath that there are deeper causes:

all Rousseau's errors in reasoning arose from sensibility, and sensibility to their charms women are very ready to forgive. When he should have reasoned, he became impassioned, and reflection inflamed his imagination instead of enlightening his understanding ... Can any other answer be given than this, that the effervescence of his imagination produced both; but had his fancy been allowed to cool, it is possible that he might have acquired more strength of mind. (Below, p. 149)

According to Mary Wollstonecraft's diagnosis, these causes are rooted in defects within Rousseau's psyche, and I find it hard to explain the glaring discrepancy between the *Second Discourse* and *Emile*, Book V in any other way. In much of his other work, Rousseau steered a sure course between reason and romanticism, between intellect and sensibility, and was able to understand both the positive and the negative sides of the imagination, which allows us to identify with others, and so take the first steps towards justice, but can also enslave us in the world of chimeras. If he gave way to enslavement by his imagination in dealing with, and writing about, women, as Mary Wollstonecraft argues persuasively that he did, then we must seek for the factor that separates his political from his sexual experience. In the case of political inequalities, Rousseau was able to use his own experience of personal dependence to construct a powerful theoretical model to overcome it. So why could he not translate his dealings with women into a more plausible picture of the possible relations between the sexes? Most of the women Rousseau encountered were his social and psychological superiors, richer, more powerful and more adept at social intrigue than he. This was true of all his great loves, starting with Madame de Warens and finishing with Sophie d'Houdentot. Only with Thérèse were the social roles reversed, though she too was no passive dependent.

But Rousseau never managed to form any kind of sexual relationship on the basis of equality. In *Emile*, Book V he translated that incapacity into an evidently specious naturalistic justification for the total dependence of women on men. He made use of the ideology of complementarism, which contemporary writers were then elaborating in order to reverse the advances already made by the most privileged women in eighteenth-century France. These were the women with whom Rousseau was in constant contact, and on whom he was dependent for much of his life, the prickly recipient of their favours and ungrateful guest on their estates. Rousseau was overawed by the high culture of these distinguished women, and he reacted against it by devising a demeaning education for the fictional Sophie, which would produce an intellectually empty adult, entirely dependent on the views of her husband and on public opinion. In politics, the contrast between the real and the possible yielded a revolutionary alternative. In sexuality, in contrast, it drove Rousseau into a crisis of *ressentiment*. The outcome was *Emile*, Book V, a travesty of his own deepest insights in the *Second Discourse*. His women critics were not slow to take him to task for it.

## Conclusion

Mary Wollstonecraft was one of the great Enlightenment feminists, writers who were, and still are, united around four key theses. First, they argue that women are identical to men with respect to those capacities – mastery of abstract thought, impartiality, creativity, etc. – in which men have claimed that women are different (i.e. inferior). Second, they argue that if women do not perform at the same level as men in a given society, it is for reasons of historically specific social conditioning, not of irreducible biological or psychological difference. Third, they argue the need for programmes of reform – political, legal, social and educational – to correct those inequalities of performance by bringing about real equality of opportunity between the sexes. Fourth, and lastly, they maintain that the respects in which men and women are genuinely not identical in nature are irrelevant to the distribution of fundamental rights.

In his *Second Discourse*, Rousseau provides powerful support for the first two theses of Enlightenment feminism: social inequalities should be permitted only where they correspond to natural ones, and since the latter are minimal, so too should be the former. But in the *Emile* Rousseau reverses the implicit feminism of the *Second Discourse*, rejecting these first two theses, and using the ideology of complementarity, he makes the egalitarian political demands of the second two theses appear absurd.

Two centuries later, Enlightenment feminism has been the vehicle of most of the victories won by women in their slow and still uncompleted march to empowerment as full members of civil society. But it has also come under attack, not only from anti-feminist reactionaries but also from certain elements within the women's movement itself, both of whom have stressed differences rather than identity. The former, following Rousseau in *Emile*, Book V, have aimed to keep women 'in their place', a place determined by their biological destiny to serve as mothers and home-makers. The latter give a positive, rather than a negative, reading of allegedly irreducibly feminine characteristics. The feminine virtues of caring, nurturing, conciliating and co-operating are contrasted unfavourably with the (allegedly) masculine concern with systems of rights, claims and justice. Even if her work does not decide conclusively between nature and nurture, the psychologist Carol

Gilligan has shown how small girls and boys certainly behave in remarkably different fashions in dealing with other people and in rationalising their dealings. Perhaps recent work on the human brain and its connection with linguistic and reasoning skills may shed more light on the question. But it is doubtful whether such empirical investigations will alter the political conclusions drawn by either side, and the debate looks set to continue. All the same, it is worth noting that, shorn of its brutal inegalitarian conclusions, Rousseau's politics of difference is closer to the programme of many contemporary feminists than anything found in the tradition of Enlightenment feminism. But that may simply tell us that those radical programmes are as bankrupt as Rousseau's was. In the long run, Mary Wollstonecraft is a better ally of the women's movement than Jean-Jacques.

## References

References to Rousseau are to one of the following English translations:
The *Second Discourse* in *The Collected Writings of Rousseau*, vol. 3, ed. R. D. Masters and C. Kelly, Hanover and London: University Press of New England, 1992.
The First Version of the *Social Contract* in *The Collected Writings of Rousseau*, vol. 4, ed. R. D. Masters and C. Kelly, Hanover and London: University Press of New England, 1994.
The *Emile* in *Emile or on Education*, trans. Alan Bloom, New York: Basic Books, 1979.
References to Mary Wollstonecraft are to *A Vindication of the Rights of Woman*, ed. Miriam Brody, London: Penguin, 1992 (which has an excellent bibliography on pp. 71–3).

## Further reading

Maurice Cranston had published two volumes of his absorbing intellectual biography of Rousseau before his death: *Jean-Jacques: the Early Life and Work of Jean-Jacques Rousseau, 1712–1754* (London: Allen Lane, 1983) and *The Noble Savage: Jean-Jacques Rousseau, 1754–1762* (London: Allen Lane, 1991). The best account of *amour propre* is in N. J. H. Dent, *Rousseau* (Oxford: Blackwell, 1988). For Rousseau's views on men and women, see J. Schwartz, *The Sexual Politics of Jean-Jacques Rousseau* (Chicago: Chicago University Press, 1984).

For a straightforward feminist critique of Rousseau, see Susan Moller Okin, *Women in Western Political Thought* (Princeton: Princeton University Press, 1979), part 3. For the eighteenth-century debate, see Elisabeth Badinter, *The Myth of Motherhood: An Historical View of the Maternal Instinct*, trans. Francine du Plessix Gray (London: Souvenir Press, 1981), and Londa Schiebinger, *The Mind has no Sex? Women in the Origins of Modern Science* (Cambridge, MA: Harvard University Press, 1989).

For the continuing debate within the feminist movement, see Carol Gilligan, *In a Different Voice: Psychological Theory and Women's Development* (Cambridge, MA: Harvard University Press, 1982), and Virginia Held, 'Liberty and Equality from a Feminist Perspective', in N. MacCormick and Z. Bankowski (eds), *Enlightenment, Rights and Revolution: Essays in Legal and social Philosophy* (Aberdeen: Aberdeen University Press, 1989).

Does Rousseau's *Second Discourse* help us to understand the *origin* of inequality between men and women?

Does Wollstonecraft vindicate the rights of woman, or only of middle-class women?

How might Rousseau respond to Wollstonecraft's critique?

Is the whole of Rousseau's political theory infected by his sexism?

# J.-J. ROUSSEAU
# From the *Second Discourse*

The first [problem] is to imagine how languages could have become necessary; for since Men had no communication among themselves nor any need of it, one can conceive neither the necessity of this invention nor its possibility were it not indispensable. I might well say, as many others do, that Languages were born in the domestic intercourse of Fathers, Mothers, and Children. But not only would that fail to resolve the objections, it would be committing the error of those who, reasoning about the state of Nature, carry over to it ideas taken from Society, and always see the family gathered in the same habitation and its members maintaining among themselves a union as intimate and permanent as among us, where so many common interests unite them. Instead, in the primitive state, having neither Houses, nor Huts, nor property of any kind, everyone took up his lodging by chance and often for only one night. Males and females united fortuitously, depending on encounter, occasion, and desire, without speech being a very necessary interpreter of the things they had to say to each other; they left each other with the same ease. The mother nursed her Children at first for her own need; then, habit having endeared them to her, she nourished them afterward for their need. As soon as they had the strength to seek their food, they did not delay in leaving the Mother herself; and as there was practically no other way to find one another again than not to lose sight of each other, they were soon at a point of not even recognizing one another. [Part I, p. 30]

Mr Locke proves at most that there could well be in a man a motive for remaining attached to a woman when she has a Child; but he does not prove at all that he must have been attached to her before the delivery and during the nine months of pregnancy. If a given woman is indifferent to the man during these nine months, if she even becomes unknown to him, why will he assist her after delivery? Why will he help her to raise a Child he does not even know belongs to him, and whose birth he neither planned nor foresaw? Mr Locke evidently supposes what is in question; for it is not a matter of knowing why the man will remain attached to the woman after delivery, but why he will become attached to her after conception. His appetite satisfied, the man no longer needs a given woman, nor the woman a given man. The man has not the least concern nor perhaps the least idea of the consequences of his action. One goes off in one direction, the other in another, and there is no likelihood that at the end of nine months they have any memory of having known each other: for this kind of memory, by which one individual gives preference to another for the act of procreation, requires, as I prove in the text, more progress or corruption in human understanding than can be supposed in man in the state of animality in question here. Another woman can therefore satisfy the new desires of the man as conveniently as the one he has already known, and another man satisfy in the same way the woman, supposing that she is impelled by the same appetite during pregnancy, which can reasonably be doubted. And if in the state of Nature the woman no longer feels the passion of love after the conception of the child, the obstacle to her Society with the man thereby becomes much greater still, since then she no longer needs either the man who impregnated her or any other. Therefore there is not, for the man, any reason to seek the same woman, nor for the woman, any reason to seek the same man. Locke's reasoning therefore falls apart, and all the Dialectic of this Philosopher has not saved him from the error committed by Hobbes and others. They had to explain a fact of the state of Nature, that is to say, of a state where men lived isolated and where a given man had no motive for living near another given man, nor perhaps to live near one another, which is much worse; and they did not think of carrying themselves back beyond the Centuries of Society, that is to say, of those times when men have always had a reason to live near one another, and when a given man often has a reason for living beside a given man or a given woman. [Note 4, pp. 89–90]

Everything begins to change its appearance. Men who until this time wandered in the Woods, having adopted a more fixed settlement, slowly come together, unite into different bands, and finally form in each country a particular Nation, unified by morals and character, not by Regulations and Laws but by the same kind of life and foods and by the common influence of Climate. A permanent proximity cannot fail to engender at length some contact between different families. Young people of different sexes live in neighboring Huts; the passing intercourse demanded by Nature soon leads to another kind no less sweet and more permanent through mutual frequentation. People grow accustomed to consider different objects and to make comparisons; imperceptibly they acquire ideas of merit and beauty which produce sentiments of preference. By dint of seeing one another, they can no longer do without seeing one another again. A tender and gentle sentiment is gradually introduced into the soul and at the least obstacle becomes an impetuous fury. Jealousy awakens

137

with love; Discord triumphs, and the gentlest of the passions receives sacrifices of human blood.

In proportion as ideas and sentiments follow upon one another and as mind and heart are trained, the human Race continues to be tamed, contacts spread, and bonds are tightened. People grew accustomed to assembling in front of the Huts or around a large Tree; song and dance, true children of love and leisure, became the amusement or rather the occupation of idle and assembled men and women. Each one began to look at the others and to want to be looked at himself, and public esteem had a value. The one who sang or danced the best, the handsomest, the strongest, the most adroit, or the most eloquent became the most highly considered; and that was the first step toward inequality and, at the same time, toward vice. From these first preferences were born on one hand vanity and contempt, on the other shame and envy; and the fermentation caused by these new leavens eventually produced compounds fatal to happiness and innocence. [Part II, p. 47]

# J. J. ROUSSEAU
## From *Emile*

### BOOK IV

As soon as man has need of a companion, he is no longer an isolated being. His heart is no longer alone. All his relations with his species, all the affections of his soul are born with this one. His first passion soon makes the others ferment.

The inclination of instinct is indeterminate. One sex is attracted to the other; that is the movement of nature. Choice, preferences, and personal attachments are the work of enlightenment, prejudice, and habit. Time and knowledge are required to make us capable of love. One loves only after having judged; one prefers only after having compared. These judgments are made without one's being aware of it, but they are nonetheless real. True love, whatever is said of it, will always be honored by men; for although its transports lead us astray, although it does not exclude odious qualities from the heart that feels it – and even produces them – it nevertheless always presupposes estimable qualities without which one would not be in a condition to feel it. This choosing, which is held to be the opposite of reason, comes to us from it. Love has been presented as blind because it has better eyes than we do and sees relations we are not able to perceive. For a man who had no idea of merit or beauty, every woman would be equally good, and the first comer would always be the most lovable. Far from arising from nature, love is the rule and the bridle of nature's inclinations. It is due to love that, except for the beloved object, one sex ceases to be anything for the other.

One wants to obtain the preference that one grants. Love must be reciprocal. To be loved, one has to make oneself lovable. To be preferred,
one has to make oneself more lovable than another, more lovable
than every other, at least in the eyes of the beloved object. This is the
source of the first glances at one's fellows; this is the source of the
first comparisons with them; this is the source of emulation, rivalries,
and jealousy. A heart full of an overflowing sentiment likes to open
itself. From the need for a mistress is soon born the need for a friend.
He who senses how sweet it is to be loved would want to be loved
by everyone; and all could not want preference without there being
many malcontents. With love and friendship are born dissensions,
enmity, and hate. From the bosom of so many diverse passions I see
opinion raising an unshakable throne, and stupid mortals, subjected
to its empire, basing their own existence on the judgments of others.
Extend these ideas, and you will see where our *amour-propre* gets the
form we believe natural to it, and how self-love, ceasing to be an
absolute sentiment, becomes pride in great souls, vanity in small
ones, and feeds itself constantly in all at the expense of their neighbors. This species of passion, not having its germ in children's hearts,
cannot be born in them of itself; it is we alone who put it there, and
it never takes root except by our fault. But this is no longer the case
with the young man's heart. Whatever we may do, these passions
will be born in spite of us. [pp. 214–15]

**BOOK V**

Now we have come to the last act in the drama of youth, but we are not
yet at the dénouement. It is not good for man to be alone. Emile is a
man. We have promised him a companion. She has to be given to
him. That companion is Sophie. In what place is her abode? Where
shall we find her? To find her, it is necessary to know her. Let us first
learn what she is; then we shall better judge what places she inhab-
its. And even when we have found her, everything will still not have
been done. 'Since our young gentleman,' says Locke, 'is ready to
marry, it is time to leave him to his beloved.' And with that he
finishes his work. But as I do not have the honor of raising a gentleman, I shall take care not to imitate Locke on this point.

### *Sophie* or the Woman

Sophie ought to be a woman as Emile is a man – that is to say, she ought
to have everything which suits the constitution of her species and her
sex in order to fill her place in the physical and moral order. Let us
begin, then, by examining the similarities and the differences of her
sex and ours.

In everything not connected with sex, woman is man. She has the same
organs, the same needs, the same faculties. The machine is constructed
in the same way; its parts are the same; the one functions as does the
other; the form is similar; and in whatever respect one considers them,
the difference between them is only one of more or less.

In everything connected with sex, woman and man are in every respect related and in every respect different. The difficulty of comparing them comes from the difficulty of determining what in their constitutions is due to sex and what is not. On the basis of comparative anatomy and even just by inspection, one finds general differences between them that do not appear connected with sex. They are, nevertheless, connected with sex, but by relations which we are not in a position to perceive. We do not know the extent of these relations. The only thing we know with certainty is that everything man and woman have in common belongs to the species, and that everything which distinguishes them belongs to the sex. From this double perspective, we find them related in so many ways and opposed in so many other ways that it is perhaps one of the marvels of nature to have been able to construct two such similar beings who are constituted so differently.

These relations and these differences must have a moral influence. This conclusion is evident to the senses; it is in agreement with our experience; and it shows how vain are the disputes as to whether one of the two sexes is superior or whether they are equal – as though each, in fulfilling nature's ends according to its own particular purpose, were thereby less perfect than if it resembled the other more! In what they have in common, they are equal. Where they differ, they are not comparable. A perfect woman and a perfect man ought not to resemble each other in mind any more than in looks, and perfection is not susceptible of more or less.

In the union of the sexes each contributes equally to the common aim, but not in the same way. From this diversity arises the first assignable difference in the moral relations of the two sexes. One ought to be active and strong, the other passive and weak. One must necessarily will and be able; it suffices that the other put up little resistance.

Once this principle is established, it follows that woman is made specially to please man. If man ought to please her in turn, it is due to a less direct necessity. His merit is in his power; he pleases by the sole fact of his strength. This is not the law of love, I agree. But it is that of nature, prior to love itself.

If woman is made to please and to be subjugatged, she ought to make herself agreeable to man instead of arousing him. Her own violence is in her charms. It is by these that she ought to constrain him to find his strength and make use of it. The surest art for animating that strength is to make it necessary by resistance. Then *amour-propre* unites with desire, and the one triumphs in the victory that the other has made him win. From this there arises attack and defense, the audacity of one sex and the timidity of the other, and finally the modesty and the shame with which nature armed the weak in order to enslave the strong.

Who could think that nature has indiscriminately prescribed the same advances to both men and women, and that the first to form desires should also be the first to show them? What a strange depravity of judgment! Since the undertaking has such different consequences for the two sexes, is it natural that they should have the same audacity in abandoning themselves to it? With so great an inequality in what each risks in the union, how can one fail to see that if reserve did not impose on one sex the moderation which nature imposes on the other, the result would soon be the ruin of both, and mankind would perish by the means established for preserving it? If there were some unfortunate region on earth where philosophy had introduced this practice – especially in hot countries, where more women are born than men – men would be tyrannized by women. For, given the ease with which women arouse men's senses and reawaken in the depths of their hearts the remains of ardors which are almost extinguished, men would finally be their victims and would see themselves dragged to death without ever being able to defend themselves.

If females among the animals do not have the same shame, what follows from that? Do they have, as women do, the unlimited desires to which this shame serves as a brake? For them, desires comes only with need. When the need is satisfied, the desire ceases. They no longer feign to repulse the male[1] but really do so. They do exactly the opposite of Augustus' daughter; they accept no more passengers when the ship has its cargo. Even when they are free, their times of good will are short and quickly pass. Instinct impels them, and instinct stops them. What will be the substitute for this negative instinct when you have deprived woman of modesty? To wait until they no longer care for men is equivalent to waiting until they are no longer good for anything.

The Supreme Being wanted to do honor to the human species in everything. While giving man inclinations without limit, He gives him at the same time the law which regulates them, in order that he may be free and in command of himself. While abandoning man to immoderate passions, He joins reason to these passions in order to govern them. While abandoning woman to unlimited desires, He joins modesty to these desires in order to constrain them. In addition, He adds yet another real recompense for the good use of one's faculties – the taste we acquire for decent things when we make them the rule of our actions. All this, it seems to me, is worth more than the instinct of beasts.

Whether the human female shares man's desires or not and wants to satisfy them or not, she repulses him and always defends herself – but not always with the same force or, consequently, with the same success. For the attacker to be victorious, the one who is attacked must permit or arrange it; for does she not have adroit means to force the aggressor to use force? The freest and sweetest of all acts does not

[1] I have already noticed that affected and provocative refusals are common to almost all females, even among animals, even when they are most disposed to give themselves. One has to have never observed their wiles not to agree with this.

admit of real violence. Nature and reason oppose it: nature, in that it has provided the weaker with as much strength as is needed to resist when it pleases her; reason, in that real rape is not only the most brutal of all acts but the one most contrary to its end – either because the man thus declares war on his companion and authorizes her to defend her person and her liberty even at the expense of the aggressor's life, or because the woman alone is the judge of the condition she is in, and a child would have no father if every man could usurp the father's rights.

Here, then, is a third conclusion drawn from the constitution of the sexes – that the stronger appears to be master but actually depends on the weaker. This is due not to a frivolous practice of gallantry or to the pround generosity of a protector but to an invariable law of nature which gives woman more facility to excite the desires than man to satisfy them. This causes the latter, whether he likes it or not, to depend on the former's wish and constrains him to seek to please her in turn; so that she will consent to let him be the stronger. Then what is sweetest for man in his victory is the doubt whether it is weakness which yields to strength or the will which surrenders. And the woman's usual ruse is always to leave this doubt between her and him. In this the spirit of women corresponds perfectly to their constitution. Far from blushing at their weakness, they make it their glory. Their tender muscles are without resistance. They pretend to be unable to lift the lightest burdens. They would be ashamed to be strong. Why is that? It is not only to appear delicate; it is due to a shrewder precaution. They prepare in advance excuses and the right to be weak in case of need.

The progress of the enlightenment acquired as a result of our vices has greatly changed the old opinions on this point among us. Rapes are hardly ever spoken of anymore, since they are so little necessary and men no longer believe in them.[2] By contrast, they are very common in early Greek and Jewish antiquity, because those old opinions belong to the simplicity of nature, and only the experience of libertinism has been able to uproot them. If fewer acts of rape are cited in our day, this is surely not because men are more temperate but because they are less credulous, and such a complaint, which previously would have persuaded simple peoples, in our days would succeed only in attracting the laughter of mockers. It is more advantageous to keep quiet. In Deuteronomy there is a law by which a girl who had been abused was punished along with her seducer if the offense had been committed in the city. But if it had been committed in the country or in an isolated place, the man alone was punished: 'For,' the law says, 'the girl cried out and was not heard.' This benign interpretation taught the girls not to let themselves be surprised in well-frequented places.

[2] There can be such a disproportion of age and strength that real rape takes place; but treating here the relation between the sexes according to the order of nature, I take them both as they ordinarily are in that relation.

The effect of these differences of opinion about morals is evident. Modern gallantry is their work. Finding that their pleasures depended more on the will of the fair sex than they had believed, men have captivated that will by attentions for which the fair sex has amply compensated them.

Observe how the physical leads us unawares to the moral, and how the sweetest laws of love are born little by little from the coarse union of the sexes. Women possess their empire not because men wanted it that way, but because nature wants it that way. It belonged to women before they appeared to have it. The same Hercules who believed he raped the fifty daughters of Thespitius was nevertheless constrained to weave while he was with Omphale; and the strong Samson was not so strong as Delilah. This empire belongs to women and cannot be taken from them, even when they abuse it. If they could ever lose it, they would have done so long ago.

There is no parity between the two sexes in regard to the consequences of sex. The male is male only at certain moments. The female is female her whole life or at least during her whole youth. Everything constantly recalls her sex to her; and, to fulfill its functions well, she needs a constitution which corresponds to it. She needs care during her pregnancy; she needs rest at the time of childbirth; she needs a soft and sedentary life to suckle her children; she needs patience and gentleness, a zeal and an affection that nothing can rebuff in order to raise her children. She serves as the link between them and their father; she alone makes him love them and gives him the confidence to call them his own. How much tenderness and care is required to maintain the union of the whole family! And, finally, all this must come not from virtues but from tastes, or else the human species would soon be extinguished.

The strictness of the relative duties of the two sexes is not and cannot be the same. When woman complains on this score about unjust man-made inequality, she is wrong. This inequality is not a human institution – or, at least, it is the work not of prejudice but of reason. It is up to the sex that nature has charged with the bearing of children to be responsible for them to the other sex. Doubtless it is not permitted to anyone to violate his faith, and every unfaithful husband who deprives his wife of the only reward of the austere duties of her sex is an unjust and barbarous man. But the unfaithful woman does more; she dissolves the family and breaks all the bonds of nature. In giving the man children which are not his, she betrays both. She joins perfidy to infidelity. I have difficulty seeing what disorders and what crimes do not flow from this one. If there is a frightful condition in the world, it is that of an unhappy father who, lacking confidence in his wife, does not dare to yield to the sweetest sentiments of his heart, who wonders, in embracing his child, whether he is embracing another's, the token of his dishonor, the plunderer of his own children's property. What does the family become in such a situation if not a society of secret enemies whom a

143

guilty woman arms against one another in forcing them to feign mutual love?

It is important, then, not only that a woman be faithful, but that she be judged to be faithful by her husband, by those near her, by everyone. It is important that she be modest, attentive, reserved, and that she give evidence of her virtue to the eyes of others as well as to her own conscience. If it is important that a father love his children, it is important that he esteem their mother. These are the reasons which put even appearances among the duties of women, and make honor and reputation no less indispensable to them than chastity. There follows from these principles, along with the moral difference of the sexes, a new motive of duty and propriety which prescribes especially to women the most scrupulous attention to their conduct, their manners, and their bearing. To maintain vaguely that the two sexes are equal and that their duties are the same, is to lose oneself in vain declaiming; it is to say nothing so long as one does not respond to these considerations:

Is it not a sound way of reasoning to present exceptions in response to such well-grounded general laws: Women, you say, do not always produce children? No, but their proper purpose is to produce them. What! Because there are a hundred big cities in the universe where women living in license produce few children, you claim that it is proper to woman's status to produce few children! And what would become of your cities if women living more simply and more chastely far away in the country did not make up for the sterility of the city ladies? In how many provinces are women who have only produced four or five children taken to be infecund![3] Finally, what does it matter that this or that woman produces few children? Is woman's status any less that of motherhood, and is it not by general laws that nature and morals ought to provide for this status?

Even if there were intervals as long as one supposes between pregnancies, will a woman abruptly and regularly change her way of life without peril and risk? Will she be nurse today and warrior tomorrow? Will she change temperament and tastes as a chameleon does colors? Will she suddenly go from shade, enclosure, and domestic cares to the harshness of the open air, the labors, the fatigues, and the perils of war? Will she be fearful[4] at one moment and brave at another, delicate at one moment and robust at another? If young people raised in Paris have difficulty enduring the profession of arms, will women, who have never endured the sun and hardly know how to walk, endure it after fifty years of softness? Will they take up this harsh profession at the age when men leave it?

---

[3] Without that, the species would necessarily fade away. In order for it to be preserved, every woman must, everything considered, produce nearly four children; for nearly half of the children who are born die before they can have others, and the two remaining ones are needed to represent the father and the mother. See if the cities will provide you with this population.

[4] The timidity of women is another instinct of nature against the double risk they run during their pregnancy.

There are countries where women give birth almost without pain and nurse their children almost without effort. I admit it. But in these same countries the men go half naked at all times, vanquish ferocious beasts, carry a canoe like a knapsack, pursue the hunt for up to seven or eight hundred leagues, sleep in the open air on the ground, bear unbelievable fatigues, and go several days without eating. When women become robust, men become still more so. When men get soft, women get even softer. When the two change equally, the difference remains the same.

In his *Republic*, Plato gives women the same exercises as men. I can well believe it! Having removed private families from his regime and no longer knowing what to do with women, he found himself forced to make them men. That noble genius had planned everything, foreseen everything. He was forestalling an objection that perhaps no one would have thought of making to him, but he provided a poor solution to the one which is made to him. I am not speaking of that alleged community of women; the often repeated reproach on this point proves that those who make it against him have never read him. I am speaking of that civil promiscuity which throughout confounds the two sexes in the same employments and in the same labors and which cannot fail to engender the most intolerable abuses. I speak of that subversion of the sweetest sentiments of nature, sacrifices to an artificial sentiment which can only be maintained by them – as though there were no need for a natural base on which to form conventional ties; as though the love of one's nearest were not the principle of the love one owes the state; as though it were not by means of the small fatherland which is the family that the heart attaches itself to the large one; as though it were not the good son, the good husband, and the good father who make the good citizen!

Once it is demonstrated that man and woman are not and ought not to be constituted in the same way in either character or temperament, it follows that they ought not to have the same education. In following nature's directions, man and woman ought to act in concert, but they ought not to do the same things. The goal of their labors is common, but their labors themselves are different, and consequently so are the tastes directing them. After having tried to form the natural man, let us also see how the woman who suits this man ought to be formed so that our work will not be left imperfect.

Do you wish always to be well guided? Then always follow nature's indications. Everything that characterizes the fair sex ought to be respected as established by nature. You constantly say, 'Women have this or that failing which we do not have.' Your pride deceives you. They would be failings for you; they are their good qualities. Everything would go less well if they did not have these qualities. Prevent these alleged failings from degenerating, but take care not to destroy them.

For their part, women do not cease to proclaim that we raise them to be vain and coquettish, that we constantly entertain them with

145

puerilities in order to remain more easily their masters. They blame on us the failings for which we reproach them. What folly! And since when is it that men get involved in the education of girls? Who prevents their mothers from raising them as they please? They have no colleges. What a great misfortune! Would God that there were none for boys; they would be more sensibly and decently raised! Are your daughters forced to waste their time in silliness? Are they made in spite of themselves to spend half their lives getting dressed up, following the example you set them? Are you prevented from instructing them and having them instructed as you please? Is it our fault that they please us when they are pretty, that their mincing ways seduce us, that the art which they learn from you attracts us and pleases us, that we like to see them tastefully dressed, that we let them sharpen at their leisure the weapons with which they subjugate us? So, decide to raise them like men. The men will gladly consent to it! The more women want to resemble them, the less women will govern them, and then men will truly be the masters.

All the faculties common to the two sexes are not equally distributed between them; but taken together, they balance out. Woman is worth more as woman and less as man. Wherever she makes use of her rights, she has the advantage. Wherever she wants to usurp ours, she remains beneath us. One can respond to this general truth only with exceptions, the constant mode of argument of the gallant partisans of the fair sex.

To cultivate man's qualities in women and to neglect those which are proper to them is obviously to work to their detriment. Crafty women see this too well to be duped by it. In trying to usurp our advantages, they do not abandon theirs. But it turns out that they are unable to manage both well – because the two are incompatible – and they remain beneath their own level without getting up to ours, thus losing half their value. Believe me, judicious mother, do not make a decent man of your daughter, as though you would give nature the lie. Make a decent woman of her, and be sure that as a result she will be worth more for herself and for us.

Does it follow that she ought to be raised in ignorance of everything and limited to the housekeeping functions alone? Will man turn his companion into his servant? Will he deprive himself of the greatest charm of society with her? In order to make her more subject, will he prevent her from feeling anything, from knowing anything? Will he make her into a veritable automaton? Surely not. It is not thus that nature has spoken in giving women such agreeable and nimble minds. On the contrary, nature wants them to think, to judge, to love, to know, to cultivate their minds as well as their looks. These are the weapons nature gives them to take the place of the strength they lack and to direct ours. They ought to learn many things but only those that are suitable for them to know.

Whether I consider the particular purpose of the fair sex, whether I observe its inclinations, whether I consider its duties, all join equally in indicating to me the form of education that suits it. Woman and man are made for one another, but their mutual dependence is not equal. Men depend on women because of their desires; women depend on men because of both their desires and their needs. We would survive more easily without them than they would without us. For them to have what is necessary to their station, they depend on us to give it to them; to want to give it to them, to esteem them worthy of it. They depend on our sentiments, on the value we set on their merit, on the importance we attach to their charms and their virtues. By the very law of nature women are at the mercy of men's judgments, as much for their own sake as for that of their children. It is not enough that they be estimable; they must be esteemed. It is not enough for them to be pretty; they must please. It is not enough for them to be temperate; they must be recognized as such. Their honor is not only in their conduct but in their reputation; and it is not possible that a woman who consents to be regarded as disreputable can ever be decent. When a man acts well, he depends only on himself and can brave public judgment; but when a woman acts well, she has accomplished only half of her task, and what is thought of her is no less important to her than what she actually is. From this it follows that the system of woman's education ought to be contrary in this respect to the system of our education. Opinion is the grave of virtue among men and its throne among women.

The good constitution of children initially depends on that of their mothers. The first education of men depends on the care of women. Men's morals, their passions, their tastes, their pleasures, their very happiness also depend on women. Thus the whole education of women ought to relate to men. To please men, to be useful to them, to make herself loved and honored by them, to raise them when young, to care for them when grown, to counsel them, to console them, to make their lives agreeable and sweet – these are the duties of women at all times, and they ought to be taught from childhood. So long as one does not return to this principle, one will deviate from the goal, and all the precepts taught to women will be of no use for their happiness or for ours.

But although every woman wants to please men and should want to, there is quite a difference between wanting to please the man of merit, the truly lovable man, and wanting to please those little flatterers who dishonor both their own sex and the one they imitate. Neither nature nor reason can bring a woman to love in men what resembles herself; nor is it by adopting their ways that she ought to seek to make herself loved. [pp. 357–65]

# MARY WOLLSTONECRAFT
## From *A Vindication of the Rights of Woman*

### Writers Who Have Rendered Women Objects of Pity

This is certainly an education of the body; but Rousseau is not the only
man who has indirectly said that merely the person of a *young*
woman, without any mind, unless animal spirits come under that
description, is very pleasing. To render it weak, and what some may
call beautiful, the understanding is neglected, and girls forced to sit
still, play with dolls and listen to foolish conversations; – the effect
of habit is insisted upon as an undoubted indication of nature. I know
it was Rousseau's opinion that the first years of youth should be
employed to form the body, though in educating Emilius he deviates
from this plan; yet, the difference between strengthening the body, on
which strength of mind in a great measure depends, and only giving
it an easy motion, is very wide.

Rousseau's observations, it is proper to remark, were made in a country
where the art of pleasing was refined only to extract grossness of vice.
He did not go back to nature, or his ruling appetite disturbed the
operations of reason, else he would not have drawn these crude infer-
ences.

In France boys and girls, particularly the latter, are only educated to
please, to manage their persons, and regulate the exterior behaviour;
and their minds are corrupted, at a very early age, by the worldly and
pious cautions they receive to guard them against immodesty. I speak
of past times. The very confessions which mere children were obliged
to make, and the questions asked by the holy men, I assert these facts
on good authority, were sufficient to impress a sexual character; and
the education of society was a school of coquetry and art. At the age
of ten or eleven; nay, often much sooner, girls began to coquette, and
talked, unreproved, of establishing themselves in the world by
marriage.

In short, they were treated like women, almost from their very birth,
and compliments were listened to instead of instruction. These weakening the mind, Nature was supposed to have acted like a
step-mother, when she formed this afterthought of creation. [pp.
179–80]

Children, he truly observes, form a much more permanent connection
between married people than love. Beauty, he declares, will not be
valued, or even seen, after a couple have lived six months together;
artificial graces and coquetry will likewise pall on the senses. Why,
then, does he say that a girl should be educated for her husband with
the same care as for an Eastern harem?

I now appeal from the reveries of fancy and refined licentiousness to
the good sense of mankind, whether, if the object of education be to
prepare women to become chaste wives and sensible mothers, the

method so plausibly recommended in the foregoing sketch be the one best calculated to produce those ends? Will it be allowed that the surest way to make a wife chaste is to teach her to practise the wanton arts of a mistress, termed virtuous coquetry, by the sensualist who can no longer relish the artless charms of sincerity, or taste the pleasure arising from a tender intimacy, when confidence is unchecked by suspicion, and rendered interesting by sense?

The man who can be contented to live with a pretty, useful companion, without a mind, has lost in voluptuous gratifications a taste for more refined enjoyments; he has never felt the calm satisfaction that refreshes the parched heart like the silent dew of heaven – of being beloved by one who could understand him. In the society of his wife he is still alone, unless when the man is sunk in the brute. 'The charm of life', says a grave philosophical reasoner, is 'sympathy; nothing pleases us more than to observe in other men a fellow-feeling with all the emotions of our own breast'.

But according to the tenor of reasoning by which women are kept from the tree of knowledge, the important years of youth, the usefulness of age, and the rational hopes of futurity, are all to be sacrificed to render women an object of desire for a *short* time. Besides, how could Rousseau expect them to be virtuous and constant when reason is neither allowed to be the foundation of their virtue, nor truth the object of their inquiries?

But all Rousseau's errors in reasoning arose from sensibility, and sensibility to their charms women are very ready to forgive. When he should have reasoned he became impassioned, and reflection inflamed his imagination instead of enlightening his understanding. Even his virtues also led him farther astray; for, born with a warm constitution and lively fancy, nature carried him toward the other sex with such eager fondness that he soon became lascivious. Had he given way to these desires, the fire would have extinguished itself in a natural manner, but virtue, and a romantic kind of delicacy, made him practise self-denial; yet when fear, delicacy, or virtue restrained him, he debauched his imagination, and reflecting on the sensations to which fancy gave force, he traced them in the most glowing colours, and sunk them deep into his soul.

He then sought for solitude, not to sleep with the man of nature, or calmly investigate the causes of things under the shade where Sir Isaac Newton indulged contemplation, but merely to indulge his feelings. And so warmly has he painted what he forcibly felt, that interesting the heart and inflaming the imagination of his readers, in proportion to the strength of their fancy, they imagine that their understanding is convinced when they only sympathize with a poetic writer, who skilfully exhibits the objects of sense most voluptuously shadowed or gracefully veiled; and thus making us feel whilst dreaming that we reason, erroneous conclusions are left in the mind.

Why was Rousseau's life divided between ecstasy and misery? Can any other answer be given than this, that the effervescence of his imagination produced both; but had his fancy been allowed to cool, it is possible that he might have acquired more strength of mind. Still, if the purpose of life be to educate the intellectual part of man, all with respect to him was right; yet had not death led to a nobler scene of action, it is probable that he would have enjoyed more equal happiness on earth, and have felt the calm sensation of the man of nature, instead of being prepared for another stage of existence by nourishing the passions which agitate the civilized man.

But peace to his manes! I war not with his ashes, but his opinions. I war only with the sensibility that led him to degrade woman by making her the slave of love.

> – Cursed vassalage,
> First idolized till love's hot fire be o'er,
> Then slaves to those who courted us before. – DRYDEN.

The pernicious tendency of those books, in which the writers insidiously degrade the sex whilst they are prostrate before their personal charms, cannot be too often or too severely exposed.

Let us, my dear contemporaries, arise above such narrow prejudices. If wisdom be desirable on its own account, if virtue, to deserve the name, must be founded on knowledge, let us endeavour to strengthen our minds by reflection till our heads become a balance for our hearts; let us not confine all our thoughts to the petty occurrences of the day, or our knowledge to an acquaintance with our lovers' or husbands' hearts, but let the practice of every duty be subordinate to the grand one of improving our minds, and preparing our affections of a more exalted state.

Beware, then, my friends, of suffering the heart to be moved by every trivial incident; the reed is shaken by a breeze, and annually dies, but the oak stands firm, and for ages braves the storm.

Were we, indeed, only created to flutter our hour out and die – why let us then indulge sensibility, and laugh at the severity of reason. Yet, alas! even then we should want strength of body and mind, and life would be lost in feverish pleasures or wearisome languor.

But the system of education, which I earnestly wish to see exploded, seems to presuppose what ought to be taken for granted, that virtue shields us from the casualties of life; and that Fortune, slipping off her bandage, will smile on a well-educated female, and bring in her hand an Emilius or a Telemachus. Whilst, on the contrary, the reward, which Virtue promises to her votaries is confined, it seems clear, to their own bosoms; and often must they contend with the most vexatious worldly cares, and bear with the vices and humours of relations for whom they can never feel a friendship.

There have been many women in the world who, instead of being supported by the reason and virtue of their fathers and brothers, have strengthened their own minds by struggling with their vices and follies; yet have never met a hero, in the shape of a husband; who, paying the debt that mankind owed them, might chance to bring back their reason to its natural dependent state, and restore the usurped prerogative, of rising above opinion, to man. [pp. 191–4]

## Some Instances of the Folly

It is not necessary to inform the sagacious reader, now I enter on my concluding reflections, that the discussion of this subject merely consists in opening a few simple principles, and clearing away the rubbish which obscured them. But, as all readers are not sagacious, I must be allowed to add some explanatory remarks to bring the subject home to reason – to that sluggish reason, which supinely takes opinions on trust, and obstinately supports them to spare itself the labour of thinking.

Moralists have unanimously agreed, that unless virtue be nursed by liberty, it will never attain due strength – and what they say of man I extend to mankind, insisting that in all cases morals must be fixed on immutable principles; and, that the being cannot be termed rational or virtuous, who obeys any authority, but that of reason.

To render women truly useful members of society, I argue that they should be led, by having their understandings cultivated on a large scale, to acquire a rational affection for their country, founded on knowledge, because it is obvious that we are little interested about what we do not understand. And to render this general knowledge of due importance, I have endeavoured to show that private duties are never properly fulfilled unless the understanding enlarges the heart; and that public virtue is only an aggregate of private. But, the distinctions established in society undermine both, by beating out the solid gold of virtue, till it becomes only the tinsel-covering of vice; for whilst wealth renders a man more respectable than virtue, wealth will be sought before virtue; and, whilst women's persons are caressed, when a childish simper shows an absence of mind – the mind will lie fallow. Yet, true voluptuousness must proceed from the mind – for what can equal the sensations produced by mutual affection, supported by mutual respect? What are the cold, or feverish caresses of appetitie, but sin embracing death, compared with the modest overflowings of a pure heart and exalted imagination? Yes, let me tell the libertine of fancy when he despises understanding in woman – that the mind, which he disregards, gives life to the enthusiastic affection from which rapture, short-lived as it is, alone can blow! And, that, without virtue, a sexual attachment must expire, like a tallow candle in the socket, creating intolerable disgust. To prove this, I need only observe, that men who have wasted great part of their lives with women, and with whom they have sought for pleasure with eager thirst, entertain the meanest opinion of the sex. Virtue, true refiner of joy! – if foolish men were to fright thee from earth, in order to give loose to all their appetites without a check – some sensual weight of taste would scale the heavens to invite thee back, to give a zest to pleasure!

**Wollstonecraft** That women at present are by ignorance rendered foolish or vicious is, I think, not to be disputed; and, that the most salutary effects tending to improve mankind might be expected from a REVOLUTION in female manners, appears, at least, with a face of probability, to rise out of the observation. For as marriage has been termed the parent of those endearing charities which draw man from the brutal herd, the corrupting intercourse that wealth, idleness, and folly, produce between the sexes, is more universally injurious to morality than all the other vices of mankind collectively considered. To adulterous lust the most sacred duties are sacrificed, because before marriage, men, by a promiscuous intimacy with women, learned to consider love as a selfish gratification – learned to separate it not only from esteem, but from the affection merely built on habit, which mixes a little humanity with it. Justice and friendship are also set at defiance, and that purity of taste is vitiated which would naturally lead a man to relish an artless display of affection rather than affected airs. But that noble simplicity of affection, which dares to appear unadorned, has few attractions for the libertine, though it be the charm, which by cementing the matrimonial tie, secures to the pledges of a warmer passion the necessary parental attention; for children will never be properly educated till friendship subsists between parents. Virtue flies from a house divided against itself – and a whole legion of devils take up their residence there.

The affection of husbands and wives cannot be pure when they have so few sentiments in common, and when so little confidence is established at home, as must be the case when their pursuits are so different. That intimacy from which tenderness should flow, will not, cannot subsist between the vicious.

Contending, therefore, that the sexual distinction which men have so warmly insisted upon, is arbitrary, I have dwelt on an observation, that several sensible men, with whom I have conversed on the subject, allowed to be well founded; and it is simply this, that the little chastity to be found amongst men, and consequent disregard of modesty, tend to degrade both sexes; and further, that the modesty of women, characterized as such, will often be only the artful veil of wantonness instead of being the natural reflection of purity, till modesty be universally respected.

From the tyranny of man, I firmly believe, the greater number of female follies proceed; and the cunning, which I allow makes at present a part of their character, I likewise have repeatedly endeavoured to prove, is produced by oppression.

Were not dissenters, for instance, a class of people, with strict truth, characterized as cunning? And may I not lay some stress on this fact to prove, that when any power but reason curbs the free spirit of man, dissimulation is practised, and the various shifts of art are naturally called forth? Great attention to decorum, which was carried to a degree of scrupulosity, and all that puerile bustle about trifles and consequential solemnity, which Butler's caricature of a dissenter brings before the imagination, shaped their persons as well as their minds in the mould of prim littleness. I speak collectively, for I know how many ornaments in human nature have been enrolled amongst sectaries; yet, I assert, that the same narrow prejudice for their sect, which women have for their families, prevailed in the dissenting part of the community, however worthy in other respects; and also that the same timid prudence, or headstrong efforts, often disgraced the exertions of both. Oppression thus formed many of the features of their character perfectly to coincidence with that of the oppressed half of mankind; for is it not notorious that dissenters were, like women, fond of deliberating together, and asking advice of each other, till by a complication of little contrivances, some little end was brought about? A similar attention to preserve their reputation was conspicuous in the dissenting and female world, and was produced by a similar cause.

Asserting the rights which women in common with men ought to contend for, I have not attempted to extenuate their faults; but to prove them to be the natural consequence of their education and station in society. If so, it is reasonable to suppose that they will change their character, and correct their vices and follies, when they are allowed to be free in a physical, moral, and civil sense.

Let women share the rights, and she will emulate the virtues of man; for she must grow more perfect when emancipated, or justify the authority that chains such a weak being to her duty. If the latter, it will be expedient to open a fresh trade with Russia for whips: a present which a father should always make to his son-in-law on his wedding day, that a husband may keep his whole family in order by the same means; and without any violation of justice reign, wielding this sceptre, sole master of his house, because he is the only thing in it who has reason: – the divine, indefeasible earthly soveriegnty breathed into man by the Master of the universe. Allowing this position, women have not any inherent rights to claim; and, by the same rule, their duties vanish, for rights and duties are inseparable.

Be just then, O ye men of understanding; and mark not more severely what women do amiss than the vicious tricks of the horse or the ass for whom ye provide provender – and allow her the privileges of ignorance, to whom ye deny the rights of reason, or ye will be worse than Egyptian taskmasters, expecting virtue where Nature has not given understanding. [pp. 324–8]

HOWARD CAYGILL

# Kant and Hegel on the state

6

Kant's and Hegel's social and political theories explore the tensions between the form and the potential of the modern state and the modern idea of political, civil and economic freedom. The focus of both their theories is the relationship between, on the one hand, the legal and political institutions of the state, and on the other hand, the social organisations and interactions between individuals characteristic of civil society. Each offered different views of the role and form of the state with regard to civil society. Kant saw the state as a 'lawful authority' which he opposed to the civil society of 'free individuals striving against each other'. Hegel, in contrast, regarded the state as a universal and rational institution, whilst civil society consisted of the partial and conflicting interests of individuals and corporate groups. However, they agreed that the relationship between the state and civil society was continually changing, and that the state could only be understood with respect to its history.

## Immanuel Kant (1724–1804)

Kant was born in the East Prussian port of Königsberg, where he studied and later taught at the university as Professor of Logic and Metaphysics. He crowned a career of teaching and writing in a number of areas ranging from physical geography to metaphysics with the publication of the *Critique of Pure Reason* (1781), *The Critique of Practical Reason* (1788) and the *Critique of Judgement* (1790). These works established him as the leading philosopher of the German Enlightenment, and were followed by a number of shorter writings on political theory and the philosophy of history during the 1790s. Before he died he was to witness, with some disquiet, the growing influence of his work on the younger generation of German philosophers.

Kant's concern with the theory of the state is evident at all stages of his writing, but becomes most prominent in the writings published during the 1790s. These include *On the Common Saying 'It May be Correct in Theory, but it does Not Apply in Practice'* (1793), *Perpetual Peace: A Philosophical Sketch* (1795) and *The Metaphysics of Morals* (1797). His interest was not merely academic, but was also the outcome of his fascination with current political events, notably the American War of Independence and the French Revolution, and also his own experience of the attack on the ideology and structure of the enlightened Prussian state of Frederick the Great following the death of the monarch in 1786. His reflections on these events may be found peppered throughout his writings on the theory of the state and the philosophy of history.

Kant's *On the Common Saying: 'This May be Correct in Theory, but it does not Apply in Practice'*, extracts from which are reproduced below (pp. 161–9), was published in the leading journal of the Prussian Enlightenment, the *Berlinische Monatsschrift* in September 1793. At this point of time the Enlightenment was under severe political pressure, with censorship being applied to writers even of the stature of Kant. Thus in this text he defends the role of political theory against its detractors, as well as putting forward his own particular political philosophy. A year later Kant, now seventy years old, was reprimanded by a royal order in council for distorting and disparaging the basic teachings of Christianity and of corrupting youth with his teaching; he was ordered to account for his actions 'or to expect unpleasant measures' for his 'continuing obstinacy'.

Kant insists that the purpose of the state is not to promote the happiness or the welfare of its citizens. With this claim he criticised a powerful and influential current of eighteenth-century German political theory, represented by Christian Wolff (1679–1754), which argued for the state's comprehensive responsibility for the happiness and welfare of civil society (see also James Mill, chapter 8). In this argument, the claims of the absolute state and its enlightened bureaucrats are given priority over those of citizens in civil society. Against this view, Kant proposes that the state be directed towards the end of establishing the best possible conditions for its citizens to exercise and enjoy their freedom. He argues that the state is required to do no more than regulate the potential conflicts which arise from the pursuit of freedom by citizens in civil society, and ensure that one citizen's freedom is not enjoyed at the expense of that of another. Accordingly, in §83 of *The Critique of Judgement* he describes the constitution as 'so regulating the mutual relations of men so that the abuse of freedom by individuals striving one against another is opposed by a lawful authority centred in a whole'. Kant described the form of state based on this principle as the *Rechtsstaat*, or state-of-law, a term which has since obtained wide currency.

In his writings of the 1790s, Kant develops two schemas for classifying states. The first considers states in terms of their 'form of sovereignty' which may be, following the traditional, Aristotelian structure of argument, autocratic, aristocratic, or democratic. The second distinguishes between states in terms of their form of government which may be either republican or despotic. A republican form of government rests on the separation of executive and legislative power, which for Kant is only possible in autocratic and aristocratic forms of sovereignty. For him democracy is 'necessarily a despotism' because it is prone to collapse together executive and legislature. Thus Kant's social and political theory is not a variant of democratic theory, as becomes strikingly evident in his discussion of the three a priori principles of the republican state: freedom, equality, and independence. However, these are formal principles, a matter of freedom and equality before the law. They do not guarantee the existence of real freedom, equality and independence. Indeed the absence of the latter is used by Kant to underwrite a distinction between 'active' and 'passive' citizens; passive citizens are those who are deemed to be dependent upon others for their livelihood, among whom Kant includes apprentices, servants, minors, all women, tradesmen, teachers and tenant farmers. For Kant, this compromised the independence of their political judgement, and disqualified them from political participation.

Another influential strand of Kant's political theory is represented by his analysis of international relations in his essay *Perpetual Peace: A Philosophical Sketch* (1795). In this Kant envisages the gradual development of a 'cosmopolitan constitution' based on a federation of states bound by treaties of non-aggression. The proposed articles of these treaties are extremely radical and include the abolition of standing armies, the forbidding of raising national debt for military purposes, respect for the principle of non-interference and the laws of war.

One of the most criticised aspects of Kant's social and political theory is the distinction he makes between private morality and public legality. In relation to the former, the individual is autonomous; the moral law is a law the individual imposes on themselves. In relation to the latter, the individual is heteronomous; public law is laid down by the state. Rousseau, by whom Kant was profoundly influenced, had maintained in his doctrine of the 'general will' that, under certain conditions, public law too can be self-imposed, so that in obeying the law 'we obey only ourselves' (see chapter 8). But the conditions under which Rousseau claims this ideal state of affairs will obtain amount to a radical form of democracy in which all citizens are active participants and in which there are no economic inequalities serious enough to render one individual dependent on another – conditions Kant rejects as incompatible with his conception of the role of the state. It is not the job of the state to interfere in civil society to ensure equality of wealth, or indeed to 'force citizens to be free' in Rousseau's ominous phrase.

All the same, the significance of this distinction has been exaggerated somewhat by Kant's critics, especially given his discussion of the 'spirit of freedom' in the extracts reproduced below. The distinction between autonomy and heteronomy was, however, central to Hegel's critique of Kant, which largely consists in bringing together the heteronomous form of the state and the ethical life of the family and civil society into an 'ethical state'. Hegel accepted Kant's (and Rousseau's) overriding concern with the problem of bringing together freedom and government, but proposed a more integrated, and indeed democratic solution.

## George William Friedrich Hegel (1770–1831)

Hegel was a leading and highly influential critic of Kant. Born in Stuttgart, the son of a civil servant, he studied at the Tübingen theological seminary and later taught philosophy at the University of Jena where he wrote his masterpiece *The Phenomenology of Spirit* (1807). Following a period as a newspaper editor and as headmaster of a grammar school, during which he wrote the *Science of Logic* (1812–16), he was appointed professor of philosophy at the University of Heidelberg (1816) and then Berlin (1818). It was here that he published his main work in political philosophy, *Elements of the Philosophy of Right*, in 1821. His last published work was a critique of the English Reform Bill.

Hegel's writings in social and political theory may be divided into two broad groups, though they frequently and fruitfully intersect. The first group comprises concrete analyses of particular governments, such as the early analysis of *The German Constitution* (written 1801–02), the *Proceedings of the Estates Assembly in the Kingdom of Wurtenberg, 1815–1816* (1817), and his last essay on *The English Reform Bill* (1831) whose publication was halted by the Prussian censor. These works combine sociological insight into current affairs with a keen sense of journalistic irony and controversy, and are vital for setting Hegel's more abstract writings in social and political philosophy in their proper context. The latter include the early texts on *Natural Law* (1802) and the *System of Ethical Life* (1802–3) and his main text in political philosophy, *Elements of the Philosophy of Right* (1821).

In the *Philosophy of Right*, Hegel moves from the most abstract notion of individual freedom to the institutions of the modern state. He begins with the basic elements of the modern idea of freedom which he describes as 'Abstract Right', namely: persons, property, contract and the criminal law. He then moves from abstract right to morality and conscience. In the third section, on 'Ethical Life', instead of distinguishing between morality and the state in the manner of Kant, Hegel proceeds to connect them. He begins with the family, discussing marriage, kinship and parenthood, and moves to civil society as the realm of the production and satisfaction of needs. The discussion of civil society is organised in terms of individual persons, their interaction in a 'system of needs' or economy, law and the courts and, finally, corporate groups, poverty and welfare. He then goes on to discuss the various powers of the state, its sovereignty and its history. The discussion of the state moves from constitutional law to a consideration of the functions of the sovereign, and of executive power with respect to internal and external affairs. On the whole, in the *Philosophy of Right*, the state and its bureaucracy are taken to represent the general interest of society, by contrast with the conflicting and partial interests of individuals and corporate groups.

Hegel's *Lectures on the Philosophy of History*, first given in 1822–23, were produced under conditions of political repression which particu-

larly affected academic freedom of speech in the university. In the
passage reproduced below (pp. 169–78), taken from the concluding
lecture of the series, Hegel assesses the significance of the two founding events of modernity: the German Reformation (Luther's break with
the church of Rome) and the French Revolution. Both events represent
developments of the modern idea of freedom, on the one hand the
subjective morality of the Reformation which makes each individual
directly answerable to God and their conscience, and on the other hand
the objective political institutions of the modern state created by the
Revolution. But each development, Hegel argues, is unstable if taken in
isolation from the other. The revolutionary change in form of government must be accompanied by a reformation or change in the ethical
sentiments of its citizens. On this basis he offers a caustic comparison
and review of the existing constitutions of France, Germany and
England.

Hegel's social and political philosophy is informed by the attempt to
reconcile the subjective freedom of morality and civil society ('disposition') with the objective morality of the institutional structure of the
modern state. Using concrete examples, he shows how modern societies have failed to achieve this synthesis. An exclusive stress upon
subjective freedom tends towards political quietism, and an exclusive
stress upon objective freedom tending towards state terror, illustrated
for Hegel by the course of the French Revolution. Informing these critical analyses is a vision of the realisation of the modern idea of freedom
in an 'ethical' state, one whose citizens possess a disposition which
'cordially recognises' the state's laws and the obligation to subordinate
their particular wills to them.

### Conclusion

Kant and Hegel represent points of transition from ancient to modern
social and political theory. They combine aspects of Plato's system of
thought (on education) and Aristotle's (on forms of government) with
the distinctively modern notion of the 'spirit of freedom' drawn from
civic republicanism and Rousseau's discussions of sovereignty and the
will. However, while Hegel strives to reconcile modern freedom with
an Aristotelian vision of the community, Kant is arguably prepared to
subordinate and even abandon community to the claims of individual
freedom. Their theories also anticipate the reflections of Tocqueville,
Marx and Durkheim on the implications of the revolutionary slogan
'liberty, equality, and fraternity' for the structure of modern state and
civil society, as well as those of Weber on the consequences of the
Reformation.

### References

The extract from Kant is taken from Immanuel Kant, *Political Writings*, ed. Hans
Reiss, trans. H. B. Nisbet, Cambridge: Cambridge University Press, 1991, pp.

73–9 & 83–6. It consists of most of *On the Common Saying 'This may be Correct in Theory, but it does not Apply in Practice'*, part II 'On the Relationship of Theory to Practice in Political Right (Against Hobbes)'.

The extract from Hegel is taken from 'The Enlightenment and Revolution', in *The Philosophy of History*, trans. J. Sibree, New York: Dover Publications, 1956, pp. 445–56.

### Further reading

The volume of Kant's *Political Writings*, ed. Hans Reiss (see above) usefully collects most of his essays on politics. Also important is Immanuel Kant, *The Metaphysics of Morals*, (trans. Mary Gregor Cambridge: Cambridge University Press, 1991). Howard Williams, *Kant's Political Philosophy* (Oxford: Blackwell, 1983) offers a clear introduction, whilst Hannah Arendt's *Lectures on Kant's Political Philosophy* (ed. R. Beiner, Brighton: Harvester Wheatsheaf, 1982) is an influential discussion of the Kantian project that casts an interesting light on her own distinctive political theory.

Hegel's main work on politics is his *Elements of the Philosophy of Right* (ed. Allen W. Wood, trans. H. B. Nisbet Cambridge: Cambridge University Press, 1991). A selection of minor pieces are collected in G. F. W. Hegel, *Hegel's Political Writings* (trans. T. M. Knox, introduced by Z. A. Pelczynski, Oxford: Clarendon Press, 1964). Shlomo Avineri, *Hegel's Theory of the Modern State* (Cambridge: Cambridge University Press, 1972) provides a clear introduction. Gillian Rose, *Hegel Contra Sociology* (London: Athlone Press, 1995) and Herbert Marcuse, *Reason and Revolution: Hegel and the Rise of Social Theory* (Boston: Harper Torch Books, 1941) are two controversial critiques. Manfred Riedel, *Between Tradition and Revolution* (Cambridge: Cambridge University Press, 1984) and Joachim Ritter, *Hegel and the French Revolution* (Cambridge, MA: Harvard University Press, 1982) are interesting historical studies by two leading German scholars.

### Seminar questions

To what extent can Kant's social and political theory be described as 'anti-democratic liberalism'?

How does Hegel relate the concept of freedom and the form of the state?

Why does Hegel deny that there 'can be a Revolution without a Reformation'?

What is the role of education in Kant's and Hegel's theories of the state?

Discuss Kant's and Hegel's critiques of the English constitution.

How does Kant's 'spirit of freedom' differ from Hegel's 'disposition'?

# I. KANT

# From *On the Common Saying: 'This May be Correct in Theory but it does not Apply in Practice'*

## ON THE RELATIONSHIP OF THEORY TO PRACTICE
## IN POLITICAL RIGHT

### (Against Hobbes)

Among all the contracts by which a large group of men unites to form a society (*pactum sociale*), the contract establishing a *civil constitution* (*pactum unionis civilis*) is of an exceptional nature. For while, so far as its execution is concerned, it has much in common with all others that are likewise directed towards a chosen end to be pursued by joint effort, it is essentially different from all others in the principle of its constitution (*constitutionis civilis*). In all social contracts, we find a union of many individuals for some common end which they all *share*. But a union as an end in itself which they all *ought to share* and which is thus an absolute and primary duty in all external relationships whatsoever among human beings (who cannot avoid mutually influencing one another), is only found in a society in so far as it constitutes a civil state, i.e. a commonwealth. And the end which is a duty in itself in such external relationships, and which is indeed the highest formal condition (*conditio sine qua non*) of all other external duties, is the *right* of men *under coercive public laws* by which each can be given what is due to him and secured against attack from any others. But the whole concept of an external right is derived entirely from the concept of *freedom* in the mutual external relationships of human beings, and has nothing to do with the end which all men have by nature (i.e. the aim of achieving happiness) or with the recognised means of attaining this end. And thus the latter end must on no account interfere as a determinant with the laws governing external right. *Right* is the restriction of each individual's freedom so that it harmonises with the freedom of everyone else (in so far as this is possible within the terms of a general law). And *public right* is the distinctive quality of the *external laws* which make this constant harmony possible. Since every restriction of freedom through the arbitrary will of another party is termed *coercion*, it follows that a civil constitution is a relationship among *free* men who are subject to coercive laws, while they retain their freedom within the general union with their fellows. Such is the requirement of pure reason, which legislates *a priori*, regardless of all empirical ends (which can all be summed up under the general heading of happiness). Men have different views on the empirical end of happiness and what it consists of, so that as far as happiness is concerned, their will cannot be brought under any common principle nor thus under any external law harmonising with the freedom of everyone.

The civil state, regarded purely as a lawful state, is based on the following *a priori* principles:

1. The *freedom* of every member of society as a *human being*.
2. The *equality* of each with all the others as a *subject*.
3. The *independence* of each member of a commonwealth as a *citizen*.

These principles are not so much laws given by an already established state, as laws by which a state can alone be established in accordance with pure rational principles of external human right. Thus:

1. Man's *freedom* as a human being, as a principle for the constitution of a commonwealth, can be expressed in the following formula. No-one can compel me to be happy in accordance with his conception of the welfare of others, for each may seek his happiness in whatever way he sees fit, so long as he does not infringe upon the freedom of others to pursue a similar end which can be reconciled with the freedom of everyone else within a workable general law – i.e. he must accord to others the same right as he enjoys himself. A government might be established on the principle of benevolence towards the people, like that of a father towards his children. Under such a *paternal government (imperium paternale)*, the subjects, as immature children who cannot distinguish what is truly useful or harmful to themselves, would be obliged to behave purely passively and to rely upon the judgement of the head of state as to how they *ought* to be happy, and upon his kindness in willing their happiness at all. Such a government is the greatest conceivable *despotism*, i.e. a constitution which suspends the entire freedom of its subjects, who thenceforth have no rights whatsoever. The only conceivable government for men who are capable of possessing rights, even if the ruler is benevolent, is not a *paternal* but a *patriotic* government (*imperium non paternale, sed patrioticum*). A *patriotic* attitude is one where everyone in the state, not excepting its head, regards the commonwealth as a maternal womb, or the land as the paternal ground from which he himself sprang and which he must leave to his descendants as a treasured pledge. Each regards himself as authorised to protect the rights of the commonwealth by laws of the general will, but not to submit it to his personal use at his own absolute pleasure. This right of freedom belongs to each member of the commonwealth as a human being, in so far as each is a being capable of possessing rights.

2. Man's *equality* as a subject might be formulated as follows. Each member of the commonwealth has rights of coercion in relation to all the others, except in relation to the head of state. For he alone is not a member of the commonwealth, but its creator or preserver, and he alone is authorised to coerce others without being subject to any coercive law himself. But all who are subject to laws are the subjects of a state, and are thus subject to the right of coercion along with all other members of the commonwealth; the only exception is a single person (in either the physical or the moral sense of the word), the head of state, through whom alone the rightful coercion of all others can be

exercised. For if he too could be coerced, he would not be the head of state, and the hierarchy of subordination would ascend infinitely. But if there were two persons exempt from coercion, neither would be subject to coercive laws, and neither could do to the other anything contrary to right, which is impossible.

This uniform equality of human beings as subjects of a state is, however, perfectly consistent with the utmost inequality of the mass in the degree of its possessions, whether these take the form of physical or mental superiority over others, or of fortuitous external property and of particular rights (of which there may be many) with respect to others. Thus the welfare of the one depends very much on the will of the other (the poor depending on the rich), the one must obey the other (as the child its parents or the wife her husband), the one serves (the labourer) while the other pays, etc. Nevertheless, they are all equal as subjects *before the law*, which, as the pronouncement of the general will, can only be single in form, and which concerns the form of right and not the material or object in relation to which I possess rights. For no-one can coerce anyone else other than through the public law and its executor, the head of state, while everyone else can resist the others in the same way and to the same degree. No-one, however, can lose this authority to coerce others and to have rights towards them except through committing a crime. And no-one can voluntarily renounce his rights by a contract or legal transaction to the effect that he has no rights but only duties, for such a contract would deprive him of the right to make a contract, and would thus invalidate the one he had already made.

From this idea of the equality of men as subjects in a commonwealth, there emerges this further formula: every member of the commonwealth must be entitled to reach any degree of rank which a subject can earn through his talent, his industry and his good fortune. And his fellow-subjects may not stand in his way by *hereditary* prerogatives or privileges of rank and thereby hold him and his descendants back indefinitely.

All right consists solely in the restriction of the freedom of others, with the qualification that their freedom can co-exist with my freedom within the terms of a general law; and public right in a commonwealth is simply a state of affairs regulated by a real legislation which conforms to this principle and is backed up by power, and under which a whole people live as subjects in a lawful state (*status iuridicus*). This is what we call a civil state, and it is characterised by equality in the effects and counter-effects of freely willed actions which limit one another in accordance with the general law of freedom. Thus the *birthright* of each individual in such a state (i.e. before he has performed any acts which can be judged in relation to right) is absolutely *equal* as regards his authority to coerce others to use their freedom in a way which harmonises with his freedom. Since birth is not an act on the part of the one who is born, it cannot create any inequality in his legal position and cannot make him submit to any coercive laws except in so far as he is a subject, along with all the others, of the one supreme legislative power. Thus no member of the commonwealth can have a hereditary privilege as against his fellow-subjects; and no-one can hand down to his descendants the privileges attached to the rank he occupies in the commonwealth, nor act as if he were qualified as a ruler by birth and forcibly prevent others from reaching the higher levels of the hierachy (which are *superior* and *inferior*, but never *imperans* and *subiectus*) through their own merit. He may hand down everything else, so long as it is material and not pertaining to his person, for it may be acquired and disposed of as property and may over a series of generations create considerable inequalities in wealth among the members of the commonwealth (the employee and the employer, the landowner and the argricultural servants, etc). But he may not prevent his subordinates from raising themselves to his own level if they are able and entitled to do so by their talent, industry and good fortune. If this were not so, he would be allowed to practise coercion without himself being subject to coercive counter-measures from others, and would thus be more than their fellow-subject. No-one who lives within the lawful state of a commonwealth can forfeit this equality other than through some crime of his own, but never by contract or through military force (*occupatio bellica*). For no legal transaction on his part or on that of anyone else can make him cease to be his own master. He cannot become like a domestic animal to be employed in any chosen capacity and retained therein without consent for any desired period, even with the reservation (which is at times sanctioned by religion, as among the Indians) that he may not be maimed or killed. He can be considered happy in any condition so long as he is aware that, if he does not reach the same level as others, the fault lies either with himself (i.e. lack of ability or serious endeavour) or with cirumstances for which he cannot blame others, and not with the irresistible will of any outside party. For as far as right is concerned, his fellow-subjects have no advantage over him.[1]

[1] If we try to find a definite meaning for the word *gracious,* as distinct from kind, beneficent, protective etc. we see that it can be attributed only to a person to whom no *coercive rights* apply. Thus only the head of the *state's government* who enacts and distributes all benefits that are possible within the public laws (for the *sovereign,* who provides them is, as it were, invisible, and is not an agent but the personified law itself), can be given the title of *gracious lord,* for he is the only individual to whom coercive rights do not apply. And even in an aristocratic government, as for example in Venice, the *senate* is the only 'gracious lord'. The nobles who belong to it, even including the *Doge* (for only the *plenary council* is the sovereign), are all subjects and equal to the others so far as the exercise of rights is concerned, for each subject has coercive rights towards every one of them. Princes (i.e. persons with a hereditary right to become rulers) are themselves called gracious lords only with future reference, an account of their claims to become rulers (i.e. by courtly etiquette, *par courtoisie*). But as owners of property, they are nonetheless fellow-subjects of the others, and even the humblest of their servants must posses a right of coercion against them through the head of state. Thus there can be no more than one gracious lord in a state. And as for

3. The *independence* (*sibisufficientia*) of a member of the commonwealth as a *citizen*, i.e. as a co-legislator, may be defined as follows. In the question of actual legislation, all who are free and equal under existing public laws may be considered equal, but not as regards the right to make these laws. Those who are not entitled to this right are nonetheless obliged, as members of the commonwealth, to comply with these laws, and they thus likewise enjoy their protection (not as *citizens* but as co-beneficiaries of this protection). For all right depends on laws. But a public law which defines for everyone that which is permitted and prohibited by right, is the act of a public will, from which all right proceeds and which must not therefore itself be able to do an injustice to any one. And this requires no less than the will of the entire people (since all men decide for all men and each decides for himself). For only towards oneself can one never act unjustly. But on the other hand, the will of another person cannot decide anything for someone without injustice, so that the law made by this other person would require further law to limit his legislation. Thus an individual will cannot legislate for a commonwealth. For this requires freedom, equality and *unity* of the will of *all* the members. And the prerqeuisite for unity, since it necessitates a general vote (if freedom and equality are both present), is independence. The basic law, which can come only from the general, united will of the people, is called the *original contract.*

Anyone who has the right to vote on this legislation is a *citizen* (*citoyen*, i.e. citizen of a state, not *bourgeois* or citizen of a town). The only qualification required by a citizen (apart, of course, from being an adult male) is that he must be his *own master* (sui iuris), and must have some *property* (which can include any skill, trade, fine art or science) to support himself. In cases where he must earn his living from others, he must earn it only by *selling* that which is his,[2] and not by allowing others to make use of him; for he must in the true sense of the word *serve* no-one but the commonwealth. In this respect, artisans and large or small landowners are all equal, and each is entitled to one vote only. As for landowners, we leave aside the question of how anyone can have rightfully acquired more land than he can cultivate with his own hands (for acquisition by military seizure is not primary acquisition), and how it came about that numerous people who might otherwise have acquired permanent property were thereby reduced to serving someone else in order to live at all. It would certainly conflict with the above principle of equality if a law were to grant them a privileged status so that their descendants would always remain feudal landowners, without their land being sold or divided by inheritance and thus made useful to more people;

gracious (more correctly *distinguished*) ladies, they can be considered entitled to this appellation by their *rank* and their *sex* (thus only as opposed to the *male* sex), and this only by virtue of a refinement of manners (known as gallantry) whereby the male sex imagines that it does itself greater honour by giving the fair sex precedence over itself.

it would also be unjust if only those belonging to an arbitrarily selected class were allowed to acquire land, should the estates in fact be divided. The owner of a large estate keeps out as many smaller property owners (and their votes) as could otherwise occupy his territories. He does not vote on their behalf, and himself has only *one* vote. It should be left exclusively to the ability, industry and good fortune of each member of the commonwealth to enable each to acquire a part and all to acquire the whole, although this distinction cannot be observed within the general legislation itself. The number of those entitled to vote on matters of legislation must be calculated purely from the number of property owners, not from the size of their properties.

Those who posess this right to vote must agree *unanimously* to the law of public justice, or else a legal contention would arise between those who agree and those who disagree, and it would require yet another higher legal principle to resolve it. An entire people cannot, however, be expected to reach unanimity, but only to show a majority of votes (and not even of direct votes, but simply of the votes of those delegated in a large nation to represent the people). Thus the actual principle of being content with majority decisions must be accepted unanimously and embodied in a contract; and this itself must be the ultimate basis on which a civil constitution is established.

It is obvious from this that the principle of happiness (which is not in fact a definite principle at all) has ill effects in political right just as in morality, however good the intentions of those who teach it. The sovereign wants to make the people happy as he thinks best, and thus becomes a despot, while the people are unwilling to give up their universal human desire to seek happiness in their own way, and thus become rebels. If they had first of all asked what is lawful (in terms of *a priori* certainty, which no empiricist can upset), the idea of a social contract would retain its authority undiminished. But it would not exist as a fact (as Danton would have it, declaring that since it does not actually exist, all property and all rights under the existing civil constitution are null and void), but only as a rational prinicple for

---

[2] He who does a piece of work (*opus*) can sell it to someone else, just as if it were his own property. But guaranteeing one's labour (*praestatio operae*) is not the same as selling a commodity. The domestic servant, the shop assistant, the labourer, or even the barber, are merely labourers (*operarii*), not *artists* (*artifices*, in the wider sense) or members of the state, and are thus unqualified to be citizens. And although the man to whom I give my firewood to chop and the tailor to whom I give material to make into clothes both appear to have a similar relationship towards me, the former differs from the latter in the same way as the barber from the wig-maker (to whom I may in fact have given the requisite hair) or the labourer from the artist or tradesman, who does a piece of work which belongs to him until he is paid for it. For the latter, in pursuing his trade, exchanges his property with someone else (*opus*), while the former allows someone else to make use of him – But I do admit that it is somewhat difficult to define the qualifications which entitle anyone to claim the status of being his own master.

judging any lawful public constitution whatsoever. And it would then be seen that, until the general will is there, the people has no coercive right against its ruler, since it can apply coercion legally only through him. But if the will is there, no force can be applied to the ruler by the people, otherwise the people would be the supreme ruler. Thus the people can never possess a right of coercion against the head of state, or be entitled to oppose him in word or deed.

We can see, furthermore, that this theory is adequately confirmed in practice. In the British constitution, of which the people are so proud that they hold it up as a model for the whole world, we find no mention of what the people are entitled to do if the monarch were to violate the contract of 1688. Since there is no law to cover such a case, the people tacitly reserve the right to rebel against him if he should violate the contract. And it would be an obvious contradiction if the constitution included a law for such eventualities, entitling the people to overthrow the existing constitution, from which all particular laws are derived, if the contract were violated. For there would then have to be a *publicly constituted*[3] opposing power, hence a second head of state to protect the rights of the people against the first ruler, and then yet a third to decide which of the other two had right on his side. In fact, the leaders (or guardians – call them what you will) of the British people, fearing some such accusation if their plans did not succeed, *invented* the notion of a voluntary abdication by the monarch they forced out, rather than claim a right to depose him (which would have made the constitution self-contradictory).

While I trust that no-one will accuse me of flattering monarchs too much by declaring them inviolable, I likewise hope that I shall be spared the reproach of claiming too much for the people if I maintain that the people too have inalienable rights against the head of state, even if these cannot be rights of coercion.

Hobbes is of the opposite opinion. According to him (*De Cive*, Chap. 7, 14), the head of state has no contractual obligations towards the people; he can do no injustice to a citizen, but may act towards him as he pleases. This proposition would be perfectly correct if injustice were taken to mean any injury which gave the injured party a *coercive right* against the one who has done him injustice. But in its general form, the proposition is quite terrifying.

The non-resisting subject must be able to assume that his ruler has no *wish* to do him injustice. And everyone has his inalienable rights, which he cannot give up even if he wishes to, and about which he is entitled to make his own judgements. But if he assumes that the ruler's attitude is one of good will, any injustice which he believes he has suffered can only have resulted through error, or through igno-

[3] No right in a state can be tacitly and treacherously included by a secret reservation, and least of all a right which the people claim to be part of the constitution, for all laws within it must be thought of as arising out of a public will. Thus if the constitution allowed rebellion, it would have to declare this right publicly and make clear how it might be implemented.

rance of certain possible consequences of the laws which the supreme authority has made. Thus the citizen must, with the approval of the ruler, be entitled to make public his opinion on whatever of the ruler's measures seem to him to constitute an injustice against the commonwealth. For to assume that the head of state can neither make mistakes nor be ignorant of anything would be to imply that he receives divine inspiration and is more than a human being. Thus *freedom of the pen* is the only safeguard of the rights of the people, although it must not transcend the bounds of respect and devotion towards the existing constitution, which should itself create a liberal attitude of mind among the subjects. To try to deny the citizen this freedom does not only mean, as Hobbes maintains, that the subject can claim no rights against the supreme ruler. It also means withholding from the ruler all knowledge of those matters which, if he knew about them, he would himself rectify, so that he is thereby put into a self-stultifying position. For his will issues commands to his subjects (as citizens) only in so far as he represents the general will of the people. But to encourage the head of state to fear that independent and public thought might cause political unrest is tantamount to making him distrust his own power and feel hatred towards his people.

The general principle, however, according to which a people may judge negatively whatever it believes was *not decreed* in good will by the supreme legislation, can be summed up as follows: *Whatever a people cannot impose upon itself cannot be imposed upon it by the legislator either.*

For example, if we wish to discover whether a law which declares permanently valid an ecclesiastical constitution (itself formulated at some time in the past) can be regarded as emanating from the actual will or intention of the legislator, we must first ask whether a people is *authorised* to make a law for itself whereby certain accepted doctrines and outward forms of religion are declared permanent, and whether the people may thus prevent its own descendants from making further progress in religious understanding or from correcting any past mistakes. It is clear that any original contract of the people which established such a law would in itself be null and void, for it would conflict with the appointed aim and purpose of mankind. Thus a law of this kind cannot be regarded as the actual will of the monarch, to whom counter-representations may accordingly be made. In all cases, however, where the supreme legislation did nevertheless adopt such measures, it would be permissible to pass general and public judgements upon them, but never to offer any verbal or active resistance.

In every commonwealth, there must be *obedience* to generally valid coercive laws within the mechanism of the political constitution. There must also be a *spirit of freedom*, for in all matters concerning universal human duties, each individual requires to be convinced by reason that the coercion which prevails is lawful, otherwise he would be in contradiction with himself. Obedience without the spirit of freedom is the effective cause of all *secret societies*. For it is a natural vocation of man to communicate with his fellows, especially in matters affecting mankind as a whole. Thus secret societies would disappear if freedom of this kind were encouraged. And how else can the government itself acquire the knowledge it needs to further its own basic intention, if not by allowing the spirit of freedom, so admirable in its origins and effects, to make itself heard?

# G. W. F. HEGEL
## From *Lectures on the Philosophy of History*

An *intellectual principle* was thus discovered to serve as a basis for the State – one which does not, like previous principles, belong to the sphere of opinion, such as the social impulse, the desire of security for property, etc. nor owe its origin to the religious sentiment, as does that of the Divine appointment of the governing power – but the principle of Certainty, which is identity with my self-consciousness, stopping short however of that of Truth, which needs to be distinguished from it. This is a vast discovery in regard to the profoundest depths of being and Freedom. The consciousness of the Spiritual is now the essential basis of the political fabric, and *Philosophy* has thereby become dominant. It has been said, that the *French Revolution* resulted from Philosophy and it is not without reason that Philosophy has been called Weltweisheit [World Wisdom], for it is not only Truth in and for itself, as the pure essence of things, but also Truth in its living form as exhibited in the affairs of the world. We should not, therefore, contradict the assertion that the Revolution received its first impulse from Philosophy. But this philosophy is in the first instance only abstract Thought, not the concrete comprehension of absolute Truth – intellectual positions between which there is an immeasurable chasm.

The principle of the Freedom of the Will, therefore, asserted itself against existing Right. Before the French Revolution, it must be allowed, the power of the grandees had been diminished by Richelieu, and they had been deprived of privileges; but, like the clergy, they retained all the prerogatives which gave them an advantage over the lower class. The political condition of France at that time presents nothing but a confused mass of privileges altogether contravening Thought and Reason – an utterly irrational state of things, and one with which the greatest corruption of morals, of Spirit was associated – an empire characterized by Destitutuion of Right. and which. when its real state begins to be recognized. becomes shameless destitution of Right. The fearfully heavy burdens that pressed upon the people, the embarrassment of the government to procure for the Court the means of supporting luxury and extravagance, gave the first impulse to discontent. The new Spirit began to agitate men's minds: oppression drove men to investigation. It was perceived that the sums extorted from the people were not expended in furthering the objects of the State, but were lavished in the most unreasonable fashion. The entire political system appeared one mass of injustice. The change was necessarily violent, because the work of transformation was not undertaken by the government. And the reason why the government did not undertake it was that the Court, the Clergy, the Nobility, the Parliaments themselves, were unwilling to surrender the privileges they possessed, either for the sake of expediency or that of abstract Right; moreover, because the government as the concrete centre of the power of the State, could not adopt as its principle abstract individual wills, and reconstruct the State on this basis; lastly, because it was Catholic, and therefore the Idea of Freedom – Reason embodied in Laws – did not pass for the final absolute obligation, since the Holy and the religious conscience are separated from them. The conception, the idea of Right asserted its authority *all at once* and the old framework of injustice could offer no resistance to its onslaught. A constitution, therefore, was established in harmony with the conception of the Right, and on this foundation all future legislation was to be based. Never since the sun had stood in the firmament and the planets revolved around him had it been perceived that man's existence centres in his head, *i.e.* in Thought, inspired by which he builds up the world of reality. Anaxagoras had been the first to say that Thought governs the World; but not until now had man advanced to the recognition of the principle that Thought ought to govern spiritual reality. This was accordingly a glorious mental dawn. All thinking beings shared in the jubilation of this epoch. Emotions of a lofty character stirred men's minds at that time; a spiritual enthusiasm thrilled through the world, as if the reconciliation between the Divine and the Secular was now first accomplished.

The two following points must now occupy our attention: 1st. The course which the Revolution in France took; 2d. How that Revolution became World-Historical.

1. Freedom presents two aspects: the one concerns its substance and purport – its objectivity – the thing itself – [that which is performed as a free act]; the other relates to the Form of Freedom, involving the consciousness of his activity on the part of the individual; for Freedom demands that the individual recognize himself in such acts, that they should be veritably his, it being his interest that the result in question should be attained. The three elements and powers of the State in actual working must be contemplated according to the above analysis, their examination in detail being referred to the Lectures on the Philosophy of Right.

(1) *Laws* of Rationality – of intrinsic Right – Objective or Real Freedom: to this category belong Freedom of Property and Freedom of Person. Those relics of that condition of servitude which the feudal relation had introduced are hereby swept away, and all those fiscal ordi-

nances which were the bequest of the feudal law – its tithes and dues, are abrogated. Real [practical] Liberty requires moreover freedom in regard to trades and professions – the permission to every one to use his abilities without restriction – and the free admission to all offices of State. This is a summary of the elements of real Freedom, and which are not based on feeling – for feeling allows of the continuance even of serfdom and slavery – but on the thought and self-consciousness of man recognizing the spiritual character of his existence.

(2) But the agency which gives the laws practical effect is the *Government* generally. Government is primarily the formal execution of the laws and the maintenance of their authority: in respect to foreign relations it prosecutes the interest of the State; that is, it assists the independence of the nation as an individuality against other nations; lastly, it has to provide for the internal weal of the State and all its classes – what is called administration: for it is not enough that the citizen is allowed to pursue a trade or calling, it must also be a source of gain to him; it is not enough that men are permitted to use their powers, they must also find an opportunity of applying them to purpose. Thus the State involves a body of abstract principles and a practical application to them. This application must be the work of a subjective will, a will which resolves and decides. Legislation itself – the invention and positive enactment of these statutory arrangements, is an application of such general principles. The next step, then, consists in [specific] determination and execution. Here then the question presents itself: what is the decisive will to be? The ultimate decision is the prerogative of the monarch: but if the State is based on Liberty, the many wills of individuals also desire to have a share in political decisions. But the *Many* are *All*; and it seems but a poor expedient, rather a monstrous inconsistency, to allow only a few to take part in those decisions, since each wishes that his volition should have a share in determining what is to be law for him. The Few assume to be the *deputies*, but they are often only the *despoilers* of the Many. Nor is the sway of the Majority over the Minority a less palpable inconsistency.

(3) This collision of subjective wills leads therefore to the consideration of a third point, that of *Disposition* – an *ex amino* acquiescence in the laws; not the mere customary observance of them, but the cordial recognition of laws and the Constitution as in principle fixed and immutable, and of the supreme obligation of individuals to subject their particular wills to them. There may be various opinions and views respecting laws, constitution and government, but there must be a disposition on the part of the citizens to regard all these opinions as subordinate to the substantial interest of the State, and to insist upon them no further than that interest will allow; moreover nothing must be considered higher and more sacred than good will towards the State; or, if Religion be looked upon as higher and more sacred, it must involve nothing really alien or opposed to the Constitution. It is, indeed, regarded as a maxim of the profoundest

171

wisdom entirely to separate the laws and constitution of the State from Religion, since bigotry and hypocrisy are to be feared as the results of a State Religion. But although the aspects of Religion and the State are different, they are radically *one*; and the laws find their highest confirmation in Religion.

Here it must be frankly stated, that with the Catholic Religion no rational constitution is possible; for Government and People must reciprocate that final guarantee of Disposition, and can have it only in a Religion that is not opposed to a rational political constitution.

Plato in his Republic makes everything depend upon the Government, and makes Disposition the principle of the State; on which account he lays the chief stress on Education. The modern theory is diametrically opposed to this, referring everything to the individual will. But here we have no guarantee that the will in question has that right dispostion which is essential to the stability of the State.

In view then of these leading considerations we have to trace the course of the *French Revolution* and the remodelling of the State in accordance with the Idea of Right. In the first instance purely abstract philosophical principles were set up: Disposition and Religion were not taken into account. The first Constitutional form of Government in France was one which recognized Royalty; the monarch was to stand at the head of the State, and on him in conjunction with his Ministers was to devolve the executive power; the legislative body on the other hand were to make the laws. But this constitution involved from the very first an internal contradiction; for the legislature absorbed the whole power of the administration: the budget, affairs of war and peace, and the levying of the armed force were in the hands of the Legislative Chamber. Everything was brought under the head of Law. The budget however is in its nature something diverse from law, for it is annually renewed, and the power to which it properly belongs is that of the Government. With this moreover is connected the indirect nomination of the ministry and officers of state etc. The government was thus transferred to the Legislative Chamber, as in England to the Parliament. This constitution was also vitiated by the experience of absolute mistrust; the dynasty lay under suspicion, because it had lost the power it formerly enjoyed and the priests refused the oath. Neither government nor constitution could be maintained on this footing, and the ruin of both was the result. A government of some kind however is always in existence. The question presents itself then, Whence did it emanate? Theoretically, it proceeded from the people; really and truly from the National Convention and its Committees. The forces now dominant are the abstract principles – Freedom, and, as it exists within the limits of the Subjective Will – Virtue. This Virtue has now to conduct the government in opposition to the Many, whom their corruption and attachment to old interests, or a liberty that has degenerated into license, and the violence of their passions, render unfaithful to virtue. Virtue is here a simple abstract principle and distinguishes the citizens into two classes only – those who are favourably disposed and those who are not. But disposition can only be recognized and judged of by disposition. *Suspicion* therefore is in the ascendant; but virtue, as soon as it becomes liable to suspicion, is already condemned. Suspicion attained a terrible power and brought to the scaffold the Monarch, whose subjective will was in fact the religious conscience of a Catholic. Robespierre set up the principle of Virtue as supreme, and it may be said that with this man Virtue was an earnest matter. *Virtue* and *Terror* are the order of the day; for Subjective Virtue, whose sway is based on disposition only, brings with it the most fearful tyranny. It exercises its power without legal formalities, and the punishment it inflicts is equally simple – *Death*. This tyranny could not last; for all inclinations, all interests, reason itself revolted against this terribly consistent Liberty, which in its concentrated intensity exhibited so fanatical a shape. An organized government is introduced, analogous to the one that had been displaced; only that is chief and monarch is now a mutable Directory of Five, who may form a moral, but have not an individual unity; under them also suspicion was in the ascendant, and the government was in the hands of the legislative assemblies; this constitution therefore experienced the same fate as its predecessor, for it had proved to itself the absolute necessity of a governmental *power*. *Napoleon* restored it as a military power, and followed up this step by establishing himself as an individual will at the head of the State: he knew how to rule, and soon settled the internal affairs of France. The *avocats*, idealogues and abstract-principle men who ventured to show themselves he sent 'to the right about', and the sway of mistrust was exhanged for that of respect and fear. He then, with the vast might of his character turned his attention to foreign relations, subjected all Europe, and diffused his liberal institutions in every quarter. Greater victories were never gained, expeditions displaying greater genius were never conducted: but never was the powerlessness of Victory exhibited in a clearer light than then. The disposition of the peoples. *i.e.* their religious disposition and that of their nationality, ultimately precipitated this colossus; and in France constitutional monarchy, with the 'Charte' as its basis, was restored. But here again the antithesis of Disposition [good feeling] and Mistrust made its appearance. The French stood in a mendacious position to each other, when they issued addresses full of devotion and love to the monarchy, and loading it with benediction. A fifteen years' farce was played. For although the *Charte* was the standard under which all were enrolled, and though both parties had sworn to it, yet on the one side the ruling disposition was a Catholic one, which regarded it as a matter of conscience to destroy the existing institutions. Another breach, therefore, took place, and the Government was overturned. At length, after forty years of war and confusion indescribable, a weary heart might fain congratulate itself on seeing a termination and tranquillization of all these disturbances. But although one main point is set at rest, there remains on

173

the one hand that rapture which the Catholic principle inevitably occasions, on the other hand that which has to do with men's subjective will. In regard to the latter, the main feature of incompatibility still presents itself, in the requirement that the ideal general will should also be the *empirically* general – *i.e.* that the units of the State, in their individual capacity, should rule, or at any rate take part in the government. Not satisfied with the establishment of rational rights, with freedom of person and property, with the existence of a political organization in which are to be found various circles of civil life each having its own functions to perform, and with that influence over the people which is exercised by the intelligent members of the community, and the confidence that is felt in them, '*Liberalism*' sets up in opposition to all this the atomistic principle, that which insists upon the sway of individual wills; maintaining that all government should emanate from their express power, and have their express sanction. Asserting this formal side of Freedom – this abstraction – the party in question allows no political organization to be firmly established. The particular arrangements of the government are forthwith opposed by the advocates of Liberty as the mandates of a particular will, and branded as displays of arbitrary power. The will of the Many expels the Ministry from power, and those who had formed the Opposition fill the vacant places; but the latter having now become the Government, meet with hostility from the Many, and share the same fate. Thus agitation and unrest are perpetuated. This collision, this nodus, this problem is that with which history is now occupied, and whose solution it has to work out in the future.

2. We have now to consider the French Revolution in its organic connection with the *History of the World*; for in its substantial import that event is World-Historical, and that contest of Formalism which we discussed in the last paragraph must be properly distinguished from its wider bearings. As regards outward diffusion its principle gained access to almost all modern states, either through conquest or by express introduction into their political life. Particularly all the Romanic nations, and the Roman Catholic World in special – *France, Italy, Spain* – were subjected to the dominion of Liberalism. But it became bankrupt everywhere; first, the grand firm in France, then its branches in Spain and Italy; twice, in fact, in the states into which it had been introduced. This was the case in Spain, where it was first brought in by the Napoleonic Constitution, then by that which the Cortes adopted – in Piedmont, first when it was incorporated with the French Empire, and a second time as the result of internal insurrection; so in Rome and in Naples it was twice set up. Thus Liberalism as an abstraction, emanating from France, traversed the Roman World; but Religious slavery held that world in the fetters of political servitude. For it is a false principle that the fetters which bind Right and Freedom can be broken without the emancipation of conscience – that there can be a Revolution without a Reformation. – These countries, therefore, sank back into their old condition – in

Italy with some modifications of the outward political condition. Venice and Genoa, those ancient aristocracies, which could at least boast of legitimacy, vanished as rotten despotisms. Material superiority in power can achieve not enduring results: Napoleon could not coerce Spain into freedom any more than Philip II could force Holland into slavery.

Contrasted with these Romanic nations we observe the other powers of Europe, and especially the Protestant nations. *Austria* and *England* were not drawn within the vortex of internal agitation, and exhibited great, immense proofs of their internal solidity. *Austria* is not a Kingdom, but an Empire, *i.e.* an aggregate of many political organizations. The inhabitants of its chief provinces are not German in origin and character, and have remained unaffected by 'ideas.' Elevated neither by education nor religion, the lower classes in some districts have remained in a condition of serfdom, and the nobility have been kept down, as in Bohemia; in other quarters, while the former have continued the same, the barons have maintained their despotism, as in Hungary. Austria has surrendered that more intimate connection with Germany which was derived from the imperial dignity, and renounced its numerous possessions and rights in Germany and the Netherlands. It now takes its place in Europe as a distinct power, involved with no other. *England*, with great exertions, maintained itself on its old foundations; the English *Constitution* kept its ground amid the general convulsion, though it seemed so much the more liable to be affected by it, as a public Parliament, that habit of assembling in public meeting which was common to all orders of the state, and a free press, offered singular facilities for introducing the French principles of Liberty and Equality among all classes of the people. Was the English nation too backward in point of culture to apprehend these general principles? Yet in no country has the question of Liberty been more frequently a subject of reflection and public discussion. Or was the English constitution so entirely a Free Constitution – had those principles been already so completely realized in it, that they could no longer excite opposition or even interest? The English nation may be said to have approved of the emancipation of France; but it was proudly reliant on its own constitution and freedom, and instead of imitating the example of the foreigner, it displayed its ancient hostiltiy to its rival, and was soon involved in a popular war with France.

The Constitution of England is a complex of mere *particular Rights* and particular privileges: the Government is essentially administrative – that is, conservative of the interests of all particular orders and classes; and each particular Church, parochial district, county, society, takes care of itself, so that the Government strictly speaking, has nowhere less to do than in England. This is the leading feature of what Englishmen call their Liberty, and is the very antithesis of such a centralized administration as exists in France, where down to the least village the Maire is named by the Ministry or their agents.

Nowhere can people less tolerate free action on the part of others than in France: there the Ministry combines in itself all administrative power, to which, on the other hand, the Chamber of Deputies lays claim. In England, on the contrary, every parish, every subordinate division and association has a part of its own to perform. Thus the common interest is concrete, and particular interests are taken cognizance of and determined in view of that common interest. These arrangements, based on particular interests, render a general system impossible. Consequently, abstract and general principles have no attraction for Englishmen – are addressed in their case to inattentive ears. – The particular interests above referred to have positive rights attached to them, which date from the antique times of Feudal Law, and have been preserved in England more than in any other country. By an inconsistency of the most startling kind, we find them contravening equity most grossly; and of institutions characterized by real freedom there are nowhere fewer than in England. In point of private right and freedom of possession they present an incredible deficiency: sufficient proof of which is afforded in the rights of primogeniture, involving the necessity of purchasing or otherwise providing military or ecclesiastical appointments for the younger sons of the aristocracy.

The *Parliament governs,* although Englishmen are unwilling to allow that such is the case. It is worthy of remark, that what has been always regarded as the period of the corruption of a republican people, presents itself here; viz. election to seats in parliament by means of bribery. But this also they call freedom – the power to sell one's vote, and to purchase a seat in parliament.

But this utterly inconsistent and corrupt state of things has nevertheless one advantage, that it provides for the possibility of a government – that it introduces a majority of men into parliament who are statesmen, who from their very youth have devoted themselves to political business and have worked and lived in it. And the nation has the correct conviction and perception that there must be a government, and is therefore willing to give its confidence to a body of men who have had experience in governing; for a general sense of particularity involves also a recognition of that form of particularity which is a distinguishing feature of one class of the community – that knowledge, experience, and facility acquired by practice, which the aristocracy who devote themselves to such interests exclusively possess. This is quite opposed to the appreciation of principles and abstract views which everyone can understand at once, and which are besides to be found in all Constitutions and Charters. It is a question whether the Reform in Parliament now on the tapis, consistently carried out, will leave the possibility of a Government.

The material existence of England is based on commerce and industry, and the English have undertaken the weighty responsibility of being the missionaries of civilization to the world; for their commercial spirit urges them to traverse every sea and land, to form connections with barbarous peoples, to create wants and stimulate industry, and first and foremost to establish among them the conditions necessary to commerce, viz. the relinquishment of a life of lawless violence, respect for property, and civility to strangers.

*Germany* was traversed by the victorious French hosts, but German nationality delivered it from this yoke. One of the leading features in the political condition of Germany is that code of Rights which was cerainly occasioned by French oppression, since this was the especial means of bringing to light the deficiencies of the old system. The fiction of an Empire has utterly vanished. It is broken up into sovereign states. Feudal obligations are abolished, for freedom of property and of person have been recognized as fundamental principles. Offices of State are open to every citizen, talent and adaptation being of course the necessary conditions. The government rests with the offical world, and the personal decision of the monarch constitutes its apex; for a final decision is, as was remarked above, absolutely necessary. Yet with firmly established laws, and a settled organization of the State, what is left to the sole arbitrament of the monarch is, in point of substance, no great matter. It is certainly a very fortunate circumstance for a nation, when a sovereign of noble character falls to its lot: yet in a great state even this is of small moment, since its strength lies in the Reason incorporated in it. Minor states have their existence and tranquillity secured to them more or less by their neighbors: they are therefore, properly speaking, not independent, and have not the fiery trial of war to endure. As has been remarked, a share in the government may be obtained by every one who has a competent knowledge, experience, and a morally regulated will. Those who know ought to govern – *hoi aristoi*, not ignorance and the presumptuous conceit of 'knowing better'. Lastly, as to Disposition, we have already remarked that in the Protestant Church the reconciliation of Religion with Legal Right has taken place. In the Protestant world there is no sacred, no religious conscience in a state of separation from, or perhaps even hostility to Secular Right.

This is the point which consciousness has attained, and these are the principal phases of that form in which the principle of Freedom has realized itself; – for the History of the World is nothing but the development of the Idea of Freedom. But Objective Freedom – the laws of *real* Freedom – demand the subjugation of the mere contingent Will – for this is in its nature formal. If the Objective is in itself Rational, human insight and conviction must correspond with the Reason which it embodies, and then we have the other essential element – Subjective Freedom – also realized. We have confined ourselves to the consideration of that progress of the Idea [which has led to this consummation], and have been obliged to forego the pleasure of giving a detailed picture of the prosperity, the periods of glory that have distinguished the career of peoples, the beauty and grandeur of the character of individuals, and the interest attaching to their fate in weal or woe. Philosophy concerns itself only with the glory of the

Idea mirroring itself in the History of the World. Philosophy escapes from the weary strife of passions that agitate the surface of society into the calm region of contemplation; that which interests it is the recognition of the process of development which the Idea has passed through in realizing itself – *i.e.* the Idea of Freedom, whose reality is the consciouseness of Freedom and nothing short of it.

That the History of the World, with all the changing scenes which its annals present, is this process of development and the realization of Spirit – this is the true *Theodicæa*, the justification of God in History. Only *this* insight can reconcile Spirit with the History of the World – viz., that what has happened, and is happening every day, is not only not 'without God', but is essentially His Work.

JOHN GREENAWAY

# Burke and de Tocqueville on conservatism

7

The origins of conservatism as a political concept, as opposed to a mere political disposition, lie in the French Revolution of 1789. Many observers quickly became appalled at the destructive effects which the revolutionaries had upon the values and the structures of the existing order. The resulting wreckage was seen to stem from the radical theories which inspired the revolutionaries (especially those of Rousseau: see chapter 8), and in reaction conservatives articulated ideas and doctrines to counter revolutionary radicalism. Conservative theorists have been profoundly sceptical about the optimistic claims of radicals to be able to reconstruct society along rational lines. In contrast to Enlightenment rationalism, conservatives have stressed the complexities and idiosyncrasies of both human behaviour and social institutions. Civilised behaviour cannot be taken for granted, and the political devices designed to sustain it are seen as fragile and easily shattered by the forces of human greed, ignorance and irrationality.

The French Revolution, nevertheless, posed a dilemma for subsequent conservatives. In rejecting its values was it possible (or expedient) to return to the political beliefs and practices of the *ancien régime*? One strand of conservatism tried to do just that. The far right in France rejected the republican tradition along with the values of equality and democracy which underpinned it and argued for a hierarchical society, crowned with a monarchy and imbued with Catholicism and traditional values. As late as the 1940s Pétain's Vichy state tried to embody such ideals. The reactionary strain of conservatism was also much reinforced by the romantic movement of the early nineteenth century which exerted great influence upon thinkers in Germany and England. This movement rediscovered the virtues of medieval Europe. Here, it was argued, had been a harmonious, 'organic' society where beliefs, social behaviour and institutions were all balanced. Romantic thinkers dreamed of recreating such a harmonious society in the modern world. Such thinking rapidly became as much directed against dislocations of the industrial revolution and the market economy as those of the political movements of the French Revolution. But here there was a dilemma. If the answer to the destructive depredations of left-wing liberals and socialists lay in the

179

reconstruction of a new order based on comprehensively reformulated values, then was this really conservatism? In the twentieth century this reconstructionist strand of the far right led to fascism and other movements, which themselves represented a degree of social and political engineering every bit as radical as those of the left.

Another solution was for conservatives to accommodate themselves to the process of change. The idea here was to accept the necessity for reform of the old order, but also to distinguish between necessary, useful reform and unnecessary, destructive upheaval. The aspiration of this strand of conservatism was to accept the fact of historical change but to do so in such a way as to preserve the essentials of the old verities. This 'liberal conservative' tradition, as we may call it, has been the dominant one in America and Britain. In due course, this strand of conservatism came to cherish the values of liberalism as much as those of conservatism in the face of the dangers posed by mass democracy, levelling egalitarianism or totalitarianism. To such instinctive conservative values as order, the defence of property and tradition were added liberal nostrums such as individual freedom, political liberty, and decentralisation. The two writers we shall be considering in this section may be considered the founding fathers of this tradition.

### Edmund Burke (1729–97)

Edmund Burke was born in Dublin, the son of an attorney. He went to London to study law in 1750 and remained there as a literary figure. As a protégé of the Whig grandee, the Earl of Rockingham, he was elected to the House of Commons in 1765. During the next decades Burke established himself as one of the leading parliamentarians of the age, active in the Whig cause and a writer of powerful pamphlets, directed against self-seeking patronage. In the 1770s he championed the cause of the American colonists, ultimately supporting their claims for independence. His chief concern in the 1780s was to bring the East India Company and the former Governor-General of Bengal, Warren Hastings, to account for maladministration and corruption. As early as 1790, long before the execution of the French king and the Terror, Burke had become concerned at the course of events in France and penned his most famous work, *Reflections on the Revolution in France*. After unsuccessful campaigns for the emancipation of Roman Catholics in Ireland, Burke left Parliament in 1794 and died three years later.

Burke's background was not that of a reactionary. He had been concerned to defend liberty and the 'balanced constitution' which, he believed, had been secured by the Glorious Revolution of 1688; the King, the Lords and the Commons all had a role to play in the polity with no one element dominant. Burke had been especially concerned to resist arbitrary government or undue corruption at the Court; but by the late 1780s he had become alarmed at the tone of the republican, democratic and anti-religious ideas being voiced by dissenters in England. In his view, government was a trust which emanated from the consent of the

people. The Commons represented the people in so far as it incorporated
the various propertied interests in the kingdom. For Burke, however, the
consent of the people was not to be expressed in democratic devices,
such as a popularly-elected national assembly. The problem with the
egalitarian radicals was that they ignored the importance of social hierarchy. Society and politics were actually complicated matters; hence
government was an art and required a ruling elite. Legislators needed
the qualities of virtue and wisdom. The common people lacked such
talents. They might be ill-educated, morally suspect or plain incompetent. By contrast landowners, having the advantage of education, leisure
and training in administering estates, were more likely to display both
competence in government and high-minded concern for the common
good. They had a long-term stake in the country, since their estates were
passed down from generation to generation. In this respect they were
unlike traders or bankers, who might have acquired wealth through
speculation and who could easily move their money from one place to
another. The strength of the English polity lay in the ability of the landed
classes to be, not as in France, a secluded elite, but in 'close connexion
and union' with other sections of society. The House of Commons represented a subtle blending of the 'illustrious' elites of the country, but was
happily moderated and led by the landed class.

The popularly-elected Third Estate in France, which was dominated
by provincial lawyers and dealers in 'paper wealth', displayed all the
dangers of democracy. In the first extract which follows, Burke points
both to the political dangers of overthrowing the natural order of a hierarchical but balanced society, and to the perils of placing power in
irresponsible hands. The best men in the Assembly were 'only men of
theory' who lacked practical experience of government; they would be
forced to become the dupes and instruments of the mass of the representatives. As the three Estates were merged into a single Assembly, the
balance of the polity was unhinged and there were no checks upon its
power. The extract ends with a fierce attack upon the effects of levelling in a political system. Egalitarianism destroyed the subdivisions in
society, what Burke termed 'the little platoons'. Such intermediary
institutions and associations in the modern state not only provide a
bulwark against tyranny but also generate civic responsibility, or
'public affections' as Burke put it.

However, the errors of the revolutionaries in France went much
deeper than this. Their fundamental mistake was to adopt a too mech-
anistic view of society and politics. They acted as if they 'had every
thing to begin anew'. Burke insists on the organically evolving character of the polity, an idea which was to become one of the central themes
of later conservative thought. Society is like an organism, a complex
interconnected whole that is greater than the sum of its parts, which
cannot be tinkered with without grave risk. Institutions work, not
because of any rational principle, but because they have evolved over
the centuries. They gain legitimacy on account of their antiquity or
'prescription'. It is simply impossible to transplant institutions or mech-

181

anisms from one political system to another. In the second extract below, Burke writes with great passion and eloquence on this point. Improvement and change is important in politics, but it should be gradual and organic, just like the work of nature. He lectures the French for neglecting to repair the old fabric of their constitution. They failed to grasp that the harmony of a political system actually arises from the clash of divergent interests and competing forces within it. Liberty is best guaranteed by the plurality of long established interests and not by abstract declarations or legislation.

The final brief extract expresses Burke's vision of the state as part of the harmonious order of things, a partnership which stretches across the generations. Civil society is a natural, organic entity, and although it has no life force or spirit of its own outside the individuals who make it up, it is not, as Locke and Hobbes held, an artificial entity, the result of a contract between pre-social individuals in the state of nature.

Burke's criticism of radical politics leads him to develop a profound scepticism about the political process and the role of the intellectual reformer. Enlightened and altruistic radicals are every bit as dangerous as dishonest or perfidious ones. Radicals, impatient for change, promise too much and become out of step with the mass of the people, who are rooted by their property and interests in the fabric of society. The result is that radical reformers seek to force through increasingly unrealistic and unpopular policies in the conviction that they have the monopoly of truth. The result is political upheavals and the loss of freedom and liberty. Revolution all too often leads to misery, oppression and despotism.

Burke sets the tone for later conservative attacks upon all attempts at rationalist social engineering. Conservatives see such efforts as utopian, speculative and 'ideological', as opposed to the conservative approach to political management which is pragmatic, based upon the real world of experience. The art of government, as Michael Oakeshott later put it, is about keeping the ship of state afloat with a contented crew, avoiding shoals and storms, and putting into convenient ports when necessary; it is not about setting a course for some far distant destination and dogmatically forcing your way there. Opponents of conservatism point out that the conservative position is itself an abstract ideological one, since it depends upon maintaining the *status quo* and the interests of the ruling class and privileged groups of the time.

Burke shows a sophisticated sense of the interconnectedness of society and the importance of history in a political system. He was aware of the need for change and reform: 'a state without the means of some change is without the means of its conservation'. However, as an analyst of social and political change, his understanding of the historical process was deficient. He had no conception that society could fundamentally transform itself, and that the values and beliefs of a polity altered in tandem with social and economic developments. By the early nineteenth century, writers like Tocqueville were beginning to think in terms of a succession of stages of human development.

Alexis de Tocqueville was born into a Norman, provincial aristocratic family which had suffered greatly during the French Revolution. In the 1820s he studied law in Paris and became interested in politics. The revolution of 1830, which replaced the reactionary, Bourbon monarchist line with the liberal, Orleanist monarchy of Louis Philippe, compromised Tocqueville's political position. He took the opportunity to visit America, ostensibly to make a study of the penal system there, but in reality to observe the workings of democracy in the New World. This research resulted in two lengthy volumes, *Democracy in America*, published to critical acclaim in 1835 and 1840. Elected to parliament in the 1840s, he made little impact as a politician until the 1848 revolutions when he played a role in suppressing the working-class insurrection. Tocqueville served Louis Napoleon as foreign minister but became repelled by his caesaristic ambitions. Leaving public life, he devoted himself to further scholarship, most notably his exploration of the causes of the French Revolution.

By the 1830s Tocqueville was convinced that only the development of representative institutions in France and the involvement of the bourgeois classes in government would ensure stability. Yet the indications were that in Europe the advance of democratic ideas was leading to instability and also centralisation and subsequent loss of liberties. In visiting America, Tocqueville had intended to examine a purely democratic society at work. He was impressed at the vibrancy and energy of American life, the lack of class consciousness, and most of all by the extensive network of local institutions and the high degree of participation in public affairs. *Democracy in America* offers an account of the complex interactions of geographical factors, political institutions, social mores and ideas in the emerging American polity. Even more ambitiously, it aims to analyse the differences between an aristocratic and a democratic society and to examine the processes of historical change.

Fundamental to Tocqueville's analysis was the belief that he lived in an era of transition, when the aristocratic or feudal order was rapidly being replaced by a democratic one rooted in the dominance of the commercial world. The latter was characterised by the sentiment of equality. It was the impact of the democratic revolution upon Europe, and especially his native France, that was Tocqueville's primary concern. He concluded that the political effects of the rise of democratic ideas and behaviour were by no means straightforward. Superficially, democracy was feared on account of its destabilising impact, its levelling effects and the tendency of the citizens to ignore those traditions and ancient practices which did so much to cement a state together. It might be possible to guard against such tendencies by constitutional devices, such as the separation of powers or the institutions of representative democracy. Far more corrosive and insidious a danger, Tocqueville believed, was posed by the growth of atomised

183

individualism in the democratic polity. Such individualism subverted interest in public affairs and eroded social bonds and structures. Citizens retreated into a private world and came to imagine that they stood on their own two feet in a self-sufficient way. This feeling was intensified by the greater social mobility of the democratic, commercial society of the new order. As traditional structures and privileges faded away, citizens would be likely to look to the centralised and impersonal bureaucratic government of the state to supply those services of administration which they, as individuals, could not provide.

A further danger was that individualism would encourage mediocrity and conformism (see also chapter 11). In an aristocratic society, a diversity of views was guaranteed by the separate classes or interests – nobles, tenant farmers, burghers, traders, peasants – but in a democratic society, where the condition of every individual and his or her way of life was essentially similar, there was no such institutional underpinning of a pluralism of opinion. Instead, individuals were forced on to their own resources and took their cue from the majority opinion. The force of 'public opinion' replaced the diversity of competing interests. Hence, paradoxically, a democratic society ran the risk of being repressive. The tyranny of the majority was a most powerful force and might well lead to stagnation and an end to progress. This process was likely to be accompanied by the growth of centralisation, as the old intermediate institutions and associations faded away. The end result, therefore, was likely to be the rise of demagogic politics exploited by would-be dictators playing upon popular passions. Tocqueville had only to point to the experiences of France under Napoleon, and later, after 1851, under Napoleon III, to show that this was no idle threat.

Tocqueville could see all these tendencies in the America which he studied. But that country also offered grounds for optimism. The American people had many advantages: the moral values of self-reliance and public spiritedness which were the legacy of the early settlers, and the long gestation period during which democratic institutions had developed. In Europe, in contrast, the democratic revolution had occurred too suddenly. In America the strong love of liberty counteracted some of the baneful effects of equality. Respect for the law and, above all, the development of vibrant, local institutions offset the dangers of an individualist culture. In short, participation was a guarantee of citizenship. All these were themes which were to be enthusiastically endorsed and developed by the liberal, John Stuart Mill, who was profoundly influenced by Tocqueville's ideas (see chapter 11).

The passages which follow show all the ambivalence of the modern liberal-conservative towards the advance of democracy. In theory democracy provides a guarantee that rulers will be chosen to act in the interest of those who elect them. The reality is that the populace lacks either the intelligence, the inclination or the time to exercise a proper judgement in selecting its rulers or in monitoring their behaviour. Politics itself is likely to become a vulgar activity from which the more refined and high-minded will shrink. The development of the mass media and the trivialisation of politics in the twentieth century add even more force to Tocqueville's argument.

The second extract shows Tocqueville's concern at the destabilising effects of individualism and equality upon the health of a political system. Modern democracy ends up by embracing a voluntary servitude of the tyranny of public opinion every bit as far-reaching as the imposed servitude of the old order of inequality which it replaced. Far from being an enlightened force, democracy will pander to the prejudices of public opinion and stand to be manipulated by zealots or advertisers.

The third extract points to the dangers of excessive centralisation and over-government. In modern democratic society, the ancient privileges and inequalities are eroded and destroyed, leaving the individual citizens and the state in naked relationship, without the harmonising and balming effects of the intermediary associations, Burke's 'little platoons'. A perennial worry of subsequent conservative writers has been that in a democracy the people would irresponsibly vote themselves benefits and privileges, which could be ill-afforded, at the ultimate sacrifice of both the well-being of the state and the self-reliance of its constituent members. All Tocqueville's anxieties were multiplied in the minds of conservative theorists who faced the challenges of socialism in the twentieth century. A common fear of conservative writers has been the tendency of the mass society towards mediocrity and conformism which result from a passive citizenry at the mercy of centralising bureaucrats.

However, Tocqueville was not wholly pessimistic. As the last sentence in the third extract makes clear, although the natural tendency in democratic society is towards centralisation, it was always possible, through 'artificial contrivance', to evolve a political system where individual independence and local liberties are valued. Tocqueville was a liberal who took a gloomy and conservative view of the developments in the Europe of his day; but America pointed to the possibility of building a network of participatory institutions and of cultivating habits of participation through education. Civil associations, the customs and lifestyle (the 'mores') of the people, and political institutions could all cross-fertilise each other in such a way as to offset the ill effects of democracy. In this respect Tocqueville anticipates twentieth-century exponents of pluralism, who argue that it is not the formal political institutions of democracy but rather the fragmentation and dispersal of power among competing pressure groups and smaller institutions which are the best guarantees of liberty in the modern state.

## Conclusion

The conservative political tradition represented by Burke and Tocqueville respects tradition, history and religion; it values order, property, diversity and strong intermediary institutions in the state. It fears centralisation and sees equality as subversive of liberty. It stresses the complexity of society and the limitations of social engineering, however enlightened its exponents. In the nineteenth century, the main concern of conservatives in Europe was the effect mass democracy would have upon the political, social and economic order. In the twentieth century, conservatives have come to terms with mass democracy. Following the lead of Disraeli in Britain, conservatives have recognised that the mass of the people are likely themselves to hold conservative or traditional opinions, especially when these are linked with appeals to patriotism or nationalism. Moreover, the extension of the franchise did not lead to the degree of political instability and social levelling which conservatives feared. Old elites and institutions proved remarkably resilient. Indeed, conservatives in both Britain and America have come to value the institutions of representative democracy in their countries as contributing to social and political stability.

The main concern of conservatives in the twentieth century has been to resist the advance of social democracy. In this battle, liberal and conservative thinkers have made much common cause. Class politics, public control of industry, large bureaucracies, social and economic planning and attempts to redistribute wealth have all been attacked as destroying individual freedom, undermining citizenship and wrecking the economy. But the attitude of conservative writers to the free market economy has been ambivalent. In America, with its stronger egalitarian political culture, there has been little tension. Conservatism in recent years has combined a vigorous defence of the free market with social conservatism, authoritarian attitudes, and often religious fundamentalism against the aspirations of progressive, 'liberal' intellectuals.

In Britain, however, the story has been more complex. Conservative thinkers and politicians from the time of Burke onwards have valued the free market as a natural part of the order of things, underpinning the social fabric and creating a pluralist, healthily balanced polity. But many twentieth-century conservatives have combined this appreciation of the beneficial effects of the market with a recognition of the dangers posed by the unqualified pursuit of wealth. Some have seen unfettered market forces as threatening to undermine community values, the family, religion, and a proper respect for social elites – all key elements of Burkean conservatism. Others, like Harold Macmillan, saw market liberalism as leading to the economic dislocations of mass unemployment and the loss of whole industries. Conservatives, they argued, had a duty to use the power of the state to mitigate the effect of the free market upon the less advantaged in the interests of the 'One Nation'. Conservatism should represent a 'middle way' between unfettered *laissez-faire* and state-controlled socialism. More recently, however, conservatives of the New Right have wholeheartedly endorsed the free market as an antidote to inefficient state planning and a generally liberating force. Drawing on the tradition of liberal political thought, but blending it with traditional conservative themes such as the need for a strong state, this brand of conservatism – of which Thatcherism is a prime example – has stressed the rationality of the market, the malign influence of powerful vested interests, and the self-serving nature of state bureaucracies which run public services in the interests of officials or producers rather than of consumers.

## Seminar questions

Can you think of some contemporary examples of institutions which work well and gain legitimacy on account of their antiquity?

On what grounds do conservatives criticise the ideas of equality and mass democracy? Which criticism do you think is the most telling and why?

Why are Burke and Tocqueville fearful of centralised government?

What criticisms might Tocqueville make of American and British society today?

What do liberal and conservative political ideas have in common, and where do they diverge?

## Further reading

Two books which provide good introductions to conservatism generally are: from an historical perspective, Noel O'Sullivan, *Conservatism* (London: Dent, 1976) and more thematically, R. Nisbet, *Conservatism* (Milton Keynes: Open University Press, 1986). Two recent works which offer a useful survey of the conservative tradition in Britain and the US are: R. Eatwell and N. O'Sullivan (eds), *The Nature of the Right* (London: Pinter, 1989) and Arthur Aughey, Greta Jones and W. T. M. Riches, *The Conservative Tradition in Britain and the United States* (London: Pinter, 1992). S. P. Huntington 'Conservatism as Ideology' (*American Political Science Review*, 51, 2, 1957) is more advanced. C. Rossiter, *Conservatism in America* (New York: Vintage Books, 1962) is a classic study. For Britain, Robert Eccleshall, *English Conservatism since the Restoration: An Introduction and Anthology* (London: Unwin, Hyman, 1990) is a useful survey. There is a vast literature on Burke, but the following will be most useful as introductory reading: Michael Freeman, *Edmund Burke and the Critique of Political Radicalism* (Oxford: Blackwell, 1980), Frank O'Gorman, *Edmund Burke: His Political Philosophy* (London: Allen & Unwin, 1973), Alfred Cobban, *Edmund Burke and the Revolt against the Eighteenth Century* (London: Allen & Unwin, 1960). The best short introduction to Tocqueville is provided in Larry Siedentop, *Tocqueville* (Oxford: Oxford University Press, 1994), but the older Hugh Brogan, *Tocqueville* (London: Collins/Fontana, 1973) remains useful. More advanced works include Jack Lively, *The Social and Political Thought of Alexis de Tocqueville* (Oxford: Oxford University Press, 1962), J. P. Mayer, *Alexis de Tocqueville* (New York: Harpers, 1960) and Marvin Zetterbaum, *Tocqueville and the Problem of Democracy*, (Stanford, CA: Stanford University Press, 1967).

# EDMUND BURKE
## From *Reflections on the Revolution in France*

**[I]**

This unforced choice, this fond election of evil, would appear perfectly unaccountable, if we did not consider the composition of the National Assembly; I do not mean its formal constitution, which, as it now stands, is exceptionable enough, but the materials of which in a great measure it is composed, which is of ten thousand times greater consequence than all the formalities in the world. If we were to know nothing of this Assembly but by its title and function, no colours could paint to the imagination any thing more venerable. In that light the mind of an enquirer, subdued by such an awful image as that of the virtue and wisdom of a whole people collected into a focus, would pause and hesitate in condemning things even of the very worst aspect. Instead of blameable, they would appear only mysterious. But no name, no power, no function, no artifical institution whatsoever, can make the men of whom any system of authority is composed, any other than God, and nature, and education, and their habits of life have made them. Capacities beyond these the people have not to give. Virtue and wisdom may be the objects of their choice; but their choice confers neither the one nor the other on those upon whom they lay their ordaining hands. They have not the engagement of nature, they have not the promise of revelation for any such powers.

After I have read over the list of the persons and descriptions elected into the *Tiers Etat*, nothing which they afterwards did could appear astonishing. Among them, indeed, I saw some of known rank; some of shining talents; but of any practical experience in the state, not one man was to be found. The best were only men of theory. But whatever the distinguished few may have been, it is the substance and mass of the body which constitutes its character, and must finally determine its direction. In all bodies, those who will lead, must also, in a considerable degree, follow. They must conform their propositions to the taste, talent, and disposition of those whom they wish to conduct: therefore, if an Assembly is viciously or feebly composed in a very great part of it, nothing but such a supreme degree of virtue as very rarely appears in the world, and for that reason cannot enter into calculation, will prevent the men of talents disseminated through it from becoming only the expert instruments of absurd projects! If what is the more likely event, instead of that unusual degree of virtue, they should be actuated by sinister ambition and a lust of meretricious glory, then the feeble part of the Assembly, to whom at first they conform, becomes in its turn the dupe and instrument of their designs. In this political traffick the leaders will be obliged to bow to the ignorance of their followers, and the followers to become subservient to the worst designs of their leaders.

To secure any degree of sobriety in the propositions made by the leaders in any public assembly, they ought to respect, in some degree perhaps to fear, those whom they conduct. To be led any otherwise than blindly, the followers must be qualified, if not for actors, at least for judges; they must also be judges of natural weight and authority. Nothing can secure a steady and moderate conduct in such assemblies, but that the body of them should be respectably composed, in point of condition in life, of permanent property, of education, and of such habits as enlarge and liberalize the understanding.

In the calling of the states general of France, the first thing which struck me, was a great departure from the antient course. I found the representation for the Third Estate composed of six hundred persons. They were equal in number to the representatives of both the other orders. If the orders were to act separately, the number would not, beyond the consideration of the expence, be of much moment. But when it became apparent that the three orders were to be melted down into one, the policy and necessary effect of this numerous representation became obvious. A very small desertion from either of the other two orders must throw the power of both into the hands of the third. In fact, the whole power of the state was soon resolved into that body. Its due composition became therefore of infinitely the greater importance.

Judge. Sir, of my surprize, when I found that a very great proportion of the Assembly (a majority, I believe, of the members who attended) was composed of practitioners in the law. It was composed not of distinguished magistrates, who had given pledges to their country of their science, prudence, and integrity; not of leading advocates, the glory of the bar; not of renowned professors in universities; – but for the far greater part, as it must in such a number, of the inferior, unlearned, mechanical, merely instrumental members of the profession. There were distinguished exceptions; but the general composition was of obscure provincial advocates, of stewards of petty local jurisdictions, country attornies, notaries, and the whole train of the ministers of municipal litigation, the fomentors and conductors of the petty war of village vexation. From the moment I read the list I saw distinctly, and very nearly as it has happened, all that was to follow.

The degree of estimation in which any profession is held becomes the standard of the estimation in which the professors hold themselves. Whatever the personal merits of many individual lawyers might have been, and in many it was undoubtedly very considerable, in that military kingdom, no part of the profession had been much regarded, except the highest of all, who often united to their professional offices great family splendour, and were invested with great power and authority. These certainly were highly respected, and even with no small degree of awe. The next rank was not much esteemed; the mechanical part was in a very low degree of repute.

Whenever the supreme authority is invested in a body so composed, it must evidently produce the consequences of supreme authority

189

placed in the hands of men not taught habitually to respect themselves; who had no previous fortune in character at stake; who could not be expected to bear with moderation, or to conduct with discretion, a power which they themselves, more than any others, must be surprized to find in their hands. Who could flatter himself that these men, suddenly, and, as it were, by enchantment, snatched from the humblest rank of subordination, would not be intoxicated with their unprepared greatness? Who could conceive, that men who are habitually meddling, daring, subtle, active, or litigious dispositions and unquiet minds, would easily fall back into their old condition of obscure contention, and laborious, low, unprofitable chicane? Who could doubt but that, at any expence to the state, of which they understood nothing, they must pursue their private interests, which they understood but too well? It was not an event depending on chance or contingency. It was inevitable; it was necessary; it was planted in the nature of things. They must *join* (if their capacity did not permit them to *lead*) in any project which could procure to them a *litigious constitution;* which could lay open to them those innumerable lucrative jobs which follow in the train of all great convulsions and revolutions in the state, and particularly in all great and violent permutations of property. Was it to be expected that they would attend to the stability of property, whose existence had always depended upon whatever rendered propery questionable, ambiguous, and insecure? Their objects would be enlarged with their elevation, but their disposition and habits, and mode of accomplishing their designs, must remain the same.

Well! but these men were to be tempered and restrained by other descriptions, of more sober minds, and more enlarged understandings. Were they then to be awed by the super-eminent authority and awful dignity of an handful of country clowns who have seats in the Assembly, some of whom are said not to be able to read and write? and by not a greater number of traders, who, though somewhat more instructed, and more conspicuous in the order of society, had never known any thing beyond their counting house? No! both these descriptions were more formed to be overborne and swayed by the intrigues and artifices of lawyers, than to become their counterpoise. With such a dangerous disproportion, the whole must needs be governed by them. To the faculty of law was joined a pretty considerable proportion of the faculty of medicine. This faculty had not, any more than that of the law, possessed in France its just estimation. Its professors therefore must have the qualities of men not habituated to sentiments of dignity. But supposing they had ranked as they ought to do, and as with us they do actually, the sides of sick beds are not the academies for forming statesmen and legislators. Then came the dealers in stocks and funds, who must be eager, at any expence, to change their ideal paper wealth for the more solid substance of land. To these were joined men of other descriptions, from whom as little knowledge of or attention to the interests of a great state was to be expected, and as little regard to the stability of any institution; men formed to be instruments, not controls. Such in general was the composition of the *Tiers Etat* in the National Assembly; in which was scarcely to be perceived the slightest traces of what we call the natural landed interest of the country.

We know that the British house of commons, without shutting its doors to any merit in any class, is, by the sure operation of adequate causes, filled with every thing illustrious in rank, in descent, in hereditary and in acquired opulence, in cultivated talents, in military, civil, naval, and politic distinction, that the country can afford. But supposing, what hardly can be supposed as a case, that the house of commons should be composed in the same manner with the Tiers Etat in France, would this dominion of chicane be borne with patience, or even conceived without horror? God forbid I should insinuate any thing derogatory to that profession, which is another priesthood, administering the rites of sacred justice. But whilst I revere men in the functions which belong to them, and would do, as much as one man can do, to prevent their exclusion from any, I cannot, to flatter them, give the lye to nature. They are good and useful in the composition; they must be mischievous if they preponderate so as virtually to become the whole. Their very excellence in their peculiar functions may be far from a qualification for others. It cannot escape observation, that when men are too much confined to professional and faculty habits, and, as it were, inveterate in the recurrent employment of that narrow circle, they are rather disabled than qualified for whatever depends on the knowledge of mankind, on experience in mixed affairs, on a comprehensive connected view of the various complicated external and internal interests which go to the formation of that multifarious thing called a state.

After all, if the house of commons were to have an wholly professional and faculty composition, what is the power of the house of commons, circumscribed, and shut in by the immovable barriers of laws, usages, positive rules of doctrine and practice, counterpoized by the house of lords, and every moment of its existence at the discretion of the crown to continue, prorogue, or dissolve us? The power of the house of commons, direct or indirect, is indeed great; and long may it be able to preserve its greatness, and the spirit belonging to true greatness, at the full; and it will do so, as long as it can keep the breakers of law in India from becoming the makers of law for England. The power, however, of the house of commons, when least diminished, is as a drop of water in the ocean, compared to that residing in a settled majority of your National Assembly. That Assembly, since the destruction of the orders, has no fundamental law, no strict convention, no respected usage to restrain it. Instead of finding themselves obliged to conform to a fixed constitution, they have a power to make a constitution which shall conform to their designs. Nothing in heaven or upon earth can serve as a control on them. What ought to be the heads, the hearts, the dispositions, that are qualified, or that dare, not only to make laws under a fixed constitiution, but at one heat to strike out a totally new constitution for a great kingdom, and in every part of it, from the monarch on the throne to the vestry of a parish? But – *'fools rush in where angels fear to tread.'* In such a state of unbounded power, for undefined and undefinable purposes, the evil of a moral and almost physical inaptitude of the man to the function must be the greatest we can conceive to happen in the management of human affairs.

Having considered the composition of the third estate as it stood in its original frame, I took a view of the representatives of the clergy. There too it appeared, that full as little regard was had to the general security of property, or to the aptitude of the deputies for their public purposes, in the principles of their election. That election was so contrived as to send a very large proportion of mere country curates to the great and arduous work of new-modelling a state; men who never had seen the state so much as in a picture; men who knew nothing of the world beyond the bounds of an obscure village; who, immersed in hopeless poverty, could regard all property, whether secular or ecclesiastical, with no other eye than that of envy; among whom must be many, who, for the smallest hope of the meanest dividend in plunder, would readily join in any attempts upon a body of wealth, in which they could hardly look to have any share, except in a general scramble. Instead of balancing the power of the active chicaners in the other assembly, these curates must necessarily become the active coadjutors, or at best the passive instruments of those by whom they had been habitually guided in their petty village concerns. They too could hardly be the most conscientious of their kind, who, presuming upon their incompetent understanding, could intrigue for a trust which led them from their natural relation to their flocks, and their natural spheres of action, to undertake the regeneration of kingdoms. This preponderating weight being added to the force of the body of chicane in the Tiers Etat, compleated that momentum of ignorance, rashness, presumption, and lust of plunder, which nothing has been able to resist.

To observing men it must have appeared from the beginning, that the majority of the Third Estate, in conjunction with such a deputation from the clergy as I have described, whilst it pursued the destruction of the nobility, would inevitably become subservient to the worst designs of individuals in that class. In the spoil and humiliation of their own order these individuals would possess a sure fund for the pay of their new followers. To squander away the objects which made the happiness of their fellows, would be to them no sacrifice at all. Turbulent, discontented men of quality, in proportion as they are puffed up with personal pride and arrogance, generally despise their own order. One of the first symptoms they discover of a selfish and mischievous ambition, is a profligate disregard of a dignity which they partake with others. To be attached to the subdivision, to love the little platoon we belong to in society, is the first principle (the germ as it were) of public affections. It is the first link in the series by which we proceed towards a love to our country and to mankind. The interests of that portion of social arrangement is a trust in the hands of all those who compose it; and as none but bad men would justify it in abuse, none but traitors would barter it away for their own personal advantage.

There were, in the time of our civil troubles in England (I do not know whether you have any such in your Assembly in France) several persons, like the then Earl of Holland, who by themselves or their families had brought an odium on the throne, by the prodigal dispensation of its bounties towards them, who afterwards joined in the rebellions arising from the discontents of which they were themselves the cause; men who helped to subvert that throne to which they owed, some of them, their existence, others all that power which they employed to ruin their benefactor. If any bounds are set to the rapacious demands of that sort of people, or that others are permitted to partake in the objects they would engross, revenge and envy soon fill up the craving void that is left in their avarice. Confounded by the complication of distempered passions, their reason is disturbed; their views become vast and perplexed; to others inexplicable; to themselves, uncertain. They find, on all sides, bounds to their unprincipled ambition in any fixed order of things. But in the fog and haze of confusion all is enlarged, and appears without any limit.

When men of rank sacrifice all ideas of dignity to an ambition without a distinct object, and work with low instruments and for low ends, the whole composition becomes low and base. Does not something like this now appear in France? Does it not produce something ignoble and inglorious? a kind of meanness in all the prevalent policy? a tendency in all that is done to lower along with individuals all the dignity and importance of the state? Other revolutions have been conducted by persons, who whilst they attempted or effected changes in the commonwealth, sanctified their ambition by advancing the dignity of the people whose peace they troubled. They had long views. They aimed at the rule, not at the destruction of their country. They were men of great civil, and great military talents, and if the terror, the ornament of their age. They were not like Jew brokers contending with each other who could best remedy with fraudulent circulation and depreciated paper the wretchedness and ruin brought on their country by their degenerate councils. The compliment made to one of the great bad men of the old stamp (Cromwell) by his kinsman, a favourite poet of that time, shews what it was he proposed, and what indeed to a great degree he accomplished in the success of his ambition:

> Still as *you* rise, the *state*, exalted too,
> Finds no distemper whilst 'tis chang'd by *you*;
> Chang'd like the world's great scene, when without noise
> The rising sun night's vulgar lights destroys.

These disturbers were not so much like men usurping power, as asserting their natural place in society. Their conquest over their
competitors was by outshining them. The hand that, like a destroying angel, smote the country, communicated to it the force and energy
under which it suffered. I do not say (God forbid) I do not say, that
the virtues of such men were to be taken as a balance to their crimes;
but they were some corrective to their effects. Such was, as I said, our
Cromwell. Such were your whole race of Guises, Condés, and
Colignis. Such the Richlieus, who in more quiet times acted in the
spirit of a civil war. Such, as better men, and in less dubious cause,
were your Henry the 4th and your Sully, though nursed in civil
confusions, and not wholly without some of their taint. It is a thing
to be wondered at, to see how very soon France, when she had a
moment to respire, recovered and emerged from the longest and
most dreadful civil war that ever was known in any nation. Why?
Because, among all their massacres, they had not slain the *mind* in
their country. A conscious dignity, a noble pride, a generous sense of
glory and emulation, was not extinguished. On the contrary, it was
kindled and inflamed. The organs also of the state, however shattered, existed. All the prizes of honour and virtue, all the rewards, all
the distinctions, remained. But your present confusion, like a palsy,
has attacked the fountain of life itself. Every person in your country,
in a situation to be actuated by a principle of honour, is disgraced and
degraded, and can entertain no sensation of life, except in a morti-
fied and humiliated indignation. But this generation will quickly
pass away. The next generation of the nobility will resemble the arti-
ficers and clowns, and money-jobbers, usurers, and Jews, who will
be always their fellows, sometimes their masters. Believe me, Sir,
those who attempt to level, never equalize. In all societies, consisting
of various descriptions of citizens, some description must be upper-
most. The levellers therefore only change and pervert the natural
order of things; they load the edifice of society, by setting up in the
air what the solidity of the structure requires to be on the ground.
The associations of taylors and carpenters, of which the republic (of
Paris, for instance) is composed, cannot be equal to the situation, into
which, by the worst of usurpations, an usurpation on the prerogatives of nature, you attempt to force them.
[...]

## [II]

You will observe, that from Magna Charta to the Declaration of Right,
it has been the uniform policy of our constitution to claim and assert
our liberties, as an *entailed inheritance* derived to us from our forefathers, and to be transmitted to our posterity: as an estate specially
belonging to the people of this kingdom without any reference whatever to any other more general or prior right. By this means our
constitution preserves an unity in so great a diversity of its parts. We
have an inheritable crown; an inheritable peerage; and an house of

commons and a people inheriting privileges, franchises, and liberties,
from a long line of ancestors.

This policy appears to me to be the result of profound reflection; or
rather the happy effect of following nature, which is wisdom without
reflection, and above it. A spirit of innovation is generally the result
of a selfish temper and confined views. People will not look forward
to posterity, who never look backward to their ancestors. Besides, the
people of England well know, that the idea of inheritance furnishes
a sure principle of conservation, and a sure principle of transmission;
without at all excluding a principle of improvement. It leaves acquisition free; but it secures what it acquires. Whatever advantages are
obtained by a state proceeding on these maxims, are locked fast as in
a sort of family settlement; grasped as in a kind of mortmain for ever.
By a constitutional policy, working after the pattern of nature, we
receive, we hold, we transmit our government and our privileges, in
the same manner in which we enjoy and transmit our property and
our lives. The institutions of policy, the goods of fortune, the gifts of
Providence, are handed down to us and from us, in the same course
and order. Our political system is placed in a just correspondence and
symmetry with the order of the world, and with the mode of existence decreed to a permanent body composed of transitory parts;
wherein, by the disposition of a stupendous wisdom, moulding together the great mysterious incorporation of the human race, the
whole, at one time, is never old, or middle-aged, or young, but in a
condition of unchangeable constancy, moves on through the varied
tenour of perpetual decay, fall, renovation, and progression. Thus, by
preserving the method of nature in the conduct of the state, in what
we improve we are never wholly new; in what we retain we are never
wholly obsolete. By adhering in this manner and on those principles
to our forefathers, we are guided not by the superstition of anti-
quarians, but by the spirit of philosophic analogy. In this choice of
inheritance we have given to our frame of polity the image of relation in blood; binding up the constitution of our country with our
dearest domestic ties; adopting our fundamental laws into the bosom
of our family affections; keeping inseparable, and cherishing with the
warmth of all their combined and mutually reflected charities, our
state, our hearths, our sepulchres, and our altars.

Through the same plan of a conformity to nature in our artificial institutions, and by calling in the aid of her unerring and powerful
instincts, to fortify the fallible and feeble contrivances of our reason,
we have derived several other, and those no small benefits, from
considering our liberties in the light of an inheritance. Always acting
as if in the presence of canonized forefathers, the spirit of freedom,
leading in itself to misrule and excess, is tempered with an awful
gravity. This idea of a liberal descent inspires us with a sense of habitual native dignity, which prevents that upstart insolence almost
inevitably adhering to and disgracing those who are the first acquir-
ers of any distinction. By this means our liberty becomes a noble

freedom. It carries an imposing and majestic aspect. It has a pedigree and illustrating ancestors. It has its bearings and its ensigns armorial. It has its gallery of portraits; its monumental inscriptions; its records, evidences, and titles. We procure reverence to our civil institutions on the principle upon which nature teaches us to revere individual men; on account of their age; and on account of those from whom they are descended. All your sophisters cannot produce any thing better adapted to preserve a rational and manly freedom than the course that we have pursued, who have chosen our nature rather than our speculations, our breasts rather than our inventions, for the great conservatories and magazines of our rights and privileges.

You might, if you pleased, have profited of our example, and have given to your recovered freedom a correspondent dignity. Your privileges, though discontinued, were not lost to memory. Your constitution, it is true, whilst you were out of possession, suffered waste and dilapidation; but you possessed in some parts the walls, and in all the foundations of a noble and venerable castle. You might have repaired those walls; you might have built on those old foundations. Your constitution was suspended before it was perfected; but you had the elements of a constitution very nearly as good as could be wished. In your old states you possessed that variety of parts corresponding with the various descriptions of which your community was happily composed; you had all that combination, and all that opposition of interests, you had that action and counteraction which, in the natural and in the political world, from the reciprocal struggle of discordant powers, draws out the harmony of the universe. These opposed and conflicting interests, which you considered as so great a blemish in your old and in our present constitution, interpose a salutary check to all precipitate resolutions; They render deliberation a matter not of choice, but of necessity; they make all change a subject of *compromise,* which naturally begets moderation; they produce *temperaments,* preventing the sore evil of harsh, crude, unqualified reformations; and rendering all the headlong exertions of arbitrary power, in the few or in the many, for ever impracticable. Through that diversity of members and interests, general liberty had as many securities as there were separate views in the several orders; whilst by pressing down the whole by the weight of a real monarchy, the separate parts would have been prevented from warping and starting from their allotted places.

You had all these advantages in your antient states; but you chose to act as if you had never been moulded into civil society, and had every thing to begin anew. You began ill, because you began by despising every thing that belonged to you. You set up your trade without a capital. If the last generations of your country appeared without much lustre in your eyes, you might have passed them by, and derived your claims from a more early race of ancestors. Under a pious predilection for those ancestors, your imaginations would have realized in them a standard of virtue and wisdom, beyond the vulgar practice of the hour; and you would have risen with the example to whose imitation you aspired. Respecting your forefathers, you would have been taught to respect yourselves. You would not have chose to consider the French as a people of yesterday, as a nation of low-born servile wretches until the emancipating year of 1789.

[…]

## [III]

Society is indeed a contract. Subordinate contracts for objects of mere occasional interest may be dissolved at pleasure – but the state ought not to be considered as nothing better than a partnership agreement in a trade of pepper and coffee, callico or tobacco, or some other such low concern, to be taken up for a little temporary interest, and to be dissolved by the fancy of the parties. It is to be looked on with other reverence; because it is not a partnership in things subservient only to the gross animal existence of a temporary and perishable nature. It is a partnership in all science; a partnership in all art; a partnership in every virtue, and in all perfection. As the ends of such a partnership cannot be obtained in many generations, it becomes a partnership not only between those who are living, but between those who are living, those who are dead, and those who are to be born. Each contract of each particular state is but a clause in the great primaeval contract of eternal society, linking the lower with the higher natures, connecting the visible and invisible world, according to a fixed compact sanctioned by the inviolable oath which holds all physical and all moral natures, each in their appointed place. This law is not subject to the will of those, who by an obligation above them, and infinitely superior, are bound to submit their will to that law. The municipal corporations of that universal kingdom are not morally at liberty at their pleasure, and on their speculations of a contingent improvement, wholly to separate and tear asunder the bands of their subordinate community, and to dissolve it into an unsocial, uncivil, unconnected chaos of elementary principles. It is the first and supreme necessity only, a necessity that is not chosen but chooses, a necessity paramount to deliberation, that admits no discussion, and demands no evidence, which alone can justify a resort to anarchy. This necessity is no exception to the rule; because this necessity itself is a part too of that moral and physical disposition of things to which man must be obedient by consent or force; but if that which is only submission to necessity should be made the object of choice, the law is broken, nature is disobeyed, and the rebellious are outlaws, cast forth, and exiled, from this world of reason, and order, and peace, and virtue, and frutiful penitence, into the antagonist world of madness, discord, vice, confusion, and unavailing sorrow.

# ALEXIS DE TOCQUEVILLE
## From *Democracy in America*

[I]

When the ranks of society are unequal, and men unlike each other in condition, there are some individuals invested with all the power of superior intelligence, learning and enlightenment, whilst the multitude is sunk in ignorance and prejudice. Men living at these aristocratic periods are therefore naturally induced to shape their opinions by the superior standard of a person or a class of persons, whilst they are averse to recognize the infallibility of the mass of the people.

The contrary takes place in ages of equality. The nearer the citizens are drawn to the common level of an equal and similar condition, the less prone does each man become to place implicit faith in a certain man or a certain class of men. But his readiness to believe the multitude increases, and opinion is more than ever mistress of the world. Not only is common opinion the only guide which private judgment retains amongst a democratic people, but amongst such a people it possesses a power infinitely beyond what it has elsewhere. At periods of equality men have no faith in one another, by reason of their common resemblance; but this very resemblance gives them almost unbounded confidence in the judgment of the public; for it would not seem probable, as they are all endowed with equal means of judging, but that the greater truth should go with the greater number.

When the inhabitant of a democratic country compares himself individually with all those about him, he feels with pride that he is the equal of any one of them; but when he comes to survey the totality of his fellows, and to place himself in contrast to so huge a body, he is instantly overwhelmed by the sense of his own insignificance and and weakness.

The same equality which renders him independent of each of his fellow citizens, taken severally, exposes him alone and unprotected to the influence of the greater number.

The public has therefore among a democratic people a singular power, of which aristocratic nations could never so much as conceive an idea; for it does not persuade to certain opinions, but it enforces them, and infuses them into the faculties by a sort of enormous pressure of the minds of all upon the reason of each.

In the United States the majority undertakes to supply a multitude of ready-made opinions for the use of individuals, who are thus relieved from the necessity of forming opinions of their own. Everybody there adopts great numbers of theories, on philosophy, morals, and politics, without inquiry, upon public trust; and if we look to it very narrowly, it will be perceived that religion herself holds her sway there, much less as a doctrine of revelation than as a commonly received opinion.

The fact that the political laws of the Americans are such that the majority rules the community with sovereign sway, materially increases the power which that majority naturally exercises over the mind. For nothing is more customary in man than to recognize superior wisdom in the person of his oppressor. This political omnipotence of the majority in the United States doubtless augments the influence which public opinion would obtain without it over the mind of each member of the community; but the foundations of that influence do not rest upon it. They must be sought for in the principle of equality itself, not in the more or less popular institutions which men living under that condition may give themselves. The intellectual dominion of the greater number would probably be less absolute amongst a democratic people governed by a king than in the sphere of a pure democracy, but it will always be extremely absolute; and by whatever political laws men are governed in the ages of equality, it may be foreseen that faith in public opinion will become a species of religion there, and the majority its ministering prophet.

Thus intellectual authority will be different, but it will not be diminished; and far from thinking that it will disappear, I augur that it may readily acquire too much proponderance, and confine the action of private judgment within narrower limits than are suited either to the greatness or the happiness of the human race. In the principle of equality I very clearly discern two tendencies; the one leading the mind of every man to untried thoughts, the other inclined to prohibit him from thinking at all. And I perceive how, under the dominion of certain laws, democracy would extinguish that liberty of the mind in which a democratic social condition is favourable; so that, after having broken all the bondage once imposed on it by ranks or by men, the human mind would be closely fettered to the general will of the greatest number.

If the absolute power of a majority were to be substituted by democratic nations, for all the different powers which checked or retarded overmuch the energy of individual minds, the evil would only have changed its symptoms. Men would not have found the means of independent life; they would simply have invented (no easy task) a new dress for servitude. There is – and I cannot repeat it too often – there is in this matter for profound reflection for those who look on freedom as a holy thing, and who hate not only the despot, but despotism. For myself, when I feel the hand of power lie heavy on my brow, I care but little to know who oppresses me; and I am not the more disposed to pass beneath the yoke, because it is held out to me by the arms of a million of men.

[II]

In Europe we are at a loss how to judge the true character and the more permanent propensities of democracy, because in Europe two conflicting principles exist, and we do not know what to attribute to the principles themselves, and what to refer to the passions which they bring into collision. Such, however, is not the case in America; there the people reigns without any obstacle, and it has no perils to dread, and no injuries to avenge. In America, democracy is swayed by its own free propensities; its course is natural, and its activity is unrestrained; the United States consequently afford the most favourable opportunity of studying its real character. And to no people can this inquiry be more vitally interesting than to the French nation, which is blindly driven onwards by a daily and irresistible impulse, towards a state of things, which may prove either despotic or republican, but which will assuredly be democratic.

### Universal suffrage

I have ready observed that Universal Suffrage has been adopted in all the States of the Union: it consequently occurs amongst different populations which occupy very different positions in the scale of society. I have had opportunities of observing its effects in different localities, and amongst races of men who are nearly strangers to each other by their language, their religion, and their manner of life; in Louisiana as well as in New England, in Georgia and in Canada. I have remarked that Universal Suffrage is far from producing in America either all the good or all the evil consequences which are assigned to it in Europe, and that its effects differ very widely from those which are usually attributed to it.

### Choice of the people and instinctive preferences of the American democracy

Many people in Europe are apt to believe without saying it, or to say without believing it, that one of the great advantages of universal suffrage is, that it entrusts the direction of public affairs to men who are worthy of the public confidence. They admit that the people is unable to govern for itself, but they aver that it is always sincerely disposed to promote the welfare of the State, and that it instinctively designates those persons who are animated by the same good wishes, and who are the most fit to wield the supreme authority. I confess that the observations I made in America by no means coincide with these opinions. On my arrival in the United States I was surprised to find so much distinguished talent among the subjects, and so little among the heads of the Government. It is a well-authenticated fact, that at the present day the most able men in the United States are very rarely placed at the head of affairs; and it must be acknowledged that such has been the result, in proportion as democracy has outstepped all its former limits. The race of American statesmen has evidently dwindled most remarkably in the course of the last fifty years.

Several causes may be assigned to this phenomenon. It is impossible, not withstanding the most strenuous exertions, to raise the intelligence of the people above a certain level. Whatever may be the facilities of acquiring information, whatever may be the profusion of easy methods and of cheap science, the human mind can never be instructed and educated without devoting a considerable space of time to those objects.

The greater or the lesser possibility of subsisting without labour is therefore the necessary boundary of intellectual improvement. This boundary is more remote in some countries, and more restricted in others; but it must exist somewhere as long as the people is constrained to work in order to procure the means of physical subsistence, that is to say, as long as it retains its popular character. It is therefore quite as difficult to imagine a State in which all the citizens should be very well-informed, as a State in which they should all be wealthy; these two difficulties may be looked upon as correlative. It may very readily be admitted that the mass of the citizens are sincerely disposed to promote the welfare of their country; nay more, it may even be allowed that the lower classes are less apt to be swayed by considerations of personal interest than the higher orders; but it is always more or less impossible for them to discern the best means of attaining the end, which they desire with sincerity. Long and patient observation, joined to a multitude of different notions, is required to form a just estimate of the character of a single individual; and can it be supposed that the vulgar have the power of succeeding in an inquiry which misleads the penetration of genius itself? The people has neither the time nor the means which are essential to the prosecution of an investigation of this kind; its conclusions are hastily formed from a superficial inspection of the more prominent features of a question. Hence it often assents to the clamour of a mountebank, who knows the secret of stimulating its tastes; whilst its truest friends frequently fail in their exertions.

Moreover, the democracy is not only deficient in that soundness of judgment which is neccessary to select men really deserving of its confidence, but it has neither the desire nor the inclination to find them out. It cannot be denied that democratic institutions have a very strong tendency to promote the feeling of envy in the human heart; not so much because they afford to every one the means of rising to the level of any of his fellow-citizens, as because those means perpetually disappoint the persons who employ them. Democratic institutions awaken and foster a passion for equality which they can never entirely satisfy. This complete equality eludes the grasp of the people at the very moment at which it thinks to hold it fast and 'flies,' as Pascal says, 'with eternal flight;' the people is excited in the pursuit of an advantage, which is more precious because it is not sufficiently remote to be unknown, or sufficiently near to be enjoyed. The lower orders are agitated by the chance of success, they are irritated by its uncertainty; and they pass from the enthusiasm of pursuit to the exhaustion of ill-success, and lastly to the acrimony of disappointment. Whatever transcends their own limits appears to be an obstacle to their desires, and there is no kind of superiority, however legitimate it may be, which is not irksome in their sight.

It has been supposed that the secret instinct, which leads the lower orders to remove their superiors as much as possible from the direction of public affairs, is peculiar to France. This, however, is an error; the propensity to which I allude is not inherent in any particular nation, but in democratic institutions in general; and although it may have been heightened by peculiar political circumstances, it owes its origin to a higher cause.

In the United States, the people is not disposed to hate the superior classes of society; but it is not very favourably inclined towards them, and it carefully excludes them from the exercise of authority. It does not entertain any dread of distinguished talents, but it is rarely captivated by them; and it awards its approbation very sparingly to such as have risen without the popular support.

Whilst the natural propensities of democracy induce the people to reject the most distinguished citizens as its rulers, these individuals are no less apt to retire from a political career, in which it is almost impossible to retain their independence, or to advance without degrading themselves. This opinion has been very candidly set forth by Chancellor Kent, who says, in speaking with great eulogiums of that part of the Constitution which empowers the executive to nominate the judges: 'It is indeed probable that the men who are best fitted to discharge the duties of this high office would have too much reserve in their manners, and too much austerity in their principles, for them to be returned by the majority at an election where universal suffrage is adopted.' Such were the opinions which were printed without contradiction in America in the year 1830.

I hold it to be sufficiently demonstrated, that universal suffrage is by no means a guarantee of the wisdom of the popular choice; and that whatever its advantages may be, this is not one of them.

[...]

## [III]

### That the sentiments of democratic nations accord with their opinions in leading them to concentrate political power

If it be true that, in ages of equality, men readily adopt the notion of a great central power, it cannot be doubted on the other hand that their habits and sentiments predispose them to recognize such a power and to give it their support. This may be demonstrated in a few words, as the greater part of the reasons, to which the fact may be attributed, have been previously stated.

As the men who inhabit democratic countries have no superiors, no inferiors, and no habitual or necessary partners in their undertakings, they readily fall back upon themselves and consider themselves as beings apart. I had occasion to point this out at considerable length in treating of individualism. Hence such men can never, without an effort, tear themselves from their private affairs to engage in public business; their natural bias leads them to abandon the latter to the sole visible and permanent representative of the interests of the community, that is to say, to the State. Not only are they naturally wanting in a taste for public business, but they have frequently no time to attend to it. Private life is so busy in democratic periods, so excited, so full of wishes and of work, that hardly any energy or leisure remains to each individual for public life. I am the last man to contend that these propensities are unconquerable, since my chief object in writing this book has been to combat them. I only maintain that at the present day a secret power is fostering them in the human heart, and that if they are not checked they will wholly overgrow it.

I have also had occasion to show how the increasing love of well-being, and the fluctuating character of property cause democratic nations to dread all violent disturbance. The love of public tranquillity is frequently the only passion which these nations retain, and it becomes more active and powerful amongst them in proportion as all other passions droop and die. This naturally disposes the members of the community constantly to give or to surrender additional rights to the central power, which alone seems to be interested in defending them by the same means that it uses to defend itself.

As in ages of equality no man is compelled to lend his assistance to his fellow-men, and none has any right to expect much support from them, every one is at once independent and powerless. These two conditions, which must never be either separately considered or confounded together, inspire the citizen of a democratic country with very contrary propensities. His independence fills him with self-reliance and pride amongst his equals; his debility makes him feel from time to time the want of some outward assistance, which he cannot expect from any of them, because they are all impotent and unsympathizing. In this predicament he naturally turns his eyes to that imposing power which alone rises above the level of universal depression. Of that power his wants and especially his desires continually remind him, until he ultimately views it as the sole and necessary support of his own weakness.

This may more completely explain what frequently takes place in democratic countries, where the very men who are so impatient of superiors patiently submit to a master, exhibiting at once their pride and their sevility.

The hatred which men bear to privilege increases in proportion as privileges become more scarce and less considerable, so that democratic passions would seem to burn most fiercely at the very time when they have least fuel. I have already given the reason for this phenomenon. When all conditions are unequal, no inequality is so great as to offend the eye; whereas the slightest dissimilarity is odious in the midst of general uniformity; the more complete is this uniformity, the more insupportable does the sight of such a difference become. Hence it is natural that the love of equality should constantly increase together with equality itself, and that it should grow by what it feeds upon.

This never-dying ever-kindling hatred, which sets a democratic people against the smallest privileges, is peculiarly favourable to the gradual concentration of all political rights in the hands of the representative of the State alone. The sovereign, being necessarily and incontestably above all the citizens, excites not their envy, and each of them thinks that he strips his equals of the prerogative which he concedes to the crown.

The man of a democratic age is extremely reluctant to obey his neighbour who is his equal; he refuses to acknowledge in such a person ablility superior to his own; he mistrusts his justice, and is jealous of his power; he fears and he contemns him; and he loves continually to remind him of the common dependence in which both of them stand to the same master.

Every central power which follows its natural tendencies courts and encourages the principle of equality; for equality singularly facilitates, extends, and secures the influence of a central power.

In like manner it may be said that every central government worships uniformity: uniformity relieves it from inquiry into an infinite number of small details which must be attended to if rules were to be adapted to men, instead of indiscriminately subjecting men to rules: thus the government likes what the citizens like, and naturally hates what they hate. These common sentiments, which, in democrtic nations, constantly unite the sovereign and every member of the community in one and the same conviction, establish a secret and lasting sympathy between them. The faults of the government are pardoned for the sake of its tastes; public confidence is only reluctantly withdrawn in the midst even of its excesses and its errors, and it is restored at the first call. Democratic nations often hate those in whose hands the central power is vested; but they always love that power itself.

Thus, by two separate paths, I have reached the same conclusion. I have shown that the principle of equality suggest to men the notion of a sole, uniform, and strong government: I have now shown that the principle of equality imparts to them a taste for it. To governments of this kind the nations of our age are therefore tending. They are drawn thither by the natural inclination of mind and heart; and in order to reach that result, it is enough that they do not check themselves in their course.

I am of opinion, that, in the democratic ages which are opening upon us, individual independence and local liberties will ever be the produce of artificial contrivance; that centralization will be the natural form of government.

# Rousseau and James Mill on democracy

8

Jean-Jacques Rousseau and James Mill represent polar opposites, both as people and as political theorists. Rousseau was passionate and extravagant; Mill was deliberate and calculating. Rousseau designed a political system intended to bring out the best in his citizens; Mill designed one to protect against the worst in their rulers. They shared some things in common: they both dallied briefly with a career in religion, and they both believed strongly in the need to connect theory and practice, to match personal beliefs to political pronouncements. Mill followed his own firm injunctions in the education and training of his son, John Stuart Mill; while Rousseau turned his strictures upon himself in the detailed self-scrutiny of his *Confessions* (1781; 1977 edn), or explored their implications in *Emile* (1762; 1974 edn). These similarities are, however, of only passing significance when set against the major differences between them.

Rousseau and Mill stand as exemplars of the two central strands in the history of democratic theory. Any idea about democracy is almost inevitably allocated to one of the two traditions of democracy. Either they belong to the school of thought that is labelled 'direct' or 'classical' or 'participatory' democracy; or they are consigned to ones labelled 'pluralist' or 'representative' or 'liberal' democracy. The appropriate allocation is determined by the answer given to the question: 'what does rule by the people mean?' With the first school of thought, 'the people' is defined as a collectivity or community with a shared interest which may be expressed or realised through active participation in the business of ruling. For the other school, the people are defined by their differences, by their individual interests, and the aim of democracy is to protect this pluralism through a system of representative and accountable authority. In this chapter, Rousseau stands as the embodiment of the first school; James Mill of the second.

## Jean-Jacques Rousseau (1712–78)

After a troubled and unsettled childhood – one unsympathetic critic described him as 'a motherless vagabond starved of warmth and affection' (Talmon, 1986, p. 38) – Rousseau was to establish himself as one of the most influential of eighteenth-century thinkers. But he was no ordinary political theorist. He was a composer as well as a writer. And as a writer, he refused to be confined to one genre. Besides his novels and political treatises (*Emile* combined both), his *Confessions* was to help fashion the modern notion of autobiography.

His political arguments ambitiously integrate ideas about sovereignty and liberty with a distinctive moral vision. And while the individual components were not always original – the 'general will', the expression most closely associated with Rousseau, was first used by Diderot – their particular combination was special. Rousseau sought to build an ancient collectivism within an emergent modernity. It is an ambition that is still pursued in the arguments of modern-day communitarians. Indeed, Charles Taylor, one of the key figures in contemporary communitarianism, sees Rousseau as trying to unite the claims of the ancient, in the guise of Stoicism, and the modern. Taylor (1989, p. 360) writes: '... very familiar ancient themes of austerity as a condition of true virtue become woven by Rousseau into a modern one, the affirmation of ordinary life'. In a similar, but not identical vein, Judith Shklar (1969, p. 3) saw Rousseau as entertaining two utopias, one old – a Spartan city – and one new – 'a tranquil household'.

The word 'democracy' makes only rare appearances in Rousseau's *Social Contract*. And when he does mention it, it receives rough treatment. He writes (Book 3, chapter 4): 'If we take the term in the strict sense, there never has been a real democracy, and there never will be.' Indeed, in the very next chapter, following his dismissal of democracy, he talks warmly of the virtues of an elected aristocracy (Book 3, chapter 5). But for all this, his *Social Contract* is regarded as 'the most novel account of democracy', and one that has spawned many imitators, who together represent the major challenge to liberal democracy (Held, 1987, p. 73).

The *Social Contract*, which is in fact the remaining fragment of a much longer political work (the rest of which Rousseau burnt in despair), addresses one central question: 'The problem is to find a form of association which will defend and protect with the whole common force the person and goods of each associate, and in which each, while uniting himself with all, may still obey himself alone, and remain as free as before' (below, p. 215). Rousseau is nothing if not ambitious. His concern is not only with order and with protecting people and their property. As the second part of the quotation makes clear, he is concerned to identify the conditions for self-rule, in which individuals will be free from control by others and subject only to their own choices and decisions. Rousseau wants, in other words, to create a political order that allows for both stability and liberty. He does not believe that order depends upon repression, nor that individual freedom creates chaos and instability. On the contrary, his argument is that freedom emerges through a particular kind of collective order. This order is represented by the term with which Rousseau is most closely identified: the General Will.

To see how Rousseau proposes to achieve this ambition, we need first to understand the version of freedom that he is invoking. We have to place Rousseau in the context of the competing versions of liberty (republican and modern) that Martin Hollis described in chapter 3. To be free, the modern liberal might claim, is to be able to do whatever one wants. But while this may capture the basic intuition, it hardly serves as a complete account. Such a definition might make a lone person on a desert island the epitome of freedom, but is that a freedom we would value? The number of things such a person could do is extremely limited. Indeed, the range of available options increases with the size of the population. Alone, you can only play patience, with two you can play chess, and so on.

Of course, as the numbers rise so do the costs. To play, you need the co-operation of others, and you may find conflicts emerging over the choice of activities or over the rules for the games. But the point is that the freedom which is to be enjoyed in the company of others is greater than that for the solitary figure, even though there are some things that you are now unable to do. But this is not the only advantage to be gained from replacing 'the private person' with a 'moral and collective body' (Book 1, chapter 6). The most important aspect of the new situation is that the rules which define collective freedom are *self-imposed*. It is, indeed, possible to achieve the collective state by authoritarian means, by imposing the rules from above, but for Rousseau true freedom is to be found in obeying rules that we impose on ourselves.

What Rousseau is proposing is a system of government which enshrines this collective version of freedom by establishing a means by which we come together with the dual purpose of both maximising and limiting our freedoms. Importantly, though, *we* set the limits; they are not imposed on us. And we accept these limits not only because they are the product of our decisions, but also because they represent the best possible list of mutually agreed options. This combination of the individual and the collective is not easily achieved. It is, after all, a fundamental problem of all political systems. Rousseau believes the answer lies in obedience to the General Will.

Imagine a group of people deliberating upon the laws and rules which are to apply to their community. Rousseau suggests that they might arrive at their decisions by asking what they *as individuals* most want. Suppose the choice is between a road building programme and a public transport programme. As individuals, we will reason that the car can be used whenever we want it, to get us to precisely where we wish to go. We will probably vote for the roads. The result, says Rousseau, will be 'the will of all'. The cost of this decision is that we build roads which become congested and generate pollution, so that we do not achieve the convenience and freedom that the car seems to promise.

Let us now imagine that the decision is taken by us *as members of the community*. In voting, we do not ask 'what do I want?', but 'what do *we* want?' We think about the collective good. This time we may vote for public transport. And this, according to Rousseau, is the General Will. Note that this decision entails some personal cost. However efficient and flexible the system of public transport, it will not take us from door to door. We will get wet waiting at bus stops, and so on. None the less, it is the best that *we* can hope for. It generates the maximum freedom for each of us by imposing limits on what we would otherwise do. These restrictions are, however, the products of our choices, choices made as social beings aware that our freedom is dependent upon co-operation with others.

Before a General Will can exist, all must agree to the social contract which creates the community. This means, Rousseau insists, 'the total alienation of each associate, with all his rights, to the whole community' (below, p. 215). Unlike Locke, Rousseau does not believe that the contract should place limits in advance on the powers of government. However, this does not mean that individuals are signing themselves into slavery, for in signing the contract and agreeing to be bound by majority decisions, 'each gives himself to all' and therefore 'gives himself to no one' (below, p. 216). We exchange the possibility of 'personal dependence', dependence on the will of another as exists in the state of nature, for dependence on the General Will, and in doing so we ensure that we obey no one but ourselves – or so Rousseau maintains. If we fail to obey the General Will, then since it is by our own decision that we have undertaken to obey it, it is entirely legitimate that the community should force us to obey. In fact in doing so, Rousseau tells us, the community is forcing us to be free! This is not tyranny but perfect democracy.

However, there are other conditions that must also be satisfied before the General Will (as distinct from the will of all) can be said to have emerged. A majority vote is not in itself enough. Rousseau insists that the community must be relatively small. We have to be able to recognise who our fellow citizens are so that we can know who 'we' are. It is also important that the community not be divided. There must be no large disparities of wealth, since these will create different interest groups who will think of their own interests and not of the common interest. For the same reason, there must be no factions or 'partial associations', which rules out political parties in the modern sense. Finally, the community must share a common culture which creates the bond which defines 'us', and without which there can be no hope of understanding each other's needs and identifying the common good.

If these conditions are met and the General Will is realised, then we have the answer to the question that Rousseau set himself at the beginning of the *Social Contract*. He has combined liberty with legitimate collective authority. Individuals recognise their common interests, and through the laws they create they define their liberties – civil liberties not mere natural liberty which is no more than the right of the strongest. It is also democracy in the sense that it allows the people to rule themselves. True, it is not liberal democracy, since the 'people' is a collective entity, not the sum of many diverse, individual interests, and no limits are placed on the power of government. But it is none the less a form of democracy which would be recognisable to the citizens who ruled Ancient Greece and to those who advocate communitarianism today.

Rousseau's argument has been the subject of much criticism. Many have seen the theory of the General Will as paving the way for dictatorship rather than democracy. Such criticisms spring in part from observation of regimes which have claimed to embody the General Will, most notably the tyranny that followed the French Revolution. 'It is not surprising', writes Talmon (1986, p. 98), 'that as a faithful disciple of Rousseau, Robespierre was not prepared to recognise the decision of a representative assembly.' Others are less willing to accept this picture of Rousseau's malign influence. It is true that Rousseau was much revered and much quoted at the time of the Revolution, but this is quite different from attributing the subsequent Terror to him (see Miller, 1984, pp. 132ff.).

However, the logic of Rousseau's argument itself gives cause for worries about tyranny. Rousseau is not simply recommending majority rule, for he allows that the people may be mistaken or deluded about the General Will and may confuse their individual interests with those of the community and fail to perceive the common interest. Brian Barry (1964), borrowing from a discovery of Condorcet's, has argued that this is in practice unlikely to result in the majority decision being in error, for given large enough numbers, even a very slight predisposition for any one individual to be right will yield a high probability that the majority will be right. As Barry shows, in a population of 1,000, each member of which is right 51 per cent of the time, the probability that the majority is right is 69 per cent. There is thus some comfort in numbers. However, the real worry is that, in allowing that the majority may be wrong about the General Will, Rousseau has allowed for the possibility of a minority claiming to be able to discern the General Will and setting out to *impose* it on the majority who are deemed to be 'in error'. Rousseau's reference to individuals being 'forced to be free' is not, of course, reassuring in this connection, even if we are told that it is being done for their own good.

Other critics have sought to undermine the very idea of a General Will. Even within Rousseau's tightly-knit, homogenous community, they argue, there is no one interest that is shared in common. And even if there were, there would be no agreement about how to achieve it. Although Joseph Schumpeter (1976) does not mention Rousseau by name, he is one of the obvious targets of Schumpeter's critique of 'classical democracy'. To return to the example I used earlier, these critics cannot be persuaded that public transport is the General Will (and even if it was, there would be no agreement over the question of how it should be run or funded). It is just such doubts that may incline us towards a more modest, less interventionist conception of democracy, one that seeks to secure the least worst outcome rather than taking the risks of pursuing the best. It is this other, protective version of democracy that James Mill advocates.

## James Mill (1773–1836)

Born into the family of a Scottish shoemaker, James Mill's early academic promise brought him the patronage and support, first, of his local minister, and then of Sir John Stuart, whose daughter he tutored. Having distinguished himself as a Greek scholar, he went into the church, a move he was soon to regret. After Stuart was elected as a Member of Parliament, Mill accompanied him to London to become a writer. It was in London that he met Jeremy Bentham and became a leading proselytiser for Benthamite utilitarianism.

Bentham (1748–1823) was a writer and social reformer whose thought was influential in a wide variety of areas, not only politics but also in philosophy and economics. He sought to apply a ruthlessly logical scheme of thought to all human practices, judging them by the degree to which they produced pleasure or pain. For Bentham, the good society was that which generated the 'greatest pleasure for the greatest number'. It is precisely this principle that Mill embraces at the beginning of his 'Essay on Government'. Bentham and Mill were to constitute the intellectual force behind the movement known as 'philosophical radicalism' (see Thomas, 1979, chapter 3). Under the guidance of Mill's son, John Stuart Mill (see chapter 11), philosophical radicalism was the label adopted by those attempting to bring about, among other things, democratic reform in Britain. Their campaign was at its height in the 1830s, when they found a forum in the press and in the House of Commons.

But for James Mill, finding a public forum for his ideas was not easy. He struggled for a long time to establish himself as writer. His efforts were eventually rewarded with the publication of his *History of British India* (1818) and, subsequently, he was appointed to the East India Company. He continued to write, and in 1820 his 'Essay on Government' was published as a supplement to the *Encyclopedia Britannica*.

The 'Essay on Government' attracted considerable attention and was reprinted several times. It was, in its condemnation of monarchy and aristocracy and in its qualified defence of representative democracy, a radical text. It was at the same time a conservative statement, not just because of the highly limited franchise (no votes for women or the poor, for example), but also as a plea on behalf of the middle classes as guardians of the common weal.

Despite its popularity, Mill's essay received a vicious mauling from Thomas Macaulay in an edition of the *Edinburgh Review*. Macaulay dismissed it as a work which 'rests altogether on false principles, and even on those false principles he [James Mill] does not reason logically' (Macaulay, 1992 edn, p. 272). Despite Macaulay's withering scorn for Mill's efforts, the 'Essay on Government' stands as an important statement of a distinct tradition in democratic theorising and one that still has resonance today. In an article on the causes and cures of famine, the economist Amartya Sen makes explicit use of James Mill to argue that

'Democracy spreads the penalty of famines from the destitute to those in authority. There is no surer way of making government responsive to the suffering of famine victims' ('How democracy can free the world of famine', *The Independent*, 2 August 1990, p. 19).

The redistribution of pain and pleasure lies at the core of Mill's account of democracy. It is an argument which has a disarming simplicity, which makes it both easily understood and easily dismissed. Its philosophical and psychological assumptions are those of utilitarianism. All individuals are motivated by the desire to seek pleasure and to avoid pain. From this premise is derived the thought that a good society is one which maximises the total quantity of pleasure experienced by the population, and similarly minimises the total quantity of pain. Mill also assumes that each individual's capacity for pleasure is unbounded. They can never get enough.

Mill's essay is an attempt to establish the role and character of government in the good utilitarian society. The explanation is, in one sense, straightforward. The need for government is established by the fact that, as utilitarian creatures, we seek always to maximise our own pleasure, a search from which there is no respite. Our desires are limitless. Labour and property constitute the key means to securing pleasure, according to Mill, so the most obvious means by which a given individual can maximise their pleasure and minimise their pain is to enslave their fellow human beings or to steal their goods and wealth. But since such practices will, of course, threaten the general happiness, there is a need to establish a mechanism for guarding against the threats posed by the competitive pursuit of individual interest. This is the role assigned to government, whose job is to manage conflict: 'its business is to increase to the utmost the pleasures, and diminish to the utmost the pains, which men derive from one another' (below, p. 222), though Mill concedes that governments cannot be held responsible for the pain that results from natural processes – earthquakes, ageing and so on.

The question then becomes, 'what kind of government will do this most effectively?' Mill considers three familiar models: democracy, aristocracy and monarchy. The first represents rule by the many; the others rule by one or a few. He dismisses them all. Monarchy and aristocracy fail for one main reason. Elite rule, by its nature, is unaccountable, and those who occupy the elite will – as good utilitarian people – pursue their own pleasures. They will take advantage of their subjects, using them to their pleasurable advantage. It is not enough, Mill says, that these people may be models of good manners and breeding. He offers the example of the English gentleman who, when allowed colonial power in the West Indies, behave in the most cruel fashion (Mill, 1992 edn, p. 15). These dangers are compounded by the fact that monarchs and aristocrats are, in fact, ill-equipped by breeding and experience to manage the affairs of state, since they know nothing of the lives of those whom they rule over.

Mass democracy, on the other hand, while ensuring that there are no unaccountable elites, fails in another crucial respect. It takes up too much time. The business of mass assemblies is extremely time consuming, and as a result the very goal for which government is instituted – to maximise productive labour (pleasure) – is sacrificed.

So it is that Mill reaches his neat compromise: representative democracy. Citizens elect those who are to represent them and to take decisions on their behalf. The incentives under which these representatives work will guarantee the greatest happiness of the greatest number. The elected elite are tied to the electors by the bonds of pain and pleasure. The representatives seek to maximise their own pleasure by being elected and re-elected. They can only achieve this result by delivering pleasure to the citizens, who will in return give them their votes.

It is important to note that in explaining the conditions under which this system will work, Mill introduces draconian restrictions on the franchise. He sees no reason, for example, why women should have the vote (their interests being identical with those of their fathers or husbands). Such limitations are intended, according to Mill, to cut down on the amount of unnecessary participation.

It is easy to condemn Mill's thesis for such prejudices. After all, contemporary critics, and later his own son, condemned the restrictions he advocated. It is, however, worth recalling that at the time Mill was writing, women were denied the vote, and less than 5 per cent of the population as whole had the vote. Equally, it may be argued that such restrictions are superfluous to Mill's central argument. The more telling criticisms may, therefore, be those which address the main features of Mill's model. Here questions are raised about the logic and practice of a utilitarian representative democracy.

The first concerns the exact status of 'democracy' in Mill's argument. The doubt can be put like this: if maximum happiness could be achieved by some non-democratic system, would there be any reason to favour democracy? In other words, is it just a happy coincidence that links pleasure to representative democracy? And those who question the idea that happiness (as opposed to, say, freedom) constitutes a proper goal for a political order, must also doubt the virtues of Mill's approach.

A more specific doubt arises in connection with Mill's assumptions about how voters will actually behave. Put simply, Mill believes that they will act like him, choosing to maintain the kind of social order that he sees as being in the best interests of all. He attributes this vision to the good sense of the 'middle rank'. But will the mass of people choose like this, guided as Mill hopes by the example of the middle class? May they not opt for the mass irrationality of the will of all? This was the fear of Mill's son, John Stuart Mill, and was the reason for his inclusion of various safeguards against 'mass mediocrity'.

Also implicit in James Mill's model of democracy is the assumption that the actions of representatives can be assessed accurately by those who vote for them. But there is sufficient evidence of agenda-setting and other such devices to suggest that voters can be misled and deceived into supporting governments who have ill-served them. In other words, Mill assumes that a representative system is also a transparent one, that the use which representatives make of their power is plain to see. If, however, these individuals use their office to obscure the true nature of their actions and to delude their constituents, then the citizen's capacity to hold representatives accountable is nullified.

## Conclusion

Whatever the weaknesses in Mill's argument, it still remains a powerful case for protective democracy, one which rests more upon assumptions about people's malign leanings than upon their benign intentions. As such, it may constitute a more realistic, if more conservative, alternative to Rousseau's utopian vision. Such a conclusion is tempting given the way in which Rousseau's ideas have been tainted, albeit unfairly, by their association with the French Revolution and with one-party democracies in emergent African states (Nursey-Bray, 1983).

However, the argument is not yet over. Rousseau's dreams and Mill's practical solutions still mark out a fault line in contemporary debates, both in academia in the disputes between libertarians and communitarians, and in debates prompted by the New Right over the proper function of government. James Mill's ideas can be detected in the arguments of the Public Choice school that so impressed the governments of Margaret Thatcher and Ronald Reagan, for example in the claim that unaccountable authority (the Civil Service, or bureaucrats generally) will always seek to advance its own interests. We can also see Mill's ideas at work in the general suspicion of government and the preference for a consumer-based democracy of shareholders and internal markets. But in reaction to these regimes, the voice of Rousseau can also still be heard, in talk of the need to rediscover community and in the arguments of those who question pluralism or who dispute conventional liberal democratic solutions to the problems of political control in the modern world (e.g. Adonis and Mulgan, 1994). For these communitarians, as for Rousseau, democracy is about active participation in collective decisions; it is about collective deliberation over choices rather than registering preferences.

## References

Adonis, A. and Mulgan, G., 'Back to Greece: the Scope for Direct Democracy', *Demos Quarterly*, issue 3, 1994, pp. 2–9.

Barry, B., 'The Public Interest', *Proceedings of the Aristotelian Society*, 38, 1964, pp. 1–18.

Collini, S., Winch, D. and Burrow, J., *That Noble Science of Politics*, Cambridge: Cambridge University Press, 1983.

Held, D., *Models of Democracy*, Cambridge: Polity, 1987.

Macaulay, T. B., 'Mill on Government', in *James Mill: Political Writings*, Cambridge: Cambridge University Press, 1992, pp. 271–303.

Mill, J., 'Essay on Government', in *James Mill: Political Writings*, Cambridge: Cambrige University Press, 1992, pp. 1–42.

Miller, J., *Rousseau: Dreamer of Democracy*, New Haven: Yale University Press, 1984.

Nursey-Bray, P., 'Consensus and Community: The Theory of African One-Party Democracy', in G. Duncan (ed.), *Democratic Theory and Practice*, Cambridge: Cambridge University Press, 1983, pp. 96–114.

Rousseau, J. J., *The Confessions*, London: Penguin, 1977; 1st pub. 1781.

Rousseau, J. J., *The Social Contract*, from *The Collected Writings of Rousseau*, vol. 4, ed. R. D. T. Masters and C. Kelly, Hanover and London, University Press of New England, 1994; 1st pub. 1762.

Rousseau, J.-J., *Emile*, London: Dent, 1974; 1st pub. 1762.

Schumpeter, J., *Capitalism, Socialism and Democracy*, London: Allen & Unwin, 1976.

Shklar, J., *Men and Citizens: A Study of Rousseau's Social Theory*, Cambridge: Cambridge University Press, 1969.

Talmon, J. L., *The Origins of Totalitarian Democracy*, London: Penguin, 1986.

Taylor, C., *Sources of the Self: The Making of Modern Identity*, Cambridge: Cambridge University Press, 1989.

Thomas, W., *The Philosophic Radicals*, Oxford: Clarendon Press, 1979.

### Further reading

The main texts for both Rousseau (*The Social Contract*) and James Mill ('Essay on Government') are short. There are several translations of *The Social Contract*, of which the best is the one edited by Roger Masters and Christopher Kelly (see references). The most accessible version of Mill's essay is published by Cambridge University Press and edited by Terence Ball (see references). This edition also includes Macaulay's critical review.

The best general commentary on Mill and Rousseau as democratic theorists is contained in David Held's *Models of Democracy*. Anthony Arblaster's short book, *Democracy* (Milton Keynes: Open University Press, 1987), provides a useful summary of the key lines of argument around democracy.

For more detailed discussion of Rousseau, see the works by James Miller and Judith Shklar, and for the most intemperate critique see J. L. Talmon (all cited in references). For a critical discussion of Mill, see C. B. Macpherson, *The Life and Times of Liberal Democracy* (Oxford: Oxford University Press, 1977), and for a richer understanding of his place in the history of ideas, see Stefan Collini *et al.* and William Thomas (see references).

### Seminar questions

Is there such a thing as the General Will? If so, what are the problems involved in identifying it?

Does democracy result from adherence to the General Will?

Is utilitarianism a safe foundation upon which to build a case for democracy?

Mill's version of representative democracy is often labelled 'protective democracy'. Who or what is he protecting?

# J. J. ROUSSEAU
## From *The Social Contract*

### BOOK I

### Chapter VI   On the Social Compact

I assume that men have reached the point where obstacles to their self-preservation in the state of nature prevail by their resistance over the forces each individual can use to maintain himself in that state. Then that primitive state can no longer subsist and the human race would perish if it did not change its manner of living.

Now since men cannot engender new forces, but merely unite and direct existing ones, they have no other means of self preservation except to form, by aggregation, a sum of forces that can prevail over the resistance; set them to work by a single motivation; and make them act in concert.

This sum of forces can arise only from the cooperation of many. But since each man's force and freedom are the primary instruments of his self-preservation, how is he to engage them without harming himself and without neglecting the cares he owes to himself? In the context of my subject, this difficulty can be stated in these terms:

'Find a form of association that defends and protects the person and goods of each associate with all the common force, and by means of which each one, uniting with all, nevertheless obeys only himself and remains as free as before.' This is the fundamental problem which is solved by the social contract.

The clauses of this contract are so completely determined by the nature of the act that the slightest modification would render them null and void. So that although they may never have been formally pronounced, they are everywhere the same, everywhere tacitly accepted and recognized, until the social compact is violated, at which point each man recovers his original rights and resumes his natural freedom, thereby losing the conventional freedom for which he renounced it.

Properly understood, all of these clauses come down to a single one, namely the total alienation of each associate, with all his rights, to the whole community. For first of all, since each one gives his entire self, the condition is equal for everyone, and since the condition is equal for everyone, no one has an interest in making it burdensome for the others.

Furthermore, as the alienation is made without reservation, the union is as perfect as it can be, and no associate has anything further to claim. For if some rights were left to private individuals, there would be no common superior who could judge between them and the public. Each man being his own judge on some point would soon claim to be so on all; the state of nature would subsist and the association would neccessarily become tyrannical or ineffectual.

Finally, as each gives himself to all, he gives himself to no one; and since there is no associate over whom one does not acquire the same right one grants him over oneself, one gains the equivalent of everything one loses, and more force to preserve what one has.

If, then, everything that is not of the essence of the social compact is set aside, one will find that it can be reduced to the following terms. *Each of us puts his person and all his power in common under the supreme direction of the general will; and in a body we receive each member as an indivisible part of the whole.*

Instantly, in place of the private person of each contracting party, this act of association produces a moral and collective body, composed of as many members as there are voices in the assembly, which receives from this same act its unity, its common *self*, its life, and its will. This public person, formed by the union of all the others, formerly took the name *City*, and now takes that of *Republic* or *body politic*, which its members call *State* when it is passive, *Sovereign* when active, *Power* when comparing it to similar bodies. As for the associates, they collectively take the name *people*; and individually are called *Citizens* as participants in the sovereign authority, and *Subjects* as subject to the laws of the State. But these terms are often mixed up and mistaken for one another. It is enough to know how to distinguish them when they are used with complete precision.

### Chapter VII  On the Sovereign

This formula shows that the act of association includes a reciprocal engagement between the public and private individuals, and that each individual, contracting with himself so to speak, finds himself engaged in a double relation, namely toward private individuals as a member of the Sovereign and toward the Sovereign as a member of the State. But the maxim of civil right that no one can be held responsible for engagements toward himself cannot be applied here, because there is a great difference between being obligated to oneself, or to a whole of which one is a part.

It must further be noted that the public deliberation that can obligate all of the subjects to the Sovereign – due to the two different relationships in which each of them is considered – cannot for the opposite reason obligate the Sovereign toward itself; and that consequently it is contrary to the nature of the body politic for the Sovereign to impose on itself a law it cannot break. Since the sovereign can only be considered in a single relationship, it is then in the situation of a private individual contracting with himself. It is apparent from this that there is not, nor can there be, any kind of fundamental law that is obligatory for the body of the people, not even the social contract. This does not mean that this body cannot perfectly well enter an engagement toward another with respect to things that do not violate this contract. For with reference to the foreigner, it becomes a simple being or individual.

But the body politic or the Sovereign, deriving its being solely from the sanctity of the contract, can never obligate itself, even toward another, to do anything that violates that original act, such as to alienate some part of itself or to subject itself to another Sovereign. To violate the act by which it exists would be to destroy itself, and whatever is nothing, produces nothing.

As soon as this multitude is thus united in a body, one cannot harm one of the members without attacking the body, and it is even less possible to harm the body without the members feeling the effects. Thus duty and interest equally obligate the two contracting parties to mutual assistance, and the same men should seek to combine in this double relationship all the advantages that are dependent on it.

Now, the Sovereign, formed solely by the private individuals composing it, does not and cannot have any interest contrary to theirs. Consequently, the Sovereign power has no need of a guarantee toward the subjects, because it is impossible for the body ever to want to harm all its members, and we shall see later that it cannot harm any one of them as an individual. The Sovereign, by the sole fact of being, is always what it ought to be.

But the same is not true of the subjects in relation to the Sovereign, which, despite the common interest, would have no guarantee of the subjects' engagements if it did not find ways to be assured of their fidelity.

Indeed, each individual can, as a man, have a private will contrary to or differing from the general will he has as a Citizen. His private interest can speak to him quite differently from the common interest. His absolute and naturally independent existence can bring him to view what he owes the common cause as a free contribution, the loss of which will harm others less than its payment burdens him. And considering the moral person of the State as a being produced by reason because it is not a man, he might wish to enjoy the rights of the citizen without wanting to fulfill the duties of a subject, an injustice whose spread would cause the ruin of the body politic.

Therefore, in order for the social compact not to be an ineffectual formula, it tacitly includes the following engagement, which alone can give force to the others: that whoever refuses to obey the general will shall be constrained to do so by the entire body; which means only that he will be forced to be free. For this is the condition that, by giving each Citizen to the fatherland, guarantees him against all personal dependence; a condition that creates the ingenuity and functioning of the political machine and alone gives legitimacy to civil engagements which without it would be absurd, tyrannical, and subject to the most enormous abuses.

## Chapter VIII  On the Civil State

This passage from the state of nature to the civil state produces a remarkable change in man, by substituting justice for instinct in his behavior and giving his actions the morality they previously lacked. Only then, when the voice of duty replaces physical impulse and

217

right replaces appetite, does man, who until that time only considered himself, find himself forced to act upon other principles and to consult his reason before heeding his inclinations. Although in this state he deprives himself of several advantages given him by nature, he gains such great ones, his faculties are exercised and developed, his ideas broadened, his feelings ennobled, and his whole soul elevated to such a point that if the abuses of this new condition did not often degrade him beneath the condition he left, he ought ceaselessly to bless the happy moment that tore him away from it forever, and that changed him from a stupid, limited animal into an intelligent being and a man.

Let us reduce the pros and cons to easily compared terms. What man loses by the social contract is his natural freedom and an unlimited right to everything that tempts him and that he can get; what he gains is civil freedom and the proprietorship of everything he possesses. In order not to be mistaken about these compensations, one must distinguish carefully between natural freedom, which is limited only by the force of the individual, and civil freedom, which is limited by the general will; and between possession, which is only the effect of force or the right of the first occupant, and property, which can only be based on a positive title.

To the foregoing acquisitions of the civil state could be added moral freedom, which alone makes man truly the master of himself. For the impulse of appetite alone is slavery, and obedience to the law one has prescribed for oneself is freedom. But I have already said too much about this topic, and the philosophic meaning of the word *freedom* is not my subject here.

## BOOK II

### Chapter I   That Sovereignty is Inalienable

The first and most important consequence of the principles established above is that the general will alone can guide the forces of the State according to the end for which it was instituted, which is the common good. For if the opposition of private interests made the establishment of societies neccessary, it is what these different interests have in common that forms the social bond, and if there were not some point at which all the interests are in agreement, no society could exist. Now it is uniquely on the basis of this common interest that society ought to be governed.

I say, therefore, that sovereignty, being only the exercise of the general will, can never be alientated, and that the sovereign, which is only a collective being, can only be represented by itself. Power can perfectly well be transferred, but not will.

Indeed, though it is not impossible for a private will to agree with the general will on a given point, it is impossible, at least, for this agreement to be lasting and unchanging. For the private will tends by its nature toward preferences, and the general will toward equality. It is even more impossible for there to be a guarantee of this agreement even should it always exist. It would not be the result of art, but of chance. The Sovereign may well say, 'I currently want what a particular man wants, or at least what he says he wants.' But it cannot say, 'What that man will want tomorrow, I shall still want,' since it is absurd for the will to tie itself down for the future and since no will can consent to anything that is contrary to the good of the being that wills. Therefore, if the people promises simply to obey, it dissolves itself by that act; it loses the status of a people. The moment there is a master, there is no longer a Sovereign, and from then on the body politic is destroyed.

This is not to say that the commands of leaders cannot pass for expressions of the general will, as long as the Sovereign, being free to oppose them, does not do so. In such a case, one ought to presume the consent of the people from universal silence. This will be explained at greater length.

## Chapter II    That Sovereignty is Indivisible

For the same reason that sovereignty is inalienable, it is indivisible. Because either the will is general or it is not (in order for a will to be general, it is not always necessary for it to be unanimous, but it is necessary that all votes be counted. Any formal exclusion destroys the generality.) It is the will of the people as a body, or of only a part. In the first case, this declared will is an act of sovereignty and constitutes law. In the second case, it is merely a private will or an act of magistracy; it is at most a decree.

But our political thinkers, unable to divide the principle of sovereignty, divide it in its object. They divide it into force and will; into legislative power and executive power; into rights of taxation, justice, and war; into internal administration and power to negotiate with foreigners. Sometimes they mix all these parts together, sometimes they separate them. They turn the sovereign into a fantastic being formed of bits and pieces. It is as though they constructed a man out of several bodies, one of which would have eyes, another arms, another feet, and nothing more. Japanese charlatans are said to cut up a child right in front of the audience; then, tossing all the parts into the air one after another, they make the child come back down alive and in one piece. The juggling acts of our political thinkers are about like that. After they have taken the social body apart by a trick worthy of a carnival, they put the peices back together in some unknown way.

This error comes from not having developed exact concepts of sovereign authority, and from having mistaken for parts of that authority what were merely emanations from it. Thus, for example, the acts of declaring war and making peace have been regarded as acts of sovereignty, which they are not, since each of these acts is not a law but merely an application of the law, a particular act which determines the legal situation, as will be clearly seen when the idea attached to the word *law* is established.

By examining the other divisions in the same way, it would be found that every time it is thought that sovereignty is divided, a mistake has been made, and that the rights that are mistaken for parts of that sovereignty are always subordinate to it and always presuppose supreme wills which these rights merely execute.

It is hard to overestimate how much this lack of precision has obscured the decisions of authors on the subject of political right when they wanted to judge the respective rights of kings and peoples on the basis of the principles they had established. In chapters III and IV of the first book of Grotius, anyone can see how this learned man and his translator Barbeyrac get entangled and trapped in their sophisms, for fear of saying too much or not enough according to their viewpoints, and of offending the interests they needed to reconcile. Grotius – taking refuge in France, discontent with his fatherland, and wanting to pay court to Louis XIII to whom his book is dedicated – spares nothing to divest the people of all their rights and to endow kings with them as artfully as possible. This would certainly have been the preference of Barbeyrac, too, who dedicated his translation to King George I of England. But unfortunately the expulsion of James II, which he calls abdication, forced him to be cautious, evasive, and equivocal so as not to make William appear to be a usurper. If these two writers had adopted the true principles, all their difficulties would have been avoided and they would always have been consistent. But they would have told the truth with regret and paid court only to the people. For truth does not lead to fortune, and the people does not confer embassies, professorships, or pensions.

### Chapter III  Whether the General Will Can Err

From the foregoing it follows that the general will is always right and always tends toward the public utility. But it does not follow that the people's deliberations always have the same rectitude. One always wants what is good for oneself, but one does not always see it. The people is never corrupted, but it is often fooled, and only then does it appear to want what is bad.

There is often a great difference between the will of all and the general will. The latter considers only the common interest; the former considers private interest, and is only a sum of private wills. But take away from these same wills the pluses and minuses that cancel each other out, and the remaining sum of the differences is the general will. (*Each interest*, says the Marquis d'Argensou, *has different principles. The agreement of two private interests is formed in opposition to the interest of a third.* He could have added that the agreement of all interests is formed in opposition to the interest of each. If there were no different interests, the common interest, which would never encounter any obstacle, would scarcely be felt. Everything would run smoothly by itself and politics would cease to be an art.)

If, when an adequately informed people deliberates, the Citizens were to have no communication among themselves, the general will would always result from the large number of small differences, and the deliberation would always be good. But when factious, partial associations at the expense of the large one, are formed, the will of each of these associations becomes general with reference to its members and particular with reference to the State. One can say, then, that there are no longer as many voters as there are men, but merely as many as there are associations. The differences become less numerous and produce a result that is less general. Finally, when one of these associations is so big that it prevails over all the others, the result is no longer a sum of small differences, but a single difference. Then there is no longer a general will, and the opinion that prevails is merely a private opinion.

In order for the general will to be well expressed, it is therefore important that there be no partial society in the State, and that each Citizen give only his own opinion. Such were the unique and sublime institutions by the great Lycurgus. If there are partial societies, their number must be multiplied and their inequality prevented, as was done by Solon, Numa, and Servius. These precautions are the only ones good for ensuring that the general will is always enlightened and that the people is not deceived.

# JAMES MILL
## From *Essay on Government*

### I. The End of Government; viz. the Good or Benefit for the Sake of which it exists

The question with respect to Government is a question about the adaptation of means to an end. Notwithstanding the portion of discourse which has been bestowed upon this subject, it is surprising to find, on a close inspection, how few of its principles are settled. The reason is, that the ends and means have not been analyzed; and it is only a general and undistinguishing conception of them, which is found in the minds of the greatest number of men. Things, in this situation, give rise to interminable disputes; more especially when the deliberation is subject, as here, to the strongest action of personal interest.

In a discourse, limited as the present, it would be obviously vain to attempt the accomplishment of such a task as that of the analysis we have mentioned. The mode, however, in which the operation should be conducted, may perhaps be described, and evidence enough exhibited to shew in what road we must travel, to approach the goal at which so many have vainly endeavoured to arrive.

The end of Government has been described in a great variety of expressions. By Locke it was said to be 'the public good;' by others it has been described as being 'the greatest happiness of the greatest number.' These, and equivalent expressions, are just; but they are defective, inasmuch as the particular ideas which they embrace are indistinctly announced; and different conceptions are by means of them raised in different minds, and even in the same mind on different occasions.

It is immediately obvious, that a wide and difficult field is presented, and that the whole science of human nature must be explored, to lay a foundation for the science of Government.

To understand what is included in the happiness of the greatest number, we must understand what is included in the happiness of the individuals of whom it is composed.

That dissection of human nature which would be necessary for exhibiting, on proper evidence, the primary elements into which human happiness may be resolved, it is not compatible with the present design to undertake. We must content ourselves with assuming certain results.

We may allow, for example, in general terms, that the lot of every human being is determined by his pains and pleasures; and that his happiness corresponds with the degree in which his pleasures are great, and his pains are small.

Human pains and pleasures are derived from two sources: – They are produced, either by our fellow-men, or by causes independent of other men.

We may assume it as another principle, that the concern of Government is with the former of these two sources; that its business is to increase to the utmost the pleasures, and diminish to the utmost the pains, which men derive from one another.

Of the laws of nature, on which the condition of man depends, that which is attended with the greatest number of consequences, is the necessity of labour for obtaining the means of subsistence, as well as the means of the greatest part of our pleasures. This is, no doubt, the primary cause of Government; for, if nature had produced spontaneously all the objects which we desire, and in sufficient abundance for the desires of all, there would have been no source of dispute or of injury among men; nor would any man have possessed the means of ever acquiring authority over another.

The results are exceedingly different, when nature produces the objects of desire not in sufficient abundance for all. The source of dispute is then exhaustless; and every man has the means of acquiring authority over others, in proportion to the quantity of those objects which he is able to possess.

In this case, the end to be obtained, through Government as the means, is, to make that distribution of the scanty materials of happiness, which would insure the greatest sum of it in the members of the community, taken altogether, preventing every individual, or combination of individuals, from interfering with that distribution, or making any man to have less than his share.

When it is considered that most of the objects of desire, and even the means of subsistence, are the product of labour, it is evident that the means of insuring labour must be provided for as the foundation of all.

The means for the insuring of labour are of two sorts; the one made out of the matter of evil, the other made out of the matter of good.

The first sort is commonly denominated force; and, under its application, the labourers are slaves. This mode of procuring labour we need not consider; for, if the end of Government be to produce the greatest happiness of the greatest number, that end cannot be attained by making the greatest number slaves.

The other mode of obtaining labour is by allurement, or the advantage which it brings. To obtain all the objects of desire in the greatest possible quantity, we must obtain labour in the greatest possible quantity; and to obtain labour in the greatest possible quantity, we must raise to the greatest possible height the advantage attached to labour. It is impossible to attach to labour a greater degree of advantage than the whole of the product of labour. Why so? Because, if you give more to one man than the produce of his labour, you can do so only by taking it away from the produce of some other man's labour. The greatest possible happiness of society is, therefore, attained by insuring to every man the greatest possible quantity of the produce of his labour.

How is this to be accomplished? for it is obvious that every man, who has not all the objects of his desire, has inducement to take them from any other man who is weaker than himself: and how is he to be prevented?

One mode is sufficiently obvious; and it does not appear that there is any other: The union of a certain number of men, to protect one another. The object, it is plain, can best be attained when a great number of men combine, and delegate to a small number the power necessary for protecting them all. This is Government.

With respect to the end of Government, or that for the sake of which it exists, it is not conceived to be necessary, on the present occasion, that the analysis should be carried any further. What follows is an attempt to analyze the means.

### III. That the requisite Securities against the Abuse of Power, are not found in any of the simple Forms of Government

There are three modes in which it may be supposed that the powers for the protection of the community are capable of being exercised. The community may undertake the protection of itself, and of its members. The powers of protection may be placed in the hands of a few. And, lastly, they may be placed in the hands of an individual. The Many, The Few, The One; These varieties appear to exhaust the subject. It is not possible to conceive any hands, or combination of hands, in which the powers of protection can be lodged, which will not fall under one or other of those descriptions. And these varieties correspond to the three forms of Government, The Democratical, the Aristocratical, and the Monarchical.

It will be necessary to look somewhat closely at each of these forms in their order.

1. THE DEMOCRATICAL – It is obviously impossible that the commu-

nity in a body can be present to afford protection to each of its members. It must employ individuals for that purpose. Employing individuals, it must choose them; it must lay down the rules under which they are to act; and it must punish them, if they act in disconformity to those rules. In these functions are included the three great operations of Government – Administration, Legislation, and Judicature. The community, to perform any of these operations, must be assembled. This circumstance alone seems to form a conclusive objection against the democratical form. To assemble the whole of a community as often as the business of Government requires performance would almost preclude the existence of labour; hence that of property; and hence the existence of the community itself.

There is another objection, not less conclusive. A whole community would form a numerous assembly. But all numerous assemblies are essentially incapable of business. It is unneccessary to be tedious in the proof of this proposition. In an assembly, every thing must be done by speaking and assenting. But where the assembly is numerous, so many persons desire to speak, and feelings, by mutual inflammation, become so violent, that calm and effectual deliberation is impossible.

It may be taken, therefore, as a position, from which there will be no dissent, that a community in mass is ill adapted for the business of Government. There is no principle more in conformity with the sentiments and the practice of the people than this. The management of the joint affairs of any considerable body of the people they never undertake for themselves. What they uniformly do is, to choose a certain number of themselves to be the actors in their stead. Even in the case of a common Benefit Club, the members choose a Committee of Management, and content themselves with a general control.

2. THE ARISTOCRATICAL – This term applies to all those cases, in which the powers of Government are held by any number of persons intermediate between a single person and the majority. When the number is small, it is common to call the Government an Oligarchy; when it is considerable, to call it an Aristocracy. The cases are essentially the same; because the motives which operate in both are the same. This is a proposition which carries, we think, its own evidence along with it. We, therefore, assume it as a point which will not be disputed.

The source of evil is radically different, in the case of Aristocracy, from what it is in that of Democracy.

The Community cannot have an interest opposite to its interest. To affirm this would be a contradiction in terms. The Community within itself, and with respect to itself, can have no sinister interest. One Community may intend the evil of another; never its own. This is an indubitable proposition, and one of great importance. The Community may act wrong from mistake. To suppose that it could from design, would be to suppose that human beings can wish their own misery.

The circumstances, from which the inaptitude of the community, as a body, for the business of Government, arises, namely, the inconvenience of assembling them, and the inconvenience of their numbers when assembled, do not necessarily exist in the case of Aristocracy. If the number of those who hold among them the powers of Government is so great, as to make it inconvenient to assemble them, or impossible for them to deliberate calmly when assembled, this is only an objection to so extended an Aristocracy, and has no application to an Aristocracy not too numerous, when assembled for the best exercise of deliberation.

The question is, whether such an Aristocracy may be trusted to make that use of the powers of Government which is most conducive to the end for which Government exists?

There may be a strong presumption that any Aristocracy monopolizing the powers of Government, would not possess intellectual powers in any very high perfection. Intellectual powers are the offspring of labour. But an hereditary Aristocracy are deprived of the strongest motives to labour. The greater part of them will, therefore, be defective in those mental powers. This is one objection, and an important one, though not the greatest.

We have already observed, that the reason for which Government exists is, that one man, if stronger than another, will take from him whatever that other possesses and he desires. But if one man will do this, so will several. And if powers are put into the hands of a comparatively small number, called an Aristocracy, powers which make them stronger than the rest of the community, they will take from the rest of the community as much as they please of the objects of desire. They will, thus, defeat the very end for which Government was instituted. The unfitness, therefore, of an Aristocracy to be entrusted with the powers of Government, rests on demonstration.

3. THE MONARCHICAL – It will be seen, and therefore words to make it manifest are unnecessary, that, in most respects, the Monarchical form of Government agrees with the Aristocratical, and is liable to the same objections.

If Government is founded upon this, as a law of human nature, that a man, if able, will take from others any thing which they have and he desires, it is sufficiently evident that when a man is called a King, it does not change his nature; so that when he has got power to enable him to take from every man what he pleases, he will take whatever he pleases. To suppose that he will not, is to affirm that Government is unneccessary; and that human beings will abstain from injuring one another of their own accord.

It is very evident that this reasoning extends to every modification of the smaller number. Whenever the powers of Government are placed in any hands other than those of the community, whether those of one man, of a few, or of several, those principles of human nature which imply that Government is at all necessary, imply that those persons will make use of them to defeat the very end for which Government exists.

## VI. In the Representative System alone the Securities for good Government are to be found

What then is to be done? For, according to this reasoning, we may be told that good Government appears to be impossible. The people, as a body, cannot perform the business of Government for themselves. If the powers of Government are entrusted to one man, or a few men, and a Monarchy, or governing Aristocracy, if formed, the results are fatal: And it appears that a combination of the simple forms is impossible.

Notwithstanding the truth of these propositions, it is not yet proved that good Government is impossible. For though the people, who cannot exercise the powers of Government themselves, must entrust them to some one individual or set of individuals, and such individuals will infallibly have the strongest motives to make a bad use of them, it is possible that checks may be found sufficient to prevent them. The next subject of inquiry, then, is the doctrine of checks. It is sufficiently conformable to the established and fashionable opinions to say, that, upon the right constitution of checks, all goodness of Government depends. To this propostition we fully subscribe. Nothing, therefore, can exceed the importance of correct conclusions upon this subject. After the developments already made, it is hoped that the inquiry will be neither intricate nor unsatisfactory.

In the grand discovery of modern times, the system of representation, the solution of all the difficulties, both speculative and practical, will perhaps be found. If it cannot, we seem to be forced upon the extraordinary conclusion, that good Government is impossible. For as there is not individual, or combination of individuals, except the community itself, who would not have an interest in bad Government, if entrusted with its powers; and as the community itself is incapable of exercising those powers, and must entrust them to some individual or combination of individuals, the conclusion is obvious. The Community itself must check those individuals, else they will follow their interest, and produce bad Government.

But how is it the Community can check? The community can act only when assembled: And then it is incapable of acting.

The community, however, can choose Representatives: And the question is, whether the Representatives of the Community can operate as a check?

## X . Objection: that the People are not capable of acting agreeably to their Interests

[...]

The question is between a portion of the community, which, if entrusted with power, would have an interest in making a bad use of it, and a portion which, though entrusted with power, would not have an interest in making a bad use of it. The former are any small number whatsoever, who, by the circumstance of being entrusted with power, are constituted an Aristocracy.

From the frequency, however great, with which those who compose the mass of the community act in opposition to their interests, no conclusion can, in this case, be drawn, without a comparison of the frequency with which those, who are placed in contrast with them, act in opposition to theirs. Now, it may with great confidence be affirmed, that as great a proportion of those who compose the Aristocratical body of any country, as of those who compose the rest of the community, are distinguished for a conduct unfavourable for their interests. Prudence is a more general characteristic of the people who are without the advantages of fortune, than of the people who have been thoroughly subject to their corruptive operation. It may surely be said that if the powers of Government must be entrusted to persons incapable of good conduct, they were better entrusted to incapables who have an interest in good government, than to incapables who have an interest in bad.

It will be said that a conclusion ought not to be drawn from the unthinking conduct of the great majority of an Aristocratical body, against the capability of such a body for acting wisely in the management of public affairs; because the body will always contain a certain proportion of wise men, and the rest will be governed by them. Nothing but this can be said with pertinency. And, under certain modifications, this may be said with truth. The wise and good in any class of men do, to all general purposes, govern the rest. The comparison, however, must go on. Of that body, whose interests are identified with those of the community, it may also be said, that if one portion of them are unthinking, there is another portion wise; and that, in matters of state, the less wise would be governed by the more wise, not less certainly than in that body, whose interests, if they were entrusted with power, could not be identified with those of the community.

If we compare in each of these two contrasted bodies the two descriptions of persons, we shall not find that the foolish part of the Democratical body are more foolish than that of the Aristocratical, nor the wise part less wise.

Though, according to the opinions which fashion has propagated, it may appear a little paradoxical, we shall probably find the very reverse.

That there is not only as great a proportion of wise men in that part of the community which is not the Aristocracy, as in that which is; but that, under the present state of education, and the diffusion of knowledge, there is a much greater, we presume, there are few persons who will be disposed to dispute. It is to be observed, that the class which is universally described as both the most wise and the most virtuous part of the community, the middle rank, are wholly included in that part of the community which is not the Aristocratical. It is also not disputed, that in Great Britain the middle rank are numerous, and form a large proportion of the whole body of the people. Another proposition may be stated, with a perfect confidence of the concurrence of all those men who have attentively considered the formation of opinions in the great body of society, or, indeed, the principles of human nature in general. It is, that the opinions of that class of the people, who are below the middle rank, are formed, and their minds are directed by that intelligent and virtuous rank, who come the most immediately in contact with them, who are in the constant habit of intimate communication with them, to whom they fly for advice and assistance in all their numerous difficulties, upon whom they feel an immediate and daily dependence, in health and in sickness, in infancy and in old age; to whom their children look up as models for their imitation, whose opinions they hear daily repeated, and account it their honour to adopt. There can be no doubt that the middle rank, which gives to science, to art, and to legislation itself, their most distinguished ornaments, the chief source of all that has exalted and refined human nature, is that portion of the community of which, if the basis of Representation were ever so far extended, the opinion would ultimately decide. Of the people beneath them, a vast majority would be sure to be guided by their advice and example.

The incidents which have been urged as exceptions to this general rule, and even as reasons for rejecting it, may be considered as contributing to its proof. What signify the irregularities of a mob, more than half composed, in the greater number of instances, of boys and women, and disturbing, for a few hours or days, a particular town? What signifies the occasional turbulence of a manufacturing district, peculiarly unhappy from a very great deficiency of a middle rank, as there the population almost wholly consists of rich manufacturers and poor workmen; with whose minds no pains are taken by anybody; with whose afflictions there is no virtuous family of the middle rank to sympathize; whose children have no good example of such a family to see and to admire; and who are placed in the highly unfavourable situation of fluctuating between very high wages in one year, and very low wages in another? It is altogether futile with regard to the foundation of good government to say that this or the other portion of the people, may at this, or the other time, depart from the wisdom of the middle rank. It is enough that the great majority of the people never cease to be guided by that rank; and we may, with some confidence, challenge the adversaries of the people to produce a single instance to the contrary in the history of the world.

DAVID HOUGHTON

# Marx and Lenin on communism

9

Communism, as understood by Marx and Lenin, signifies both a form of society and a political movement aimed at bringing societies of that form about. The defining feature of a communist society is that in it, all means of production – factories, machinery, land and raw materials – are owned and controlled by the community as a whole. It is not to be thought of as a simple society whose members, out of either virtue or necessity, live frugal, austere lives, sleeping in dormitories, eating in refectories and sharing all their worldly goods. On the contrary, it will be an economically advanced society, with the capacity to provide all its members with the means to live diverse and fulfilling lives.

The means of production must be collectively owned, Marx and Lenin believe, because private ownership is the source of all major social ills. It divides societies into classes with irreconcilably conflicting interests. It enables owners to dominate, oppress and exploit non-owners. It condemns some to impoverished lives and daily drudgery while permitting others to live in leisured luxury. It has a disfiguring effect on society as a whole as first politics and law, and then morality, art and even philosophy, are recruited in the defence of class interests.

As a political movement, modern communism has two features of note. Firstly, it believes that it has history on its side. It holds that the various property systems which are to be found in history – slavery, feudalism, capitalism – all emerged in order to increase society's productive potential. Hence, once societies have acquired the technical capacity to provide for the reasonable needs of all, a point which it is supposed will be reached under advanced capitalism, private property will have served its historical function and become redundant. Secondly, it holds that, once this historical point is reached, it will be in the interests of the great majority of the population, the proletariat or propertyless wage labourers, to overthrow the existing capitalist (or bourgeois) system of production and property and to institute a system of common ownership and co-operative production. In theory, then, the task of the communist movement is little more than the consciousness-raising one of pointing out these facts and 'scientific' insights.

Modern communism is a radical political philosophy, believing as it does that structural conflict is not endemic to human society, that, accordingly, the state as an organised coercive force for suppressing conflict will not be forever necessary and the problems which orthodox political philosophies, with their different theories of justice, have attempted to solve are problems that in future need not arise. It combines extreme pessimism about the possibility of social harmony under conditions of economic scarcity with wide-eyed optimism about the power of technical innovation and human ingenuity to overcome these conditions, and about the benefits that will result from overcoming them. However, unlike anarchism (see chapter 10), it believes that the good society, the 'truly human' society, cannot be built overnight and that repressive measures and the use of force are certain to be needed in the building of it. A transition period will be necessary after capitalism before the full benefits of communism can be enjoyed.

The experience of would-be communist governments in the twentieth century has shown that merely abolishing private ownership of the means of production has no liberating effect and fails to prevent the domination and oppression of one social group by another. Marx and Lenin still owe us an account of what exactly is meant by 'collective' or 'social' ownership and control and how it is to be achieved.

### Karl Marx (1818–83)

Karl Marx was born in Trier, Germany. As a student in Berlin he came under the influence of Hegel's philosophy and associated himself with the radical Young Hegelian movement. Barred from an academic career by his anti-establishment views, he turned to journalism and edited a radical newspaper until it was banned by the Prussian authorities. Converted by this stage to communist ideas, he moved to Paris which was then the centre of socialist thought and activity. There he began his long association with Frederick Engels, and together they worked out their materialist theory of history, which retained Hegel's dialectical account of social change but located the source of change in the economic development of society, a development which they believed would naturally lead to communism. Expelled from Paris, Marx moved to Brussels where he joined the Communist League and, with Engels' help, drew up its 1848 manifesto. In the reactionary aftermath of the continental uprisings of 1848 he was forced to take refuge in England, there to spend the rest of his life. The next decade he devoted to studying the economic workings of capitalism, conducting most of his research in the British Museum, and in 1867 he published the first volume of his masterpiece, *Capital*. Between 1864 and 1872 he was a leading figure in the International Working Men's Association until a rift with Bakunin and the anarchists led to its dissolution. The latter part of his life was marred by ill health, prompting him on one occasion to make the wry remark that the bourgeoisie would have good reason to rue his carbuncles. However, he lived long enough to see the formation of the German Social Democratic Party, the first political party proper to espouse his ideas. He is buried in Highgate Cemetery, London.

It is ironic that the so-called communist regimes of the twentieth century should have found themselves condemned for their denial of freedom and democracy, since it was Marx's own commitment to these two values, and his belief that they could never be adequately realised in Western liberal democracies that first led him to communism. This is one of the main themes of his early writings, in particular the essay from which the first reading comes, *On the Jewish Question*, written in 1843 shortly after his conversion to communism.

Marx was fond of developing his own ideas by way of criticising some opponent, and here he begins with an attack on the views of his former university tutor, Bruno Bauer. Bauer had written two pamphlets responding unsympathetically to the demand of German Jews for equal civil rights with Christians. All Germans, Bauer argued, should combine in the struggle for a political order in which they could participate as free and equal citizens, but they would first need to renounce their separate religious identities, Jewish or Christian, in order to achieve that. Marx, whose father had been obliged to renounce his Jewish faith to keep his post in the Prussian civil service, observed, in reply, that no greater religious differences could be found anywhere than in the United States although it had the kind of secular constitution Bauer was advocating. His main point, however, was to argue that the emancipation which Bauer wanted to see in Germany, the emancipation which the American and French revolutions of 1776 and 1789 had achieved, was merely a 'political emancipation' that left people in bondage in their everyday working lives. It fell far short of 'human' emancipation and it failed to address those social evils to which, in fact, the religious preoccupations so deplored by Bauer were a natural response.

Marx did not deny that the results of the French Revolution represented an advance on the old order. With its declaration of the Rights of the Citizen it had turned public affairs, the affairs of state, into the affairs of the people. All citizens were declared to have equal rights to political participation, irrespective of wealth or social status. Yet, on the other hand, not only did vast social and economic inequalities remain in place, they were now identified as belonging to a private sphere outside the range of political interference and control. For what the French Revolution had done was to perfect a separation that is peculiar to the modern, post-feudal world, the separation of state and 'civil society', of 'public' political and 'private' economic life (see chapter 6). In feudal society no such separation existed. The political and economic were intertwined. But with the breakdown of the old feudal order economic activity had been gradually freed of traditional constraints and encumbrances. The state indeed played a necessary part in this process since it was needed to supply a framework for the emergent 'free' market economy, protecting private property and acting to prevent force and fraud, but otherwise civil society, ordered on market principles, was left to regulate itself. The Rights of Man, included alongside the Rights of the Citizen in the French Declaration of Rights, sanctified this separation. The right to private property, which meant the right to the unrestricted accumulation of capital and the right to buy and sell labour-power on the market, effectively removed the economic sphere from political interference and direction (see also chapter 4). So the Rights of the Citizen were not as valuable as they might have first appeared. The juxtaposed Rights of Man had severely reduced their significance.

This separation of state and civil society had had a disastrous effect, Marx believed, on human behaviour, attitudes and relations. The ethos of the market-place had turned people into ruthlessly self-seeking individuals, for whom others were to be regarded either as rivals or as resources to be used. It had produced a fragmented, atomised society and the Rights of Man seemed only to reflect and reinforce this egoistic mentality, expressing a conception of society as made up of naturally self-serving beings. This was even evident in the language which advocates of these rights used to describe them, referring to them as 'bastions' or 'bulwarks' as if other people were naturally to be thought of potential assailants or trespassers who had to be kept at bay.

In addition, the market had turned people's talents and creative capacities, the means by which they expressed their own identities, into commodities that could be bought and sold. The value of people was now measured in terms of their marketable assets, their selling or purchasing power. More and more aspects of life had become commercialised. Everything, and everybody, had come to have its price. The market had 'left remaining no other nexus between man and man than naked self-interest, than callous "cash payment"' (Marx, in McLellan, 1977, p. 223).

The German philosopher Hegel who, like Marx, took self-interest to be an inadequate basis for a healthy society, believed that the state, properly constituted, would rise above the egoism of the market and assert the good of society as a whole. A professional bureaucracy could, he thought, act in the role of a 'universal class'. In Marx's opinion this is a forlorn hope. If everyday life is permeated by selfish concerns, they will come to permeate the political realm as well. 'As far as the individual bureaucrat is concerned, the aim of the state becomes his private aim, in the form of a race for higher posts, of careerism' (Marx, in McLellan, 1977, p. 31). Nor can ordinary members of society be expected to lead a double life, first pursuing their own interests as agents in a market economy and then preoccupying themselves with the general good in their role as citizens. It is not surprising if they escape from this psychological bind by allowing the real empirical self to triumph and using their political rights for what they are worth as further means for pursuing their own interests. Indeed, this instrumentalist approach to citizenship is precisely what one finds in many liberal theorists (see, for example, James Mill in chapter 8).

But why is a society which recognises the Rights of Man and the Rights of the Citizen, that is to say, a liberal democratic society, incapable of producing human *emancipation*? To understand Marx's answer we need to grasp his conception of freedom. For Marx freedom is not the negative liberal notion of being left alone, free from the interference of others (see chapter 11). It is the more positive notion of having control over those conditions which determine the quality of one's life. It is freedom understood as self-determination. Marx's claim, then, is that societies governed by liberal democratic principles deny their members this power of self-determination. They do so, he believes, in two significant ways.

Firstly, they do so by upholding the right of individuals to accumulate means of production and to buy and sell labour-power, so creating two classes of people one of which can exercise systematic domination over the other – a class of capitalists who own sufficient means of production to enable them to live off the proceeds of hiring labour to work for them, and a class of wage labourers who, lacking sufficient means of production of their own, must sell their labour-power in order to live. It is true that the latter are formally free in a way that the direct producers of earlier societies, slaves and serfs, were not. The wage labourer enters into a voluntary contract with the capitalist. Nevertheless, propertyless workers have no realistic alternative but to accept capitalists' terms of employment. This means not only that they surrender a share of what they produce to the unproductive owners – Marx calls this 'exploitation' – but also that they surrender control over their working lives. Since Marx believed that it was through free, creative labour, self-regulated work, that we express both our generic identity as a species and our own personal individuality, capitalism is seen as denying working people their essential means of self-fulfilment, thus 'alienating' them from themselves. By upholding the capitalist economy, liberal democracy leaves workers without control over their working lives and in that respect fails to deliver on its promise of emancipation.

But secondly, by endorsing the 'free' market economy, liberal democracy makes all members of society, both capitalists and workers, 'the playthings of alien forces' (below, p. 246). For in a market economy, people's life chances depend on the unpredictable play of market forces. Workers will lose their jobs and owners their businesses if the work done becomes unprofitable, and this can depend on such contingencies as a change in consumer tastes or the invention of a new technology. Capitalism is prone to crises of recession and mass unemployment, crises that can ruin the lives of capitalists and wage labourers alike. Paradoxically, while it had brought so much of the natural world within human control, capitalism had left society itself at the mercy of impersonal, quasi-natural forces. The market economy is but one example of an institution which human beings have created but which has then come to take over and tyrannise them, (money would be another example).

So, Marx concludes, the principles of liberal democracy turn out to constitute a set of flawed, indeed incompatible, ideals. The freedom liberalism offers is compromised because it permits the subordination of one economic grouping to the power of another and then leaves all parties exposed to the anarchy of the market. And the democracy it offers is a sham because, when combined with economic liberalism, it removes the most important aspects of life, the most important decisions a society can make, from the scope of democratic control. The rights of the citizen are marginalised.

In the end it turns out that the political ideals which Bauer applauds have much the same value and purpose as the religious faith he decries. Both offer illusory compensations for the deficiencies of real, down-to-earth existence. The liberal democratic state provides the illusion of an ethereal political community while leaving people engaged in ruthless competition with one another in their daily lives. It promises a legal and political equality while supporting gross inequalities of wealth and social status. It offers power to the people while restricting it to a narrowly circumscribed political realm. And just as the imaginary joys of heaven that religion promises reduce people's resolve to improve their earthly lot, so do the shadowy forms of liberty, equality and fraternity that the modern state provides.

What then is the alternative? How is human emancipation to be achieved? It can be achieved, Marx thinks, only through a radical social transformation, a revolutionary change in the way societies produce their wealth. Nothing less is needed than the institution of a communist society in which productive resources, instead of being privately owned, become common property, subject to collective control, and in which the anarchy of the market is replaced by rational economic planning, and economic competition replaced by co-operative production.

But how convincing is Marx's attack on liberal democracy and the conception of the Rights of Man? A defender might reply that there is no essential connection between the basic idea of individual rights and human selfishness or between it and the capitalist market economy. The point behind these rights, whatever their implications with regard to property, is to allow individuals scope to decide important matters for themselves free from political and societal interference. What underlies liberal thinking is a belief that individual autonomy is valuable and should be protected irrespective of the nature of a person's own interests and goals and whether they are self-centred or not. To extend the principle of democratic decision-making to all areas of life would be to threaten that value and, in J. S. Mill's phrase, to expose individuals and minorities to 'the tyranny of the majority' (see chapter 11). A government that takes upon itself the direction of the whole of society is a totalitarian one, however democratically constituted it may be.

Now it is not Marx's intention to reject the ideal of individual self-determination. He envisages communism, not as a society in which differences in interests and personality are suppressed and people dedicate themselves wholly to some common cause, but as one in which individual diversity flourishes. His point appears to be that individual empowerment and self-development are achievable only in the context of a socialised, co-operative economy. But this leaves us with a puzzle.

'Human emancipation' involves, it seems, three objectives which do not obviously harmonise: (1) rational economic planning, to reduce the elements of chance and contingency which disrupt people's lives; (2) comprehensive democratisation; (3) local and individual autonomy, allowing factories and individual workers a large say in what they produce and how they produce it. But can grass-roots democratic decision-making result in a coherent overall policy? And what room would a plan for the economy as a whole leave for the work-force in a particular factory to make key decisions about what they do? It should be noted that the term 'economic democracy' is itself ambiguous between two very different ideas: popular macro-economic control, whereby the whole electorate decides on targets for the economy at large, and popular micro-economic control, where workers are left free to manage their own factories. What is clear is that if these three objectives are to be reconciled, boundary markers will be needed, defining which parties are responsible for which decisions. Rights will have a place after all.

These problems aside, Marx does not tell us what political institutions and machinery will be required to put into practice this goal of human emancipation, to enable people to 'absorb the abstract citizen of the state' into their real lives and to organize their 'own forces as social forces'. For a possible answer, we turn to Lenin's *The State and Revolution*.

### Vladimir Ilich Lenin (1870–1923)

Lenin, whose real name was Vladimir Ilich Ulyanov, was born in Simbirsk, Russia. Brought up, like Marx, in a bookish, liberal-minded, middle-class family, he was first schooled in revolutionary ways by his elder brother, Alexander, who was executed for his part in a plot to assassinate the tsar. Himself exiled to Siberia for subversion, Lenin was obliged, on release in 1900, to conduct his political activities from abroad, spending fifteen of the next seventeen years as an *émigré* in Switzerland. During that time he established a reputation as a leading Marxist authority, edited an underground newspaper *Iskra* ('The Spark') and, most significantly, formed the Bolshevik faction of the Russian Social Democratic Party, turning it into a centralised, disciplined 'vanguard' movement composed of professional activists. After the overthrow of the tsar in February 1917, Lenin, who had been opposed to Russian involvement in the war, was able to persuade the German government to secure his return to Russia inside a sealed train. Accused on his return of being a German agent, he retreated to Finland, but in October of the same year, with the provisional Russian government in crisis, Lenin's well-organised Bolshevik party was able to exploit the general chaos and, supported by the soviets (the workers' and soldiers' councils), he seized power in a bloodless coup. So Lenin became leader of the world's first socialist government. However, the opposition both internal and external that the new soviet state had to

235

face, and the urgent tasks of modernisation that it had to undertake, meant that by the time of Lenin's death it had assumed a highly authoritarian and repressive character. Consequently, both Leninist ideas and practice are seen by many to mark a significant departure from the humanist and libertarian themes of Marx's own thinking. But there is no doubt that it was Lenin who turned Marxism into a world movement, both through the success of the Bolshevik revolution he had led and through the subsequent influence that his Soviet Communist Party was able to exert over communist parties elsewhere.

*The State and Revolution* was written in the summer of 1917 while Lenin was in hiding in Finland, only a few months before he was to lead the successful Bolshevik revolution in Russia. The main concern of the book is with the question of whether the democratic institutions that exist in modern Western societies can be used to bring about socialism. Could not universal franchise result in a socialist majority in parliament, and would not that majority then be in a position to engineer a radical transformation of the social and economic system?

To this question Lenin gives a firmly negative answer. He begins by setting out a conception of the state that is familiar from the writings of Marx and Engels, the conception of the state as an instrument of class domination, an 'organ of class rule'. The state comes into being as a result of the irreconcilable class antagonisms that exist in society. Its defining characteristic is the possession of organised coercive power and its historical function is to use that power to suppress class struggle, thereby securing the position of the economically dominant class. But can that really be said of parliamentary democracy? Is it not an intrinsically neutral apparatus which can be captured by a majority working class and used for socialist ends? Marx himself in his later years suggested that in countries with institutions like those in Britain and America workers might 'achieve their aims by peaceful means' (Marx, in McLellan, 1977, p. 594).

Lenin, however, thought otherwise. Universal franchise may, in theory, have potentially revolutionary implications, but there are numerous ways in which this revolutionary potential can be frustrated in practice. Firstly, the economic power of the bourgeoisie, ranging from its control of newspapers to its ownership of meeting places, enables it to make much more effective use of its democratic political rights. Secondly, the representative nature of parliamentary democracy means that members of parliament are not bound in their actions by any popular mandate and can go their own way without fear of immediate recall. But what above all, in Lenin's judgement, makes parliamentary democracy a conservative force is the fact that real power lies not with the legislature, with parliament, but with the executive from which it is separated. Parliament is a 'hollow talking-shop'. The 'real business of state' is conducted 'behind the scenes', in 'the departments, chancelleries and general staffs'. The bureaucracy, the government machine consisting of officials who are unelected and not accountable to the people, can frustrate and subvert the will of parliament, thus ensuring that the interests of the bourgeoisie from whose ranks these officials are likely to be drawn will remain protected. Parliamentary democracy, then, with its gestures towards majority rule and popular power, acts as 'the best possible political shell for capitalism'.

Lenin, it should be noted, wrote *The State and Revolution* at the same time as Weber was writing his *Parliament and Government in a Reconstructed Germany* (see chapter 12). He differs from Weber in seeing a professional bureaucracy, not as a technical necessity arising out of the scale and complexity of modern society but as a political device aimed to secure the position of the bourgeoisie against the threat posed to it by the extension of the franchise. Marx, both in his earlier and in his later writings, had been readier than Lenin to allow that the executive power of the state could act as an agent in its own right, pursuing its own interests rather than those of the dominant economic class, apparently rising above the economic struggle and playing one class off against another (see especially his account of the 'Bonapartist' state of Napoleon III in *The Eighteenth Brumaire of Louis Bonaparte*). But, like Lenin, he saw a professional bureaucracy as technically dispensable, as an 'appalling parasitic body which enmeshes the body of ... society like a net and chokes all its pores' (Marx, in McLellan, 1977, p. 316), and again, like Lenin, he saw its continuing existence as an obstacle to the development of a socialist society.

So whether or not the workers were able to capture the bourgeois state by peaceful means, both men were agreed that the bourgeois state would have to be 'smashed' before socialism could be built. 'The working class cannot simply lay hold of the ready-made state machinery and wield it for its own purposes', Marx wrote and Lenin repeated. Having destroyed these bourgeois political institutions, the working class would, then, have to replace them with its own workers' state. It was not, as anarchists believed (see chapter 10), the state itself that was the source of social oppression but economic class division. A 'dictatorship of the proletariat', i.e. a state exercising its coercive power on behalf of the working class, would first be needed to eliminate the basis of class division, expropriating the capitalist class and ensuring that it did not mount a successful counter-revolution. Only when a classless socialist economy had been constructed could the state as a coercive instrument of class domination be expected to disappear.

But how was this new workers' state to be constituted? Lenin takes up a suggestion Marx had made. It should be modelled on the Paris Commune of 1871 to which Marx had paid tribute in his essay *The Civil War in France*, describing it as 'the political form at last discovered under which to work out the economic emancipation of labour' (Marx, in McLellan, 1977, p. 544). The Paris Commune had been a form of government and administration set up by the people of Paris after they had been armed to defend the city against the encircling Prussian army. It was ruthlessly suppressed within a few months by the national government which had earlier retreated to Versailles.

The Paris Commune had three features of note. Firstly, it did away with the apparatus of unelected full-time bureaucrats, replacing them with elected short-term officials who were paid average wages. It ensured that there was no separate body of state functionaries to form an interest group of their own. The communards, Marx said, had exposed the mystique of power, 'the whole sham of state mysteries and state pretensions' which made out the business of government to be above the heads of ordinary people. No Greek or Roman statesman, Marx earlier observed, had been required to take examinations. Secondly, it established a pyramid-shaped structure of decision-making with power flowing from the base up. Applied on a national scale, it would have meant that local communes and work-places, while retaining responsibility for their own affairs, elected delegates to serve on regional councils which in turn elected delegates to serve on a national committee. Delegates were to be bound by the instructions, the mandate, of those who elected them. Lenin drew a comparison here with the Russian soviets, the councils of workers, soldiers and peasants which had formed spontaneously in the uprising of 1905. Finally, the commune state was to concern itself with all aspects of social life, including, most importantly, economic affairs.

In these three ways the commune state achieved a more radical form of popular government than was possible under liberal parliamentary democracy. It involved the people in all areas of government, including administration; it gave the people a more direct role in decision-making and it extended the principle of democratic decision-making to all spheres of social activity. It seemed to fulfil what Marx had envisaged in *On the Jewish Question* when he contrasted 'human emancipation' with merely political emancipation.

True to his word, Lenin instituted a quite new kind of political order after the Bolshevik revolution, but the state that emerged in the following years was far removed from the radically democratic ideal of the Paris Commune. It was an autocratic one-party state with supreme power resting in the hands of a self-selected elite, a state that assumed total authority over its subjects, that suppressed political dissent and criticism both inside and outside the party and that carried out ruthless social experiments in the cause of modernisation. The workers' councils, supposedly the main organs of popular power, were taken over and turned into docile instruments of central government. Bakunin's prophecy that the workers' state would lead to a new 'red' bourgeoisie had come all too true (see chapter 10).

Why was the reality so different from the ideal that Lenin had advocated, with apparent sincerity, only months before? Some will point to the unfavourable circumstances in which the Russian revolution took place. The conditions of economic and political backwardness in Russia were far from those Marx had envisaged for a majority proletarian revolution and the subsequent building of socialism. Others will say that the means employed to bring about the revolution were bound to have an effect on the nature of the outcome that followed. The kind of party organisation that Lenin thought necessary for spearheading the revolution – a closed, centralised, disciplined, hierarchical party – was bound to be reflected in the character of the post-revolutionary state. The very same factors that made that type of structure seem appropriate before the revolution – the need for decisive action, for quick responses to the changing course of events – would also make it seem appropriate afterwards. The vanguard party would become a power elite. There is even a hint of this in the pages of *The State and Revolution*, where Lenin describes the workers' party as 'the vanguard of the proletariat, capable of assuming power and of *leading the whole people* to socialism, of directing and organizing the new order, of being the teacher, guide and leader' (below, p. 252).

But another explanation is that these historical developments resulted from problems inherent in the theory of the commune state itself, defects in the model which meant that any attempt to implement it would have disastrous consequences and produce a travesty of what was originally intended. For how can decisions made in hundreds of local communities and work-places be expected to add up to a coherent national policy? How can grass-roots democracy of itself generate a rational plan for the economy as a whole? This is even harder to understand if elected members of regional and national committees have no independent power to negotiate or reach a compromise, no authority to depart from what was decided by those who elected them. Problems then arise about how to co-ordinate this multitude of local decisions, leaving those at the apex of the pyramid with a more or less free hand to solve them. Decisions made by the rank and file could serve as no more than inputs into the process, supplying information about local preferences that might or might not be taken into account in the shaping of overall policy. But since justice could not be done to them all, there was no guarantee that heed would be taken of any of them. Certainly no principled way of taking diverse preferences into account was built into the model, and no constraints were placed on how the resulting co-ordination problem might be solved. Of course, different policy options might be presented to the rank and file for them to vote on, but these presumably would be drawn up by those at the top who would thus have the power to set the agenda. There is no space in the model for any competitive party system that might be expected to generate alternative programmes of action for the electorate to choose between.

Not surprisingly, then, the pyramid structure gets easily transformed from one in which decision-making power travels from the bottom upwards into one in which it travels from the top downwards – the commune state degenerates into a system in which fundamental decisions are made by a central committee and all lower bodies are turned into 'transmission belts' for converting policy made at the top into action on the ground. The pyramid structure remains in place, but its function now is to involve all and sundry in the execution of policy and not in its creation.

239

It is interesting that Lenin at the end of his life, aware that things had gone wrong, should have expressed such disappointment at the failure to involve ordinary people in the tasks of administration. Administration could not, after all, be reduced to the simple functions of accounting and control as he had supposed in *The State and Revolution* (below, p. 259), and the regime continued to rely heavily on the expertise of professional officials. But it did not occur to him to express the same disappointment at the failure to involve ordinary people in the making of policy, as if participatory democracy meant getting the people to participate in the implementation of decisions rather than in the making of them. There is evidence in *The State and Revolution* that Lenin took democracy proper to mean government for the people rather than government by the people – his question 'democracy for whom?' (below, p. 260) is ominous – and one should bear in mind that he sought to justify his centralised vanguard party by claiming that party intellectuals, equipped with a 'correct' theoretical consciousness, i.e. a 'correct' (= Marxist) understanding of society and social change, were in a better position to know where the true interests of the working class lay than were the workers themselves. This seems a long way from Marx's belief in the 'self-emancipation' of the proletariat, with its implication that the workers could educate, organise, liberate and then govern themselves. But whatever contribution Lenin's own ideas had made to its perversion, it does seem that the radically democratic ideal of the commune state was not a realisable one.

## Concluding remarks

Communism seems not, after all, to have history on its side. According to the classical Marxist theory there are two conditions for a successful communist revolution, an objective one – a high level of industrialisation – and a subjective one – revolutionary enthusiasm among the masses. Countries that have satisfied one of the conditions have invariably not satisfied the other, and Lenin's Russia was no exception.

So communism has to argue its case like any other political theory, presenting us with a blueprint of the alternative society it envisages. If it disdains, in Marx's phrase, 'writing recipes for the cookshops of the future', it must at least provide us with the map of a workable kitchen, and that, we have argued here, it fails to do.

Still, whatever the defects of communism as a constructive theory, the critique of liberal democracy and the attack on the complacent apologists of capitalism that we find in Marx's early writings, like *On the Jewish Question*, are as fresh, relevant and potent today as on the day they were written.

## Reference

McLellan, David (ed.), *Karl Marx: Selected Writings*, Oxford: Oxford University Press, 1977.

Most of Marx's major writings are published in the Pelican Marx Library, edited by Quentin Hoare. A good single volume selection is that of McLellan referred to above. D. McLellan's *The Thought of Karl Marx* (2nd ed, London: Macmillan, 1980) is a useful study guide, with relevant passages from Marx's writings collected under topic headings. There are many introductory text books on Marx. The shortest and liveliest is P. Singer's *Marx* (Oxford: Oxford University Press, 1980). More probing is Jon Elster's *An Introduction to Karl Marx* (Cambridge: Cambridge University Press, 1986). Michael Evans's *Karl Marx* (London: Allen and Unwin, 1975) has copious references to the Marxian corpus. Two important books on Marx's political theory are Schlomo Avineri's *The Social and Political Thought of Karl Marx* (Cambridge: Cambridge University Press, 1968) and Richard N. Hunt's two-part *The Political Ideas of Marx and Engels* (London: Macmillan, 1974 and 1984). Michael Levin's *Marx, Engels and Liberal Democracy* (Basingstoke: Macmillan, 1989) touches on many of the issues discussed in this chapter. Two interesting works on the relationship between Marxism and issues in ethics and political philosophy are Allen E. Buchanan's *Marx and Justice* (Totowa, NJ, Rowman and Littlefield, 1982) and Steven Lukes' *Marxism and Morality* (Oxford: Clarendon, 1985).

A good single volume selection of Lenin's writings is to be found in Robert C. Tucker's *The Lenin Anthology* (New York: Norton, 1975). Robert Conquest's *Lenin* in the Fontana modern masters series (London: Fontana, 1972) provides a useful introduction to Lenin's life and works. *Lenin's Political Thought* is comprehensively covered by Neil Harding in a two-volume work of that name ((London: Macmillan, 1977 and 1981). A. J. Polan's *Lenin and the End of Politics* (London: Methuen, 1984) gives a more hostile account.

**Seminar questions**

Do you think that Marx's critique of liberal democracy is a fair one? If not, why not?

Would there be any need for individual rights in a society in which there were no conflicts of interest between its members? Could such a society ever exist? Would all conflicts of interest disappear if either (a) there were no shortage of economic resources or (b) people were not selfish? Can you think of any current conflicts that do not have their roots in either economic scarcity or human selfishness?

Some people think that the culture of rights undermines the spirit of community. They contrast societies in which people are bound by natural ties of kinship, affection and sociability with societies in which relationships are structured by a formal system of rights embedded in a legal code. The German sociologist Ferdinand Tönnies called the first kind of society a Gemeinschaft, the second kind a Gesellschaft. Do you think the two kinds of relationship are necessarily opposed? Or do you think that rights and community can coexist?

If there were no framework of law, the distinction between crime (violation of the law) and other forms of deviant behaviour, e.g. eccentricity and non-conformity, would disappear. Do you think that would be a good thing? If not, why not?

'In a people's court unpopular defendants would not get a fair trial.'
Is this a good argument, do you think, in favour of retaining an
independent professional judiciary?

Adjudicate between Lenin and Weber on the need for a professional
bureaucracy in modern societies.

## KARL MARX
### From *On the Jewish Question*

The German Jews desire emancipation. Which emancipation do they
want? *Civic*, that is, *political* emancipation.

Bruno Bauer replies to them: nobody in Germany is politically emancipated. We ourselves are not free. How are we supposed to liberate
you? You Jews are *egoists* if you demand a special emancipation for
youselves as Jews. You have to participate as Germans in the political emancipation of Germany, as human beings in the emancipation
of humanity, and not perceive the special form of your oppression
and your humiliation as an exception to the rule, but rather as confirmation of the rule.

Or do the Jews demand equality with the *Christian subjects*? In that case
they recognise the *Christian state* to be justified, they acknowledge the
regime of general subjugation. Why should your special yoke
displease you when you are satisfied with the general yoke? Why
should the Germans take an interest in the liberation of the Jews
when the Jews take no interest in the liberation of the Germans?

The *Christian* state knows only *privileges*. In this state the Jews have the
privilege of being Jews. As Jews they have rights which the
Christians do not have. Why do they desire rights which they do not
have and which the Christians enjoy?

If the Jew wishes to be emancipated from the Christian state, he
demands that the Christian state renounce its *religious* prejudice.
Does the Jew renounce his religious prejudice? Does he, then, have
the right to demand of another that he abjure religion in this way?
[...] Bauer demands on the one hand that Jews give up Judaism – in
fact, that man give up religion in general – in order to be emancipated
as *citizens of the state*. On the other hand he takes the *political* abolition of religion to be logically equivalent to the abolition of religion
*in toto*. The state which presupposes religion is not yet a true, an
actual state.

It is on this point that the *one-sided* formulation of the Jewish question
stands out.

It is by no means sufficient to ask: who should do the emancipating?
who should be emancipated? There is a third thing that criticism has
to do. It has to ask: what *sort of emancipation* is at issue? What conditions flow from the nature of the desired emancipation? Only the

critique of *political emancipation* itself was the definitive critique of the Jewish question and its true dissolution into the *'general question of the times'*.

Because Bauer does not raise the question to this level, he falls into contradictions. He poses conditions that are not founded in the nature of *political* emancipation itself. He raises questions that are not part of his task, and he resolves issues that leave his question unanswered. When Bauer says of the opponents of Jewish emancipation, 'their only error was that they presupposed the Christian state as the only true one and did not subject it to the same criticism with which they treated Judaism', then we find Bauer's error in the fact that he subjects to criticism only the 'Christian state' and not the 'state simply', that he does not examine the *relationship of political emancipation to human emancipation,* and therefore poses conditions whose sole explanation lies in an uncritical confusion of political emancipation with general human emancipation. If Bauer asks the Jews: from your standpoint do you have the right to desire *political emancipation?* then we ask in return: does the standpoint of *political* emancipation have the right to demand of the Jews the abolition of Judaism, and of mankind in general the abolition of religion?

The Jewish question has a different formulation according to which state the Jews happen to be in. In Germany, where no political state, no state as state, exists, the Jewish question is a purely *theological* question. The Jew finds himself in *religious* opposition to a state which recognises Christianity as its basis. This state is a theologian *ex professo.* The critique here is a critique of theology, a two-edged critique, a critique of the Christian and of the Jewish theology. But in this fashion we are still involved in theology, however *critically* we may be involved in it.

In France, in a *constitutional* state, the Jewish question is a question of constitutionalism, a question of the *half-heartedness of the political emancipation.* Because the *semblance* of a state religion, even if in a mute and self-contradictory formulation, is maintained here in the shape of a *religion of the majority,* the relationship of the Jews to the state maintains the *semblance* of a religious, theological opposition.

Only in the North American free states – at least in a part of them – does the Jewish question lose its *theological* significance and become a truly *secular* question. Only where the political state exists in its complete development can the relationship of the Jews, and in general of religious persons, to the political state – that is, the relationship of religion to the state – step forth in its proper characteristics and its pure form.

The critique of this relationship ceases to be a theological critique as soon as the state ceases to relate to religion in a *theological* manner, as soon as it relates as a state, i.e. relates *politically* to religion. The critique then becomes a *critique of the political state.* At this point, where the question ceases to be *theological,* Bauer's critique ceases to be critical. 'There exists in the United States neither a state religion nor a religion declared to be that of the majority, nor is there preeminence of one cult over another. The state stands apart from all cults.' (*Marie ou l'esclavage aux Etats-unis etc.*, par G. de Beaumont, Paris, 1835, p. 214) Indeed, there are several North American states in which 'the constitution does not impose any religious belief or any religious practice as a condition of political privilege' (*ibid.* p. 224). Nevertheless, 'in the United States people do not believe that a man without religion can be an honest man' (*ibid.*, p. 224). Nevertheless, North America is the preeminent land of religiosity, as Beaumont, Tocqueville, and the Englishman, Hamilton, tell us with one voice. However the North American states only serve as an example. The question is: how does *accomplished* political emancipation relate to religion? If we find not only the existence, but the *vigorous* and *flourishing* existence, of religion in the very land of accomplished political emancipation, then we have proof that the existence of religion does not contradict the accomplishment of the state. But since the existence of religion is the existence of a defect, the source of this defect can only be sought in the *nature* of the state itself. We then no longer regard religion as the *basis*, but rather only as the *phenomenon* of a secular limitedness. We therefore explain the religious bias of free citizens of a state as resulting from their secular bias. We do not insist that they must abolish their religious limitation in order to abolish their secular limitations. We contend that they will abolish their religious limitation as soon as they abolish their secular limitations. We do not turn secular questions into theological ones; we turn theological questions into secular ones. After history has long enough been reduced to superstition, we are going to reduce superstition to history. The question of *the relationship of political emancipation to religion* becomes for us the question of the *relationship of political emacipation to human emancipation*. We criticise the religious weakness of the political state by criticising the political state in its *secular* construction, *apart* from its religious weaknesses. We humanise this issue by making the contradicition of the state with *a specific religion*, say, *Judaism*, into a contradiction of the state with *specific secular* elements, and the contradiction of the state with *religion in general* into a contradiction of the state with its *presuppositions* in general.

The *political* emancipation of the Jews, of the Christians, of *religious* persons in general, is the *emancipation of the state* from Judaism, from Christianity, from *religion* in general. In its form, in a fashion proper to its nature, the state as *state* emancipates itself from religion in that it emancipates itself from *state religion*, i.e. in that the state as state acknowldeges no religion, in that the state rather acknowledges itself as state. *Political* emancipation from religion is not the completed, contradiction-free emancipation from religion, because political emancipation is not the completed, contradiction-free form of *human* emancipation.

The restricted character of political emancipation immediately appears in the fact that the *state* can free itself of a limitation without the human being *truly* being free of it, in the fact that the state can be a Communism *free state* without the man being a *free man*.

The *state*, therefore, can have emancipated itself from religion even if the *vast majority* is still religious. And the *vast majority* does not cease being religious by being *privately* religious.

But the attitude of the state, namely the *free state* towards religion is, still, only the attitude towards religion of the *people* who form the state. It follows from this that man frees himself from a barrier *politically*, via the *medium of the state*, in that, in contradiction with himself, he raises himself above it partially, in an *abstract* and *limited* fashion. Further, it follows that in freeing himself *politically* he frees himself in a round-about way, through a *medium*, even if a *necessary medium*. Finally, it follows that even if the person proclaims himself an atheist through the mediation of the state, i.e. if he proclaims the state to be atheistic, he still remains locked in a religious frame of reference, precisely because he recognises himself only in this round-about way, through a medium. Religion is precisely the recognition of the human being in a round-about fashion, through a *mediator.* The state is the mediator between man and human freedom. Just as Christ is the mediator whom the human being burdens with all of his divinity, all of his *religious constraint*, so too is the state the mediator into which he places all of his non-divinity, all of his *human spontaneity.*

The *political* elevation of the person over religion shares all the advantages and disadvantages of political elevation in general. The state *qua* state annuls, for example, *private property*; in a *political* fashion the person declares private property to be *superseded* as soon as he supersedes the *census* in favour of active and passive eligibility for elections, as this has been done in many North American states. From a political standpoint, *Hamilton* interprets this quite correctly thus: *'The masses have been victorious over the property owners and the moneyed classes.'* Is not private property ideally superseded when individuals without property become the legislators of those with property? The census is the final *political* form of recognition of private property.

Nevertheless, the political annulment of private property does not supersede private property, but on the contrary presupposes it. The state dissolves distinctions of *birth*, of *social rank*, of *education*, and of *occupation* if it declares birth, social rank, education, and occupation to be *non-political* distinctions; if without consideration of these distinctions it calls on every member of the nation to be an *equal* participant in the national sovereignty; if it treats all elements of the actual life of the nation from the point of view of the state. Nevertheless the state allows private property, education, occupation to *function* and affirm their *particular* nature in *their own* way, i.e. as private property, education, and occupation. Far from superseding these factual distinctions, the state's existence presupposes them: it feels itself to be *political state* and can affirm its *universality* only in opposition to these factors.

The perfected political state is essentially the *species life* of man in opposition to his material life. All presuppositions of this *egoistic* life are retained *outside* the sphere of the state in *civil society*, but as attributes of civil society. Where the political state has attained its true development, man leads – and not only in thought, in consciousness, but also in *reality*, in *life* – a double life, a heavenly one and an earthly one, a life in the *political community*, in which he counts as a *communal being*, and a life in *civil society* in which he acts as a *private individual*, views other people as means, debases himself to the status of a means, and becomes the plaything of alien forces. The political state relates just as spiritually to civil society as heaven does to earth. It stands in the same opposition, and overcomes it in the same way as religion overcomes the limitedness of the secular world, i.e. by recognising, restoring, and allowing itself to be governed by civil society. Man is his *immediate* reality, in civil society, is a secular being. Here, where he counts for himself and others as a real individual, he is a *false* semblance. In the state, on the other hand, where man counts as a species-being, he is an imaginary member of an illusory sovereignty, is robbed of his actual individual life, and is filled with an unreal universality.

*Political* emancipation is to be sure a great advance, but it is certainly not the final form of human emancipation in general. Rather it is the final form of human emancipation *within* the previous order of things: Obviously we are speaking here of actual, practical emancipation.

Man emancipates himself *politically* from religion in that he banishes it from public right to the realm of private right. Religion is no longer the spirit of the *state*, in which man functions as a species-being – even if in a limited fashion, in a particular form and in a particular sphere – in society with other men; it becomes the spirit of *civil society*, of the sphere of egoism, of the *bellum omnium contra omnes*. It is no longer the essence of the *community*, but rather the essence of the *separation*. It has become the expression of the *diremption* of man from his *communal being*, from himself and other men – as it *originally* was. It is but the abstract acknowledgement of a particular folly, of a *private whim*, of caprice. The infinite splintering of religion in North America, for example, has already given it the *external* form of a purely individual matter. It has been relegated to the numerous private interests and, as the communal essence, exiled from the community. But let no one delude himself about the boundaries of political emancipation. The diremption of man into a *public* and a *private* man, the *dislocation* of religion out of the state into civil society, is not just a state, but rather the *completion* of political emancipation, which neither does nor tries to supersede the *actual* religiosity of man.

Indeed, is it not the so-called *Christian* state, which recognises Christianity as its basis, its state religion, and which therefore has an exlusive relationship to other religions, that is the perfected Christian state, but rather the *atheistic* state, the *democratic* state, the state that relegates religion to the ranks of the other elements of civil society. The state which is still theological and which testifies officially to its adherence to Christianity, which does not yet dare to proclaim itself a *state*, does not succeed in expressing in its *reality* as a state, in *secular, human* form, the *human* basis whose rapturous expression is Christianity. The so-called Christian state is simply the *non-state*, because it is not Christianity as religion, but only the *human background* of the Christian religion that can fulfill itself in real human creations.

But the religious spirit also cannot be *actually* secularised, for what is it but the *unsecular* form of a state of development of the human spirit? The religious spirit can only be secularised insofar as the stage of development of the human spirit whose religious expression it is steps forth and constitutes itself in its *secular* form. This occurs in the *democratic* state. Not Christianity, but rather the *human ground* of Christianity is the basis of this state. Religion remains the ideal, unworldly consciousness of its members because it is the ideal form of the *human stage of development* which is achieved in it [i.e. in the democratic state].

The members of the political state are religious through the dualism between individual life and species-life, between the life of civil society and political life; religious in that man relates to the life of the state, which is foreign to his actual individuality, as though it were his true life; religious in so far as religion here is the spirit of civil society, the expression of the separation and the distancing of man from man. Political democracy is Christian in that in it man – not only one man, but every man – has value as a *sovereign* being, the highest being, but this is man in his uncultivated, unsocial aspect, man in his accidental existence, man just as he is, corrupted by the entire organisation of our society, lost to himself, alienated, under the domination of inhuman relationships and elements – in a word, man who is not yet an actual species-being. The fantasy, the dream, the postulate of Christianity, namely the sovereignty of man – but man as an alien being, different from actual man – is in democracy a sensuous reality, presence, secular maxim.

We have therefore shown that the political emancipation from religion allows the continued existence of religion, even if not a privileged religion. The contradiction in which the adherent of a particular religion finds himself with his state citizenship is only a *part* of the universal *secular contradiction between the political state and civil society*. The completion of the Christian state is the state which acknowledges itself to be a state and abstracts from the religion of its members. The emancipation of the state from religion is not the emancipation of actual man from religion.

Therefore we do not, with Bauer, say to the Jews: you cannot be politically emancipated without radically emancipating yourselves from Judaism. Rather we tell them: because you can be politically emancipated without fully and definitively withdrawing from Judaism, *political emancipation* itself is not *human* emancipation. If you Jews want to be politically emancipated without emancipating yourselves

247

humanly, the imperfection and contradiction lies not only in you, it lies in the *essence* and the *category* of political emancipation.

[...]

Let us look for a moment at the so-called human rights, and indeed human rights in their authentic form, the form in which they are found among their *discoverers*, the North Americans and the French! In part these human rights are *political* rights, rights which are exercised only in community with others. *Participation* in the *community* and specifically in the *political* community, in the state, constitutes their content. They fall under the category of *political freedom*, under the category of the *rights of citizenship*, which, as we have seen, in no way presupposes an unconditional and positive supersession of religion, nor therefore of Judaism. The other part of the rights of man remain to be considered, the *rights of man* in so far as they differ from the rights of citizen.

Among these rights we find the freedom of conscience, the right to exercise the cult of one's choice. The *privilege of belief* is expressly recognised, either as a *human right* or as the consequence of a human right, of freedom.

The incompatibility of religion with human rights is so little grounded in the concept of human rights that the right to be *religious*, and to be religious in the way one chooses, to practice one's particular religion, is in fact to be numbered expressly among human rights. The *privilege of belief* is a *universal human right*.

The *droits de l'homme*, the rights of man, human rights, as *such* are different from the *droits du citoyen*, from the rights of the citizen. Who is the *homme* who differs from the *citizen?* None other than the *member of civil society*. Why is the member of civil society called 'man', man pure and simple, and why are his rights called *human rights?* How are we to explain this fact? From the relationship of the political state to civil society, from the nature of political emancipation.

Above all we confirm the fact that the so-called *human rights*, the *droits de l'homme* in contrast to the *droits du citoyen*, are nothing but the rights of the *member of civil society*, i.e. of egoistic man, of the man who is separated from other men and from the community. Let the most radical constitution, that of 1793 speak:

**Declaration of the Rights of Man and of the Citizen**

Art. 2 These rights etc. (the natural and imprescriptable rights) are: *equality, liberty, security, property*.

In what does *liberty* consist?

Art 6. 'Liberty is the power belonging to man to do everything that does not harm the rights of another', or according to the Declaration of Human Rights of 1791: 'Liberty consists in being able to do everything that does not harm another'.

Freedom, then, is the right to do and to pursue what does not harm another. The limit within which everyone can operate in a way not harmful to others is determined by law, like the boundary between

two fields is determined by the fencepost. This is the freedom of man
as a monad isolated and withdrawn into himself.

[...]

But the human right of freedom is not based on the connection of man
with man, but much more on the separation of man from man. It is
the *right* of this separation, the right of the individual who is *limited*,
enclosed within himself.

The practical application of the human right of freedom is the right of
*private property*.

In what consists the right of private property?

Art. 16 (Constitution of 1793). 'The right of *property* is that which
belongs to each citizen to enjoy and to dispose *as he pleases* of his
goods, of his revenues, of the fruit of his labour and of his industry'.

The human right of private property is thus the right to enjoy and
dispose of one's wealth arbitrarily (as one pleases), without relation
to other men, independently of society, the right of personal use. That
individual freedom together with this application of it constitutes the
basis of civil society. It allows each man to find in the others not the
*actualisation*, but much more the *limit* of his freedom. But above all it
proclaims the human right to 'enjoy and to dispose *as he pleases* of his
goods, of his revenues, of the fruit of his labour and of his industry'.

There still remain the other human rights, equality and security.

Equality here, in its non-political significance, is nothing but the parity of
the *liberté* described above, namely: that every human as such is
equally considered to be a self-based monad. The Constitution of 1795
defines the concept of this parity, in keeping with its meaning thus:

Art. 3 (Constitution of 1795). 'Equality consists in the fact that the law
is the same for all, whether it protects or punishes'.

And Security?

Art. 8 (Constitution of 1793). 'Security consists in the protection
accorded by society to each of its members for the conservation of his
person, of his rights, and of his properties'.

*Security* is the highest social concept of civil society, the concept of the
*police*, the concept that the entire society exists only to guarantee each
of its members the preservation of his person, of his rights, and of his
property. In this sense Hegel calls civil society 'the state of necessity
and of the understanding' [*Philosophy of Right* §183].

Civil society does not by the concept of security transcend its egoism.
Much more so is security the *insuring* of its egoism.

None of the so-called human rights then goes beyond the egoistic man,
beyond man as member of civil society, namely withdrawn into his
private interests and his private will, separated from the community.
Not only is man not considered in these human rights to be a species-
being, but also species-life itself, society, appears to be a context
external to the individuals, and a restriction of their original independence. The one tie that holds them together is natural necessity,
need and private interest, the conservation of their property and their
egoistic person.

It is curious that a nation that begins to liberate itself, to tear down all barriers between the various national groupings and to found a political community, that such a nation solemnly proclaims (Declaration of 1791) the privileges of egoistic man, separated from his fellow man and from the community, indeed even repeats this proclamation at a moment when only heroic sacrifice can save the nation and is therefore imperative, at an instant when relinquishing every interest of civil society has to be the order of the day and egoism must be punished as a crime. (Declaration of the Rights of Man, etc. of 1793.) This fact becomes even more curious if we consider that citizenship in the state, that the *political community*, is even reduced by the political emancipators to the status of mere *means* for the preservation of these so-called human rights, in other words that the citizen is declared to be the servant of the egoistic man and the sphere in which man functions as a communal being is degraded and subordinated to the sphere in which he functions as a partial being; finally, that it is not man as citizen but man as bourgeois who is taken to be the *real* and *true* human being.

The puzzle is easily solved.

Political emancipation is also the *dissolution* of the old society, on which rests the state which is estranged from the people – the sovereign power. Political revolution is the revolution of civil society. What was the character of the old society? One word characterises it: *feudalism*. The old civil society had *immediately a political* character, i.e. the elements of civil life, e.g. property or the family, or the form and manner of labour, were raised in the form of estate ownership, of the social orders and corporations, to elements in the life of the state. In these forms they determined the relationship of the single individual to the *whole of the state*, i.e. his *political* relationship, i.e. his relationship of division and exclusion from the other component parts of society. For that organisation of the life of the people did not elevate property or labour to the status of social elements, but rather completed their *separation* form the state as a whole and constituted them as *special* particular societies within society. Thus the functions and conditions of the life of civil society were still political, although political in the feudal sense, i.e. they separated the individual from the whole of the state, they transformed the *particular* relationship of his guild to the whole of the state into his own general relationship to the life of the people, just as his specific civil activity and situation were transformed into his general activity and situation. As a consequence of this organisation, the unity of the state, along with its consciousness, will, and activity, the universal power of the state, likewise necessarily appears to be a *particular* concern of a ruler separated from his people and surrounded by his servants.

The political revolution that toppled this sovereign power and raised state matters to the status of concerns of the people, which constituted the political state as a *universal* concern, i.e. as an actual state, necessarily destroyed all social orders, corporations, guilds and privileges,

which were just so many expressions of the separation of the people
from their community. With that the political revolution *abolished* the
*political character of civil society*. It broke civil society down into its
simple components, on the one hand the *individuals,* on the other the
*material* and *spiritual elements* that constituted the content of life, the
civil situation of these individuals. It released the political spirit which
had been, as it were, divided, dispersed, and decomposed in the
various cul-de-sacs of feudal society; it collected this spirit out of this
helter-skelter dispersion, freed it from its confusion with civil life, and
constituted it as the sphere of the community, of the *universal* concern
of the people in an ideal independence from those *particular* elements
of civil life. The *specific* activity and *specific* situation of life were
debased to merely individual significance. They no longer formed the
universal relationship of the individual to the whole of the state.
Public affairs as such became the universal affair of each individual
and the political function became his universal function.
But the completion of the state's idealism was at the same time the
completion of civil society's materialism. The shedding of the political yoke was at the same time the shedding of the ties that restrained
the egoistic spirit of civil society. Political emancipation was at the
same time the emancipation of civil society from politics, from even
the *semblance* of a universal content.
Feudal society was dissolved into its basis, into man, but into man as
he was truly its basis, into *egoistic* man.
This man, the member of civil society, is now the basis, the presuppo-
sition, of the *political* state. He is recognised as such by the state in
the rights of man.
But the freedom of egoistic man and the recognition of this freedom is
really the recognition of the *unbridled* movement of the spiritual and
material elements which form the content of his life.
Man, therefore, was not freed from religion, he received the freedom of
religion. He was not freed from property. He received the freedom of
property. He was not freed from the egoism of trade, he received the
freedom of trade.
The *constitution of the political state* and the dissolution of civil society into
independent *individuals* – whose relationship is Right, just as men's
relationship within the estate and guild was *privilege* – is completed in
*one and the same act*. But man as a member of civil society, *unpolitical*
man, necessarily appears to the *natural* man. The rights of man appear
to be natural rights, for *self-conscious activity* is concentrated on the
*political act*. Egoistic man is the *passive* and merely *discovered* result of
the dissolved society, an object of *immediate certainty*, and thus a *natural*
object. The *political revolution* dissolves civil life into its components,
without *revolutionising* these components themselves and subjecting
them to criticism. It relates to civil society, to the world of need, of
labour, of private interests, and of private right as to the *basis of its existence, its fundamental premise,* hence its *natural basis*. Finally, man in his
capacity as member of civil society counts as the *genuine* man, as the

*homme* in contrast to the *citoyen*, because he is man in his sensuous, individual, and *immediate* existence, while *political* man is only abstract, artificial man, man as an *allegorical, moral* person. Actual man is recognised only in the form of the *egoistic* individual, and true man only in the form of the *abstract citoyen*.

Every emancipation *leads* the human world and its relationships *back to man himself*.

Political emancipation is the reduction of man on the one hand to the member of civil society, to the *egoistic, independent* individual, and on the other to the *citizen of the state*, to the moral person.

Only when the actual individual man absorbs the abstract citizen of the state into himself and has become in his empirical life, in his individual labour, in his individual relationships, a *species-being;* only when he has recognised and organised his 'own forces' as *social* forces and therefore no longer separates the social force from himself in the form of *political* force; only then is human emancipation completed.

## V. I. LENIN
### From *The State and Revolution*

The state is a special organization of force; it is an organization of violence for the suppression of some class. What class must the proletariat suppress? Naturally, only the exploiting class, i.e. the bourgeoisie. The labouring people need a state only to suppress the resistance of the exploiters, and only the proletariat is in a position to direct this suppression, to carry it out; for the proletariat is the only class that is consistently revolutionary, the only class that can unite all the labouring and exploited people in the struggle against the bourgeoisie, in its complete overthrow.

The exploiting classes need political rule in order to maintain exploitation, i.e. in the selfish interests of an insignificant minority against the vast majority of the people. The exploited classes need political rule in order completely to abolish all exploitation, i.e. in the interests of the vast majority of the people and against the insignificant minority consisting of the contemporary slave-owners, i.e. the landlords and the capitalists.

[...]

The proletariat needs state power, the centralized organization of force, the organization of violence both to crush the resistance of the exploiters and to *lead* the enormous mass of the population – the peasantry, the petty bourgeoisie, the semi-proletarians – in the work of 'establishing' a socialist economy.

By educating the workers' party, Marxism educates the vanguard of the proletariat which is capable of assuming power and *of leading the whole people* to socialism, of directing and organizing the new order, of being the teacher, the guide, the leader of all the labouring and exploited people in the task of constructing their social life without the bourgeoisie and against the bourgeoisie. By contrast, the now prevalent opportunism selects from the workers' party and trains the representatives of the better-paid workers, who are cut off from the working masses and who 'get along' fairly well under capitalism and sell their birthright for a mess of pottage, i.e. renounce their role as revolutionary leaders of the people against the bourgeoisie.

'The state, i.e. the proletariat organized as the ruling class': this theory of Marx is inseparably bound up with all he taught about the revolutionary role of the proletariat in history. The culmination of this role is the proletarian dictatorship, the political rule of the proletariat.

But if the proletariat needs a state as a *special* organization of violence *against* the bourgeoisie, the following question suggests itself by way of conclusion: is it conceivable that such an organization can be created without first abolishing, destroying the state machine created by the bourgeoisie *for itself*?

[...]

It is well known that several months before the Commune, in autumn 1870, Marx warned the workers of Paris that any attempt to overthrow the government would be the folly of desperation. But when, in March 1871, a decisive battle was imposed upon the workers and they accepted the challenge when the uprising had become a fact, Marx greeted the proletarian revolution with the greatest of joy despite the unfavourable auguries.

[...]

Marx, however, was not only enthusiastic about the heroism of the Communards who, as he put it, 'stormed the heavens'. He regarded the mass revolutionary movement, even though it did not achieve its aim, as an historical experience of enormous importance, as a certain advance on the part of the worldwide proletarian revolution, as a practical step which was more important than hundreds of programmes and arguments. To analyse this experience, to draw tactical lessons from it, to re-examine his theory in the light of it: this was the task set for himself by Marx.

The only 'correction' Marx thought it necessary to make to *The Communist Manifesto* was made on the basis of the revolutionary experience of the Paris Communards.

The last preface to the new German edition of *The Communist Manifesto*, as signed by both its authors, is dated 24 June 1872. In this preface the authors Karl Marx and Friedrich Engels say that the programme of *The Communist Manifesto* 'has in some places become outdated', and they continue:

[The Commune] demonstrated in particular that 'the working class cannot simply lay hold of the ready-made state machine, and deploy it for its own purposes.'

[...]

Marx subjected the experience of the Commune, scanty as it was, to the most attentive analysis in *The Civil War in France*. Let us quote the most important passages of this work.

[...]

The direct antithesis to the Empire was the Commune ... It was a particular form [of] a republic that was to eliminate not only the monarchical form of class rule but also class rule itself.

[...]

What did this 'particular' form of proletarian, socialist republic consist of? What was the state it was beginning to create?

The Commune was formed from municipal councillors chosen through universal suffrage in the various wards of Paris. They were responsible and instantly recallable. The majority of them naturally consisted of workers or acknowledged representatives of the working class ...

The police, until then the agent of the state government, was quickly stripped of its political functions and turned into the responsible and instantly recallable organ of the Commune ... So, too, were the bureaucrats of all other branches of the administration ... Beginning with the members of the Commune downwards, the public service had to be done at *a workman's wages*. All privileges and financial allowances for representative work given to the highest holders of state office disappeared along with those offices ... Having eradicated the standing army and the police, those instruments of material power for the old government, the Commune was anxious to break the instrument of spiritual oppression, the power of the priests ... The posts in the judiciary lost their former appearance of independence ... Henceforward they were to be elective, responsible and recallable.

Thus the Commune appears to have replaced the smashed state machine 'only' by fuller democracy: the abolition of the standing army; the provision that all officials should be elected and subject to recall. But as a matter of fact this 'only' signifies a gigantic replacement of certain institutions by other institutions of an essentially different kind. This is precisely one of those instances of 'quantity becoming transformed into quality': democracy, introduced as fully and consistently as is at all conceivable, is transformed from bourgeois democracy into proletarian democracy; from a state (= a special force for the suppression of a particular class) into something which is no longer a state in the proper sense.

It is still necessary to suppress the bourgeoisie and its resistance. This was particularly necessary for the Commune; and one of the reasons for its defeat was that it did not do this with enough decisiveness. But the organ of suppression is now the majority of the population, and not a minority as always occurred under slavery, serfdom and wage slavery. And as soon as it is the majority of the people *itself* which suppresses its oppressors, a 'special force' for suppression is *no longer necessary*! In this sense the state *begins to wither away*. Instead

of the special institutions of a privileged minority (privileged offi-
caldom, the high command of the standing army), the majority itself
can directly undertake this, and the more the functions of the state
power are undertaken by the people as a whole, the less need is left
for such a power.

In this respect a certain measure of the Commune highlighted by Marx
is especially noteworthy: the abolition of all financial allowances for
persons chosen as political representatives and of all financial privileges accorded to officials: the reduction of the pay for *all* servants of
the state to the level of *'a workman's wages'*. This expresses, in the
sharpest possible way, the break between bourgeois democracy and
proletarian democracy, between the democracy of the oppressors and
the democracy of the oppressed classes, between the state as a *'special
force'* for the suppression of a particular class and the suppression of
the oppressors by the *general force* of the majority of the people – the
workers and the peasants. And it is precisely on this especially
obvious point, arguably the most important as regards the problem
of the state is concerned, that the teachings of Marx have been the
most forgotten! In popular commentaries, whose number is legion,
this is not mentioned. It is 'good form' to keep silent about it as if it
were old-fashioned *'naïveté'*, just as the Christians, after receiving the
position of a state religion, 'forgot' the *'naïveté'* of primitive
Christianity with its democratic-revolutionary spirit.

The reduction of the pay of the highest state officials seems to be 'simply'
a demand of a naïve, primitive democratism. One of the 'founders' of
modern opportunism, the former social-democrat Eduard Bernstein,
has often exerted himself to repeat the vulgar bourgeois jeers at 'primitive' democratism. Like all opportunists and like today's Kautskyites,
he has utterly failed to understand that, firstly, the transition from
capitalism to socialism is *impossible* without a certain 'return' to 'primitive' democratism (for how else can the majority of the population and
then the whole population, including every one of its members,
proceed to discharge state functions?); secondly, that 'primitive
democratism' on the basis of capitalism and capitalist culture is not the
same as primitive democratism in prehistoric or precapitalist times.
Capitalist culture has *created* large-scale production, factories, rail-
ways, the postal service, telephones and so forth, and *on this basis* the
great majority of the functions of the old 'state power' have become so
simplified and can be reduced to such very simple operations of registering, filing and checking that these functions will become entirely
accessible to all literate people, that these functions will be entirely
performable for an ordinary 'workman's wages' and that these functions can (and must) be stripped of every shadow of association with
privilege or peremptory command.

Complete electivity of all officials without exception; their subjection to
recall *at any time;* the reduction of their salaries to the level of an ordinary 'workman's wages'; these simple and 'self-evident' democratic
measures, while completely uniting the interests of the workers and

the majority of the peasants, at the same time serve as a bridge from captialism over to socialism. These measures impinge on the state-based and purely political reconstruction of society; but, of course, they acquire their full meaning and significance only in connection with the 'expropriation of the expropriators' being either accomplished or prepared, i.e. with the transition of captialist private ownership of the means of production into social ownership.

[...]

The Commune [Marx wrote] had to be not a parliamentary but a working institution passing and executing laws at the same time ...

Instead of deciding once every three or six years which member of the ruling class should represent and suppress [*ver – und zertreten*] the people in parliament, universal suffrage was to serve the people organized in communes in the search for the workers, foremen, and bookkeepers for their enterprise just as individual suffrage serves every other employer for this purpose.

Thanks to the dominance of social-chauvinism and opportunism, this remarkable criticism of parliamentarianism made in 1871 also now belongs to the 'forgotten words' of Marxism. Cabinet ministers and professional parliamentarians, the traitors to the proletariat and the 'businesslike' socialists of our day have left all criticism of parliamentarianism completely to the anarchists, and this wonderfully rational foundation is used by them to denounce *all* criticism of parliamentarianism as 'anarchism'!!

[...]

For Marx, however, revolutionary dialectics were never the empty fashionable phrase, the toy rattle, which Plekhanov, Kautsky and others have made of it. Marx knew how to break mercilessly with anarchism for its inability to use even the 'pig-sty' of bourgeois parliamentarianism especially when there is quite obviously no revolutionary situation in sight; but at the same time he knew how to subject parliamentarianism to truly revolutionary-proletarian criticism.

To decide once every few years which member of the ruling class is to repress and crush the people in parliament: this is the real essence of bourgeois parliamentarianism not only in parliamentary-constitutional monarchies but also in the most democratic republics.

But if we pose the question of the state and if we examine parliamentarianism as one of the state's institutions, from the viewpoint of the tasks of the proletariat in *this* field, what is the way out of parliamentarianism? How can we do without it?

Again and again it needs repeating: the lessons of Marx, based on the study of the Commune, have been so much forgotten that present-day 'social-democrats' (viz. present-day traitors to socialism) find any criticism of parliamentarianism, other than anarchist or reactionary criticism of it, quite incomprehensible.

The way out of parliamentarianism is not, of course, the elimination of representative institutions and electivity but the conversion of the

representative institutions from talking shops into 'working' institutions. 'The Commune had to be not a parliamentary but a working
institution, passing and executing laws at the same time ...'

'Not a parliamentary but a working' institution: this strikes right
between the eyes of the present-day parliamentarians and parliamentary 'lap-dogs' of social-democracy! Look at any parliamentary
country, from America to Switzerland, from France to England,
Norway and so forth; in these countries, the real business of 'state' is
done behind the scenes and is carried on by departments, chancelleries, general staffs. Parliaments are only places where chattering
goes on with the special purpose of fooling the 'common people'.
This is so true that even in the Russian republic, a bourgeois-demo-
cratic republic, all these sins of parliamentarianism have immediately
revealed themselves even before the republic managed to set up a
real parliament. Heroes of rotten philistinsim such as the Skobelevs
and Tseretelis, the Chernovs and Avksentevs, have even succeeded
in polluting the Soviets after the fashion of the most disgusting bourgeois parliamentarianism and in converting them into mere talking
shops. In the Soviets, the 'socialist' gentlemen-cum-ministers are
duping credulous rustics with phrase-mongering and resolutions. In
the government, a sort of permanent quadrille is performed so that,
on the one hand, as many Socialist Revolutionaries and Mensheviks
as possible may have their turn at putting their snouts in 'the trough',
the lucrative and prestigious official posts, and so that, on the other
hand, the 'attention of the people' may be engaged. Meanwhile it is
inside the chancelleries and general staffs that they 'work' on the
business of 'state'.

[...]

The Commune replaces the venal and rotten parliamentarianism of
bourgeois society with institutions in which freedom of opinion and
discussion do not degenerate into deception, for the parliamentarians themselves have to work, have to execute their own laws, have
to test their results in real life and to answer directly to their electors.
Representative institutions remain, but parliamentarianism *does not
exist* here as a special system, as the division of labour between the
legislative and the executive, as a privileged position for the
deputies. We cannot imagine democracy, even proletarian democracy, without representative institutions, but we can and *must*
imagine democracy without parliamentarianism if our criticisms of
bourgeois society are not mere empty words for us, if the aspiration
to overthrow the rule of the bourgeoisie is our serious and sincere
desire, and not a 'ballot-box' phrase for catching workers' votes, as it
is with the Mensheviks and Socialist Revolutionaries and as it is with
the Scheidemanns and Legiens, the Sembats and Vanderveldes.

It is extremely instructive that, in speaking of the functions of *those*
bureaucrats who are necessary for the Commune and for proletarian
democracy, Marx compares them to the workers of 'any other
employer', i.e. of the ordinary capitalist enterprise, with its 'workers,

foremen and bookkeepers'.

There is no touch of utopianism in Marx in the sense that he made up or invented a 'new' society. No, he studies the *birth* of the new society *out of* the old, the forms of transtition from the latter to the former as a natural-historical process. He takes the actual experience of a mass proletarian movement and tries to draw practical lessons from it. He 'learns' from the Commune, just as all the great revolutionary thinkers were not afraid to learn from the experience of the great movements of the oppressed class, and never addresses pedantic 'sermons' to them (such as 'they should not have taken to arms' à la Plekhanov or 'a class must put limits on itself' à la Tsereteli).

There can be no talk of eradicating the bureaucracy at once, everywhere and completely. That is utopia. But to *smash* the old bureaucratic machine at once and to begin immediately to construct a new one that facilitates the gradual eradication of all bureaucracy: this is *not* utopia, this is the experience of the Commune, this is the direct, immediate task of the revolutionary proletariat.

Capitalism simplifies the functions of 'state' administration'; it makes it possible to have done with 'bossing' and to reduce the whole business to an organization of proletarians (as the ruling class) which will hire 'workers, foremen and bookkeepers' in the name of the whole of society.

We are not utopians. We do not have 'dreams' about dispensing *at once* with all administration, with all subordination; these anarchist dreams, based upon a misunderstanding of the tasks of the dictatorship of the proletariat, are essentially alien to Marxism, and in practice serve only to postpone the socialist revolution until people have themselves become different. No, we want the socialist revolution with people as they are now, with people who cannot dispense with subordination, with control, with 'foremen and bookkeepers'.

But the subordination must be to the armed vanguard of all the exploited and labouring people, to the proletariat. A start can and must be made at once, overnight, to replace the specific 'bossing' by state bureaucrats with the simple functions of 'foremen and bookkeepers', functions which are already fully accessible to ordinary urban inhabitants at their present level of development and are fully performable for a 'workman's wages'.

*We ourselves*, the workers, will organize large-scale production on the basis of what has already been created by captialism, relying on our own experience as workers, establishing strict, iron discipline supported by the state power of the armed workers; we will reduce state officials to the role of simple executors of our instructions, to the role of responsible, recallable and modestly paid 'foremen and bookkeepers' (together, of course, with technicians of all sorts, types and degrees). This is *our* proletarian task, this is what we can and must *start* with in accomplishing the proletarian revolution. Such a start, on the basis of large-scale production, will of itself lead to the gradual 'withering away' of all bureaucracy, to the gradual creation of an

258

order, an order without question marks, an order bearing no similarity to wage slavery, an order in which the ever simpler functions of control and accounting will be performed by each person in turn, will then become a habit and will finally die out as the *special* functions of a special stratum of people.

A sharp-witted German social-democrat of the 1870s called the *postal service* a model for the socialist economic system. This is very true. At present the postal service is a business organized on the lines of a state-*capitalist* monopoly. Imperialism is gradually transforming all trusts into organizations of a similar type. Over the 'common' labouring people, who are overworked and starved, the same bourgeois bureaucracy still stands in place. But the mechanism of society's economic management is already to hand. We have only to overthrow the capitalists, to crush the resistance of these exploiters with the iron hand of the armed workers, to smash the bureaucratic machine of the modern state – and we shall have a well-equipped mechanism of a high technical quality, freed from the 'parasite', a mechanism which can very easily be set in motion by the united workers themselves, who will hire technicians, foremen and bookkeepers and pay them *all*, and indeed *all* 'state' officials in general, a workman's wage. Here is a concrete, practical task, immediately fulfillable in relation to all trusts, a task that will relieve labouring people of exploitation and take account of the experiment already begun by the Commune (especially in the area of state construction).

To organize the *whole* national economy on the lines of the postal service, so that the technicians, foremen, bookkeepers, as well as *all* officials, shall receive salaries no higher than 'a workman's wage', under the control and leadership of the armed proletariat – this is our immediate aim. It is such a state, resting on such an economic foundation, that we need. This is what will bring about the eradication of parliamentarianism and the preservation of representative institutions. This is what will rid the labouring classes of the prostitution of these institutions by the bourgeoisie.

[…]

Democracy for an insignificant minority, democracy for the rich: this is the democratism of capitalist society. If we look more closely into the mechanism of capitalist democracy, we shall see everywhere, both in the 'petty' – supposedly petty – details of the suffrage (residential qualification, exclusion of women etc.) and in the techniques of the representative institutions, in the real obstacles to the right of assembly (public buildings are not for 'beggars'!) as well as in the purely capitalist organization of the daily press and so on and so forth, we shall see restriction after restriction upon democracy. These restrictions, exclusions, exceptions, obstacles for the poor, seem petty, especially in the eyes of anyone who has never known want himself and never been in close contact with the oppressed classes in their mass life (and nine-tenths, if not ninety-nine hundredths, of bourgeois publicists and politicians are of such a kind); but the sum total of these restrictions excludes and shoves out the poor from politics, from active participation in democracy.

Marx grasped the *essence* of capitalist democracy magnificently when, in analysing the experience of the Commune, he spoke as follows: the oppressed are allowed once every few years to decide which particular representatives of the oppressing class shall represent and repress them in parliament!

But from this capitalist democracy – which is inevitably narrow and stealthily shoves aside the poor, and is therefore pervasively hypocritical and false – a progressive development does not occur simply, directly and smoothly towards 'ever greater democracy' as the liberal professors and petty-bourgeois opportunists claim. No, a progressive development, i.e. towards communism, occurs through the dictatorship of the proletariat and cannot occur otherwise, for the *resistance* of the exploiter-capitalists cannot be *broken* by anyone else or by any other path.

And the dictatorship of the proletariat, i.e. the organization of the vanguard of the oppressed as the ruling class for the suppression of the oppressors, cannot lead simply to an expansion of democracy. *Alongside* an immense expansion of democratism which *for the first time* becomes democratism for the poor, democratism for the people and not democratism for the rich, the dictatorship of the proletariat imposes a series of exclusions from freedom in relation to the oppressors, the exploiters, the capitalists. We must suppress them in order to free humanity from wage slavery; their resistance must be crushed by force: it is clear that where there is suppression, where there is coercion, there is no freedom and no democracy.

[...]

Democracy for the gigantic majority of the people, and suppression by force, i.e. the exclusion from democracy of the exploiters and oppressors of the people: this is the transformation witnessed in democracy in the *transition* from capitalism to communism.

Only in communist society, when the resistance of the capitalists has been definitively crushed, when the capitalists have disappeared, when there are no classes (i.e. when there is no difference between the members of society in their relation to the social means of production), *only* then does 'the state ... disappear' and does it *'become possible to speak of freedom'*. Only then will a truly complete democracy, democracy without any exceptions whatever, become possible and be realized. And only then will democracy begin to *wither away* because of the simple fact that, relieved of capitalist slavery, of countless horrors, savageries, absurdities and infamies of capitalist exploitation, people will gradually *become accustomed* to observing the elementary rules of social intercourse that have been known for ages and repeated for thousands of years in all copybooks – and to observing them without force, without compulsion, without subordination, *without the special apparatus* for compulsion which is called the state.

TONY KEMP-WELCH

# Bakunin and Kropotkin on anarchism

# 10

The essence of anarchism is a critique of the modern state. Anarchists seek a stateless order (*anarkhos* from Greek meaning 'without ruler'), which they assert will not be mere chaos or disorder but will engender new forms of community and solidarity. The origins of their doctrine are usually attributed to the English libertarian William Godwin (*An Enquiry Concerning the Principles of Political Justice*, 1793) and to Rousseau (see chapters 5 and 8), who declared that 'man was born free and is everywhere in chains' and considered that political institutions have corrupted an otherwise innocent and pure human nature. Abolition of such institutions, anarchists argue, will restore this original purity. Since it is hard to see how this ultimate goal could be achieved through purely peaceful evolution, the popular image of anarchists as bomb-throwing terrorists is not entirely false. Anarchists have sometimes used violence in pursuit of their ends, most famously in the conspiracies to assassinate the Tsar so chillingly portrayed in Dostoyevsky's *The Possessed*. Yet anarchist doctrines are so various and diverse that they can accommodate both the terrorist and the pacifist, including the greatest Russian writer, Lev Tolstoy. This Tolstoyan pacifist tradition, which stretches forward through Gandhi, the peace movements and civil rights movements of the 1960s (Martin Luther King), to the non-violent uprisings in Eastern Europe of 1989 is, however, beyond the scope of this volume.

The magnitude of the anarchist project has always been inversely proportional to the ability of anarchists to act. Anarchist organisation is almost a contradiction in terms. The manifold difficulties of *Demanding the Impossible* (Marshall, 1992) will here be explored through the lives and writings of two Russian anarchists, Bakunin and Kropotkin.

## Mikhail Bakunin (1814–76)

Bakunin was born in Russia but travelled to Paris in his twenties and came into his own during the upheavals in European capitals of 1848, when he managed to be in several countries in successive months, usually as an orator but also as the founder of clandestine, and frequently imaginary, societies. He was extradited to Russia and spent

ten years in prison and Siberia before fleeing abroad. He reached
London in 1861. Bakunin took no part in the founding of the socialist
First International but retired to backward Italy, a country he considered ripe for revolution. For Bakunin, the oppressed in Italy and above
all Russia were potentially revolutionary. He called Russians 'socialist
by instinct, revolutionary by nature'. He referred principally to the
peasantry and he devised numerous Slavophile projects to promote
their liberation. He became implacably hostile to the Marxian prospec-
tus, which he dubbed 'state communism'. In his view, such a regime
would be supported only by the better-off workers – as organised in the
International – while his brand of anarchism appealed to the genuinely
revolutionary paupers who had nothing to lose. He constantly harked
back to the uprisings of Russian peasants – Pugachev and Stenka Razin
– as expressions of elemental and instinctive forces which would
simply be smothered under Marx's new state despotism and 'scientific
socialism'. Marx also opposed the bourgeois state, though for other
reasons (see chapter 9), and expected a socialist revolution to diminish
the state (Engels writes of its 'withering away'), but Marx also saw the
revolution as bringing with it a greatly expanded economic centralisation. For Bakunin this was a contradiction within Marxism, and he
deserves the credit for having identified it long before it was laid bare
under Stalinism.

In rejecting 'scientific socialism', Bakunin was asserting the primacy
of 'life' over ideas. In a famous aphorism, he accused Marx of 'ruining
the workers by making theorists of them'. For Bakunin, men make their
own history, as Marx had said, but not according to his prophecy or to
the tendencies he claimed to have uncovered. On the contrary, the
future was unknowable, since social science, he rightly said, was in its
infancy. For Bakunin, history works out instinctively from life itself.
Life, blocked by the state, takes place naturally in society, which is
nothing less than the instinctive ties that bind human beings together.
To abolish the state is not to abolish all forms of co-operation. On the
contrary, Bakunin argues, new forms of voluntary association can and
must be built up from below. People have an instinctive solidarity. The
state fears and opposes this natural sociability by hardening into an
oppressive solidarity of its own. Bakunin wants to abolish its essential
instruments: the state itself, public administration, law, jurisprudence
and the family. His utopia will enjoy complete freedom of opinions,
including false ones, untrammelled rights to assembly and an absence
of repressive legislation. Crime, if any, will be treated as a symptom of
disease and treated accordingly. Inheritance will be abolished and in
due course equality attained. The ensuing anarchy is no mere abstract
ideal, but the actual realisation of humanity as it is meant to be.

Bakunin's ideal society would be a federation of independent
communes resulting from 'the radical overthrow of all presently existing religious, political, economic and social organisations and
institutions' (*Principles and Organization of the International Brotherhood*).
An anarchist social revolution will burst out spontaneously among the

people 'crushing all that opposes the impetuous flow of popular life in order to create new forms of free community from the very depths of the people's being'. It will destroy the 'centralist state, lackey and *alter ego* of the Church, and as such the permanent source of poverty, degradation and subjugation of the people' (Kelly, 1982, p. 177). This will usher in a new world in which authority has been abolished, the expedient principles of *raison d'état* proscribed, and all ranks and privileges removed. The need for violence is less veiled than glorified: 'There can be no revolution without passionate destruction – destruction which is fruitful and salvatory – through it alone the new world arises'.

Such hopes were fortified by the outbreak of the Franco-Prussian War in July 1870. Bakunin believed that a French uprising against both the German invader and the national government would sweep aside the state and install an anarchist federation of free communes. This done, supporting revolutions were sure to follow. They would start in Spain and Italy and then spread through the Austrian Empire to the Slavonic nations of Poland and Russia. In September 1870, he argued that France could only be saved by a spontaneous anarchist uprising of 'popular' elements to defeat the enemy (*Lettre à un français sur la crise actuelle*). To enable this to happen, the peasantry would have to be converted to the revolutionary cause. Another necessary preliminary might be assassinating a select list of famous persons. Only the bandit was a genuine revolutionary. A later tract, which he described as his 'testament', blamed the failure of social uprising in France on the radical bourgeoisie, who had forestalled it by their 'cult of the state'.

For a brief moment, the Paris Commune installed a revolutionary regime: electing officials and magistrates, replacing the police and army by popular militias, disestablishing the Church and introducing a maximum wage and free education (see also chapter 9). To Marx this seemed the consummation of the hopes of the International. To Bakunin it was just the joyous spectacle of the free citizenry of Paris doing their own thing. The latter view was closer to the truth. However, the crushing of the Commune by Bismarck ushered in reaction everywhere, removing revolution from the European agenda for the rest of the nineteenth century. Bakunin's subsequent reflections on the defeat of the Paris Commune were more sophisticated. Marxists and Comptean positivists were now blamed for fostering a new aristocracy of the intellect. This self-appointed elite attempted 'to use the people as material for social experiments'. They sought to institute 'government by scientists' in order to perpetuate their own power. This became a common complaint by anarchists, foreshadowing the 'New Class' analysis of the Soviet Union by the Polish anarchist Machajski, by Trotsky and later Milovan Djilas.

Marx himself was thrice damned by Bakunin as German, Jewish and formerly Hegelian. One outcome of their deteriorating relationship was Bakunin's expulsion from the First International in the autumn of 1872 by majority vote. Marx himself removed the International to America, where it lingered on for some years. A rival International of Bakunin's followers fell to pieces a few years later. In September 1873, despairing of political activity – 'rolling the stone of Sisyphus against the forces of reaction which are triumphing everywhere' – Bakunin announced his retirement from revolutionary politics. He died in disappointment three years later. Thereafter, the locus of revolutionary activity shifted eastwards, especially to Russia.

In the first of the extracts reproduced below, *The Paris Commune and the Idea of the State* (published posthumously in German in 1878), Bakunin highlights a number of key themes. The opening section restates his view that only an anarchist uprising could save invaded France. His preamble ends with a somewhat unconvincing apologia for putting pen to paper. He then defends his notion of freedom as an unfettered utopia 'built on the ruin of all Churches and all States'. Equality is established by the 'spontaneous organisation' of work on a communal and freely co-operative basis. He criticises the Marxian project of a revolutionary seizure of power by organised workers as bound to perpetuate the tyranny of the state, indeed adding to it the burden of rule by 'superior intellects'. For Bakunin, it is the fact, rather than the form, of government that is the origin of evil.

The Paris Commune had been defeated in the name of 'Law and Order'. His text is written as an outcry against its crushing by 'monarchic and clerical reaction'. In a highly-charged passage, intended as an introduction to a longer work on *L' Empire knouto-germanique et la révolution sociale*, the author indulges in a series of romantic fantasies and charmingly absurd generalisations. He then reflects on the appropriate relationship between leader and the masses in a popular revolution. Nothing should be initiated except by the people themselves. To ignore spontaneity – 'the natural power of the masses' – would simply result in the replacement of one oppressive state by another. Amplification of this view may be found in Bakunin's *Statism and Anarchy* (published in Russian in 1873). This counter-poses the state and the social revolution as 'two poles whose antagonism forms the very essence of contemporary existence'. No system or doctrine was adequate to embrace the popular ideal. Social revolution must be unsullied by prior theorising. In particular, the Marxist wager on the revolutionary potential of the working class was likely to be lost: workers, being potentially bourgeois, could easily be bought off by economic concessions. There was no particular role for elitist intellectuals. Students were recommended to leave the universities – doomed to destruction – in order to 'melt' into the masses. Young seminarists and nihilists could overcome their alienation through revolt. In revolution, they would merge with the people: the peasantry and the 'great popular rabble' of have-nots and dispossessed.

The remainder of his vision is encapsulated in our second extract. The state must be abolished as a precondition for human emancipation. It is a dead weight upon the people, kept in power only through police, army and bureaucracy. The 'future social organisation', which must necessarily be left undefined, will be shaped by a succession of free and voluntary associations. Starting at the local level, these will gradually accumulate upwards, thus reconstituting European, and subsequently world, society on the basis of 'liberty, reason, justice and work'. The whole process will culminate in 'a great federation, international and universal' in which eternal peace and harmony prevail.

## Peter Kropotkin (1842–1921)

Kropotkin came to anarchism by a circuitous route. Born into the Russian nobility, he was selected at the age of eight by Tsar Nicholas for the Corps de Page, an elite military school in St Petersburg. He was prepared for admission by private tuition. On graduating at twenty, he could choose any branch of the armed services, and selected an obscure Cossack regiment in Eastern Siberia. He made exploratory trips along the Amur river and in Manchuria, reports of which won him membership, by election, of the Russian Geographical Society, and later secretaryship of its geological section. He resigned his commission, returned to St Petersburg and then travelled abroad to Sweden, Switzerland and Belgium. He was drawn towards the Bakuninist faction of the International, and joined them after they had been expelled from the movement. On his return to Russia, he became politically active in working-class districts of the capital (under a pseudonym) but was arrested and imprisoned in the Peter and Paul fortress. He escaped to Western Europe and after various adventures was arrested in France for anarchist activities. Following three years' imprisonment, he settled in Harrow and Bromley, Kent, for the next thirty.

He began to publish his theory of *Mutual Aid* in 1890, his main statement of anarchist philosophy. In contrast to Malthusian and Darwinian ideas of 'natural selection', carried out by a struggle for survival in which many competitors were bound to fail, Kropotkin identified co-operation as a distinctive trait of many successful species: 'Sociability is the greatest advantage in the struggle for life'. The struggle for existence takes place against adverse circumstances rather than against other individuals. Intellectual activity is inherently social and the fact of living together in society helps to engender a communal sense of justice. He too regarded the Paris Commune as seminal, declaring in *The Conquest of Bread* (1892) that it was the first attempt to implement a decentralised and federal society. Like all anarchists, he makes a sharp distinction between society and the state which is seen as unequal and oppressive.

In contrast to Bakunin's futuristic utopia, Kropotkin's idyll *The State: Its Historic Role*, written for a Paris audience in 1896, harks back to premodernity. Far from seeing the state as the summation of contemporary achievement, he argues that the free towns and communities of the Middle Ages represent a period of greater human liberty. Medieval institutions, in which human beings could find self-realisation, should not be regarded as outmoded and anachronistic. Their displacement by the emerging European nation states, from the time of Renaissance

Italy, was not an advance. On the contrary, only through the restoration of these earlier associations could freedom be regained.

In the extract *The State: Its Historic Role* reproduced below, Kropotkin outlines the origins of the state. The first human societies were based on mutual aid; tribal morality was the product of custom and tradition and not imposed by authority. In medieval Europe, guilds were formed, often comprising professional craftsmen, and these in turn established free cities in which individual rights were strictly respected. These promising initiatives were crushed by the modern state, which subjected them to centralisation and domination. Thereafter, men 'fell in love with authority' and readily contributed to the formation of institutions that oppressed them.

In 1897, Kropotkin travelled to America and published his *Memoirs of a Revolutionist*. On the outbreak of the First World War, he took the Allied position and split the anarchist movement. After the February 1917 Revolution, he was offered posts in the Provisional Government but declined. After the October Revolution he was respectfully received by Lenin, whose invitation to correspond was taken up. His angry *Letter to Lenin* of 21 December 1920 is also reproduced below.

### Conclusion

As the letter to Lenin shows, Kropotkin accurately foretold the fate of socialism in the Soviet Union. But he died in time and was buried in Moscow on 8 February 1921. Anarchists displayed their distinctive black and scarlet flags at his funeral. He remained honoured in Russia, but Marx's opponent Bakunin did not, and all remnants of anarchist movements were rapidly eliminated. Apart from a few teenagers under Gorbachev - charmingly innocent of the doctrines they proclaimed - they have not reappeared in Russia.

Elsewhere anarchism as a political movement has not fared well. Its few moments of glory (for example, in the Spanish Civil War) were short-lived. In the United States, the right-wing tradition of anarcho-capitalism, inaugurated by Lysander Spooner, re-emerged fitfully in the 1980s and early 1990s. The successful Solidarity movement in Poland (1980-81) had anarcho-syndicalist elements, and also contained other influences such as the Church which anarchists denounce. But these were merely flickers of a perhaps extinguished flame. It is perhaps not surprising to find there are so few open followers of a doctrine which finds itself at such odds not only with all other political theories – above all Marxism - but with most of the prevalent assumptions of the twentieth century.

### References

Kelly, Aileen, *Mikhail Bakunin: A Study in the Psychology and Politics of Utopianism*, Oxford: Clarendon Press, 1982.

Marshall, Peter, *Demanding the Impossible: A History of Anarchism*, London: Harper Collins, 1992.

The extracts reproduced below are taken from Michael Bakunin, *Selected Writings*, ed. Arthur Lehning, London: Jonathan Cape, 1973, pp. 195–200 and 204–6 and P. A. Kropotkin, *Selected Writings on Anarchism and Revolution*, ed. Martin A. Miller, Cambridge, MA and London: MIT Press 1970, pp. 211–14, 259–64, 335–7.

## Further reading

The standard life of Bakunin remains E. H. Carr, *Mikhail Bakunin* (London: Macmillan, 1937; 2nd edn 1975). The best Western account of Kropotkin's life can be found in Paul Avrich, *The Russian Anarchists* (Princeton, N J: Princeton University Press, 1963). The most recent, and encyclopaedic, account of the anarchist movement as a whole is Peter Marshall, *Demanding the Impossible: A History of Anarchism* (see references) which generously acknowledges such predecessors as George Woodcock, *Anarchism: A History of Libertarian Ideas and Movements* (Harmondsworth: Penguin, 1962 2nd edn 1986) and James Joll, *The Anarchists* (London: Eyre & Spottiswoode, 1964; 2nd edn 1979).

The more political issues are discussed in April Carter, *The Political Theory of Anarchism* (London: Routledge & Kegan Paul, 1971) and David Miller, *Anarchism* (Dent 'Modern Ideologies' series, London: Dent, 1984). For an early statement of the anarchist position, see Lysander Spooner, *Natural Law; or, the Science of Justice* (Boston, MA: A. Williams, 1882), and for a Marxist riposte, see E. J. Hobsbawm's *Primitive Rebels* (Manchester: Manchester Unuversity Press, 1971).

## Seminar questions

Is anarchy synonymous with mere disorder?

What were the main theoretical disputes between Bakunin and Marx?

How did Bakunin explain the failure of the Paris Commune?

With what does Kropotkin contrast the modern state?

'There is nothing more authoritarian than revolution' (Engels). Comment in the light of anarchist doctrines.

## MIKHAIL BAKUNIN
### From *The Paris Commune and the Idea of the State*

This work, like all the writings which I have published until now – so far there have been few enough – is a product of events. It is the natural continuation of my *Letters to a Frenchman* (September 1870), in which I had the easy and sad privilege of foreseeing and predicting the horrible misfortunes which are today assailing France and, along with her, the whole civilized world; misfortunes against which there has been and remains only one remedy now: *the Social Revolution*.

To prove this truth – from now on indisputable – from the historical development of society and from the very events taking place before our eyes in Europe, in such a way as to make it acceptable to all men of good will, and by all sincere seekers of the truth – and then to set forth frankly without reticence or equivocation the philosophical principles as well as the practical goals which make up, so to speak, the essence of the activist spirit, the basis and the aim of what we call the Social Revolution – such is the object of the present work.

The task which I have set for myself is not easy, I know, and I might be accused of presumption if I brought into this work the least personal conceit. But there is none of that, I can assure the reader. I am neither a scholar nor a philosopher, nor even a writer by profession. I have written very little during my life and I have never done so, as it were, except in self-defence, and only when a passionate conviction compelled me to overcome the repugnance which I feel instinctively for parading my private self in public.

Who am I then, and what is it that compels me to publish this work at the present time? I am a passionate seeker of the truth, and none the less persistent an enemy to the harmful untruths which the *law and order party* (that official representative, privileged and self-seeking, of all the religious, metaphysical, political, legal, economic and social villainies, past and present) still has the arrogance to make use of today so as to brutalize and enslave the world. I am a fanatical lover of freedom, considering it as the unique environment within which the intelligence, dignity and happiness of mankind may develop and increase. I am not speaking of that freedom which is purely formal, doled out, measured and regulated by the State, an everlasting lie which in reality never represents anything but the privilege of a few based on the enslavement of everyone else. Nor do I mean that individualistic, egotistical, malicious and illusory freedom, extolled by the school of J.-J. Rousseau, as by all the other schools of bourgeois liberalism, which considers the so-called rights of everyone, represented by the State as the limit of the rights of each individual, and which in fact leads of necessity and without exception to the reduction of the rights of the individual to zero. No, I mean the only

freedom which is truly worthy of that name, the freedom which
consists in the full development of all the material, intellectual and
moral powers which are found in the form of latent capabilities in
every individual. I mean that freedom which recognizes only those
restrictions which are laid down for us by the laws of our own nature;
so, properly speaking, there are no restrictions, since these laws are
not imposed by some outside legislator situated maybe beside us or
maybe above us, they are immanent in us and inherent in us and
constitute the very basis of all our being, as much material as intellectual and moral. Thus, instead of trying to find a limit for them, we
should consider them as the real conditions of and the real reason for
our freedom.

I mean that freedom of the individual which, far from stopping as if
before a boundary in face of the freedom of others, on the contrary
finds in that freedom its own confirmation and extension to infinity;
the unlimited freedom of each in the freedom of all, freedom in solidarity, freedom in equality; triumphant freedom, victorious over
brute force and the principle of authority which was never anything
but the idealized expression of brute force; freedom which, after
overthrowing all the heavenly and earthly idols, will establish and
organize a new world, that of humanity in solidarity, built on the ruin
of all Churches and all States.

I am a convinced supporter of *economic and social equality*, because I know
that, outside that equality, freedom, justice, human dignity, morality,
and the well-being of individuals, just as much as the prosperity of
nations, will never be anything but lies. But, supporter though I may
be of freedom, this first condition of humanity, I think that equality
must be established in the world by the spontaneous organization of
work and of the collective ownership of producers' associations,
freely organized and federated in the communes, and by the equally
spontaneous federation of these communes, but not by the overriding and enslaving activity of the State.

This is the point which mainly divides the revolutionary socialists or
collectivists from the authoritarian communists who are supporters
of the absolute power of the State. Their goal is the same: both the
one and the other faction equally desire the creation of a new social
order based solely on the organization of collective work, inevitably
imposed on one and all by the very nature of things, in economic
conditions which are equal for all, and upon the collective appropriation of the instruments of labour.

Only the communists imagine they will be able to attain this by the
development and the organization of the political power of the
working classes, principally of the urban proletariat, with the help of
bourgeois radicalism, while the revolutionary socialists, enemies of
every tie and every alliance of an equivocal nature, think on the
contrary that they will not be able to attain this goal except by the
development and organization, not of the political but of the social
(and, by consequence, anti-political) power of the working masses as

Bakunin  much in the towns as in the countryside, including all the men of good will who, breaking with their past in the upper classes, might sincerely wish to join with them and wholly accept their programme.

From this two different methods are derived. The communists believe they should organize the workers' strength to take over the political power of the States. The revolutionary socialists organized with a view to the destruction, or, if one wants a more polite word, the liquidation, of the States. The communists are supporters of the principle and practice of authority; the revolutionary socialists have no faith except in freedom. Both the one and the other, equally supporters of science which is to destroy superstition and replace belief, differ in the former wishing to impose it, and the latter striving to propagate it; so that human groups, convinced of its truth, may organize and federate spontaneously, freely, from the bottom up, by their own momentum according to their real interests, but never according to any plan laid down in advance and imposed upon the *ignorant masses* by some superior intellects.

The revolutionary socialists think that there is much more practical and intellectual common sense in the instinctive aspirations and in the real needs of the masses of the people than in the profound intelligence of all these doctors and teachers of mankind who, after so many fruitless attempts to make humanity happy, still aspire to add their own efforts. The revolutionary socialists think the opposite: that mankind has allowed itself to be governed long enough, too long, and that the origin of its unhappiness does not reside in this or that form of government but in the very principle and fact of government, whatever kind it may be.

Finally this is the same, already historic, contradiction which exists between the scientific communism developed by the German school and accepted in part by the American and English socialists on the one hand, and the Proudhonism widely developed and pushed right to these, its final consequences, on the other, accepted by the proletariat of the Latin countries[1] Revolutionary socialism has just attempted its first demonstration, both splendid and practical, in the *Paris Commune*.

I am a supporter of the Paris Commune, which, because it was massacred and drowned in blood by the executioners of monarchic and clerical reaction, has therefore become all the more lively and powerful in the imagination and heart of the European proletariat. I am above all a supporter of it because it was a bold and outspoken negation of the State.

It is a tremendously significant historical fact that this negation of the State should have been manifested particularly in France, which has been until now the country par excellence of political centralization,

---

[1] It is equally accepted and will be accepted yet more by the essentially non-political instinct of the Slav peoples.

and that it should have been above all precisely Paris, the historic fountain-head of this great French civilization, which should have taken the initiative. Paris, taking off it own crown and proclaiming its own downfall with enthusiasm so as to give freedom and life to France, to Europe, to the whole world! Paris, affirming once more its historic ability to take the lead, and showing to all the enslaved peoples (and which popular masses indeed are not slaves?) the unique way of emancipation and salvation! Paris, striking a moral blow at the political traditions of bourgeois radicalism and providing a real basis for revolutionary socialism! Paris, earning once more the curses of all the reactionary gangs of France and Europe! Paris, being buried in its ruins so as to pronounce a solemn contradiction to triumphant reaction; saving by its catastrophe the honour and future of France, and proving to a comforted mankind that, if life, intelligence and moral power have disappeared from the upper classes, they have remained energetic and full of potential in the proletariat! Paris, inaugurating the new era, that of the final and complete emancipation of the masses of the people and of their solidarity, henceforth a matter of fact, across and despite State frontiers. Paris, destroying patriotism and building on its ruins the religion of humanity! Paris, proclaiming itself humanist and atheist: and replacing the fictions of religion by the great realities of social life and faith in science, replacing the lies and injustices of religious, political and legal morality by the principles of freedom, justice, equality and fraternity, these eternal fundamentals of all human morality! Heroic Paris, rational and faithful, confirming its energetic faith in the destinies of mankind even in its glorious downfall and destruction, and leaving that faith much more energetic and lively for the generations to come! Paris, soaked in the blood of its most generous-hearted children - there indeed is mankind crucified by the international and co-ordinated reaction of all Europe, under the immediate inspiration of all the Christian Churches and that high priest of iniquity, the Pope. But the next international and solidarist revolution of the people will be the resurrection of Paris.

Such is the true meaning, and such are the immense beneficial consequences, of the two months of the existence and the fall, for ever memorable, of the Paris Commune.

[...]

Contrary to that authoritarian communist type of thinking – in my opinion completely erroneous – that a Social Revolution can be decreed and organized, whether by a dictatorship or whether by a constituent assembly resulting from some political revolution, our friends, the socialists of Paris, thought that it could not be made or brought to its full development except by the spontaneous and continuous action of the masses, the groups and the associations of the people.

Our friends in Paris were a thousand times right. For indeed, where is that head, however brilliant it may be, or if one wishes to speak of a collective dictatorship, were it formed by many hundreds of individuals endowed with superior faculties, where are those brains powerful enough and wide-ranging enough to embrace the infinite multiplicity and diversity of the real interests, aspirations, wishes and needs whose sum total constitutes the collective will of a people, and to invent a social organization which can satisfy everybody? This organization will never be anything but a Procrustean bed which the more or less obvious violence of the State will be able to force unhappy society to lie down on. That is what has always happened until now, and it is precisely this old system of organization by force that the Social Revolution must put an end to, by giving back their complete freedom to the masses, groups, communes, associations, individuals even, and by destroying once and for all the historic cause of all the violent acts, the power, and the very existence, of the State. The State must carry away in its fall all the injustices of the juridical law with all the lies of the various religions, this law and these religions never having been anything but the enforced consecration (as much ideological as actual) of all the violence represented, guaranteed and licensed by the State.

It is clear that freedom will never be given to mankind, and that the real interests of society, of all the groups and local organizations as well as all the individuals who make up society, will only be able to find real satisfaction when there are no more States. It is clear that all the so-called general interests of society, which the State is alleged to represent and which in reality are nothing but the constant and general negation of the positive interests of the regions, communes, associations and the largest number of individuals subjected to the State, constitute an abstraction, a fiction, a lie, and that the State is like one great slaughter-house, and like an immense graveyard where, in the shadow and under the pretext of this abstraction, there come all the real aspirations, all the living initiatives of a nation, to let themselves be generously and sanctimoniously sacrificed and buried. And since no abstraction ever exists by itself or for itself, since it has neither legs to walk on, nor arms to create with, nor stomach to digest this mass of victims which it is given to devour, it is plain that, in exactly the same way that the religious or heavenly abstraction, God, represents in reality the very positive and very real interests of a privileged caste, the clergy (its terrestrial counterpart), so the political abstraction, the State, represents the no less real and positive interests of the class which is principally if not exclusively exploiting people today and which is moreover tending to swallow up all the others, the bourgeoisie. And just as the clergy is always divided and today is tending to divide itself all the more into a very powerful and a very rich minority and a majority which is very subordinate and rather poor, so, in the same way, the bourgeoisie and its diverse social and political organizations in industry, agriculture, banking and commerce, just as in all the administrative, financial, judicial, university, police and military functions of the State, is tending to weld itself further each day into a truly dominant oligarchy and a countless mass of creatures who are more or less vainglorious and more or less fallen, living in a perpetual illusion and pushed back inevitably more and more into the proletariat by an irresistable force, that of present-day economic development, and reduced to serving as blind instruments of this all-powerful oligarchy.

The abolition of the Church and of the State must be the first and indispensable condition of the real emancipation of society; after which (and only after which) it can, and must, organize itself in a different fashion, but not from top to bottom and according to an ideal plan, dreamt up by a few wise men or scholars, or even by force of decrees put out by some dictatorial force or even by a national assembly, elected by universal suffrage. Such a system, as I have already said, would lead inevitably to the creation of a new State, and consequently to the formation of a governmental aristocracy, that is, an entire class of people, having nothing in common with the mass of the people. Certainly, that class would begin again to exploit the people and subject them under the pretext of the common good or in order to save the State.

The future social organization must be made solely from the bottom upwards, by the free association or federation of workers, firstly in their unions, then in the communes, regions, nations and finally in a great federation, international and universal. Then alone will be realized the true and life-giving order of freedom and the common good, that order which, far from denying, on the contrary affirms and brings into harmony the interests of individuals and of society.

# P. A. KROPOTKIN
## From *The State: Its Historic Role*

In taking the state and its historic role as the subject for this study, I think I am satisfying a need much felt at the present time: to examine in depth the very concept of the state; to study its essence, its past role, and the part it may be called upon to play in the future.

It is above all over the question of the state that socialists are divided. Two main currents can be discerned in the factions that exist among us, which correspond to differences in tempermanent as well as in ways of thinking, but above all to the extent that one believes in the coming revolution.

There are those, on the one hand, who hope to achieve the social revolution through the state by preserving and even extending most of its powers to be used for the revolution. And there are those like ourselves who see in the state, both in its present form, in its very essence, and in whatever guise it might appear, an obstacle to the social revolution, the greatest hindrance to the birth of a society

273

based on equality and liberty, as well as the historic means designed to prevent this blossoming. The latter work to abolish the state and not to reform it.

It is clear that the division is a deep one. It corresponds with two divergent currents which in our time are manifest in all philosophical thought, in literature as well as in action. And if the prevailing views on the state remain as obscure as they are today, there is no doubt whatsoever that when – and we hope, soon – communist ideas are subjected to practical application in the daily life of communities, it will be on the question of the state that the most stubborn struggles will be waged.

Having so often criticized the state as it is today it becomes necessary to seek the reason for its emergence, to study in depth its past role, and to compare it with the institutions that it has replaced.

First of all let us be agreed as to what we wish to include in the term the state.

There is, of course, the German school which enjoys confusing state with society. The best German thinkers and many among the French are guilty of this confusion because they cannot conceive of society without a concentration of the state; and because of this anarchists are usually accused of wanting to 'destroy society' and of advocating a return to 'the permanent war of each against all.'

Yet to argue this is to overlook altogether the advances made in the domain of history during the last thirty-odd years; it is to overlook the fact that man lived in societies for thousands of years before the state had been heard of; it is to forget that so far as Europe is concerned the state is of recent origin – it barely goes back to the sixteenth century; finally, it is to ignore that the most glorious periods in man's history are those in which civil liberties and communal life had not yet been destroyed by the state, and in which large numbers of people lived in communes and free federations.

The state is only one of the forms adopted by society in the course of history. Why then make no distinction between what is permanent and what is accidental?

Then again the state has also been confused with government. Since there can be no state without government, it has sometimes been said that what one must aim at is the absence of government and not the abolition of the state.

However, it seems to me that in state and government we have two concepts of a different order. The state idea means something quite different from the idea of government. It not only includes the existence of a power situated above society, but also of a territorial concentration as well as the concentration of many functions of the life of societies in the hands of a few. It carries with it some new relationships between members of society which did not exist before the establishment of the state. A whole mechanism of legislation and of policing has to be developed in order to subject some classes to the domination of others.

This distinction, which at first sight might not be obvious, emerges especially when one studies the origins of the state.

Indeed, there is only one way of really understanding the state, and that is to study its historic development, and this is what we will try to do.

The Roman Empire was a state in the real sense of the word. It remains to this day the legist's ideal. Its organs covered a vast domain with a tight network. Everything flowed toward Rome: economic and military life, wealth, education, even religion. From Rome came the laws, the magistrates, the legions to defend the territory, the prefects, and the gods. The whole life of the empire went back to the senate – later to the Caesar, the all-powerful, omniscient god of the empire. Every province, every district had its capitol in miniature, its small portion of Roman sovereignty to govern every aspect of daily life. A single law, imposed by Rome, dominated the empire which did not represent a confederation of fellow citizens but was simply a herd of subjects.

Even now, the legist and the authoritarian still admire the unity of that empire, the unitarian spirit of its laws and, as they put it, the beauty and harmony of that organization.

But the disintegration from within, hastened by the barbarian invasion; the extinction of local life, which could no longer resist the attacks from outside on the one hand nor the cancer spreading from the center on the other; the domination by the rich who had appropriated the land to themselves and the misery of those who cultivated it – all these causes reduced the empire to a shambles, and on these ruins a new civilization was developed which is ours.

So, if we ignore the civilizations of antiquity, and concentrate our attention on the origins and developments of this young barbarian civilization, right up to the times when, in its turn, it gave birth to our modern states, we will be able to capture the essence of the state. This is better than if we had directed our studies to the Roman Empire or to that of Alexander of Macedonia, or to the despotic monarchies of the East.

In taking these powerful barbarian overthrowers of the Roman Empire as our point of departure, we will be able to retrace the evolution of our whole civilization from its beginnings up to the stage of the state. [...]

If one goes a little deeper into these different categories of phenomena which I have barely touched upon in this short outline, one will understand why – seeing the state as it has been in history, and as it is in essence today – and convinced that a social institution cannot lend itself to all the desired goals, since, like every organ, it developed according to the function it performed, in a definite direction and not in all possible directions – one will understand, I say, why the conclusion we arrive at is for the abolition of the state.

We see in it the institution, developed in the history of human societies, to prevent direct association among men, to shackle the development of local and individual initiative, to crush existing liberties, to prevent their new blossoming – all this in order to subject the masses to the will of the minorities.

And we know an institution which has a long past going back several thousand years cannot lend itself to a function opposed to the one for which and by which it was developed in the course of history.

To this unshakable argument for anybody who has reflected on history the reply we receive is almost infantile: 'The state exists and it represents a powerful ready-made organization. Why not use it instead of wanting to destroy it? It operates for evil ends – agreed; but the reason is that it is in the hands of the exploiters. If it were taken over by the people, why would it not be used for better ends, for the good of the people?'

Always the same dream – that of the Marquis de Posa in Schiller's drama, seeking to make an instrument of emancipation out of absolutism; or again the dream of the gentle Abbé Pierre in Zola's *Rome* seeking to make of the church the lever for socialism.

Take a concrete example in France. All thinking people must have noticed the striking fact that the Third Republic, in spite of its republican form of government, has remained monarchist in essence. We all have reproached it for not having republicanized France – I do not only say that it has done nothing for the *social* revolution, but that it has not even introduced the morality or simply the *republican* outlook. For the little that has been done in the past twenty-five years to democratize social attitudes or to spread a little education has been done everywhere, in all the European monarchies, under pressure from the times through which we are passing. Then where does this strange anomaly of a republic which has remained a monarchy come from?

It arises from the fact that France has remained a state, and just where it was thirty years ago. The holders of power have changed the name but all that huge ministerial scaffolding, all that centralized organization of white-collar workers, all this aping of the Rome of the Caesars which has developed in France, all that huge organization to assure and extend the exploitation of the masses in favor of a few privileged groups, which is the essence of the state institution – all that has remained. And those cogs continue as in the past to exchange their fifty documents when the wind has blown down a tree onto the highway and to transfer the millions deducted from the nation to the coffers of the privileged. The official stamp on the documents has changed; but the state, its spirit, its organs, its territorial centralization, its centralization of functions, its favoritism, its role as creator of monopolies have remained. Like an octopus they go on spreading their tentacles over the country.

The republicans, and I am speaking of the sincere ones – had cherished the illusion that one could 'utilize the organization of the state' to effect a change in the republican direction, and these are the results. Whereas it was necessary to break up the old organization, *shatter the state* and rebuild a new organization, by beginning from the very

foundations of society – the liberated village commune, federalism,
groupings from simple to compound, free workingmen's associations – they thought of using the 'organization that already existed.'
And, not having understood that one does not make an historical
institution follow in the direction which one seeks to indicate – in the
opposite direction to the one it has taken over the centuries – they
were swallowed up by the institution.

And this happened, though in this case it was not even a question yet
of changing the whole of the economic relations in society! The aim
was merely to reform only some aspects of political relations between
men.

But after such complete failure, and in the light of such a pitiful experiment, there are those who still insist on telling us that the conquest
of powers of the state by the people will suffice to accomplish the
social revolution! – that the old machine, the old organism, slowly
developed in the course of history to crush freedom, to crush the
individual, to establish oppression on a legal basis, to create monop-
olists, to lead minds astray by accustoming them to servitude – will
lend itself perfectly to its new functions: that it will become the
instrument, the framework for the germination of a new life, to found
freedom and equality on economic bases, for the destruction of
monopolies, the awakening of society and the advance toward a
future freedom and equality!

What a sad and tragic mistake! To give full scope to socialism entails
rebuilding from top to bottom a society dominated by the narrow
individualism of the shopkeeper. It is not as has sometimes been said
by those indulging in metaphysical woolliness just a question of
giving the worker 'the total product of his labor'; it is a question of
completely reshaping all relationships, from those which exist today
between every individual and his churchwarden or his stationmas-
ter to those which exist between neighborhoods, hamlets, cities and
regions. In every street, in every hamlet, in every group of men gathered around a factory or along a section of the railway line, the
creative, constructive, and organizational spirit must be awakened in
order to rebuild life – in the factory, in the village, in the store, in
production, and in distribution of supplies. All relations between
individuals and great centers of population have to be made all over
again, from the very day, from the very moment one alters the existing commercial or administrative organization.

And they expect this immense task, requiring the free expression of
popular genius, to be carried out within the framework of the state
and the pyramidal organization which is the essence of the state!
They expect the state whose very *raison d'être* is the crushing of the
individual, the hatred of initiative, the triumph of *one* idea which
must be inevitably that of mediocrity – to become the lever for the
accomplishment of this immense transformation! ... They want to
direct the revival of a society by means of decrees and electoral
majorities ... How ridiculous!

**Kropotkin** Throughout the history of our civilization, two traditions, two opposing tendencies have contronted each other: the Roman and the popular traditions; the imperial and the federalist; the authoritarian and the libertarian. And this is so, once more, on the eve of the social revolution.

Between these two currents, always manifesting themselves, always at grips with each other – the popular trend and that which thirsts for political and religious domination – we have made our choice.

We seek to recapture the spirit which drove people in the twelfth century to organize themselves on the basis of free agreement and individual initiative as well as of the free federation of the interested parties. And we are quite prepared to leave the others to cling to the imperial, the Roman, and canonical tradition.

History is not an uninterrupted natural development. Again and again development has stopped in one particular territory only to emerge somewhere else. Egypt, the Near East, the Mediterranean coasts, central Europe have all in turn been centers of historical development. But every time the pattern has been the same, beginning with the phase of the primitive tribe, followed by the village commune, then by the free city, finally to die with the advent of the state.

In Egypt, civilization begins with the primitive tribe. It advances to the village commune and later to the period of the free cites, later still to the state which, after a period in which it flourishes, leads to death.

Development starts afresh in Syria, in Persia, and in Palestine. It follows the same pattern: the tribe, the village commune, the free city, the all-powerful state and ... death!

A new civilization then comes to life in Greece. Always through the tribe. Slowly it reaches the level of the village commune and then of the republican cities. In these cities civilization reaches its heights. But the East communicates its poisonous breath, its despotic traditions. War and conquests build up the empire of Alexander of Macedonia. The state asserts itself, grows, destroys all culture and again ... it is death!

In its turn Rome starts civilization over again. Once more one finds at the beginning the primitive tribe, then the village commune followed by the city. At this phase Rome was at the height of its civilization. But then come the state and the empire and then ... death!

On the ruins of the Roman Empire, Celtic, Germanic, Slavonic and Scandinavian tribes once more take up the threads of civilization. Slowly the primitive tribe develops it institutions and manages to build up the village commune. It lingers in this phase until the twelfth century when the republican city arises, and this brings with it the blossoming of the human spirit, proof of which are the masterpieces of architecture, the grandiose development of the arts, the discoveries which lay the foundations of natural sciences. But then the state emerges ... and then – death!

Yes: death – or renewal! *Either* the state forever, crushing individual and local life, taking over in all fields of human activity, bringing with it its wars and its domestic struggles for power, its palace revolutions which only replace one tyrant by another, and inevitably at the end of this development there is ... death! *Or* the destruction of the state, and new life starting again in thousands of centers on the principle of the lively initiative of the individual and groups and that of free agreement.

The choice lies with you!

# P. A. KROPOTKIN
## Letter to Lenin

Dmitrov, 4 March, 1920

Esteemed Vladimir Ilich,

Several employees of the postal-telegraph department have come to me with the request that I bring to your attention information about their truly desperate situation. As this problem concerns not only the commissariat of mail and telegraphs alone, but the general condition of everyday life in Russia, I hasten to fulfill their request.

You know, of course; that to live in the Dmitrov district on the salary received by these employees is *absolutely impossible*. It is impossible even to buy a bushel of potatoes with this [salary]; I know this from personal experience. In exchange they ask for soap and salt, of which there is none. Since [the price] of flour has gone up – if you manage to get any – it is impossible to buy eight pounds of grain and five pounds of wheat. In short, without receiving provisions, the employees are doomed to a very real famine.

Meanwhile, along with such prices, the meager provisions which the postal and telegraph employees received from the Moscow postal and telegraph supply center (according to the decree of August 15, 1918: eight pounds of wheat to an employee or to employees, and five pounds of wheat to incapacitated members of a family) *have not been delivered for two months already*. The local supply centers cannot distribute their provisions, and the appeal of the employees (125 persons in the Dmitrov area) to Moscow remains unanswered. A month ago one of the employees wrote you personally, but he has received no answer thus far.

I consider it a duty to testify that the situation of these employees is truly desperate. The majority are *literally starving*. This is obvious from their faces. Many are preparing to leave home without knowing where to go. And in the meantime, I will say openly that they carry out their work conscientiously; they have familiarized themselves with [their jobs] and to lose such workers would not be in the interests of local life in any way.

I will add only that whole categories of other Soviet employees can be found in the same desperate condition.

279

**Kropotkin**  In concluding, I cannot avoid mentioning something about the general situation to you. Living in a great center – in Moscow – it is impossible to know the true conditions of the country. To know the truth about current experiences, one must live in the provinces, in close contact with daily life, with its needs and misfortunes, with the starving – adults and children – with running back and forth to offices in order to get permission to buy a cheap kerosene lamp, and so forth.

There is now one way out of these trials for us. It is necessary to hasten the transition to more normal conditions of life. We will not continue like this for long, and we are moving toward a bloody catastrophe. The locomotives of the Allies, the export of Russian grain, hemp, flax, hides, and other things that are so indispensable to us will not help the population.

One thing is indisputable. Even if the dictatorship of the party were an appropriate means to bring about a blow to the capitalist system (which I strongly doubt), *it is nevertheless harmful for the creation of a new socialist system.* What are necessary and needed are local institutions, local forces; but there are none, anywhere. Instead of this, wherever one turns there are people who have never known anything of real life, who are committing the gravest errors which have been paid for with thousands of lives and the ravaging of entire districts.

Consider the supply of firewood, or that of last season's spring seed ...

Without the participation of local forces, without an organization from below of the peasants and workers themselves, it is impossible to build a new life.

It would seem that the soviets should have served precisely this function of creating an organization from below. But Russia has already become a Soviet Republic only in name. The influx and taking over of the people by the 'party,' that is, predominently the newcomers (the ideological communists are more in the urban centers), has already destroyed the influences and constructive energy of this promising institution – the soviets. At present, it is the party committees, not the soviets, who rule in Russia. And their organization suffers from the defects of bureaucratic organization.

To move away from the current disorder, Russia must return to the creative genius of local forces which, as I see it, can be a factor in the creation of a new life. And the sooner that the necessity of this way is understood, the better. People will then be all the more likely to accept [new] social forms of life. If the present situation continues, the very word 'socialism' will turn into a curse. This is what happened to the conception of 'equality' in France for forty years after the rule of the Jacobins.

With comradely greetings,

P. Kropotkin

# J. S. Mill and Durkheim on individualism

# 11

The English philosopher John Stuart Mill and the French sociologist Emile Durkheim both offer a defence of liberty and the rights of the individual, but apart from the fact that they agree in rejecting the social contract tradition, the perspectives from which they consider the issue could hardly be more different. Even so, their political conclusions are basically complementary. For Mill, liberty is a necessary condition of the full development of the individual as a human being, while Durkheim argues – with a typically French enjoyment of the appearance of paradox – that a shared respect for the rights of the individual is a condition of the maintenance of social solidarity and the authority of the collective in modern society.

## John Stuart Mill (1806–73)

J. S. Mill was the son of James Mill (see chapter 8), a close associate of Jeremy Bentham, the founder of the utilitarian movement. Mill wrote extensively on the nature of scientific method, and was especially concerned with the application of scientific method to the study of society. However, he is best known as the author of two essays, *On Liberty*, published in 1859, and *Utilitarianism*, published in 1861. He took an active part in the political reform movement of the 1830s and in later attempts to extend the franchise, particularly to women. He was in fact an early campaigner for women's rights, publishing *The Subjection of Women* in 1869. In 1865 he stood for parliament as a 'working man's candidate' and, much to his and everyone else's surprise, he won the seat and served for three years.

Mill's *On Liberty*, extracts from which are reproduced below, must be one of the most eloquent defences of the liberty of the individual in any language. Like his father, Mill was a strong advocate of representative democracy, but he did not see democracy as itself any guarantee of liberty, for it means 'not the government of each by himself, but of each by all the rest'. We must be on our guard against the tyranny of the majority. Thus Mill follows Locke (see chapter 4) in insisting that there are limits to the extent to which any government is entitled to interfere with the lives of individuals. However, the most serious threat to individual liberty comes, he believes, from public opinion and custom, for they can impose

> a social tyranny more formidable than many kinds of political oppression, since it leaves fewer means of escape, penetrating much more deeply into the details of life, and enslaving the soul itself. (Below, p. 293)

Mill seeks to identify a sphere of thought and action within which individuals should be free to follow their own judgement and tastes and to 'pursue their own good in their own way'. Mill's 'harm' principle, as it has come to be known, insists that one individual's liberty may be restricted only where this is necessary to prevent harm to others. Society is not entitled to prohibit a form of behaviour simply because the majority disapproves of it, and nor can restrictions on liberty be justified on the grounds that they are for the individual's own good.

The essay is of most interest for its account of *why* we should value liberty. Mill rejects any appeal to natural or 'abstract' rights (e.g. in the manner of Locke), nor is he content to claim that it is simply self-evident that liberty is a good thing. As a utilitarian he sees utility or happiness as the ultimate ground of appeal on all ethical questions, though this is not the simple thought it might seem. Sometimes Mill tells us that by happiness he means, following Bentham, 'pleasure and the absence of pain' (*Utilitarianism*, p. 257), but he also tells us that we must be concerned with

> utility in the largest sense, grounded on the permanent interests of a man as a progressive being. (Below, p. 295)

What Mill has in mind is the fact that human beings are capable of development and improvement, both as a species and as individuals. Our chief goal, he tells us, must be 'the highest and most harmonious development of [our] powers' (below, p. 297). The theme of human perfectibility is prominent in Rousseau's writing (see chapter 5) and in Christian thought generally. In fact Mill's thinking here owes more to Aristotle than to Bentham, though it is an Aristotle filtered through the German and English romantic movements, which had a strong influence on Mill. The good life is not a life of passive enjoyment but rather a life in which our natural powers are developed and exercised to the full.

What makes this a distinctively *liberal* conception of the good life is, firstly, Mill's belief that each individual possesses his or her own unique potential for self-development. There is not just one model of self-development, and Mill assumes that everyone (not just an elite, as in Aristotle) is capable of worthwhile self-development of some kind. Secondly, Mill places a high value on the fact of each individual making their *own* choices and following their *own* inclinations rather than slavishly following custom. This is, for Mill, an essential component in any worthwhile form of self-development. Both these ideas find expression in the claim that the goal of self-development is 'individuality'. As Mill uses this term it means, not mere eccentricity, being different for the sake of being different, but rather a certain sort of autonomy, the capacity to make judgements and choices that are genuinely one's own and not merely a reflection of the judgements and choices of others. Mill's argument is that liberty, in the sense of freedom from pressure to conform to the views of others, is a necessary condition of the exercise and development of certain central human faculties which are employed in making choices:

The human faculties of perception, judgement, discriminative feeling, mental activity, and even moral preference, are exercised only in making a choice. He who does anything because it is the custom makes no choice. (Below, p. 298)

To employ Isaiah Berlin's famous distinction between two kinds of liberty, Mill's argument is that negative liberty (freedom from interference) is a necessary condition of the development of positive liberty (autonomy), for the latter is not something we are born with. (See also chapter 3).

For Mill, we are each born with our own unique potential, but full individuality can be achieved only by 'self-culture', by gaining control over one's own impulses and making oneself into the person one would ideally wish to be. Mill does not deny that social influences play a significant role in making us what we are, but he believes that, given the right conditions, we are each capable of taking a hand in the formation of our own character and thus acquiring the power of making choices that are genuinely our own. The 'right conditions' here include negative liberty, i.e. freedom from undue pressure from others. But other people also have a positive role to play. To acquire a mind of one's own is not to cut oneself off from being influenced by others. If our opinions are to be more than mere prejudices, Mill tells us (*On Liberty*, chapter 2), we must understand the reasons for holding them, and we can come to do that only through being forced to defend our opinions against those who hold contrary opinions. Furthermore, to be capable of exercising our own judgement is to be capable of recognising when we are mistaken, which implies, once again, that we must be ready to listen to criticism. We acquire autonomy, Mill is saying, through coming to participate in a form of rational debate in which each individual is free to express his or her own opinions, while at the same time recognising an obligation to take account of the opinions of others. The autonomous individual is a rational individual, and the rational individual is the product of a certain kind of society, a society in which individuals are tolerant but mutually critical.

Nowadays, those who argue that we should be free to choose our own plan of life often do so on the grounds that which way of life is 'best' is a subjective matter to which there is no right answer. It is important to see that this is not Mill's position. Mill certainly believes that there is more than *one* right answer to this question – which way of life is right for a given individual depends on the specifics of their circumstances and character – but he does not believe that *all* answers are equally right. As far as the case for liberty is concerned, Mill sees no fundamental difference between the sphere of thought and the sphere of action. There are truths concerning the nature of the good life just as there are truths on other matters. The argument for individual liberty is partly that no one can claim to know with certainty what these truths are, hence the need for further 'experiments in living' and for the truth of one opinion to be tested against alternative views, and partly that playing an active role in choosing one's own plan of life is a vital ingredient in any fully human life. It is because Mill is himself so sure on this last point that he believes that individuals should be free to choose their own plan of life even if this means that they are likely to make mistakes.

Those for whom true freedom means spontaneity in the sense of following the impulses of the moment, will of course be unhappy with the suggestion that we should follow any sort of *plan* of life, whether of our own or anyone else's choosing. Mill believes that those who have chosen their own plan of life will be persons of energy and strong impulses, but it is clear that for him the truly free individual is someone who has at some point reflected carefully on the kinds of choices they face. For Mill, as for Rousseau and Kant (see chapters 6 and 8), true liberty is rational self-mastery.

Since Mill believes that the main threat to liberty comes not from government but from public opinion, his solution is a transformation in public opinion to be brought about through education and rational persuasion. (He is an 'idealist' in the sense that he believes that social change comes about through changes in ideas, and not, as Marx maintained, the other way round.) Mill wants to see many different conceptions of the good life flourish, but that in itself is not enough. Without abandoning our own convictions, and without abandoning the right to criticise or seek to persuade those who disagree with us, it is vital that we accept the right of others to pursue their own considered plan of life. It is also important that we are ready to listen to opposing views and accept that our own conception of the good life may need to be reconsidered.

### Emile Durkheim (1858–1917)

More than anyone else, Emile Durkheim was responsible for establishing sociology and anthropology as the empirical disciplines we know today. The son of French Jewish parents, he held academic posts in Bordeaux and later at the Sorbonne in Paris. Politically, he was committed to the liberal and individualist ideals of the French Revolution of 1789, but was keenly aware that the reality of nineteenth-century French society fell short of those ideals. As a sociologist, his chief concern was with the basis of social solidarity, which he believed could not be explained by reference to individual rationality as in the social contract tradition, or indeed by reference to any supposed feature of human nature. A related concern was with the implications of the rise of individualism, which Durkheim saw as the result of a historical trend towards the increasing internal differentiation of society (*The*

*Division of Labour*, 1893). While Mill saw modern society as a threat to individuality, Durkheim saw the value we attach to individuality as one of the distinctive products of modern society. In his classic study of the social causes of suicide (*Suicide*, 1897), Durkheim identified some of the costs of increasing individualism. But as the essay reproduced below ('Individualism and the Intellectuals', 1898) makes clear, he does not believe that it is either desirable or possible to return to older, more authoritarian forms of social order, as the conservative forces in French politics were seeking to do. For Durkheim, the individualist ideals of the French Revolution are the only possible basis of social solidarity in modern society.

Written at the time of the Dreyfus affair, 'Individualism and the Intellectuals' was Durkheim's only intervention in contemporary politics. Dreyfus, a Jewish officer in the French army, had been convicted of espionage by a military court without the opportunity to present a defence. Durkheim was a member of a group of intellectuals protesting at what they saw as a serious miscarriage of justice. An article by a prominent conservative writer maintained that these intellectuals, in insisting on the overriding importance of the rights of the individual, were advocating anarchy and threatening to undermine military discipline and the authority of the state. Durkheim's response was to argue that it is those who turn a blind eye to injustice and to violations of individual rights who threaten the authority of the state.

Durkheim begins his argument by distinguishing between two kinds of individualism. The first, the 'utilitarianism of Spencer and the economists', is simply a reflection of individual egoism and does indeed amount to anarchism because it is fundamentally hostile to the idea of collective authority. The second, the individualism which Durkheim wishes to defend, is that of Kant and Rousseau and involves a commitment to a universal principle of respect for the rights of all individuals. Being a moral principle, it is has a special impersonal authority that cannot derive from merely egoistic desires. On this point, Durkheim is not saying anything that Mill would disagree with, but Durkheim parts company with Mill and any form of utilitarianism when he tells us, echoing Kant, that the rights of the individual take precedence over calculations of interest, even where those calculations concern the interests of the majority. On the view Durkheim is defending, there is a sense in which the rights of the individual are sacred. Indeed Durkheim goes so far as to describe this individualism as a kind of religion – 'the cult of the individual'.

At the same time, Durkheim is at pains to emphasise that the individualism he supports is not opposed to 'the rights of the collectivity' and does not lead to anarchism. This individualism is committed, like that of Mill, to the 'autonomy of reason', the right of each individual to be guided by their own reason. But this does not imply a rejection of all authority. The point is only that 'my intellect requires reasons for bowing to the authority of others' (below, p. 306). Respect for authority will be forthcoming as long as that authority is rationally based. On

285

scientific matters, for example, I may properly defer to the judgement of the relevant experts without suffering any loss of rational autonomy. But there are some questions, for example those concerning fundamental human rights, which are within the competence of 'every man of good sense' and where deference to authority is out of place.

Up to this point, Durkheim shows himself a faithful follower of Kant and Rousseau, but there is one key respect in which he parts company with them. For those eighteenth-century writers, the moral law is a rule which each individual imposes on him- or herself, and its authority derives from the individual's own reason. For Durkheim, by contrast, it is an essential feature of moral ideas that they possess a higher authority than the will or consent of the individual, and that, Durkheim believes, can only mean the authority of society. The new religion of individualism, like all religions and all moral codes, is social in origin and it is from society that it derives its authority. Moreover, society gives rise to moral and religious ideas because society *needs* them, because they perform a social function:

a society cannot hold together unless there exists among its members a certain intellectual and moral community. (Below, p. 307)

Social order depends upon the existence of what Durkheim elsewhere calls a 'collective consciousness', a shared way of understanding the world. There must of course be a shared understanding of the rights and obligations attaching to the various roles and statuses within society, but there must also be a shared view of human nature and of the kind of life that is proper for a human being, and a shared view of the universe at large and of our place within it. It is the function of these more general shared ideas to provide a legitimation for the institutions of society by representing them as natural and just, in the way, for example, that medieval Christianity served to legitimate the institutions of feudal society.

Thus both Durkheim and Mill recognise the power which public opinion exerts over the individual, but while Mill sees it as a threat to individual freedom, Durkheim sees it as essential to the maintenance of social order. At first sight, Durkheim's insistence on the need for a shared way of seeing things would seem to support a conservative political stance – commonly accepted religious and moral views should not be challenged for fear of undermining social order – which would put Durkheim and Mill on opposite sides of the political fence. The expectation that Durkheim is arguing for conservative political conclusions is reinforced by his use of the same organic metaphor as Burke (see chapter 7): society is like an organism, a complex interconnected whole in which each part plays an important role in sustaining the whole and should not, therefore, be tinkered with.

But matters are not so simple. For a start, Mill too acknowledges that social order requires shared values which are held as sacred and treated, in practice, as beyond question (see *A System of Logic*, VI, X, p. 5). In Mill's ideal society, these values will include the principles of individual freedom and equality, but he accepts that in moving towards this ideal we cannot question all existing values at once. At any given time, there will need to be some shared values that are currently beyond question and which provide the basis of social stability.

Durkheim's view is also more complex. Social order depends on shared ideas, but different ideas are appropriate to different stages of social development. In primitive societies, social solidarity depends upon the collective consciousness imposing a strict, detailed and uniform code of conduct on all individuals. Modern industrial society differs from primitive society most fundamentally in possessing a much higher degree of internal differentiation, both in the sense of a greater degree of division of labour and also a greater variety and degree of specialisation of institutions within society. There is, Durkheim believes, a general historical trend towards increasing social differentiation arising, ultimately, from increases in population density and improvements in transport and communications. Where Mill sees a trend towards increasing uniformity and regimentation, Durkheim sees a trend towards increasing individuality. A shared understanding of the world is still important in modern society, but increasing social differentiation makes it both impossible and unnecessary for the collective consciousness to dominate the lives of individuals in the way it does in primitive society.

It is no longer *necessary* that the collective consciousness dominates the lives of individuals in modern society because a high degree of social differentiation brings with it a high degree of interdependence between the various parts of society, and that is itself an important source of social solidarity (Durkheim calls this 'organic' solidarity). Such domination of the individual by the collective consciousness is *impossible* in modern society because the increasing division of labour gives rise to great differences between the life experiences of different individuals, which in turn give rise to differences in the way they view the world. The collective consciousness can no longer impose either a uniform way of seeing things or a uniform code of conduct on all individuals. It ceases to prescribe the details of daily life and confines itself to laying down certain general principles whose interpretation and application in particular cases is necessarily left to the judgement of individuals. The result is a progressive freeing of the individual from the grip of the collective consciousness. The religious freedom which individuals enjoy in modern society is just one aspect of a growing freedom they possess to think and act according to their own judgement. Indeed, we are approaching the point where

the members of a social group will no longer have anything in common other than their humanity ... The communion of minds can no longer form around particular rites and prejudices ... In consequence, there remains nothing that men may love and honour in common apart from man himself. (Below, p. 307–8)

All societies need a shared religion in the sense that they need to agree on what is of fundamental and overriding importance to them, but soon the only thing we can agree is sacred will be individual human beings and their rights. In these circumstances, if the state violates those rights, it weakens our sense of their sacredness and thus threatens 'the sole link which binds us one to another'. It undermines the only ideas which can legitimate the authority of the modern state.

It is worth comparing Durkheim with Marx (see chapter 9) on this issue. Marx would readily agree that the cult of the individual and the idea of individual rights (especially property rights) have their origins in the needs of modern society, by which Marx understood capitalism. But for Marx, capitalist society is merely a step on the way towards communism in which there will be no class conflict and no need for 'bourgeois' notions of individual rights. It seems that for Marx, just as the state will wither away, so will the need for any shared principles of justice or morality. For Durkheim, that thought is absurd. Any society needs agreement on *some* principles of justice and morality, socialist society every bit as much as capitalist society. Moreover, Durkheim believes that history is pushing society in the direction of further differentiation, whether we like it or not (and whether capitalism stays or not). To reverse the trend towards individualist ideas we would need to

arrest the tendency of societies to become ever more extended and centralised, and stem the unceasing growth of the division of labour. Such an undertaking, whether desirable or not, infinitely surpasses human powers. (Below, p. 308)

For Durkheim, then, the idea of the sacredness of the individual is an idea that modern society needs, and it is therefore an idea that is here to stay.

It might seem that in appealing to the inevitable course of history, Durkheim is vulnerable to an objection that is often levelled at Marxism. If history can be relied upon to ensure the eventual triumph of individualism (or communism), why should we need to engage in political battles on its behalf? But that is less of a difficulty for Durkheim than it may be for Marx. In predicting the eventual triumph of individualist ideas, Durkheim assumes that individuals will exercise their own judgement in rejecting ideas that are no longer credible to them given their own experience and understanding of society. The ideas that will triumph are those that are acceptable to individual reason. Moreover, in a time of rapid social change, the new ideas that are needed may take some time to establish themselves. It is the task of intellectuals and politicians to articulate and defend the new consensus upon which the stability of the new kind of society depends. Thus there is a clear political role for supporters of individualism in hastening the adaptation of the collective consciousness to the needs of modern society.

'Individualism and the Intellectuals' is not very specific about the political content of the individualism it defends, but it is clear that

Durkheim is not proposing the kind of libertarianism, now associated with the political right, which urges a minimal role for the state. A concern for social justice is an essential component in Durkheim's conception of respect for the sacredness of the individual, and it is the task of the state to give effective expression to this concern. Elsewhere he suggests that a form of socialism would be the best expression of a commitment to the sacredness of the individual. However, it is perhaps fair to say that the sociological argument deployed in 'Individualism and the Intellectuals' leaves such questions open. If the idea of the sacredness of the individual can be interpreted in more than one way, then no one interpretation is uniquely recommended. If we want to extract a more specific conclusion from this line of argument, we need to ask ourselves which interpretation of individualism will *best* promote social solidarity, and that means asking which interpretation can most recommend itself to the judgement of the citizens of a modern state.

## Conclusion

Durkheim is surely right to see collective authority as depending on a set of shared ideas which represent that authority as legitimate. The further claim that in a modern, highly differentiated society these shared ideas must focus on respect for the individual is also plausible and stands as a warning against the temptation to compromise individual rights when the authority of the state is perceived to be under threat. It is not clear that Durkheim has demonstrated that the ideas of individualism will eventually triumph. Perhaps they will not be strong enough for the task and the attempt to hold large modern societies together will collapse. But as a way of turning the tables on the conservative enemies of liberty in modern society, Durkheim's argument is highly effective. It is the conservative, not the liberal, who threatens to undermine social order and stability.

Note that Durkheim's own argument is directed towards showing that it is socially useful to encourage and uphold the belief that the individual is sacred, not that the individual is indeed sacred. The task of establishing the latter thesis he leaves, by implication, to Kant and Rousseau. However, J. S. Mill does offer us a direct defence of individualist values, and one which has the advantage, over Kant at least, that it makes no reference to God and is thus arguably more in tune with the needs of modern secular society. Whatever our differences, Mill hopes that we will all agree that the important thing is that all individuals should be able to develop and exercise their powers to the full, with a special priority being given to the power of choosing and judging for ourselves. Thus Mill's defence of individualist values appeals to a view of human nature, and a view of the good life for a human being, which he hopes we can all be persuaded to share.

There is nothing here that Durkheim would want to quarrel with, but not everyone will be persuaded. Even if we accept Mill's Aristotelian

289

emphasis on the importance of developing the key powers that distinguish us as human beings, we may not agree with Mill about the identity of those key powers. Thus Aristotle himself sees a life of intellectual contemplation as representing the highest development of our powers, while Marx sees human fulfilment as lying in the development of our capacity for free, creative labour, our capacity for making things. For a contemporary liberal like John Rawls (see 1993, Introduction), it is Mill's advocacy of a specific conception of the good life that is worrying. Isn't Mill contradicting his own liberal principles in ruling out certain ways of life as unsatisfactory? For Rawls, a defence of liberal principles in a modern, multicultural society like the United States must be addressed to everyone regardless of their individual conception of the good life. Mill's reply would be that he does not deny an individual's right to choose his or her own way of life, but the fundamental ground for insisting on that right is the liberal conviction that choosing for oneself is a vital ingredient in any satisfactory way of life. If that means that liberals cannot be tolerant of the way of life practised by certain minority groups, for example those that insist on arranged marriages, then so be it. Whether Rawls succeeds in his own attempt to defend liberal principles without relying on a specifically liberal view of the good life must be left for the reader to judge.

Suppose, however, we are persuaded by Mill's advocacy of individuality and are ready to accept his liberal view of the good life. We may still wonder whether freedom from constraint, and in particular freedom from pressure to conform to the views of others, is the best way of fostering the development of individuality in the sense that concerns Mill. We have already noted that Mill acknowledges a role for a certain kind of pressure from others, the challenge represented by opposing views and especially the pressure of reasoned criticism, in fostering individual autonomy. Durkheim would go further: the very concepts that make thought possible are social in origin. They constitute the community's standards for the correct use of language and the correct classification of things, and their authority is a form of social authority. All development of the intellect involves discipline, the observance of rules of correct thought. This is clearly true of modern scientific rationality, and it is arguable that it is also true of the kind of rational autonomy that is of concern to Mill. To be capable of thinking for ourselves is to be capable of imposing the necessary discipline on our own thoughts, and that is something we are in a position to do only if we have internalised a discipline that was first imposed upon us by others, and imposed upon us, moreover, before we were in a position to understand the need for it. From which it follows that subjection to pressure to conform to shared standards of correct thought and action is a necessary condition of acquiring a mind of one's own, and thus a necessary condition of the development of individuality in Mill's sense. A degree of social discipline, it can be argued, is a condition of rational autonomy.

This Durkheimian thought finds support in the writings of the

philosopher Wittgenstein and in empirical studies of child development, but it is a thought that Mill can probably accept without serious
damage to his argument for individual liberty. Mill explicitly restricts
the scope of his discussion to 'human beings in the maturity of their
faculties' who are 'capable of being improved by free and equal discussion' (below, p. 295), so he has no problem allowing that we can impose
rules on children in order to foster their development. Mill can also
accept that, even in a community in which there is free and equal
discussion, the individual will, and should, experience some degree of
pressure to conform to the views of others. But none of this affects
Mill's key claim, that if mature individuals are to be free to exercise
their own judgement, then pressure to conform to the views of others
must not go beyond that exerted by rational persuasion.

Finally, it is worth noting that if, like Mill, we value individuality and
see the highest good as consisting in everyone being able to develop
their own unique potential to the full, then there are other aspects of
modern society that should concern us. A highly differentiated society,
even one that takes a tolerant view of what individuals get up to in their
private lives, may still not be a society that offers them full scope for
self-development. It also matters what kinds of roles and occupations
society makes available to its citizens. The most enduring obstacle to
self-development may be, not the despotism of custom and the pressure of public opinion, but rather the constraints imposed on us by the
demands of our roles, both at home and at work. As Weber and Michels
point out (see chapter 12 below), bureaucracy is a central feature of
modern society and is a sworn enemy of liberty and individuality, not
least for those employed within it. Self-development is too important a
matter to be confined to our leisure hours, and it is also, for most of us,
too large a task to be pursued effectively without the support and co-
operation of others. The social and political conditions necessary for the
successful cultivation of individuality go far beyond ensuring that we
are free from the interference of those who disapprove of our chosen
way of life.

## References

Durkheim, Emile, 'Individualism and the Intellectuals', originally published in
     *Revue bleue*, 4th series, X (1898), pp. 7–13
Mill J. S., '*On Liberty*' and '*Utilitarianism*', both in *Utilitarianism*, ed. Mary
     Warnock, London: Fontana, 1962
Mill, J. S., *A System of Logic* London: Longman, 1970 (1st pub. 1843).
Rawls, John, *Political Liberalism*, New York: Columbia University Press, 1993.

## Further reading

The extract from Mill's *On Liberty* reproduced below includes key sections from
chapter 1 and most of chapter 3. The rest of the essay is of course well worth
reading, and chapter 2 ('Of the Liberty of Thought and Discussion') is particularly relevant to the theme of individuality. One of the best discussions of this

aspect of Mill's thought is to be found in chapter 5 of C. L. Ten, *Mill on Liberty* (Oxford: Oxford University Press, 1980). Isaiah Berlin's distinction between positive and negative liberty, and his own reflections on Mill, are to be found in his 'Two Concepts of Liberty' (in Berlin, *Four Essays on Liberty*, Oxford: Oxford University Press, 1969). That essay can also be found, along with other useful discussions of Mill and the full text of 'On Liberty', in John Gray and G. W. Smith (eds), *J S Mill On Liberty in Focus* (London: Routledge, 1991).

Durkheim's ideas on individualism are developed in *The Division of Labour* and in *Suicide*, useful extracts from which can be found in K. Thompson (ed.), *Readings from Emile Durkheim* (London: Routledge, 1985). For a quick overview of Durkheim's approach, see Anthony Giddens, *Durkheim* (London: Fontana, 1978). Discussions of the theme of this chapter can be found in Joseph Neyer's 'Individualism and Socialism in Durkheim' (in Emile Durkheim *et al.*, *Essays on Sociology and Philosophy*. ed. K. H. Wolf, New York: Harper and Row, 1960) and in Richard Bellamy *Liberalism and Modern Society* (Cambridge: Polity Press, 1992), chapters 2 and 3. For anticipations of Durkheim's view of the role of religion, see J.-J. Rousseau, *The Social Contract* (trans. Maurice Cranston, Harmondsworth: Penguin, 1968) Book IV, chapter 8 'The Civil Religion'.

More general discussions of the theme of individualism can be found in Georg Simmel, *On Individuality and Social Forms* (Chicago: University of Chicago Press, 1971), chapters 15 and 18, Steven Lukes *Individualism* (Oxford: Blackwell, 1973). For a contemporary discussion of the basis of liberal ideas, see John Rawls, *Political Liberalism* (New York: Columbia University Press, 1993).

### Seminar questions

Does Mill make out a persuasive case for valuing individuality?

Is Mill right when he claims that there are just two requisites for the development of individuality: 'freedom and variety of situations'?

Why does Durkheim think that it is those who disregard the rights of individuals who threaten social order?

Does Durkheim succeed in showing that 'it is possible, without contradiction, to be an individualist while asserting that the individual is the product of society, rather than its cause'?

# J. S. Mill
## From *On Liberty*

### CHAPTER I   INTRODUCTORY

The subject of this Essay is [...] Civil, or Social Liberty: the nature and
limits of the power which can be legitimately exercised by society
over the individual.

Like other tyrannies, the tyranny of the majority was at first, and is still
vulgarly, held in dread, chiefly as operating through the acts of the
public authorities. But reflecting persons perceived that when society
is itself the tyrant – society collectively over the separate individuals
who compose it – its means of tyrannising are not restricted to the
acts which it may do by the hands of its political functionaries.
Society can and does execute its own mandates: and if it issues wrong
mandates instead of right, or any mandates at all in the things with
which it ought not to meddle, it practises a social tyranny more
formidable than many kinds of political oppression, since, though
not usually upheld by such extreme penalties, it leaves fewer means
of escape, penetrating much more deeply into the details of life, and
enslaving the soul itself. Protection, therefore, against the tyranny of
the magistrate is not enough: there needs protection also against the
tyranny of the prevailing opinion and feeling; against the tendency
of society to impose, by other means than civil penalties, its own
ideas and practices as rules of conduct on those who dissent from
them; to fetter the development, and, if possible, prevent the formation, of any individuality not in harmony with its ways, and compels
all characters to fashion themselves upon the model of its own. There
is a limit to the legitimate interference of collective opinion with individual independence: and to find that limit, and maintain it against
encroachment, is as indispensable to a good condition of human
affairs, as protection against political despotism.

But though this proposition is not likely to be contested in general
terms, the practical question, where to place the limit – how to make
the fitting adjustment between individual independence and social
control – is a subject on which nearly everything remains to be done.
All that makes existence valuable to any one, depends on the enforcement of restraints upon the actions of other people. Some rules of
conduct, therefore, must be imposed, by law in the first place, and by
opinion on many things which are not fit subjects for the operation
of law. What these rules should be is the principal question in human
affairs; but if we except a few of the most obvious cases, it is one of
those which least progress has been made in resolving. No two ages,
and scarcely any two countries, have decided it alike; and the decision of one age or country is a wonder to another. Yet the people of
any given age and country no more suspect any difficulty in it, than
if it were a subject on which mankind had always been agreed. The
rules which obtain among themselves appear to them self-evident

293

and self-justifying. This all but universal illusion is one of the examples of the magical influence of custom, which is not only, as the proverb says, a second nature, but is continually mistaken for the first. The effect of custom, in preventing any misgiving respecting the rules of conduct which mankind impose on one another, is all the more complete because the subject is one on which it is not generally considered necessary that reasons should be given, either by one person to others or by each to himself. People are accustomed to believe, and have been encouraged in the belief by some who aspire to the character of philosophers, that their feelings, on subjects of this nature, are better than reasons, and render reasons unnecessary. The practical principle which guides them to their opinions on the regulation of human conduct, is the feeling in each person's mind that everybody should be required to act as he, and those with whom he sympathises, would like them to act. No one, indeed, acknowledges to himself that his standard of judgment is his own liking; but an opinion on a point of conduct, not supported by reasons, can only count as one person's preference; and if the reasons, when given, are a mere appeal to a similar preference felt by other people, it is still only many people's liking instead of one. To an ordinary man, however, his own preference, thus supported, is not only a perfectly satisfactory reason, but the only one he generally has for any of his notions of morality, taste, or propriety, which are not expressly written in his religious creed; and his chief guide in the interpretation even of that.

[...]

The object of this Essay is to assert one very simple principle, as entitled to govern absolutely the dealings of society with the individual in the way of compulsion and control, whether the means used be physical force in the form of legal penalties, or the moral coercion of public opinion. That principle is, that the sole end for which mankind are warranted, individually or collectively, in interfering with the liberty of action of any of their number, is self-protection. That the only purpose for which power can be rightfully exercised over any member of a civilised community, against his will, is to prevent harm to others. His own good, either physical or moral, is not a sufficient warrant. He cannot rightfully be compelled to do or forbear because it will be better for him to do so, because it will make him happier, because, in the opinion of others, to do so would be wise, or even right. These are good reasons for remonstrating with him, or reasoning with him, or persuading him, or entreating him, but not for compelling him, or visiting him with any evil in case he do otherwise. To justify that, the conduct from which it is desired to deter him must be calculated to produce evil to some one else. The only part of the conduct of any one, for which he is amenable to society, is that which concerns others. In the part which merely concerns himself, his independence is, of right, absolute. Over himself, over his own body and mind, the individual is sovereign.

It is, perhaps, hardly necessary to say that this doctrine is meant to apply only to human beings in the maturity of their faculties. We are not speaking of children, or of young persons below the age which the law may fix as that of manhood or womanhood. Those who are still in a state to require being taken care of by others, must be protected against their own actions as well as against external injury. For the same reason, we may leave out of consideration those backward states of society in which the race itself may be considered as in its nonage. The early difficulties in the way of spontaneous progress are so great, that there is seldom any choice of means for overcoming them; and a ruler full of the spirit of improvement is warranted in the use of any expedients that will attain an end, perhaps otherwise unattainable. Despotism is a legitimate mode of government in dealing with barbarians, provided the end be their improvement, and the means justified by actually effecting that end. Liberty, as a principle, has no application to any state of things anterior to the time when mankind have become capable of being improved by free and equal discussion.

[...]

It is proper to state that I forego any advantage which could be derived to my argument from the idea of abstract right, as a thing independent of utility. I regard utility as the ultimate appeal on all ethical questions; but it must be utility in the largest sense, grounded on the permanent interests of a man as a progressive being. Those interests, I contend, authorise the subjection of individual spontaneity to external control, only in respect to those actions of each, which concern the interest of other people. If any one does an act hurtful to others, there is a *prima facie* case for punishing him, by law, or, where legal penalties are not safely applicable, by general disapprobation.

[...]

There is a sphere of action in which society, as distinguished from the individual, has, if any, only an indirect interest; comprehending all that portion of a person's life and conduct which affects only himself, or if it also affects others, only with their free, voluntary, and undeceived consent and participation. When I say only himself, I mean directly, and in the first instance; for whatever affects himself, may affect others through himself; and the objection which may be grounded on this contingency, will receive consideration in the sequel. This, then, is the appropriate region of human liberty. It comprises, first, the inward domain of consciousness; demanding liberty of conscience in the most comprehensive sense; liberty of thought and feeling; absolute freedom of opinion and sentiment on all subjects, practical or speculative, scientific, moral, or theological. The liberty of expressing and publishing opinions may seem to fall under a different principle, since it belongs to that part of the conduct of an individual which concerns other people; but, being almost of as much importance as the liberty of thought itself, and resting in great part on the same reason, is practically inseparable from it. Secondly,

295

the principle requires liberty of tastes and pursuits; of framing the plan of our life to suit our own character; of doing as we like, subject to such consequences as may follow: without impediment from our fellow-creatures, so long as what we do does not harm them, even though they should think our conduct foolish, perverse, or wrong. Thirdly, from this liberty of each individual, follows the liberty, within the same limits, of combination among individuals; freedom to unite, for any purpose not involving harm to others: the persons combining being supposed to be of full age, and not forced or deceived.

No society in which these liberties are not, on the whole, respected, is free, whatever may be its form of government; and none is completely free in which they do not exist absolute and unqualified. The only freedom which deserves the name, is that of pursuing our own good in our own way, so long as we do not attempt to deprive others of theirs, or impede their efforts to obtain it. Each is the proper guardian of his own health, whether bodily, *or* mental and spiritual. Mankind are greater gainers by suffering each other to live as seems good to themselves, than by compelling each to live as seems good to the rest.

Though this doctrine is anything but new, and, to some persons, may have the air of a truism, there is no doctrine which stands more directly opposed to the general tendency of existing opinion and practice. Society has expended fully as much effort in the attempt (according to its lights) to compel people to conform to its notions of personal as of social excellence.

[...]

There is in the world at large an increasing inclination to stretch unduly the powers of society over the individual, both by the force of opinion and even by that of legislation; and as the tendency of all the changes taking place in the world is to strengthen society, and diminish the power of the individual, this encroachment is not one of the evils which tend spontaneously to disappear, but, on the contrary, to grow more and more formidable. The disposition of mankind, whether as rulers or as fellow-citizens, to impose their own opinions and inclinations as a rule of conduct on others, is so energetically supported by some of the best and by some of the worst feelings incident to human nature, that it is hardly ever kept under restraint by anything but want of power; and as the power is not declining, but growing, unless a strong barrier of moral conviction can be raised against the mischief, we must expect, in the present circumstances of the world, to see it increase.

## CHAPTER III   OF INDIVIDUALITY, AS ONE OF THE ELEMENTS OF WELL BEING

Such being the reasons which make it imperative that human beings should be free to form opinions, and to express their opinions without reserve; and such the baneful consequences to the intellectual, and through that to the moral nature of man, unless this liberty is either conceded, or asserted in spite of prohibition; let us next examine whether the same reasons do not require that men should be free to act upon their opinions – to carry these out in their lives, without hindrance, either physical or moral, from their fellow-men, so long as it is at their own risk and peril. [...] That mankind are not infallible; that their truths, for the most part, are only half-truths; that unity of opinion, unless resulting from the fullest and freest comparison of opposite opinions, is not desirable, and diversity not an evil, but a good, until mankind are much more capable than at present of recognising all sides of the truth, are principles applicable to men's modes of action, not less than to their opinions. As it is useful that while mankind are imperfect there should be different opinions, so it is that there should be different experiments of living; that free scope should be given to varieties of character, short of injury to others; and that the worth of different modes of life should be proved practically, when any one thinks fit to try them. It is desirable, in short, that in things which do not primarily concern others, individuality should assert itself. Where, not the person's own character, but the traditions or customs of other people are the rule of conduct, there is wanting one of the principal ingredients of human happiness, and quite the chief ingredient of individual and social progress.

In maintaining this principle, the greatest difficulty to be encountered does not lie in the appreciation of means towards an acknowledged end, but in the indifference of persons in general to the end itself. If it were felt that the free development of individuality is one of the leading essentials of well-being; that it is not only a co-ordinate element with all that is designated by the terms civilisation, instruction, education, culture, but is itself a necessary part and condition of all those things; there would be no danger that liberty should be undervalued, and the adjustment of the boundaries between it and social control would present no extraordinary difficulty. But the evil is, that individual spontaneity is hardly recognised by the common modes of thinking as having any intrinsic worth, or deserving any regard on its own account. The majority, being satisfied with the ways of mankind as they now are (for it is they who make them what they are), cannot comprehend why those ways should not be good enough for everybody; and what is more, spontaneity forms no part of the ideal of the majority of moral and social reformers, but is rather looked on with jealousy, as a troublesome and perhaps rebellious obstruction to the general acceptance of what these reformers, in their own judgment, think would be best for mankind. Few persons, out of Germany, even comprehend the meaning of the doctrine which Wilhelm von Humboldt, so eminent both as a *savant* and as a politician, made the text of a treatise – that 'the end of man, or that which is prescribed by the eternal or immutable dictates of reason, and not suggested by vague and transient desires, is the highest and most harmonious development of his powers to a complete and consistent whole;' that, therefore, the object 'towards which every human being must ceaselessly direct his efforts, and on which especially those who design to influence their fellow-men must ever keep their eyes, is the individuality of power and development;' that for this there are two requisites, 'freedom and variety of situations;' and that from the union of these arise 'individual vigour and manifold diversity,' which combine themselves in 'originality.'[1]

Little, however, as people are accustomed to a doctrine like that of Von Humboldt, and surprising as it may be to them to find so high a value attached to individuality, the question, one must nevertheless think, can only be one of degree. No one's idea of excellence in conduct is that people should do absolutely nothing but copy one another. No one would assert that people ought not to put into their mode of life, and into the conduct of their concerns, any impress whatever of their own judgment, or their own individual character. On the other hand, it would be absurd to pretend that people ought to live as if nothing whatever had been known in the world before they came into it; as if experience had as yet done nothing towards showing that one mode of existence, or of conduct, is preferable to another. Nobody denies that people should be so taught and trained in youth as to know and benefit by the ascertained results of human experience. But it is the privilege and proper condition of a human being, arrived at the maturity of his faculties, to use and interpret experience in his own way. It is for him to find out what part of recorded experience is properly applicable to his own circumstances and character. The traditions and customs of other people are, to a certain extent, evidence of what their experience has taught *them*; presumptive evidence, and as such, have a claim to his defence: but, in the first place, their experience may be too narrow; or they may not have interpreted it rightly. Secondly, their interpretation of experience may be correct, but unsuitable to him. Customs are made for customary circumstances and customary characters; and his circumstances or his character may be uncustomary. Thirdly, though the customs be both good as customs, and suitable to him, yet to conform to custom, merely *as* custom, does not educate or develop in him any of the qualities which are the distinctive endowment of a human being. The human faculties of perception, judgment, discriminative feeling, mental activity, and even moral preference, are exercised only in making a choice. He who does anything because it is the custom makes no choice. He gains no practice either in discerning or in desiring what is best. The mental and moral, like the muscular powers, are improved only by being used. The faculties are called into no exercise by doing a thing merely because others do it, no more than by believing a thing only because others believe it. If the grounds of an opinion are not conclusive to the person's own reason, his reason cannot be strengthened, but is likely to be weakened, by his adopting

[1] *The Sphere and Duties of Government*, from the German of Baron Wilhelm von Humboldt, pp. 11–13.

it: and if the inducement to an act are not such as are consentaneous to his own feelings and character (where affection, or the rights of others, are not concerned) it is so much done towards rendering his feelings and character inert and torpid, instead of active and energetic.

He who lets the world, or his own portion of it, choose his plan of life for him, has no need of any other faculty than the ape-like one of imitation. He who chooses his plan for himself, employs all his faculties. He must use observation to see, reasoning and judgment to foresee, activity to gather materials for decision, discrimination to decide, and when he has decided, firmness and self-control to hold to his deliberate decision. And these qualities he requires and exercised exactly in proportion as the part of his conduct which he determines according to his own judgment and feelings is a large one. It is possible that he might be guided in some good path, and kept out of harm's way, without any of these things. But what will be his comparative worth as a human being? It really is of importance, not only what men do, but also what manner of men they are that do it. Among the works of man, which human life is rightly employed in perfecting and beautifying, the first in importance surely is man himself. Supposing it were possible to get houses built, corn grown, battles fought, causes tried, and even churches erected and prayers said, by machinery – by automatons in human form – it would be a considerable loss to exchange for these automatons even the men and women who at present inhabit the more civilised parts of the world, and who assuredly are but starved specimens of what nature can and will produce. Human nature is not a machine to be built after a model, and set to do exactly the work prescribed for it, but a tree, which requires to grow and develop itself on all sides, according to the tendency of the inward forces which make it a living thing.

It will probably be conceded that it is desirable people should exercise their understandings, and that an intelligent following of custom, or even occasionally an intelligent deviation from custom, is better than a blind and simply mechanical adhesion to it. To a certain extent it is admitted that our understanding should be our own: but there is not the same willingness to admit that our desires and impulses should be our own likewise; or that to possess impulses of our own, and of any strength, is anything but a peril and a snare. Yet desires and impulses are as much a part of a perfect human being as beliefs and restraints: and strong impulses are only perilous when not properly balanced; when one set of aims and inclinations is developed into strength, while others, which ought to co-exist with them, remain weak and inactive. It is not because men's desires are strong that they act ill; it is because their consciences are weak. There is no natural connection between strong impulses and a weak conscience. The natural connection is the other way. To say that one person's desires and feelings are stronger and more various than those of another, is merely to say that he has more of the raw material of human nature and is therefore capable perhaps of more evil, but certainly of more good. Strong impulses are but another name for energy. Energy may be turned to bad uses; but more good may always be made of an energetic nature, than of an indolent and impassive one. Those who have most natural feeling are always those whose cultivated feelings may be made the strongest. The same strong susceptibilities which make the personal impulses vivid and powerful, are also the source from whence are generated the most passionate love of virtue, and the sternest self-control. It is through the cultivation of these that society both does its duty and protects its interests: not by rejecting the stuff of which heroes are made, because it knows not how to make them. A person whose desires and impulses are his own – are the expression of his own nature, as it has been developed and modi-fied by his own culture – is said to have a character. One whose desires and impulses are not his own, has no character, no more than a steam-engine has a character. If, in addition to being his own, his impulses are strong, and are under the government of a strong will, he has an energetic character. Whoever thinks that individuality of desires and impulses should not be encouraged to unfold itself, must maintain that society has no need of strong natures – is not the better for containing many persons who have much character – and that a high general average of energy is not desirable.

In some early states of society, these forces might be, and were, too much ahead of the power which society then possessed of disciplin-ing and controlling them. There has been a time when the element of spontaneity and individuality was in excess, and the social principle had a hard struggle with it. The difficulty then was to induce men of strong bodies or minds to pay obedience to any rules which required them to control their impulses. To overcome this difficulty, law and discipline, like the Popes struggling against the Emperors, asserted a power over the whole man, claiming to control all his life in order to control his character – which society had not found any other suffi-cient means of binding. But society has now fairly got the better of individuality; and the danger which threatens human nature is not the excess, but the deficiency, of personal impulses and preferences. [...] In our times, from the highest class of society down to the lowest, every one lives as under the eye of a hostile and dreaded consorship. Not only in what concerns others, but in what concerns only them-selves, the individual or the family do not ask themselves – what do I prefer? or, what would suit my character and disposition? or, what would allow the best and highest in me to have fair play, and enable it to grow and thrive? They ask themselves, what is suitable to my position? what is usually done by persons of my station and pecu-niary circumstances? or (worse still) what is usually done by persons of a station and circumstances superior to mine? I do not mean that they choose what is customary in preference to what suits their own inclination. It does not occur to them to have any inclination, except for what is customary. Thus the mind itself is bowed to the yoke: even in what people do for pleasure, conformity is the first thing thought of; they like in crowds; they exercise choice only among things commonly done: peculiarity of taste, eccentricity of conduct, are shunned equally with crimes: until by dint of not following their own nature they have no nature to follow: their human capacities are withered and starved: they become incapable of any strong wishes or native pleasures, and are generally without either opinions or feelings of home growth, or properly their own. Now is this, or is it not, the desirable condition of human nature?

[...]

There is no reason that all human existence should be constructed on some one or some small number of patterns. If a person possesses any tolerable amount of common sense and experience, his own mode of laying out his existence is the best, not because it is the best in itself, but because it is his own mode. Human beings are not like sheep; and even sheep are not undistinguishably alike. A man cannot get a coat or a pair of boots to fit him unless they are either made to his measure, or he has a whole warehouseful to choose from: and is it easier to fit him with a life than with a coat, or are human beings more like one another in their whole physical and spiritual conformation than in the shape of their feet? If it were only that people have diversities of taste, that is reason enough for not attempting to shape them all after one model. But different persons also require different conditions for their spiritual development; and can no more exist healthily in the same moral, than all the variety of plants can in the same physical, atmosphere and climate. The same things which are helps to one person towards the cultivation of his higher nature are hindrances to another. The same mode of life is a healthy excitement to one, keeping all his faculties of action and enjoyment in their best order, while to another it is a distracting burthen, which suspends or crushes all internal life. Such are the differences among human beings in their sources of pleasure, their susceptibilities of pain, and the operation on them of different physical and moral agencies, that unless there is a corresponding diversity in their modes of life, they neither obtain their fair share of happiness, nor grow up in the mental, moral, and aesthetic stature of which their nature is capable.

[...]

The depotism of custom is everywhere the standing hindrance to human advancement, being in unceasing antagonism to that disposition to aim at something better than customary, which is called, according to circumstances, the spirit of liberty, or that of progress or improvement. The spirit of improvement is not always a spirit of liberty, for it may aim at forcing improvements on an unwilling people; and the spirit of liberty, in so far as it resists such attempts, may ally itself locally and temporarily with the opponents of improvement; but the only unfailing and permanent source of improvement is liberty, since by it there are as many possible independent centres of improvement as there are individuals.

# EMILE DURKHEIM
## From *Individualism and the Intellectuals*

I

There is a preliminary ambiguity which must be cleared up first of all. In order to facilitate the condemnation of individualism, it has been confused with the narrow utilitarianism and utilitarian egoism of Spencer and the economists. This is to take the easy way out. It is not hard, in effect, to denounce as an ideal without grandeur that narrow commercialism which reduces society to nothing more than a vast apparatus of production and exchange, and it is only too clear that all social life would be impossible if there did not exist interests superior to the interests of individuals. Nothing is more just than that such doctrines should be treated as anarchical, and with this attitude we are in full agreement. But what is inadmissible is that this individualism should be presented as the only one that there is or even that there could be. Quite the contrary; it is becoming more and more rare and exceptional. The practical philosophy of Spencer is of such moral poverty that it now has scarcely any supporters. As for the economists, even if they once allowed themselves to be seduced by the simplicity of this theory, they have for a long time now felt the need to temper the rigour of their primitive orthodoxy and to open their minds to more generous sentiments. M. de Molinari is almost alone, in France, in remaining intractable and I am not aware that he has exercised a great influence on the ideas of our time. In truth, if individualism had no other representatives, it would be quite pointless to move heaven and earth in this way to combat an enemy that is in the process of quietly dying a natural death.

However, there exists another individualism over which it is less easy to triumph. It has been upheld for a century by the great majority of thinkers: it is the individualism of Kant and Rousseau, that of the *spiritualistes*, that which the Declaration of the Rights of Man sought, more or less successfully, to translate into formulae, that which is currently taught in our schools and which has become the basis of our moral catechism. It is true that it has been thought possible to attack this individualism under cover of the first type, but that differs from it fundamentally and the criticisms which apply to the one could not be appropriate to the other. So far is it from making personal interest the object of human conduct, that it sees in all personal motives the very source of evil. According to Kant, I am only certain of acting well if the motives that influence me relate, not to the particular circumstances in which I am placed, but to my quality as a man *in abstracto*. Conversely, my action is wicked when it cannot be justified logically except by reference to the situation I happen to be in and my social condition, my class or caste interests, my passions, etc. That is why immoral conduct is to be recognized by the sign that it is closely linked to the individuality of the agent and cannot be universalized without manifest absurdity. Similarly, if, according to Rousseau, the general will, which is the basis of the social contract, is infallible, if it is the authentic expression of perfect justice, this is because it is a resultant of all the particular wills; consequently it constitutes a kind of impersonal average from which all individual considerations have been eliminated, since, being divergent and even antagonistic to one another, they are neutralized and cancel each other out. Thus, for both these thinkers, the only ways of acting that are moral are those which are fitting for all men equally, that is to say, which are implied in the notion of man in general.

This is far indeed from that apotheosis of comfort and private interest, that egoistic cult of the self for which utilitarian individualism has justly been reproached. Quite the contrary: according to these moralists, duty consists in averting our attention from what concerns us personally, from all that relates to our empirical individuality, so as uniquely to seek that which our human condition demands, that which we hold in common with all our fellow men. This ideal goes so far beyond the limit of utilitarian ends that it appears to those who aspire to it as marked with a religious character. The human person, whose definition serves as the touchstone according to which good must be distinguished from evil, is considered as sacred, in what one might call the ritual sense of the word. It has something of that transcendental majesty which the churches of all times have given to their Gods. It is conceived as being invested with that mysterious property which creates an empty space around holy objects, which keeps them away from profane contacts and which draws them away from ordinary life. And it is exactly this feature which induces the respect of which it is the object. Whoever makes an attempt on a man's life, on a man's liberty, on a man's honour inspires us with a feeling of horror, in every way analogous to that which the believer experiences when he sees his idol profaned. Such a morality is therefore not simply a hygienic discipline or a wise principle of economy. It is a religion of which man is, at the same time, both believer and God.

But this religion is individualistic, since it has man as its object, and since man is, by definition, an individual. Indeed there is no system whose individualism is more uncompromising. Nowhere are the rights of man affirmed more energetically, since the individual is here placed on the level of sacrosanct objects; nowhere is he more jealously protected from external encroachments, whatever their source. The doctrine of utility can easily accept all kinds of compromises, without denying its fundamental axiom; it can allow that individual liberties should be suspended whenever the interest of the greatest number demands this sacrifice. But there is no possible compromise with a principle which is thus put above and beyond all temporal interests. There is no reason of State which can excuse an outrage against the person when the rights of the person are placed above the State. If, therefore, individualism by itself is a ferment of moral dissolution, one can expect to see its anti-social essence as lying here.

One can now see how grave this question is. For the liberalism of the eighteenth century which is, after all, what is basically at issue, is not simply an armchair theory, a philosophical construction. It has entered into the facts, it has penetrated our institutions and our customs, it has become part of our whole life, and, if we really must rid ourselves of it, it is our entire moral organization that must be rebuilt at the same time.

## II

Now, it is a remarkable fact that all these theorists of individualism are no less sensitive to the rights of the collectivity than they are to those of the individual. No one has insisted more emphatically than Kant on the supra-individual character of morality and law. He sees them rather as a set of imperatives that men must obey because they are obligatory, without having to discuss them; and if he has sometimes been reproached for having carried the autonomy of reason to excess, it could be equally said, with some truth, that he based his ethics on an act of unreasoning faith and submission. Besides, doctrines are judged above all by their products, that is to say by the spirit of the doctrines that they engender. Now Kantianism led to the ethics of Fichte, which was already thoroughly imbued with socialism, and to the philosophy of Hegel whose disciple was Marx. As for Rousseau, one knows how his individualism is complemented by an authoritarian conception of society. Following him, the men of the Revolution, in promulgating the famous Declaration of Rights, made France one, indivisible, centralized, and perhaps one should even see the revolutionary achievement as being above all a great movement of national concentration. Finally, the chief reason for which the *spiritualistes* have always fought against utilitarian morality is that it seemed to them to be imcompatible with social necessities.

Perhaps it will be said that this eclecticism is self-contradictory? Certainly, we do not propose to defend the way in which these different thinkers have set about combining these two aspects in the construction of their systems. If, with Rousseau, one begins by seeing the individual as a sort of absolute who can and must be sufficient unto himself, it is obviously difficult then to explain how civil society could be established. But here it is a question of ascertaining, not whether such and such a moralist has succeeded in showing how these two tendencies may be reconciled, but rather whether they are in principle reconcilable or not. The reasons that have been given for establishing their complementarity may be worthless, and yet that complementarity may be real. The very fact that they are generally to be found together in the same thinkers offers at least a presumption that they are contemporaneous with one another; whence it follows that they must depend on a single social condition of which they are probably only different aspects.

And, in effect, once one has ceased to confuse individualism with its opposite , that is to say, with utilitarianism, all these apparent contradictions vanish as if by magic. This religion of humanity has all that is required to speak to its believers in a tone that is no less imperative than the religions it replaces. Far from confining itself to indulging our instincts, it offers us an ideal which infinitely surpasses nature; for we do not naturally have that wise and pure reason which, dissociated from all personal motives, would make laws in the abstract concerning its own conduct. Doubtless, if the dignity of the individual derived from his individual qualities, from those particular characteristics which distinguish him from others, one might fear that he would become enclosed in a sort of moral egoism that would render all social cohesion impossible. But in reality he receives this dignity from a higher source, one which he shares with all men. If he has the right to this religious respect, it is because he has in him something of humanity. It is humanity that is sacred and worthy of respect. And this is not his exclusive possession. It is distributed among all his fellows, and in consequence he cannot take it as a goal for his conduct without being obliged to go beyond himself and turn towards others. The cult of which he is at once both object and follower does not address itself to the particular being that constitutes himself and carries his name, but to the human person, wherever it is to be found, and in whatever form it is incarnated. Impersonal and anonymous, such an end soars far above all particular consciences and can thus serve as a rallying-point for them. The fact that it is not remote from us (for the very reason that it is human) does not prevent it from dominating us.

Now all that societies require in order to hold together is that their members fix their eyes on the same end and come together in a single faith; but it is not at all necessary that the object of this common faith be quite unconnected with individual persons. In short, individualism thus understood is the glorification not of the self, but of the individual in general. Its motive force is not egoism but sympathy for all that is human, a wider pity for all sufferings, for all human miseries, a more ardent desire to combat and alleviate them, a greater thirst for justice. Is this not the way to achieve a community of all men of good will? Doubtless it can happen that individualism is practised in quite a different spirit. Certain people use it for their own personal ends, as a means for disguising their egoism and escaping more easily from their duties towards society. But this deceptive misuse of individualism proves nothing against it, just as the utilitarian fictions of religious hypocrites prove nothing against religion.

But I now immediately come to the great objection. This cult of man has for its first dogma the autonomy of reason and for its first rite freedom of thought. Now, it will be said, if all opinions are free, by what miracle will they then be harmonious? If they are formed without knowledge of one another and without having to take account of one another, how can they fail to be incoherent? Intellectual and moral anarchy would then be the inevitable consequence of liberalism. Such is the argument, always being refuted and always reappearing, which the perennial adversaries of reason take up periodically, with a perseverance that nothing can discourage, each time a passing weariness of the human spirit puts it more at their mercy. Certainly, it is true that individualism does not go without a certain intellectualism; for liberty of thought is the first of all liberties. But why has it been seen to have as a consequence this absurd self-infatuation which would confine each within his own desires and would create a gap between men's minds? What it demands is the right for each individual to know those things that he may legitimately know. It does not sanction unlimited right to incompetence. Concerning a question on which I cannot pronounce with expert knowledge, my intellectual independence suffers no loss if I follow a more competent opinion. The collaboration of scientists is only possible thanks to this mutual deference. Each science continuously borrows from its neighbours propositions which it accepts without verifying them. The only thing is that my intellect requires reasons for bowing to the authority of others. Respect for authority is in no way incompatible with rationalism provided that authority be rationally based.

This is why, when one seeks to summon certain men to rally to a sentiment that they do not share, it is not sufficient, in order to convince them, to remind them of that commonplace of banal rhetoric, that society is not possible without mutual sacrifices and without a certain spirit of subordination. It is still necessary to justify *in this particular case* the submission one asks of them, by showing them their incompetence. When, on the other hand, it is a matter of one of those questions which pertain, by definition, to the common judgment of men, such an abdication is contrary to all reason and, in consequence, contrary to duty. For, in order to know whether a court of justice can be allowed to condemn an accused man without having heard his defence, there is no need for any special expertise. It is a problem of practical morality concerning which every man of good sense is competent and about which no one ought to be indifferent. If, therefore, in these recent times, a certain number of artists, but above all of scholars, have believed that they ought to refuse to assent to a judgment whose legality appeared to them to be suspect, it is not because, as chemists or philologists, philosophers or historians, they attribute to themselves any special privileges, or any exclusive right of exercising control over the case in question. It is rather that, being men, they seek to exercise their entire right as men and to keep before them a matter which concerns reason alone. It is true that they have shown themselves more jealous of this right than the rest of society; but that is simply because, as a result of their professional activities, they have it nearer to heart. Accustomed by the practice of scientific method to reserve judgment when they are not fully aware of the facts, it is natural that they give in less readily to the enthusiasms of the crowd and to the prestige of authority.

Not only is individualism distinct from anarchy; but it is henceforth the only system of beliefs which can ensure the moral unity of the country.

One often hears it said that only a religion can bring about this harmony. This proposition, which modern prophets feel it necessary to utter in a mystical tone of voice, is really no more than a simple truism over which everyone can agree. For we know today that a religion does not necessarily imply symbols and rites in the full sense, or temples and priests. All this external apparatus is merely its superficial aspect. Essentially, it is nothing other than a system of collective beliefs and practices that have a special authority. Once a goal is pursued by a whole people, it acquires, as a result of this unanimous adherence, a sort of moral supremacy which raises it far above private goals and thereby gives it a religious character. On the other hand, it is clear that a society cannot hold together unless there exists among its members a certain intellectual and moral community. However, having recalled this sociological truism, one has not advanced very far. For if it is true that religion is, in a sense, indispensable, it is no less certain that religions change, that yesterday's religions could not be that of tomorrow. Thus, what we need to know is what the religion of today should be.

Now, all the evidence points to the conclusion that the only possible candidate is precisely this religion of humanity whose rational expression is the individualist morality. To what, after all, should collective sentiments be directed in future? As societies become more voluminous and spread over vaster territories, their traditions and practices, in order to adapt to the diversity of situations and constantly changing circumstances, are compelled to maintain a state of plasticity and instability which no longer offers adequate resistance to individual variations. These latter, being less well contained, develop more freely and multiply in number; that is, everyone increasingly follows his own path. At the same time, as a consequence of a more advanced division of labour, each mind finds itself directed towards a different point of the horizon, reflects a different aspect of the world and, as a result, the contents of men's minds differ from one subject to another. One is thus gradually proceeding towards a state of affairs, now almost attained, in which the members of a single social group will no longer have anything in common other than their humanity, that is, the characteristics which constitute the human person in general. This idea of the human person, given different emphases in accordance with the diversity of national temperaments, is therefore the sole idea that survives, immutable and impersonal, above the changing tides of particular opinions, and the sentiments which it awakens are the only ones to be found in almost all hearts. The communion of minds can no longer form around particular rites and prejudices, since rites and prejudices have been swept away in the natural course of things. In consequence, there remains nothing that men may love and honour in common, apart from man himself. This is why man has become a god for man, and it is why he can no longer turn to other gods without being untrue to himself. And just as each of us embodies something of humanity, so each individual mind has within it something of the divine, and thereby finds itself marked by a characteristic which renders it sacred and inviolable to others. The whole of individualism lies here. That is what makes it into the doctrine that is currently necessary. For, should we wish to hold back its progress, we would have to prevent men from becoming increasingly differentiated from one another, reduce their personalities to a single level, bring them back to the old conformism of former times and arrest, in consequence, the tendency of societies to become ever more extended and centralized, and stem the unceasing growth of the division of labour. Such an undertaking, whether desirable or not, infinitely surpasses all human powers.

What, in any case, are we offered in place of this individualism that is so disparaged? The merits of Christian morality are extolled to us and we are subtly invited to rally to its support. But are those who take this position unaware that the originality of Christianity has consisted precisely in a remarkable development of the individualist spirit? While the religion of the Ancient City was entirely made up of material practices from which the spiritual element was absent, Christianity expressed in an inward faith, in the personal conviction of the individual the essential condition of godliness. It was the first to teach that the moral value of actions must be measured in accordance with intention, which is essentially private, escapes all external judgment, and which only the agent can competently judge. The very centre of the moral life was thus transferred from outside to within and the individual was set up as the sovereign judge of his own conduct having no other accounts to render than those to himself and to his God. Finally, in completing the definitive separation of the spiritual and the temporal, in abandoning the world to the disputes of men, Christ at the same time opened the way for science and freedom of thought. In this way one can explain the rapid progress made by scientific thought from the date that Christian societies were established. Let no one therefore denounce individualism as the enemy that must be opposed at all costs! One only opposes it so as to return to it, so impossible is it to escape. Whatever alternative is offered turns out to be a form of it. The whole question, however, is to know how much of it is appropriate, and whether some advantage is to be gained by disguising it by means of symbols. Now, if individualism is as dangerous as people say, it is hard to see how it could become inoffensive or salutary, by the mere fact of having its true nature hidden with the aid of metaphors. And, on the other hand, if that restricted individualism which constitutes Christianity was necessary eighteen centuries ago, it seems probable that a more developed individualism should be indispensable today; for things have changed in the interval. It is thus a singular error to present individualist morality as antagonistic to Christian morality; quite the contrary, it is derived from it. By adhering to the former, we do not disown our past; we merely continue it.

We are now in a better position to understand the reason why certain people believe that they must offer an unyielding resistance to all that seems to them to threaten the individualist faith. If every attack on the rights of an individual revolts them, this is not solely because of sympathy for the victim. Nor is it because they fear that they themselves will suffer similar acts of injustice. Rather it is that such outrages cannot rest unpunished without putting national existence in jeopardy. It is indeed impossible that they should be freely allowed to occur without weakening the sentiments that they violate; and as these sentiments are all that we still have in common, they cannot be weakened without disturbing the cohesion of society. A religion which tolerates acts of sacrilege abdicates any sway over men's minds. The religion of the individual can therefore allow itself to be flouted without resistance, only on penalty of ruining its credit; since it is the sole link which binds us one to another, such a weakening cannot take place without the onset of social dissolution. Thus the individualist, who defends the rights of the individual, defends at the same time the vital interests of society; for he is preventing the criminal impoverishment of that final reserve of collective ideas and sentiments that constitutes the very soul of the nation. He renders his country the same service that the ancient Roman rendered his city when he defended traditional rites against reckless innovators.

[...]

## IV

In truth, it is to be feared that this campaign has been mounted with a certain lack of seriousness. A verbal similarity has made it possible to believe that *individualism* necessarily resulted from *individual*, and thus egoistic, sentiments. In reality, the religion of the individual is a social institution like all known religions. It is society which assigns us this ideal as the sole common end which is today capable of providing a focus for men's wills. To remove this ideal, without putting any other in its place, is therefore to plunge us into that very moral anarchy which it is sought to avoid.[1]

All the same, we should not consider as perfect and definitive the formula with which the eighteenth century gave expression to indi-

---

[1] This is how it is possible, without contradiction, to be an individualist while asserting that the individual is a product of society, rather than its cause. The reason is that individualism itself is a social product, like all moralities and all religions. The individual receives from society even the moral beliefs which deify him. This is what Kant and Rousseau did not understand. They wished to deduce their individualist ethics not from society, but from the notion of the isolated individual. Such an enterprise was impossible, and from it resulted the logical contradictions of their systems.

vidualism, a formula which we have made the mistake of preserving in an almost unchanged form. Although it was adequate a century ago, it is now in need of being enlarged and completed. It presented individualism only in its most negative aspect. Our fathers were concerned exclusively with freeing the individual from the political fetters which hampered his development. Freedom of thought, freedom to write, and freedom to vote were thus placed by them among the primary values that it was necessary to achieve, and this emancipation was certainly the necessary condition for all subsequent progress. However, carried away by the enthusiasm of the struggle, solely concerned with the objective they pursued, they ended by no longer seeing beyond it, and by converting into a sort of ultimate goal what was merely the next stage in their efforts. Now, political liberty is a means, not an end. It is worth no more than the manner in which it is put to use. If it does not serve something which exists beyond it, it is not merely useless: it becomes dangerous. If those who handle this weapon do not know how to use it in fruitful battles, they will not be slow in turning it against themselves.
[...]
Thus, we can no longer subscribe to this negative ideal. It is necessary to go beyond what has been achieved, if only to preserve it. Indeed, if we do not learn to put to use the means of action that we have in our hands, it is inevitable that they will become less effective. Let us therefore use our liberties in order to discover what must be done and with the aim of doing it. Let us use them in order to alleviate the functioning of the social machine, still so harsh to individuals, in order to put at their disposal all possible means for developing their faculties unhindered, in order, finally, to work towards making a reality of the famous precept: to each according to his works! Let us recognize that, in general, liberty is a delicate instrument the use of which must be learnt, and let us teach this to our children; all moral education should be directed to this end. One can see that we will not be short of things to do. However, if it is certain that we will henceforth have to work out new objectives, beyond those which have been attained, it would be senseless to renounce the latter so as to pursue the former more easily, for necessary advances are only possible thanks to those already achieved. It is a matter of completing, extending, and organizing individualism, not of restricting it or struggling against it. It is a matter of using and not stifling rational faculties. They alone can help us emerge from our present difficulties; we do not see what else can do so. In any case, it is not be meditating on the *Politique tirée de l'Écriture sainte* that we will ever find the means of organizing economic life and introducing more justice into contractual relations!

# ALAN SCOTT

# Weber and Michels on bureaucracy

12

With Max Weber and those influenced by him – for example, Robert Michels, Joseph Schumpeter and Carl Schmitt – we arrive at a highly disillusioned picture of modern political life, in which concerns with democratic representation, or indeed with the just state, recede into the background and the concepts of 'power', 'rule' and 'domination' take centre stage.

## Max Weber (1864–1920)

Weber was born into a national-liberal bourgeois family in Erfurt, an industrial town near Jena and Weimar in south-east Germany. Despite periods of mental breakdown he had a glittering academic career. He became Professor of Economics, first in Freiburg (1894) and then in Heidelburg (1899). He was later Professor of Sociology in Vienna (1918) and finally of Economics again in Munich (1919). Weber was close to the political as well as the academic establishment, and was a leading figure in the debate about the Weimar Constitution.

Max Weber's writings have usually, and rightly, been interpreted as a critical response to Marx, though they are also in many respects a development of Marx's insights. In his methodological writings Weber criticised the kind of committed social science associated with Marxism. He argued that the social scientist should remain 'value free', or should at least abstain from making explicit value judgements. In his best-known work, *The Protestant Ethic and the Spirit of Capitalism*, he tries to undermine what he sees as Marx's overly economic explanation of the rise of capitalism. Marx ignores or underestimates the importance of the cultural context in which capitalism emerged and the simple fact that the activities of capitalists themselves embody culturally-specific beliefs and values. In his writings on inequality and class, Weber assails what he takes to be Marxism's mistaken view that people who have nothing more in common than the fact that they sell their labour for wages could possibly develop a community of interests or pursue common social and political aims. In terms of their 'life-chances' (another Weberian concept which has passed into common usage) and their 'market situation' (i.e. the rewards they can command for their labour), the conditions of wage labourers are too diverse for one real-istically to expect the emergence of a common 'class consciousness'.

Similarly, Weber's political writings, with which we are concerned here, have Marxism as one of their major targets (I shall suggest that liberalism is the other). Weber is particularly concerned to show that the state is not a mere instrument of class domination, but has a set of interests of its own and a power base relatively autonomous from that of the capitalist class, on the basis of which it can pursue those inter-ests. It is important to recognise at the outset that Weber is not saying that there is *no* relationship between economic and political privilege, any more than his Protestant ethic thesis is suggesting that the emer-gence of capitalism has nothing to do with 'material' economic factors. In both cases he is arguing that the relationships (between economics and politics, or between culture and capitalism) are too complex to be captured by any model of simple 'reflection' or causal 'determination'. How does he develop this argument with respect to politics and the state?

Weber's first argument concerns the nature of the state's power base. He accepts Marx's thesis that the capitalist enterprise rests upon its successful 'monopoly of the means of production', and that this monopoly has come about through the 'primitive accumulation' of those means; simply expressed, capitalism must wrest the means of production (e.g. tools, land, workshops) from the hands of working people as it sets about turning them into wage labourers whose only chance of subsistence consists in selling their labour in return for temporary access to those means of production and wages. But Weber goes on to argue that the development of the modern state parallels this process. Just as capitalism holds a monopoly over the means of produc-tion, so too the modern state has acquired a monopoly over the means of violence (or 'coercion'). Indeed, Weber defines the state as that insti-tution which has a legitimate monopoly over the means of coercion within a given territory. This means simply that the state is the only body which can legally employ violence, for example in war-making or legally-sanctioned punishment. Furthermore, just as capitalism has emerged only in the process of primitive accumulation of the means of production, so too has the modern state emerged through the primitive (and often no less bloody) accumulation of the means of violence. Autonomous warriors (e.g. European knights or Japanese samurai), feudal lords who were able to raise and support their own armies or armed retinue, criminal organisations (e.g. triads, organised drug traf-fickers, or terrorist organisations), all must have their access to instruments of coercion removed and their violent activity made illegal or subject to state control in order for state power to be consolidated. In other words, populations have to be *pacified* in the course of devel-opment of the modern nation state. The state, if it is to remain stable, cannot tolerate the presence of competing claims to the use of coercion within its territory. Where there are such competitors, for example as in the case of the Italian mafia, this competition is both a symptom of and a contributor to the weakness of the state. The emergence of the state is thus associated with institutional changes such as the spreading of a uniform legal regulation throughout the territory and of a judiciary to administer it, the raising of an army in the state's employ, and the emergence of a state-controlled police force, a civil service, the imposition of taxation to finance the above, etc.

With respect to Weber's critique of Marxism, the significance of the state's monopoly over the means of coercion is that it constitutes a power base autonomous from capitalism, outside the economic sphere. Indeed, in so far as the monopoly of the means of coercion requires economic resources — to which the modern state can gain access through taxation — the interests of the state and those of capitalism are to a degree competing and conflicting. But for Weber the relationship is also complementary. On the one hand, the state's need for revenue gives it an interest in sustaining and protecting commercial activity. On the other, the desire of commerce for a stable and predictable political and legal environment makes the successful monopoly of coercion a valuable precondition for commercial activity, though we should not forget here that many violent criminal activities also have a commercial aspect (e.g. the international drug trade).

The second main strand of Weber's argument concerns the nature of political 'rule' or 'domination' (*Herrschaft*) in modern societies. Modern states are characterised, he argues, by 'bureaucratic domination' and by 'legal-rational legitimation'. As Weber notes (below, p. 322): 'in a modern state real rule ... lies unavoidably in the hands of the civil service'. Famously, Weber distinguishes between three socio-political forms and the types of 'legitimation' which accompany them.

However, to understand this point we need consider another aspect of Weber's definition of the state. He defines the state not simply as that institution which has a monopoly over the means of coercion, but rather as that institution which has a *legitimate* monopoly over these means. It was Weber's view that rule (*Herrschaft*) cannot be maintained through force (*Macht*) alone; rather the effective and sustained exercise of power has to some degree to be recognised as *legitimate* by those over whom it is exercised. The constant use of force is resource intensive. 'Do this, or I'll hit you!' requires my presence; much more effective, then, to gain your co-operation through your acceptance that I have legitimate authority to tell you what to do. The state does not merely have *power* over us, it also has *authority*; that is to say there are at least some areas of our lives where we recognise the right of the state to exercise its power over us. Such authority can be legitimised in a number of ways: through an appeal to tradition ('things have always been done this way'), through personal charisma (obedience because of the real or imagined qualities of an individual — 'the authority of the extraordinary and personal *gift of grace* ..., the absolute personal devotion and personal confidence in revelation, heroism, or other qualities of individual leadership' (Weber in Gerth and Mills, 1948, p. 79), or through an appeal to proper procedure, legality, consistency in the application of rules, and so on. Weber regarded this last form of legitimation – which he called 'legal-rational' – as the characteristic form of legitimacy in modern societies. It is associated above all with one organisational form, bureaucracy.

Why are appeals to legal-rational legitimation considered by Weber to be characteristically 'modern'? In the *Protestant Ethic* and elsewhere, Weber argues that modern societies are characterised by the predominance of a particular kind of rationality. Modern social forms both encourage and presume an attitude of instrumental calculation. As our belief in tradition, magic and religion declines, so we lose any fixed or absolute standards with which to orient ourselves and guide our actions. Weber seems to accept that Nietzsche's famous dictum 'God is dead' should be the starting-point for an understanding of modernity. The death of God means the loss of externally validated standards and purposes, and in their absence we adopt an attitude of instrumental calculation, we become 'instrumentally rational'. Weber refers to this loss of externally validated (e.g. religious) reference points, and the substitution of an instrumental attitude, as a process of 'disenchantment' (*Entzauberung*) and 'rationalisation'. The capitalist enterprise with its emphasis on efficiency, profitability and calculation (even risks are 'calculated') is one of the two typically modern embodiments of this rationalist spirit. The other is bureaucracy.

Bureaucracies are characterised by 'impersonal' relations of sub - and superordination. As a bureaucrat I have, at least formally, only that authority which attaches to my office. Furthermore, the spheres in which I can exercise my authority – my area of competence – is precisely circumscribed by institutional rules and the relationship that my position (my 'office') has to others within the organisation. Finally, my authority has to be exercised in a particular way, namely through those procedures prescribed by the rules of the organisation. Paper, particularly the memo, is the chief mechanism through which commands are transmitted and by which decision-making processes and responsibility are traced. Bureaucracy for Weber implies an impersonal and formalised organisation that is essentially hierarchical; commands flow downwards, and those lower down in the hierarchy are mere functionaries. Thus the civil servant is one who is trained to implement commands:

The honour of the civil servant is vested in his ability to execute conscientiously the order of the superior authorities, exactly as if the order agreed with his own conviction. (Weber in Gerth and Mills, 1948, p. 95)

The image to which Weber returns again and again is that of the machine. The bureaucracy is a 'living machine', a 'congealed spirit', the '[machine] housing of servitude', etc. (below, p. 324). Efficiency and obedience are the key principles of bureaucracy:

Organized domination [*Herrschaftsbetrieb*, literally 'an enterprise of domination'], which calls for continuous administration, requires that human conduct be conditioned to obedience towards those masters who claim to

Weber offers a number of reasons for regarding the modern state and private business as parallel organisations: 'the modern state is just as much a "business" as a factory is' (below, p. 322). In the first place, they embody the same formal and instrumental rationality; rational calculation of cost, benefits and risks are the principles underlying decision-making in both spheres. Secondly, Weber argues that just as the worker has been stripped of the 'means of production', so too has the functionary in a bureaucracy been stripped of the means of administration and, within a modern army, the soldier the means of warfare. Weber thus extends Marx's analysis to the non-economic sphere by arguing that the modern office worker or soldier is just as dependent upon the bureaucracy or army to supply his or her 'means of production' as the worker is upon the factory owner. Finally, extending this point, employees in an office and modern soldiers are exposed to, or are subjects of, the same type of rational discipline which subjugates the will of the individual worker. Although Weber seeks the origins of this form of rational discipline in ancient army discipline and in monastic life in the Middle Ages, he argues that in its modern, developed form it has been honed to perfection on the factory floor.

Weber's analysis of bureaucracy, rationalisation and discipline is closely connected with his view of politics. In the first place, and most obviously, the organs of modern government are themselves bureaucracies, large-scale organisations run by civil servants in which decisions are made on a routine daily basis. But even more important is the effect of these bureaucratic organisations on society as a whole. According to Weber we are increasingly subjected to rational bureaucratic domination and discipline. To experience such discipline, one does not need to be a civil servant *within* the bureaucracy, it is enough to be a citizen in a bureaucratically governed state. Bureaucracy, and the forms of rationality and obedience it embodies, come to shape the society in its entirety; the society becomes totally administered. For example, Weber argues that 'bureaucracy inevitably accompanies modern *mass democracy* in contrast to the democratic self-government of small homogeneous units' (Weber in Gerth and Mills, 1948, p. 224). This realisation makes Weber deeply sceptical of the possibility of real democratic participation within the formally democratic structures of modern mass democracy:

The *demos* [the people] itself, in the sense of the inarticulate mass, never 'governs' larger associations; rather it is governed, and its existence only changes the way in which the executive leaders are selected and the measure of influence which the *demos*, or better, which the social circles from its midst are able to exert upon the content and the direction of admin istrative activities by supplementing what is called 'public opinion'. 'Democratization', in the sense here intended, does not necessarily mean an increasingly active share in the authority of the social structure. (Weber in Gerth and Mills, 1948, p. 225)

This analysis of bureaucracy and what some have called the 'totally administered society' provides Weber with the intellectual tools with which to criticise the assumptions of both Marxism and liberalism. Marxism, he argues, mistakenly assumes that the abolition of economic class inequality would mean the disappearance of *all* forms of inequality, for in Weber's view political inequality has a distinct source from economic inequality: political inequality derives from the state's monopoly over the means of coercion rather than the means of production. Thus it simply does not follow that the abolition of private ownership will result in the abolition of relationships of domination and subordination. Indeed, Weber goes on to argue most powerfully that the abolition of economic class differences would strengthen the hand of the state. Under capitalism, the state bureaucracies have at least a powerful competitor in the form of the bureaucracies of large economic enterprises. Where the means of production are socialised, economic as well as political power would be concentrated in the hands of the state. Under these conditions subordinate groups are even less autonomous than under capitalism. Weber's speech on the topic of socialism, given only a few months after the Russian Revolution (below, pp. 327–8), is extraordinarily prescient in its analysis of the unintended consequences of the socialist 'collective economy' model, and in its prediction that socialism would create both a new form of class conflict – between worker and state – and greater economic inefficiencies.

Weber was not just a critic of Marxism and socialism; he was also highly critical of the assumptions that lie behind liberal political theories. Although politically a liberal in the context of Germany in the late nineteenth and early twentieth centuries, Weber's analysis of bureaucracy and the administered society led him to the view that liberalism confuses the *form* of representative democracy with its *substance*. The organs of representative government – parliaments, regular elections, competitive party systems and the rest – are, he believes, less powerful and important than the routine decision-making going on within the executive. Weber argues that these democratic political institutions have less to do with representing the popular will than with providing a *legitimation* for decisions already taken and for the ever-increasing power of the state. The classical 'solutions' of liberalism – for example balance of power – are not insignificant for Weber (see below), but they do not begin to address the real source of power in modern societies. In the modern 'mass state', it is necessary to elicit at least the tacit support of some sections of the subject population. The elaborate structures of representation have this as their true aim rather than the free formation of a popular political will. Joseph Schumpeter (1883–1950) was later to reiterate this point, arguing that modern mass politics should be interpreted as competition for mass support *between* competing political elites (Schumpeter, 1943). Weber and Schumpeter are reminding us that questions of rule and leadership do not lose their significance within representative or 'liberal' democracies.

Weber offers us a very disillusioned – even pessimistic – account of the nature of the modern state and of the possibilities for democratic control within it. This is most evident where his analysis is applied to the very bodies – political parties and social movements – which are allegedly the bearers of popular political will. Here the argument is that, within the modern bureaucratically dominated state, even these organisations of 'political will formation' become hierarchical and undemocratic. Although Weber himself frequently made this point, its most famous advocate is Robert Michels, a friend of Weber's to whom Weber acted as intellectual mentor, and to whom we now turn.

## Robert Michels (1876–1936)

Born into a bourgeois family in Cologne, Michels completed a doctorate from the University of Halle before studying in France and Italy (which later became his adopted home). He started out as a socialist with strong syndicalist leanings, highly critical of the 'petit bourgeois' politics of the German and Italian socialist parties, but his politics later shifted to the far right and he came to support Mussolini's fascists. Michels' best-known work *Zur Soziologie des Parteiwesens in der modernen Demokratie* (translated as *Political Parties*, 1959) was an account and critique of 'oligarchical' tendencies in the German Social Democratic Party.

At the time he developed his ideas on political parties, Michels was still – unlike Weber – a socialist. His disenchantment with the timidity and 'petit bourgeois' character of the then still theoretically revolutionary Social Democratic Party in Germany led Michels to develop his theory that political parties inevitably developed 'oligarchical' tendencies as they became larger and better organised. Michels' famous 'iron law of oligarchy' (below, pp. 329–33) identifies a tendency within political parties – even, or especially, subversive ones – to acquire a leadership (the 'oligarchy') which becomes increasingly cut off from the mass of its supporters. Such parties, Michels argues, become on the one hand increasingly authoritarian in the way in which they impose the leaders' will on the membership in the name of 'party discipline', and on the other hand increasingly timid and ineffectual in the pursuit of their original political goals.

Michels' analysis of political parties neatly complements Weber's general political analysis. Today we even speak of 'party machines', that is we attribute to parties those same mechanical qualities which Weber attributed to bureaucratic organisations in general. Where Michels and Weber differ is in the significance they ascribe to these developments. As a syndicalist socialist, Michels is deeply disappointed with the failure of subversive parties to deliver on their democratic promise. As a national liberal, Weber is by no means convinced that this lack of direct democratic control is a bad thing:

These modern forms are the children of democracy, of mass franchise, of the necessity to woo and organise the masses, and develop the utmost unity of direction and the strictest discipline. (Weber in Gerth and Mills, 1948, p. 102)

Weber thought that Michels' analysis, while substantially sound, was naively utopian. For Weber, party and bureaucratic discipline was a means of resisting less responsible, and therefore less desirable, forms of popular democracy:

The state-political *danger* of mass democracies lies mainly in the possibility of a strong primarily *emotional* element in politics. The 'masses' as such ... 'think no farther than the day after tomorrow'. (Weber, 1988 edn, pp. 403–4)

Weber's political concern is less with questions of *representation* or *participation* (so central to both liberal and socialist thought) than with *leadership*. The question 'how is responsible leadership possible in a modern bureaucratic mass state?' is more central to him than is the issue of democracy itself. For Weber, the danger of bureaucratic domination is not so much that it fails to be 'democratically accountable', but rather that it undermines the possibility of imaginative, effective and responsible political leadership.

We are on dangerous ground here. Weber's political analysis was influential in the development of 'elite theory' and, at least superficially, its emphasis on leadership might be thought to be anti-democratic, or even to have an 'elective affinity' with fascism. To make matters worse, the writings of other elite theorists, notably Vilfredo Pareto (1848–1923), greatly influenced Italian fascism. Worse still, Robert Michels, who although German lived in Italy, himself became a convert to Mussolini's fascist cause while another of Weber's followers, the enormously influential constitutional theorist Carl Schmitt (1888–1985), joined the German Nazi Party in 1933 and justified the Nazi seizure of power as a 'legal revolution' (Mehring, 1992, p. 102).

Weber's early death in 1920 deprives us of his reaction to the emergence of fascism and national socialism, but it would in any case be wrong to read Weber as some kind of theoretical proto-fascist, even if a concern with leadership and 'leadership quality' *can* lead in this direction. Weber's preoccupation with leadership has both a theoretical grounding – in his analysis of bureaucracy – and a practical political concern in the context of Germany as it emerged from the First World War. Weber believed that the kind of 'objective', slow, calculated and mechanically implemented decision-making characteristic of bureaucracy was anathema to effective politics, which had to be imaginative as well as responsible. Although he is critical of naively taking at face value the institutions and mechanisms of liberal democracy, he does see them as serving two important functions: they enable political leaders to mobilise mass support for their political projects against the inert government bureaucracy, while at the same time giving the population the opportunity of periodically rejecting those projects. Thus while modern representative democracy does not literally *represent*, it can at least check the excesses of both the bureaucratic state organs and the professional politician. Representative democracy offers at least a chance that the responsible politician may give a positive lead in decision-making, and offers the populace the negative power of occasionally saying 'we don't like this'. What we have here is not so much an attack on liberal democracy, but rather a very guarded and hard-headed defence based on an analysis which is not itself classically liberal.

However, Weber was also aware of the weakness of representative bodies in the face of bureaucracy. The solution which he suggested to the drafters of the Weimar Constitution, though one they did not adopt, was that the power of bureaucracy could more effectively be checked by a 'plebiscitary presidency' — i.e. by a president elected on popular mandate, by popular acclaim. Weber's hope here was that this mandate would give the president the personal authority *vis-à-vis* the executive and the institutions of the state bureaucracy which parliaments, on his analysis, lacked ('members of parliament are normally nothing better than well-disciplined "yes" men': Weber in Gerth and Mills, 1948, p. 106). Such a president, who in contrast to the impersonal bureaucracy takes *personal* responsibility, *may* be able to offer leadership, in that he or she can counter the power of bureaucracy and stand above parliament, with its debilitating principle of compromise between competing economic and social interests:

A President elected by the people as head of the executive and of official patronage, and possibly holder of a delaying veto, and the power to dissolve parliament and to call a plebiscite is the Palladium of a true democracy which is not helpless surrender to a clique but rather subordination to an elected leader. ('Der Reichspräsident', 1988 edn, p. 501)

We might read this suggestion as an attempt to combine 'legal-rational authority' with 'charismatic authority', an attempt to balance the one with the other by *institutionalising* charismatic authority.

Weber's proposal of the plebiscitary presidency is indicative of his approach to 'normative' political issues. He starts, not from an abstract notion of the ideal society or ideal state (or even of a just society or just state), but from a very concrete sociological analysis of the nature of political institutions. His message to political analysts echoes Aristotle's message to Plato: if you want to discuss where we should go next, begin by understanding the position we are in now. Even then, you can hope at best for an accommodation of that which you believe desirable with the immutable reality of your situation. This was Weber's own version of the 'objective' and disillusioned analytical approach which he believed is both our fate and our responsibility in a modern rationalised society.

## Conclusion

What does Weber still offer us? Even if, as some of his contemporary critics already argued, Weber's account of the power of bureaucracy is

319

overblown, or if his suggestion of the plebiscitary president is unrealistic (or even potentially dangerous), his analytical attack on questions of politics has as its starting-point, not a political ideal, but what Marx called the 'real material conditions of existence'. Furthermore, he points to the importance of analysing the practical and *unintended*, but nevertheless very real, implications of attempts to implement political ideals and to embody them in institutional arrangements and actual social relations. Whether we accept the substance of his analysis or not, it should at least sensitise us to the frequent disharmony between our political aims and the actual practical implications of our attempts to realise them, to the disjunction between the form of political life and its substance. Reading Weber is thus itself a contribution to the process of our disenchantment.

## References

The first extract is taken from Max Weber, 'Parlament und Regierung im neugeordeten Deutschland' (Parliament and government in a newly ordered Germany), in J. Winckelmann (ed.), *Max Weber: Gesammelte politische Schriften*, trans Alan Scott, Tübingen: J. C. B. Mohr, 1988 1st pub. 1921.

The second extract is taken from 'Socialism', in W. Runciman (ed.), *Max Weber: Selections in Translation*, trans. E. Matthews, Cambridge: Cambridge University Press, 1978.

The third extract is taken from Robert Michels, 'Der konservative Grundzug der Partei-Organisation' (The conservative character of party organization), in A. Eleutheropulos and Baron von Engelhardt (eds), *Monatsschrift für Sociologie*, 1, 1909, trans. Alan Scott.

Gerth, H. and Mills, C. Wright (eds), *From Max Weber*, London: Routledge, 1948.

Mehring, R., *Carl Schmitt: zur Einführung*, Hamburg: Junius Verlag, 1992.

Michels, R. *Political Parties*, New York: Dover, 1959, 1st pub. 1911.

Schumpeter, J. A. *Capitalism, Socialism and Democracy*, London: Allen & Unwin, 1943.

Weber, M. *The Protestant Ethic and the Spirit of Capitalism*, London: Unwin, 1930.

Weber, M. *Economy and Society*, Berkeley: University of California Press, 1968.

## Further reading

The best-known selection of Weber's writings is still H. Gerth and C. Wright Mills (eds), *From Max Weber* (London: Routledge and Kegan Paul, 1948), but possibly more useful is W. G. Runciman (ed.), *Max Weber: Selections in Translation* (Cambridge: Cambridge University Press, 1978). Fortunately, there is now also a very good translation of many of Weber's political pieces: P. Lassman and R. Speirs (eds), *Weber: Political Writings* (Cambridge: Cambridge University Press, 1994). The most famous political essay, 'Politics as a Vocation', can be found in all of the above (though in an edited form in the Runciman selection). 'Politics and Government in a Reconstructed Germany' is published as appendix II to volume III of Weber's *Economy and Society* and in Lassman and Speirs (as are the pieces on socialism and the *Reichspräsident*). Many of Weber's political writings in their original language are collected in the *Gesammelte politische Schriften*, edited by Johannes Winkelmann (Tübingen: J. C. B. Mohr, 1988; 1st pub. 1921). There is a vast secondary literature on Weber, and no shortage of general introductions. Perhaps the best of these is Dirk Käsler's *Max Weber: an Introduction to*

*His Life and Work* (Cambridge: Polity Press, 1988). One of the best discussions of his political concerns is David Beetham's *Max Weber and the Theory of Modern Politics* (Cambridge: Polity Press, 1985; 1st pub. 1974). See also, Wolfgang Mommsen's influential *Max Weber and German Politics, 1890–1920* (Chicago: Chicago University Press, 1988; 1st pub. 1959). For a discussion of Weber's critique and defence of liberalism, see Richard Bellamy's *Liberalism and Modern Society* (Cambridge: Polity Press, 1992), chapter 4. A critique of his concept of legitimation and his typology of legitimate authority can be found in David Beetham, *The Legitimation of Power* (London: Macmillan, 1991).

In addition, there are a number of useful comparisons between Weber and Marx, for example, Derek Sayer's *Capitalism and Modernity* (London: Routledge, 1991) and the classic essay by Karl Löwith: *Karl Marx and Max Weber* (London: Allen & Unwin, 1982; 1st pub. 1932).

The classic statement of Michels' 'iron law of oligarchy' is his *Political Parties* (New York: Dover, 1959). An account of Michels' political and intellectual development can be found in Beetham, 'From Socialism to Fascism: the Relationship between Theory and Practice in the Work of Robert Michels'(*Political Studies*, 25, 1977, pp. 3–24 and 161–81). On the intellectual relationship between Weber and Michels, see Mommsen 'Robert Michels and Max Weber: Moral Conviction Versus the Politics of Responsibility', in Mommsen and Osterhammel (eds), *Max Weber and His Contempories* (London: Allen & Unwin, 1987).

## Seminar questions

Is modern mass democracy compatible with bureaucratic domination?

Does Weber's account of the nature of bureaucracy and the bureaucratic state, with its emphasis on hierarchy and obedience to commands from above, underestimate the potential for resistance and subversion?

Must the inclusion of the masses in politics lead to irresponsible, emotional or short-sighted decision-making? (You might discuss here the notorious practice of 'tax bribes', the authoritarian mass movements of the 1930s, or more recent ecological and peace movements.)

Does the fate of communist revolutions confirm Weber's view that the abolition of the private ownership of the means of production merely increases the power of the state over civil society?

Do you agree that the main point of the mechanisms of representative democracy is not to make politics accountable but rather to lend legitimacy to routine administrative decisions?

Is the so-called 'iron law of oligarchy' an iron law?

# MAX WEBER
## From *Parliament and Government in a newly ordered Germany*

### Rule by Civil Servants and Political Leadership

In a modern state real *rule* [*Herrschaft*], which is exercised neither through parliamentary speeches nor in the pronouncements of the monarch but in the *operation of the administration* which affects everyday life, lies necessarily and unavoidably in the hands of the *civil service*. This is so in military as well as civilian officialdom because even the high-ranking modern army officer conducts battles from his 'office'. Just as the so-called progress of capitalism has been the unambiguous measure of modernization of the economy since the Middle Ages, so the progress towards a bureaucratic civil service relying on employment, salary, pension, promotion, specialist education and division of labour, fixed responsibilities, adherence to regulations, and hierarchical sub- and superordination is just as unambiguously the measure of the modernization of the state whether monarchical or democratic, at least where the state is not a small canton with circulating administration but a large mass state. To the advantage of the salaried civil servants, democracy, just like the absolutist state, precludes administration by feudal or patrimonial or patrician means or by other honourary or hereditary dignitaries. Salaried civil servants decide on all our daily requirements and grievances. Here those with military power, officers, are no different in decisive respects from civilian civil servants. The modern mass army is a *bureaucratic* army. The officer – unlike the knight, condottiery, chieftain or Homeric hero – is a special category of civil servant. The army's ability to fight rests upon service discipline. The onward march of bureaucracy is little different within local administration, all the more so where the community is large or has unavoidably lost its local autonomy and link to the locality due to the technically or economically conditioned emergence of interest groups of any kind. And in the church it was not the much-discussed Doctrine of Infallibility but rather the Universal Piskopate which was the important principle of the outcome of 1870 [Vatican Council]. It created a 'chaplinocracy' and, in contrast to the Middle Ages, made the Bishop and the Priest into the simple civil servants of the Curia's central administration. Nor is it any different in contemporary private enterprise, particularly large ones. The number of white-collar employees grows statistically faster than that of workers, and it is a quite laughable illusion of our *littérateurs* that there is slightest difference between mental labour in private offices and that within government bureaux.

In essence they are the same. Viewed social scientifically, the modern state is just as much a 'business' as factory is. Precisely herein lies its historical specificity. The relations of domination are similarly deter-

mined in each case. Just as the relative independence of the crafts-
man or small-scale home producer, the land-owning farmer, the
commendator, the knight and the vassal rested upon the fact that
they were owners of the tools, stocks, financial means, or weapons
with which they carried out their economic, political or military functions and with which they sustained themselves while doing so, so
too the hierarchical dependency of the worker, employee, technical
worker, university lecturer *and* government civil servant and soldier
equally rests upon the fact that the tools, stocks, and financial means
necessary for their business and economic survival are concentrated
in the hands of, in one case, the employers, in the other the political
masters. Russian soldiers, for example, do not *want*, by-and-large, to
carry on the war. But they had to because the material means of war
and the provisions from which they lived were at the disposal of
people who were just as able use them to force soldiers into the
trenches as the capitalist owner of the economic means of production
is able to force the worker into the factory or down the mine-shaft.
This essential economic precondition: the 'separation' of the worker
from the means of activity (the means of production in the economy,
of war in the army, of administration in public administration, of
research in the university and laboratory, of finance in all cases) is the
decisive *common* basis of the modern power-political and cultural-
political and military state enterprise *and* of the capitalist private
enterprise. In both cases disposal over these means is in the hands of
that power which every *instrument of bureaucracy* (judge, civil servant,
army officer, foreman, employee, non-commissioned officer) directly
*obeys* or from which it awaits orders; which gives all structures the
same characteristics and whose existence and function is cause as
well as effect of every 'concentration of the means of activity', or
rather, whose form it is. Increasing 'socialization' today unavoidably
means growing bureaucratization.

Historically too, the 'progress' towards the bureaucratic state, towards
rationally codified rights and rationally thought-out juridical and
administrative rules, is now closely connected with modern capitalist development. The modern capitalist enterprise rests essentially on
*calculation*. It requires for its existence a judiciary and administration
whose workings can at least in principle be *rationally calculated*
according to fixed general norms in the same way as the expected
performance of a machine can be calculated. It can no more be accom-
modated with what is popularly called 'cadi justice' – i.e. with justice
according to the judge's feeling of appropriateness in *individual* cases
or with other irrational principles of judicial procedures as existed
everywhere in the past and still does in the Orient today – than it can
with the patriarchal traditional-governed administration of the theo-
cratic or patrimonial bands of Asia or of our own past in which there
existed arbitrary will and mercy governed by unbroken, holy but
irrational tradition. The fact that this 'cadi justice' and its accompanying administration, because of its irrational character, can often be

*bought,* allows the existence and often the flourishing of the capitalism of traders, of state suppliers and of every type of pre-rational capitalism as it has been known the world over for four thousand years: particularly adventure- and pirate-capitalism arising out of politics, war, and administration as such. That which is however specific to *modern* capitalism, in contrast to ancient forms of capitalist money-making – the strict rational *organization of work* on the grounds of *rational technique* – arises *nowhere* within this kind of irrationally constructed state form, and could not arise within it. This is because modern forms of business with their standing capital and their exact calculation are too susceptible to irrationalities of justice and the administration ... [pp. 320–3]

[Weber goes on to analyse modern political parties as examples of 'rational' agents in which party discipline dominates (cf. the extract from Michels below). He observes that 'bureaucracy is by no means the only modern organizational form just as the factory is by no means the only productive form of enterprise. But both are those forms which stamp on our present age and the forceable future.' (Wilkelmann, 1988 edn, p. 330)]

A lifeless machine is *congealed spirit*. Only because it is this does it have the power to press people into its service and to dominate and determine their everyday working lives, as is the case in the factory. A *congealed spirit* is also that *living machine* represented by the bureaucratic organization with its specialization and trained skilled work, its demarcation of responsibilities, its regulations and hierarchically sub-divided relations of obedience. In conjunction with the dead machine, this living machine is creating the housing of future servitude. Like the fellahin [peasants] in the Ancient Egyptian state, people may one day have no option but to fit into this housing *if a purely technical – i.e. a rational – civil service administration and provision affords the final and only value determining the manner in which their affairs are to be conducted.* Bureaucracy achieves this incomparably better than any others structure of domination. And this housing, which our clueless *littérateurs* praise, supplemented by the close ties of every individual to the workplace (we can see the first instances of this in so-called 'welfare facilities'); to class (through increasing rigidity of ownership); and perhaps in the future to occupation (through the 'liturgical' meeting of governmental requirements – i.e. ascribing governmental tasks to occupationally segregated groups), will become even more infrangible when in the social sphere, as in the corvée states of the past, an 'estate' organization of the governed becomes affiliated to the bureaucracy (and that means in truth subordinated to it). An 'organic' social organization will loom upon us; that is an Oriental-Egyptian one, but in contrast to this it will be as strictly rational as a machine. Who will deny that such a *possibility* may lie in the lap of the future? This has often been said, and the hazy picture of this possibility casts its shadow over the production of our *littérateurs*. Let us assume for a moments that exactly this possibility is our unavoidable fate. Who would then not wish to laugh at the anxiety of our *littérateurs* that future political and social development could grant us *too much* 'individualism' or 'democracy' or some such, and that 'true freedom' will appear only when the current 'anarchy' of our economic production and 'party activity' of our parliamentary is *put aside* in favour of 'social order' and 'organic formation'; that means the pacifism of social powerlessness under the wing of the only totally secure *inescapable* power: bureaucracy in state and economy!

In light of the basic fact of the unstoppable march of bureaucratization the question of the future form of political organizations can only be formulated as follows:

1. How in the face of this over-powering tendency towards bureaucratization is it *still possible* to save *at all* in *any form* a remnant of 'individual' freedom of manoeuvre? For it is in the end a gross self-deception to believe that even the conservatives among us would wish to live at all without the achievements of the age of 'Rights of Man'. But this question does not interest us here because we have other concerns.

2. How can, in light of the growing indispensability and thus growing power of the *state* civil service which interests us here, *any* kind of weapon be found which empowers us to effectively control and keep in its place the enormous power of this class whose significance continues to grow? How will democracy, even in this restricted sense, be *possible at all*? But this too is not the only question which occupies us because:

3. A third question, and the most important of all, derives from the observation of that which bureaucracy as such does not accomplish. It is easy to establish that it does have performance limitations in the area of state-political business just as it does in the private sector. The *leading* spirit, the 'entrepreneur' here, the politician there, is something other than a 'civil servant', not only in form, but also in substance. The 'entrepreneur' also sits in an 'office'. Likewise the army commander. The army commander is also an officer and in form no different form other officials. And the director general of an large enterprise is the salaried official of a limited company. So even his legal status is no different in principle from other officials. This is also the case in political life with leading politicians. The chief minister is *formally* an official with a salary leading to a pension. And the circumstance in every constitution in the world that he can be dismissed and can resign at any time distinguishes his work status only outwardly from that of most but not all other officials. More noteworthy is the fact that for him *alone no specialist educational qualification of any sort* is required as it is for other civil servants. This suggests that on the basis of his position he is something different from other civil servants just as the entrepreneur and general director are within the private sector. Or rather it suggests that he *should*

be different. And so it is indeed. When someone in charge is in the *spirit* of his performance a 'civil servant', even a hard-working one – i.e. used to following regulations and commands dutifully – he is useless whether at the top of a private or state enterprise ... [pp. 332–4]

Modern parliaments are in the first instance the representatives of those who are *ruled* through bureaucracy. A particular minimum of inner assent – at least among the most important classes of the ruled – is a precondition for the survival of every, even the best organized, rule. Parliament is today the means through which this minimum assent is externally manifested. For particular acts of the public authorities a form of agreement through legislation is obligatory after advice from parliament. This is so above all for the budget. Today, as ever since the emergence of estates' prerogatives, control of the form of state's revenue collection – budget right – has been the decisive means of parliamentary power. Clearly, so long as a parliament can exercise pressure on the administration only by refusing to supply revenue, or by withholding agreement to legislative proposals, or by being able to lend support to inconsequential applications of complaint by the population against administration, it is excluded from participation in political leadership. It can and will then only pursue 'negative politics'. That means it will stand opposed to the administration as though it were an enemy power, and it will in turn be fed with a minimum of information and viewed as a constraint and a gathering of impotent moaners and know-alls. The bureaucracy on the other hand will be viewed by parliament and the electorate as a bunch of strivers and henchmen ranged against the people who are the object upon which they practice their vexatious and largely unnecessary skills. Matters are different where Parliament has succeeded in making administrative leaders either come from its ranks (*'a parliamentary system'* in the true sense) or in which in order to remain in power they are required to secure the explicit confidence of the majority, or at least avoid a vote of no-confidence (*parliamentary selection* of the leader). Here on this basis they are exhaustively answerable to parliament, or its committees, (*parliamentary answerability* of the leader) and must conduct administration according to regulations approved by parliament (*parliamentary control of administration*). In this case the leaders of the decisive parties in the parliament are a necessary positive co-bearer of state power. Parliament is then a positive factor along side the monarch whose power to co-determine policies no longer stems, at least exclusively, from his royal prerogative but from his, under all circumstances very considerable, influence (which in any case varies according to his political astuteness and determination to achieve his goals). In this case one speaks, rightly or wrongly, of a 'popular democracy' [*Volksstaat*], whereas a parliament of the ruled which confronts the ruling bureaucracy with negative politics represents the rules of the game of an 'authoritarian state'. What interests us here is the *practical* significance of the position of parliament.

One may love the parliamentary process or hate it, but one will *not* be able to dispose of it. [pp. 339–40]

# MAX WEBER
## From *Socialism*

In positive terms, however, what would socialism, as opposed to the present system, amount to? In the widest sense of the word, what is usually referred to also as a 'collective economy'. That is, first of all, an economy without profit, in other words, without the direction of production by private enterpreners on their own account and at their own risk. Instead, the economy would be in the hands of the officials of a public corporation, who would take over control in respects to be discussed presently. Secondly, and in consequence, an end to the so-called anarchy of production, that is, to competition between entrepeneurs. There is at present, especially in Germany, a good deal of discussion about whether the war has already in reality taken us halfway along the road towards such a 'collective economy'. In view of this, it should be briefly remarked that there are two fundamentally different principles which might underlie the form of organisation of a particular nation's organised economy. The first is the principle nowadays referred to as 'state interventionism', which is undoubtedly familiar to all those good men who work in enterprises which are involved in the war effort. It is based on collaboration between the combined enterpreneurs in a particular branch of the economy and state officials, either military or civilian. By this means, the supply of raw materials, the provision of credit, prices and commercial intelligence can be extensively regulated in accordance with a plan, and the state can participate both in the profits and in the decision-making of these combines. It is believed that the entrepeneur is then supervised by these officials and that production is controlled by the state. Thus, by this system, we should already have 'true', 'genuine' socialism, or at least be on the way towards it. In Germany, however, this theory has encountered widespread scepticism. I have no opinion to offer on the question of what may be true in wartime. Everyone who can count, however, knows that in peacetime, when we shall not be facing ruin, there cannot be such extensive control as there is at present, and that in peacetime this kind of state intervention, involving compulsory cartelisation of entrepreneurs in every sector and state participation in these cartels, so that the state takes a share of profits in return for extensive rights of control, would not in fact mean the control of industry by the state so much as the control of the state by industry. Indeed, this would

327

take a very disagreeable form. Within the combines, the state representatives would sit at the same table as the managers of factories, who would be greatly superior to them in knowledge of the particular industry, in commercial training and in their personal stake in the industry. In Parliament, however, the workers' representatives would sit and demand that the state representatives concern themselves with high wages and low prices, as, they would say, they had the power to do. On the other hand, moreover, in order not to ruin its finances, the state, participating as it did in the profits and losses of the combine, would naturally have an interest in keeping prices high and wages low. And finally, the private members of the combine would expect the state to guarantee them the profitablility of their enterprises. In the eyes of the working class such a state would thus appear as a class state in the truest sense of the word, and I doubt whether that is politically desirable; I doubt even more whether it would be wise to represent this state of affairs to the workers as 'true' socialism, tempting though this thought may certainly seem. For the workers would very soon discover by experience that the lot of the mine worker is not the slightest bit different whether the mine is privately or publicly owned. In the mines of the Saar, the worker's life is just the same as in a private mine: when the company is badly managed, so that it does not make much of a profit, then it also goes badly for the men. The difference, however, is that strikes against the state are impossible, so that in this form of state socialism the essential dependence of the worker is increased. That is one of the reasons why the Social Democrats reject this kind of 'state intervention' in the economy, or this form of socialism in general. The collective element in such a case is merely the cartel. Profit is still the decisive factor, as it was before; the important question which decides the direction to be taken by the economy is still that of the gains to be made by the individual entrepreneurs who have combined to form the cartel, of whom the state exchequer has now become one. The unfortunate thing would be that, whereas at present the political bureaucracy of the state and the economic bureaucracy of private enterprise, of the cartels, the banks and the large firms, exist alongside each other as separate bodies, so that, in spite of everything, economic power can be held in check by political, in the situation envisaged both sets of officials would form a single body with a solidarity of interests and would no longer be under control. At all events, profit as the goal of production would not have been abolished. The state as such, however, would have to share the burden of the workers' hatred, which at present is directed against the entrepreneurs.

# ROBERT MICHELS
## From: *The Conservative Character of Party Organization*

This democratic external form of the basis of party-political life can easily blind us to the inclination towards aristocracy, or better oligarchy, which underlies every party organization. A particularly effective and apt area in which to observe this tendency is provided by the inner nature of democratic parties, and among them especially the social-revolutionary worker's party. In conservative parties, except during elections, the tendency towards oligarchy is blatant; it corresponds to these parties' oligarchical character. But subversive parties display the same features no less convincingly. Observation here is, however, more valuable because revolutionary parties, their origins and their aims represent the negation of this tendency; they come into being in opposition to it. The appearance of the same disposition within their own heart is therefore a very powerful indication of the ever-present oligarchical traits in every human instrumental organization.

The form in which every new social movement is crystallized displays a democratic countenance. All new upwardly-striving class parties, before starting off on their march to seize power, incessantly present to the world earnest manifestos to the effect that they wish not so much to free themselves but rather the whole of humanity from the oppression of a tyrannical minority and replace an unjust regime with a just one. As the new bourgeoisie began their great struggle with the aristocracy and clergy, they started with a solemn declaration of the *Droits de l'Homme* [Rights of Man] and threw themselves into the battle with the slogan: '*Egalité, Liberté, Fraternité!*' Today we can hear for ourselves another powerful class movement, that of wage labourers, proclaiming that they may be employing the antagonism within today's economic system in order to lead this class struggle, but that the class struggle itself has the eventual aim of creating a classless, humanitarian and fraternal society.

But the victorious bourgeoisie of the *Droits de l'Homme* may have instituted the republic, though not democracy; and *Egalité, Liberté, Fraternité* are today at most still to be read over the doorways of French prisons; and the *La Kommune*, which was the first at least occasionally successful attempt to create a proletarian-socialist rule, had despite its basic communist principles even in times of financial difficulty faithfully protected the Bank of France just like any other consortium of unyielding capitalists. We have had revolutions, but not democracies.

If, however, the social-revolutionary and democratic parties theoretically view their main purpose of existence as the struggle against oligarchy in all its forms, how can it therefore be explained that they develop this self-same tendency? We see our task in the unprejudiced analytical answering of this question.

A class which places specific demands on society and which seeks to realize a complex of ideologies and 'ideals' deriving from the economic functions which it performs requires organization on both economic and on political terrain. Organization which rests upon the principle of least effort – that is on maximum savings of energy – is the most suitable weapon of the weak in their struggle against the strong. This struggle can take place only where there is solidarity. The social democrats – these fanatically loyal enthusiasts of the idea of organization – therefore expound an argument which corresponds to the results of the scientific study of parties when they argue against the theories of anarcho-individualists that the employers would like nothing better than to see the disintegration and division of the working class. Indeed the individual, at least when a member of the working class, is at the mercy of the whim of the economically strong. The principle of organization must therefore be viewed as the *conditio sine qua non* of carrying out the social struggle of the masses.

The masses' lack of organization which plays into the hands of their opponents is the Scylla in opposition to which is the politically necessary principle of organization. But organization in turn brings with it the all the danger of Charybdis. Indeed, the source from which the conservative riverlets flows into the lowlands of democracy, in order from time to time to cause flooding rendering the plain unrecognizable, is called *organization*. Who says organization, says the tendency to oligarchy. At the heart of organization lies a deeply aristocratic trait. By creating a solid structure the machinery of organization causes decisive changes in the organized masses. It turns the relationship of the leader to the mass on its head. At first the leader is only the servant of the mass. The basis of the organization is the equality of all those organized. All members of the organization have equal rights claims. All have the right to vote. All can be elected. In the organization the basic demands of the *Droits de l'Homme* are theoretically met. All offices are the outcome of the election and all officers are under the permanent control of the whole and can at any time be revoked and dismissed. The democratic party principle guarantees to the largest possible number of people influence and participation in the administration of the common cause. But technical specialization, which is the necessary consequence of every expanding organization, creates the necessity for so-called executive direction and transfers all decision-making capacities from the mass to the leaders where these capacities are re-ascribed to the special leadership quality of the leaders alone. The leaders, who are originally the organs for implementing the will of the masses, become autonomous in that they emancipate themselves from the masses. Organization decisively completes the division of every party into a leading minority and a led majority.

The party, or rather every organization in-so-far as it has a fixed structure, is good fertile soil for the emergence of differentiation. The more

the official party apparatus spreads and divides (that is the more
members it gets, the more its coffers fill and the party press grows)
the more popular rule will be squeezed and replaced by all-powerful committees and commissions. Particularly in the large industrial
centres in which the workers' party sometimes reaches hundreds of
thousands of members it is no longer possible to deal with the business of this giant body without a system of representation. With the
growth of organization the tasks of the administration grow, they
become less transparent and the circle of duties widens and divides.
The membership must by and by forego in ever larger measure regulating for themselves or even checking on administrative matters.
They will leave these tasks to the hired representatives, to paid functionaries, and must content themselves with a summary report or
commissioning auditors. Democratic control shrinks into an ever
narrower circle. More and more functions which were carried out by
an elected body are given over to executive committees. There
emerges a huge framework of complicated structure. Responsibilities
divide and re-divide; the principle of the division of labour rules.
There develops a clearly demarcated hierarchy. Exact adherence to
official channels becomes the first tenet of the party catechism.

So far the oligarchical bureaucratic character of the party organization
is unquestionably the result of a practical technical necessity. It is an
unavoidable product of the principle of organization.

But the modern political party is also a fighting organization. As such
it has to obey the laws of tactics. The basic law of tactics is speed of
response. Democracy is however incompatible with speed of
response. The great social revolutionary leader Ferdinand Lassalle
already recognized this when he argued that the existing personal
dictatorship within his organization should be declared theoretically
justified and recognized as practically necessary; the followers
should unquestioningly follow their leader and the whole body
should represent a hammer in the hand of its president. That was the
imperative of political necessity, at least in the early period of the still
virginal awkwardness of the workers' movement, and was the only
method of securing power and prestige from the bourgeoisie parties.
In centralism lay the guarantee of speed of decision. Lay, and lies. A
large organization is already a cumbersome apparatus. The distances
and the loss of time which would result, were one to present to the
masses individual day to day problems which require a quick decision in such a way that they might attain even a limited ability for
judging these issues, makes democracy in its undoctored original
form impossible. This is so because one could only pursue with it a
politics of procrastination and lost opportunity, and a political party
would thereby lose its ability to make alliances and its necessary
political flexibility. Democracy is therefore not suitable for the day-
to-day running of a political party. A party at war – even a small war
– requires a hierarchical formation without which it might be
compared to the wild amorphous hoards of negro armies (*sic*) whose

331

art of war failed when met by well-disciplined battalions of soldiers drilled in the European fashion.

Thus emerges – out of technical administrative as well as tactical grounds – a professional leadership which on the basis of the authority ascribed to it deals autonomously with matters which concern the mass. The masses delegate a small number of individuals who permanently represent them.

The beginnings of the building of a professional leadership means however the beginning of the end of democracy ...

The last link in the long chain of manifestations which gives political parties – even where they adorn themselves with the title 'revolutionary' – their conservative character is grounded in their relationship to the state. Established to overcome the centralized power of the state, they themselves have become mightily centralized. They become a party of government, that is a party which is organized like a government in miniature hoping one day to take over full-scale government. The political revolutionary party is a state within a state, established with the open aim of hollowing out and undermining the current state in order to replace it with one different from top to bottom. Organization theoretically serves this explicit current state purpose in which the single justification of the parties existence lies: to prepare suitably and systematically the work of destruction of the organs of state in their present form. The subversive party organizes the social revolution through its cadres. Thus we have all the effort to establish their position, to broaden the administrative apparatus, to pile up capital. Every new district organizer, every new party secretary, recruited is theoretically a new agent of the revolution; every new section a new battalion; every Thousand Gulden Note gained through membership fee, made through the press or by voluntary contributions a new resource for the struggle against the opponent. But the leaders of this revolutionary body within the authority state organized as it is with the same means, radiating the same iron self-discipline as all the rest, cannot but recognize that their organization standing in opposition to the state's official organization – whatever wonders it performs on the this organizational basis – it is still only a weak diminutive achievement and that therefore in the foreseeable future, barring exceptional circumstances, every attempt to attain power must end in a crushing defeat. The logical consequence of this recognition is that the exact converse arises to that which guided the party's founders as they lifted the party from the depths. Instead of a party whose organizational strength and power grows and gains revolutionary dynamic, we can today observe the opposite: there is an inner connection between the growth of the party and the growth of caution and anxiety in its politics ...

It is clear – and the history of the international workers' movement supports our theses with a hundred examples – that in this way the party with an expanding organization is ever more immobilized.

That is, it loses its revolutionary momentum; becomes heavy and
cumbersome; lazy not only in action but also in thought. They bind
themselves ever tighter to the so-called 'glorious old tactic'; that is
the tactic which had made them great, and their wariness of aggres-
sive action of any kind becomes even more formidable ... Now that
there are the three million organized workers a bureaucracy has been
called into being which in terms of sense of duty, punctuality and
deferential apathetic obedience rivals that of the state itself; the
coffers are full, complex financial and spiritual interests has spread
across the whole land.

# Index